# EXPORTING GOOD GOVERNANCE

*Temptations and Challenges
in Canada's Aid Program*

Jennifer Welsh and Ngaire Woods,
editors

Wilfrid Laurier University Press
[WLU]

We acknowledge the financial support of the Government of Canada through the Book Publishing Industry Development Program for our publishing activities. We acknowledge the financial support of the Centre for International Governance Innovation.

Library and Archives Canada Cataloguing in Publication

Exporting good governance : temptations and challenges in Canada's aid program / edited by Jennifer Welsh and Ngaire Woods.

Co-published with the Centre for International Governance Innovation.
Includes bibliographical references and index.

ISBN 978-1-55458-029-3

1. Economic assistance, Canadian—Political aspects—Developing countries.
2. Conditionality (International relations)—Developing countries.  3. Economic assistance, Canadian—Developing countries.  I. Welsh, Jennifer M. (Jennifer Mary), 1965–
II. Woods, Ngaire  III. Centre for International Governance Innovation.

HC60.E98 2007             338.91'7101724             C2007-903512-4

Cover photograph by Alistair Williamson, Ottawa, ON. Cover design by Brian Grebow/BG Communications. Text design by P.J. Woodland.

♾

Printed in Canada

# EXPORTING GOOD GOVERNANCE

The Centre for International Governance Innovation (CIGI) was founded in 2001 to provide solutions to pressing governance challenges. CIGI strives to build ideas for global change through world-class research and dialogue with practitioners, which provide a basis for advising decision-makers on the character and desired reforms of multilateral governance. CIGI's purpose is to conduct research of international significance, and to strengthen the intellectual capacity to understand and propose innovative solutions to global challenges. For more information please visit www.cigionline.org.

# CONTENTS

### III
### THE IMPLICATIONS

# FOREWORD

## Maureen O'Neil

The essays collected in this volume cover a good number of the "temptations and challenges" Canada faces as it attempts to support good governance and democratic development in developing countries. Against a changing global politics and development assistance regime, these studies force us to reassess the goals and aspirations of aid.

In his essay, Ian Smillie reminds us of the continuing "bi-polarity" of Canadian foreign policy—the romantic desire to improve the world set against narrower attention to serving our national interest.

In 2005, when these papers were first being prepared, the political mood in Canada was experiencing a policy moment when the two were conflating—especially because more democracy was seen by some as an outlet for the discontent of the "excluded"—the excluded who, it was hypothesized, might become terrorists if they were not included, as full citizens, in the political life of their own countries.

If the trade-off is between romantic aspirations (the search for justice, equity, and the alleviation of poverty) and "realism" (serving "national self-interest"), Canada's dilemmas do not set it apart from those of other Western countries. The goals of development assistance are in themselves quintessentially aspirational, reflecting the belief (as the Gates Foundation says it so succinctly) that "every life is of equal value" and that something can be done to improve the lives of those living in misery. More particularly, aid proceeds from the belief that something can be done from outside the political and geographic boundaries within which the miserable are living.

The interplay of altruism and self-interest has played out for half a century in the transfer of taxpayers' dollars from rich countries to the rest. Alongside the aid has been an internationalization of the concepts underpinning developed countries' national experiences of redistribution, economic development, and law-making—the whole panoply of policy instruments that established democracies used to create fairer societies. As a result, the thinking that has underpinned development programs has relied from the beginning on the policy experiences of quite different polities and economies. That said, the growth of a cadre of development professionals in OECD countries who worked almost exclusively on "development" in poor countries has sometimes been such that the professionals have not actually been that familiar with the ways in which their *own* countries accomplished policy change domestically—the interplay of interests, ideas, and politics that results in changed policies and programs.

There has been very little reflection on the impact of development transfers of one kind or another on the political development of ex-colonies or other poor countries. As we know well, one of the reasons why the development aid kept flowing was the cold war. One might say that the "truth telling" about politics in developing countries didn't start seriously until the late 1980s, with much greater vigour after the fall of the Berlin Wall in 1989.

In Canada little attention was paid to democracy and human rights within development programming until the mid-1980s, when two reports were issued: the report of the 1986 Special Joint (Hockin-Simard) Committee of Parliament, *Independence and Internationalism*, and the 1987 review of Canadian aid policy and programmes by Gisèle Côté-Harper and John C. Courtney. These studies—which promoted a holistic conception of human rights that included political, social, and economic dimensions—laid the groundwork for the subsequent creation of the International Centre for Human Rights and Democratic Development (Rights & Democracy). Rights & Democracy, created as a Crown corporation with an international Board, is one of the "might have beens" of Canadian foreign and development policy, given only small budgets and largely ignored by governments of all political stripes for the last two decades.[1]

In many ways, concerns for democracy and human rights were overtaken by the growing concerns of development agencies about the importance of public sector and political reforms needed in aid-receiving countries. CIDA was soon spending annually hundreds of times the budget of Rights & Democracy on good governance and democratic development. All OECD countries resolved to help developing countries improve their public sector management, their "rule of law," their policy decision-making processes, their election management, and so forth.

Where does Canada sit within this? Canadian prime ministers have responded to the rock star flattery of Bono: "the world needs more Canada." Does it really? What can Canada usefully do as a global actor through all the policy levers at its disposal to support democratic development and human rights—whether expenditures, foreign policy decisions, multilateral support, military engagement, debt relief, trade decisions?

These essays explore this complex, highly charged question. They also appear in the wake of the July 2007 report of the House of Commons Standing Committee on Foreign Affairs and International Development, "Advancing Canada's Role in International Support for Democratic Development," which argues that new policy directions and new instruments are needed if Canada is to "make a difference." But too often, we do not know what we are talking about when we set off down the democratic assistance path. Our aspirations blind us to lessons of experience or to seeking out what those lessons are. We certainly have not systematically assembled or assimilated thoughtful analysis of our experience (and expenditures) to date. We have more hypotheses about external intervention in other people's politics than conclusions.

Nonetheless, we must continue trying to help. These essays are a beginning. They probe the aspirations of aid for "good governance" and evaluate how these have been implemented in practice in several countries. They remind us that before leaping in with good intentions, a considerable task of analysis and reflection needs to be done.

*—Maureen O'Neil*
President, International Development Research Centre

## Note

1 Declaration of interest: Maureen O'Neil served as Chair of the Board of the International Centre for Human Rights and Democratic Development from 1996 to 1997.

▲

# INTRODUCTION

## Jennifer Welsh and Ngaire Woods

Good governance has become the Holy Grail of foreign aid. Previously, development assistance agencies focused more narrowly on ensuring the right economic policies in aid-receiving countries. Now they are in wide agreement that yet more important than policies are institutions. By the end of the 1990s, a series of studies commissioned by the World Bank had demonstrated a connection between good governance and economic growth (Dollar and Kraay 2000; Islam and Montenegro 2002; Knack and Keefer 1995). Donor governments and multilateral institutions swiftly internalized the implications and sought ways to focus their development assistance on countries that demonstrated a capacity to govern well. Yet more importantly, donors began to investigate and experiment with how they might promote good governance using foreign aid. By the turn of the new century, virtually all major bilateral and multilateral aid agencies—including the US Agency for International Development (USAID), the British Department for International Development (DFID), the Japan International Cooperation Agency (JICA), and the Canadian International Development Agency (CIDA)—had moved away from a pure focus on "economic development" to a new emphasis on the promotion of "good governance."

Traditionally, good governance for development economists has not meant democracy. It is not about elections, political parties, parliaments, or democratic accountability. Good governance, in the parlance of the World Bank and the IMF, deliberately strives to avoid such political connotations. For these multilateral institutions, it is a much narrower concept, one that focuses on institutions that underpin the functioning of free markets—for example, on the rule of law, the protection of property rights, competent bureaucracies, and effective restraints on corruption. Yet despite efforts to avoid overtly political interventions, both institutions have strayed into the task of institution building. In its governance indicators, the World Bank uses indices to capture six dimensions: voice and accountability, political instability and violence, government effectiveness, regulatory burden, rule of law, and graft (Kaufmann, Kraay, and Zoido-Lobaton 1999). These elements of governance have been identified as vital for promoting and supporting markets, investment, and economic growth. As a result, good governance has slipped into development assistance programs, introducing an attention to institutions that was previously confined to democracy promotion.

The appearance of good governance on the development assistance agenda poses a great temptation for Canada and other constitutional democracies. Those with a strong tradition of accountable government, an effective bureaucracy, stable and assured property rights, and a sound rule of law have good reasons to want to implant these same institutions in other countries. They have served rich and stable countries well—so, too, they could serve others. Critics of this approach argue, however, that good governance has become a framework for creating a "Westernized" world, one wedded to a particular model of capitalist development (Schmitz 1995). Others have raised concerns about the use of aid conditionality to promote good governance, asserting that it compromises an established norm of international relations—namely, self-determination (Collingwood 2003).

Before this normative debate can be addressed, however, a more immediate set of questions presents itself. *Can* good governance be exported? Now that development assistance is being focused on strengthening or achieving good governance in developing countries, is there any evidence that aid actually helps?[1]

This book investigates whether aid for good governance can work. It begins by describing the changing context and imperatives driving development assistance, before exploring the good governance agenda and how various donors have attempted to operationalize it. It then focuses on the experience of one particular country, to assess what lessons might be learned from Canada's efforts to build governance capacity through its aid program. While Canada's budget for development assistance is at best "medium-sized" relative to larger players such as the United States and the United Kingdom, and while Canada has only recently begun to reverse the substantial cutbacks that were made in the early 1990s, this country has a long history of engagement with recipient countries in Africa, Asia, and the Caribbean. Moreover, though in some ways Canada is a unique donor—particularly in terms of the relative lack of concentration in its aid program—it also exhibits characteristics common to other members of the OECD. Most notable among these is the degree to which it now channels its aid through multilateral institutions and seeks to harmonize its activities with those of other like-minded donors. These factors combine to make Canada an interesting test case for an analysis of the promotion of good governance.

## Structuring the Research

The first three chapters of this book examine the context in which good governance programming is taking place, including the aspirations of aid agencies and how they conceptualize good governance. Chapters 1 and 2, by Ngaire Woods and Sue Unsworth, were originally presented at a meeting at the International Development Research Centre in Ottawa in March 2005, convened by the Global Economic Governance Program. There, senior officials and scholars discussed the background papers that later formed the basis of the first two chapters; they also made several important contributions that gave rise to—and deeply affected—the subsequent research.

Ashraf Ghani, Afghanistan's finance minister in the first post-Taliban government, discussed how donors want to strengthen the institutions of governance in developing countries yet at the same time are circumventing and even competing against those institutions. During his tenure as finance minister, he watched donors arrive in Kabul expecting—in effect—to govern. Instead of strengthening his capacity as finance minister, they undermined him by hiring his best human resources (sometimes as drivers), by imposing their own priorities, and by insisting on their own processes. Coordination among donors evolved into a battle among them as to who should govern what. Sidelined in all this was the fledgling interim government of Afghanistan, which desperately needed to establish its own political legitimacy and sovereignty. It is no surprise, then, that Ghani's priority for donors is that first and foremost they take sovereignty seriously. In his understanding, sovereignty entails not only the legitimate monopoly over the use of violence within a country, but also an accountable and capable government that can control the public budget, provide economic and social rights to citizens, create and regulate a market, and enforce the rule of law.

Florence Kuteesa, Uganda's former budget director, provided a glimpse of life in the cockpit of an aid-receiving country. Donors' demands and exigencies take many forms: they not only set priorities but also often change them; they not only set detailed reporting requirements but also require different reports even for the same areas of expenditure. In good-governance programming a large number of donors are aspiring to achieve their own particular goals. Moreover, donors are operating through several channels simultaneously. In other words, Canada or the United Kingdom "speaks" to Uganda not only through CIDA or DFID but also through the World Bank, the IMF, the UNDP, the Global Fund, and so forth. The coordination problem is deeply rooted in the internal workings of individual donor governments: departments of defence, finance, development, foreign affairs, and trade compete with one another and project competing priorities through whichever international agency they control.

Gerald Helleiner picked up and expanded on this theme by sharing his experience as a key actor in Tanzania's efforts better to coordinate donors. In that aid-receiving country, an Independent Monitoring Group was set up to carry out independent assessments of donors. Relying on peer pressure and accountability among the donors themselves, this group delivered more effective coordination and better alignment with local priorities. Donors have responded in various ways to the Tanzanian system; generally, though, peer pressure has encouraged even the most reluctant to get involved in monitoring one another's activities in-country. Helleiner's contribution also highlights that donors' willingness to coordinate their activities often depends on changes in government (such as the election of the Labour government in the United Kingdom in 1997) and on the particular management structures in place within a donor country (i.e., as these structures relate to the decentralization of aid agencies to the field).

Duncan Snidal drew on his expertise as a theorist of international cooperation to sketch a political economy framework for analyzing foreign aid. His main assertion was that coordination problems in the realm of development assistance stem from disincentives to cooperation among donors. For example, uncertain outcomes are a characteristic of aid programs; even so, donors may have incentives to hide their failures and may therefore fail to learn from them. Poor coordination can arise because it is hard to align administrative rules even when policies and objectives are the same across donors; or because donors have multiple objectives, lack shared priorities, or lack coherence between aid and non-aid policies. Snidal suggested that the appropriate response is not to focus on "good" and "bad" motives and incentives, but rather to think about how incentives can best be harnessed to deliver the best results.

Finally, Canada's then Minister for International Cooperation Aileen Carroll spoke of Canada's goals and aspirations. She highlighted the need for Canada to coordinate its aid better with other donors, to focus its aid program more on fewer recipient countries where it could make a stronger impact, and to concentrate more on good governance. All of these goals were central to Canada's 2005 International Policy Statement—the first comprehensive review in a decade of Canadian foreign, defence, and development policy. The minister's remarks, combined with her announcement that Canada would be strengthening its focus on good governance, spurred us to undertake the second part of the research reported in this volume: a series of case studies examining what can be learned from Canada's past experience in good governance.

The cases were chosen with two considerations in mind. The first was amount of aid: we selected countries to which Canada has devoted a significant portion of its aid efforts over the past five to ten years. Ghana, Vietnam, and Bangladesh all meet this criterion (as consistent members of Canada's "top 20" list of aid-receiving countries); furthermore, they have been the focus of a series of initiatives specifically directed at good governance. The second consideration related to the context of "failing states": we chose countries where donor governments are engaged in a broad set of development and security activities under the banner of post-conflict reconstruction. Clearly, Haiti and Afghanistan are two such countries. Indeed, in 2002 and 2003, Afghanistan received the largest amount of aid that Canada has ever given a recipient country; and in 2004, Haiti was identified as Canada's "most important long-term development assistance beneficiary in the Americas." We included the final case, Mauritius, for the sake of comparison: as a country that has enjoyed good governance relative to other developing countries, it offers an opportunity to examine whether donors have actually made any difference, or whether other factors and interventions have been more influential in Mauritius's success.

Authors already familiar with these six cases were invited to work on a common template of questions concerning aid and good governance promotion. A second meeting with high-level officials and scholars was held in Ottawa in October 2005 to discuss the case studies. Having taken to heart Florence Kuteesa's insights regarding coordination within donor governments, we were careful to ensure participation from Canada's departments of justice, defence, foreign affairs, finance, and international development. The input of these officials was crucial for the authors as they set about revising their chapters for this book. In particular, we benefited greatly from the detailed feedback and information provided by CIDA's policy and country specialists.

## The Findings

Chapter 1 examines the context in which governments and multilateral institutions are delivering aid for good governance. Specifically, it reflects on the implications for aid of the new security imperatives that emerged in the wake of the 9/11 attacks on the United States. In her analysis of the impact of 9/11 on aid flows and aid priorities, Ngaire Woods focuses on several major donors and the changing trends in their aid policies. New security commitments are exerting pressure on aid budgets, albeit with a time lag. Furthermore, there is evidence that aid goals are being compelled to change now that regional and global security is displacing human security as a priority. The results highlight two points: the need for aid flows that are less volatile, more predictable, and longer term; and the need for aid agencies to beware of the pitfalls of the "growing cacophony of donors," each demanding a different set of conditions, meetings, and reports, and together eroding rather than strengthening the possibilities for good governance.

Chapter 2 discusses the challenges of trying to export good governance. Sue Unsworth dissects donors' aspirations for good-governance aid and highlights the problems arising from those aspirations. She also investigates whether a "governance first" agenda—that is, efforts to place good governance before economic development—can actually work. Her chapter pushes donors and policy-makers to think harder about the conditions in which the opposite might be true: economic growth and development may well drive institution building. Her analysis offers no easy solutions; indeed, she warns that unless donors question the bedrock assumptions about good governance, their good intentions may get derailed in the current rush to increase aid budgets and meet Millennium Development Goals (MDGS). Deploying her own experience as a good governance advisor to Britain's Department for International Development, and its analysis of how specific changes have been brought about within countries, she draws out crucial starting points for any agency seeking to promote good governance through its aid policy. These starting points include the importance of local ownership, the need for more realistic timelines for change, and a better understanding of the political economy constraints to development (at both local and global levels).

Canada's experience with exporting good governance is the subject of chapter 3. Ian Smillie examines how Canada's approach to good governance has evolved since early attempts to integrate human rights into foreign policy in the 1980s and the euphoric years of democracy promotion in the wake of European communism's collapse in the 1990s. He shows that Canada's good governance agenda has broadened from these early roots to include not only the engagement of civil society and the creation of competent and transparent organs of government (such as a professional public service), but also the more complex tasks of conflict prevention, peacebuilding, and security-sector reform. That same agenda has also become linked to the notion of "human security," which aims to place the rights and safety of individuals (not just states) at the heart of Canadian foreign, defence, and development policy. Smillie's "report card" for Canada's good governance programs is mixed. He calls on policy-makers to develop a more comprehensive understanding of local conditions in aid-receiving countries—and of the particular histories that created them—and to establish a central place in Ottawa where lessons relating to good governance can be "rolled up, spelled out, shared, and remembered."

The general insights provided in this book's first section are borne out in the six cases examined in later chapters. In chapter 4, Nilima Gulrajani assesses the impact of Canadian efforts to enhance good *economic* governance in Vietnam, through stand-alone technical assistance projects (in areas such as legal reform, judicial training, and environmental management) and multidonor funding arrangements (aimed primarily at financial management modernization and public service reform). In so doing, she highlights the difficult trade-offs for donors when it comes to creating states that are both effective in facilitating capitalist development and democratically accountable to their citizens. In the case of Vietnam, CIDA's "state-centric" approach has prioritized effectiveness as a goal by focusing on cooperation with government agencies (such as the Prime Minister's Research Commission and the Ministry of Justice) rather than on civil society organizations or social movements.

Chapter 5, on Bangladesh, examines how Canada has in other contexts privileged democratic accountability. Fahimul Quadir describes the shift in Canadian aid policy toward this high-priority recipient country from support for relief and rehabilitation to the creation of an enabling environment for economic growth and human security. CIDA has chosen to partner with Bangladesh's civil society (in particular, its private-sector organizations) for delivering services to the poor, largely out of frustration with a Bangladeshi state that consistently lacks transparency and accountability.

Chapter 6, Peter Arthur and David Black's case study of Ghana, offers another example of a country where Canada has chosen to emphasize the more "technocratic" side of governance reform—with a particular focus on economic policy-making—rather than more ambitious initiatives aimed at political reform. The authors identify some positive results from CIDA's efforts (especially its water projects); they also note that the agency's move toward budget support programs is being watched with interest by other donors. Yet, as with Gulrajani, they suggest that better governance in a technocratic sense may ultimately depend on more robust democratic accountability, even if the results of trying to deepen democracy are indirect and fit less neatly with short-term donor preferences.

Chapters 7 and 8 consider "failed" or "failing" states, where unique considerations apply and where priorities revolve around basic security and survival for the local population. In their analysis of Afghanistan, Scott Gilmore and

Janan Mosazai suggest that donors operating in former zones of conflict should adopt a different development approach—one driven more explicitly by the donor's strategic and geopolitical interests rather than by the recipient country's preferences. Directly challenging the "harmonization and alignment" agenda recently endorsed by OECD donors, they argue that the Canadian government's reconstruction efforts in Afghanistan have been hampered by its policy of working through multilateral organizations (which makes it more difficult to set Canadian priorities and to measure Canada's contribution) and of responding to the development needs as articulated by the Afghan government. In their view, Canada's engagement in Afghanistan would have been enhanced had decision makers in Ottawa initially identified specific *Canadian* interests in the region and within the coalition. This would have led to more effective coordination of Canada's defence, diplomatic, and development initiatives on the ground, including its governance projects.

Robert Muggah's case study on Haiti offers a different perspective on the challenges of promoting good governance in so-called failed states. His chapter shows how development assistance policy can become distorted by donors' broader concerns for regional and international security—largely because such concerns are subject to rapid change, whereas building good governance requires time and sustained commitment. With respect to Haiti, Canada's approach to good governance (along with those of other high-profile donors such as the United States) changed dramatically over the years, from efforts to shore up democratic gains in the mid-1990s, to the reinforcement of public institutions in the late 1990s, to more radical efforts that bypassed the state altogether and that attempted to strengthen opposition groups and civil society. This later phase (2000–3) was accompanied by donors' concerted efforts to apply strict conditions on all ODA to the Haitian government, ostensibly to induce more transparency and accountability. Muggah argues that while these shifting priorities were partly the product of useful (and painful) lessons learned by donors operating in Haiti, they have more often reflected the changing interests, prescriptions, and policy fashions emanating from offices in Ottawa, Paris, and Washington. The result has been a mismatch between top-down donor agendas and political realities on the ground.

Richard Sandbrook's contribution on Mauritius (chapter 9) seeks to find out why relatively good governance has prevailed in this country when so much of sub-Saharan Africa has fallen prey to neopatrimonial politics. Given that donors have exerted very little influence on Mauritius's evolution, the answer lies in a set of unique historical circumstances—including its well-established mercantile and agrarian bourgeoisie and its robust civil society (all inherited from the colonial period). As a result of these findings, Sandbrook advises those interested in fostering good governance to focus more on building the underlying conditions for an effective and accountable state, and less on direct capacity-building.

Chapters 10 and 11 move away from the detailed discussion of Canada's good governance programming in particular countries, to the more general question of how the government could better coordinate the delivery of aid. Bernard Wood begins his chapter by reminding us that development assistance policy operates within certain parameters of governance in the broadest sense—that it involves not only particular decision-making institutions and arrangements but also the goals and priorities assigned to this particular policy field by the relevant actors in the donor country. In analyzing Canada, Wood argues that the most important parameters and the most chronic weaknesses in the making and delivery of aid policy lie at the very heart of the Ottawa's management process, which is where strategic directions are set. In particular, he points to a series of powerful incentives and interactions among the actors on the Canadian side of the development cooperation equation that make it extremely difficult to foster recipient-country "ownership." There are opportunities for Canada to enhance its aid delivery—for example, it could concentrate on fewer recipient countries and deploy more CIDA officials to the field; more dramatic improvements in aid effectiveness, however, will require reform at the "centre" of government.

One lesson running through all the cases in this book is that Canada's contribution, even if further concentrated, can never be more than a fraction of a recipient country's aid receipts. Put another way, what other donors do and whether Canada's contributions are coordinated with those of others has a huge impact on Canada's good governance promotion. In light of this, in chapter 11, Paolo de Renzio and Sarah Mulley examine the high-level process for improving cooperation and coordination among donors and the implications of that process for good governance. Their analysis highlights that the approaches to harmonizing and aligning donors as facilitated by the OECD/DAC have resulted in some modest gains, but that substantial progress will not be made without more recipient-country ownership and leadership.

For the Canadian government, the key challenge is how to square these new OECD directions with accountability to its own key constituency (the Canadian public), with coherency in its aid program, and with Canadian values as broadly conceived. In the Conclusion, Jennifer Welsh draws on this book's findings to outline (a) the objectives that could guide Canada's good-governance policy, and (b) the programs and delivery mechanisms would best allow it to fulfill its commitment to make better governance a priority. Her key recommendation is that Ottawa be driven by a concern for concrete development outcomes, rather than by a desire to replicate a particular form of liberal democracy in other parts of the world. This more modest objective would help ensure that the government as a whole (and CIDA in particular) addresses rather than papers over the complex relationships among governance, economic growth, and the just distribution of economic and social goods. It might also help counteract the temptation to reach for the latest fad in governance promotion, and instill a more sophisticated appreciation for the processes of change occurring in the developing countries with which Canada seeks to partner.

## Note

1  There is a growing literature which casts a skeptical eye on the impact of Western foreign aid. For a recent example, see Easterly (2006).

▲

# I

**THE CONTEXT**

▼

# 1

## THE CHANGING POLITICS OF AID

### Ngaire Woods

Aid for good governance is much in the news. Wealthy countries promised dramatically to increase aid to the world's poorest countries at the G8 meeting in Gleneagles in 2005, agreeing to double aid for Africa by 2010, and noted that according to the OECD, aid for all developing countries could increase by around $50 billion per year by 2010 (Gleneagles G8 Communiqué, 8 July 2005 at www.g8.gov.uk). Promoting good governance is at the heart of these new commitments. To quote the G8 in 2007: "Good governance in Africa is vital to peace, stability, sustainable development, and growth. Without good governance, all other reforms will have limited impacts" (Heiligendamm G8 Communiqué, 8 June 2007 at www.g8.utoronto.ca).

The promises being made by wealthy countries need to be set in a broader context. After 9/11 the global security agenda shifted. Suddenly the top priority was the War on Terror in Afghanistan and Pakistan—in fact, anywhere where extremists might be contributing to international terrorist activities. Soon after, the invasion of Iraq signalled a new approach to containing and disarming states thought to have weapons of mass destruction (WMD). Inevitably demoted were efforts to prevent or resolve conflicts within poorer states, such as the one currently raging in the Darfur region of Sudan.

These developments magnified three existing challenges to foreign aid. First, donors may hijack foreign aid to pursue their own security goals instead of helping the world's poor. Second, the wars in Afghanistan and Iraq and the broader War on Terror have been extremely costly, diverting and reducing other aid budgets. Generous promises of increased aid have not translated into real new flows. "Aid to Sub-Saharan Africa has stalled," concluded the OECD DAC in 2006 (OECD DAC 2006a, Figure 2.2), while the World Bank reports that net ODA disbursements in fact declined by US$3 billion in 2006 (World Bank 2007a, p. 55). The third challenge to aid is that major donors are failing to coordinate their aid programs through existing multilateral institutions, choosing instead to establish their own new mechanisms and pursue their own priorities. The result is competition and clashes among priorities, which has led to chaos in many of the poorest recipient countries with regard to how aid is being delivered. This chapter assesses the scope for more aid and good governance promotion in the context of the emerging aid policies of the United States, Japan, the United Kingdom, and the European Union.*

## The New Security Imperatives and the Risks to Foreign Aid

New security concerns rapidly came to dominate foreign policy after 9/11. Inevitably those concerns spilled over into aid policy. Foreign aid has always been influenced by donors' geostrategic interests. Once a government allocates money to foreign aid, a range of national and commercial interests heavily influence how much aid is given and how it is disbursed (Alesina and Dollar 1990).[1] Even so, researchers have found that a genuine moral vision underpins development assistance (Lumsdaine 1993). Furthermore, efforts to improve aid policies were already under way in the 1990s.

The end of the Cold War inspired a lively debate about how to make aid more effective (Burnside and Dollar 1997; Easterly, Levine, and Roodman 2003; Hansen and Tarp 2000). This dovetailed with a resolve among donor governments to ensure that the aid they were giving was put to better use. A consensus emerged that aid would be most effective if donors forged better partnerships with recipient governments and if those governments in turn had greater "ownership" of policies. The new shared goals of development assistance were formally expressed as the Millennium Development Goals. At a global summit on financing for development in Monterrey in 2002, governments pledged to reduce poverty, disease, illiteracy, and human insecurity throughout the world.

Security concerns were part of the rethinking of development assistance even in the 1990s. Countries' internal conflicts were ruining the lives of their most vulnerable people and destroying hope for human development. The Cold War had distorted foreign aid by channelling it toward geostrategic goals. In the 1990s concerted efforts were made to refocus on human security (UNDP 2002). The links between poverty and security were widely recognized, as expressed by Britain's development minister: "poverty is both a cause and an effect of human insecurity in developing countries" (Benn 2004). The lesson of the 1990s was that tackling poverty and insecurity together would require aid that fosters sound and effective governance. But that is no easy task.

Civil wars and post-conflict reconstruction programs pose a serious challenge to donors. Typically, these situations require emergency relief. Donors act as quickly as they can to get food, peacekeepers, and/or medical supplies directly to people on the ground. In so doing, they often override local institutions. The risk is that emergency relief efforts of this sort can establish patterns of assistance that keep local officials dependent on donors. When this happens, they will not grow their own institutions. Exacerbating the problem, emergency assistance often dries up quickly, leaving governments on the ground with neither the resources nor the legitimacy to begin governing. Here, interventions in Afghanistan are instructive.

A large part of the assistance sent to Afghanistan was for emergency relief. Beyond that, donors did not pledge enough for reconstruction, nor have they disbursed what they pledged. By March 2003, Afghanistan had received the lowest per capita aid for post-conflict reconstruction (less than Kosovo, East Timor, Bosnia, Palestine, Rwanda, and Haiti had received), and a large proportion of that aid had been emergency assistance (McKechnie 2003). Of the total amount disbursed between January 2002 and February 2004, at least one-third went to emergency relief rather than reconstruction (Rubin et al. 2003). Of some US$1,352 million committed to that country for March 2003 to March 2004, only $536 million was actually disbursed.[2]

Equally problematic in Afghanistan was the lack of coordination among donors. In November 2001 the Afghanistan Reconstruction Steering Group (ARSG), chaired jointly by the United States, the European Union, Japan, and Saudi Arabia, was established to give overall direction to reconstruction. The Afghanistan Reconstruction Implementation Group (ARIG) was intended to be a forum for implementing projects through the Asian Development Bank, the Islamic Development Bank, the UN, the World Bank, and the Afghan Support Group (ASG). Over time the ARIG and the ASG developed a consultative role; the ARSG, however, was unable to raise sufficient donor funds. In 2002 the Afghan government founded its own Afghanistan Assistance Coordination Authority, which subsequently ran into resistance from specific ministries. Also, in May 2002 the Afghanistan Reconstruction Trust Fund was founded, and many donors began channelling non-humanitarian assistance through it. The result was problems of coordination among donors—problems that are certainly not unprecedented. Indeed, a scholarly account of the similar lack of donor coordination in Bosnia-Herzegovina raises the same issues (Cousens 2002).

Donors have long recognized that multiple countries and agencies often pursue similar goals in a country and trip over one another. The result is duplication, waste, and overwhelming red tape in terms of reporting requirements and loan negotiations. The problem is being documented by the OECD Development Assistance Committee (DAC), including a set of studies on the lack of coordination among donors.[3]

When individual donor countries insist on doing things their own way, waste results. In this regard, it is worth noting that donor governments have already created multilateral mechanisms for disbursing aid. These include organizations such as the World Bank and its concessional arm the International Development Association, the United Nations Development Programme, the World Health Organization, and the Food and Agriculture Organization. These specialized agencies combine technical expertise with the pooled resources of states; their purpose is to facilitate cooperation. Yet the multilateral aid agencies risk becoming even more marginalized as larger proportions of donor aid budgets are spent by national agencies—or "bilaterally," in the aid jargon—rather than through multilaterals.

Adding to the mess, donors' goals are often at odds. Some examples: the fiscal rectitude promoted by one agency is achieved at the expense of the poverty reduction sought by another; the national security sought by one branch of a donor government is at odds with the human rights and development projects promoted by another. The lack of coherence in priorities is not the result of a lack of understanding or knowledge; what drives these seemingly perverse and counterproductive actions are competing objectives, as well as the competing incentives faced by each national and multilateral agency involved in disbursing aid.

Donors have begun to recognize that incoherence is a problem. The World Bank, the IMF, and a few donors using sector-wide approaches (SWAPS) have been attempting to enhance coordination and coherence. In Canada, the Netherlands, Australia, the United Kingdom, and the United States, efforts have been under way to weave the various diplomatic, military, and development initiatives into a more coherent and effective response to failing states (Harmer and Macrae 2004). What donors are *failing* to do is allow space for recipient governments to define their own priorities and set down frameworks that would compel donors to act better.

Paradoxically, to the extent that real coherence is in fact emerging, it is focused not on a development agenda, but rather on addressing global and regional security imperatives—imperatives that often run counter to the pursuit of human security and development.

In the following sections of this chapter I analyze the shifting priorities of major donors, their approaches to funding those new priorities, and the mechanisms they are applying to deliver aid.

## The United States:
## More Aid, More Security, and More Institutions

The United States is the world's largest provider of global development aid. In 2004–5 it accounted for 25.4 percent of official development aid, having more than doubled aid since 2002 (OECD DAC 2006a, Table 8). The top seven recipients of US official development aid in 2004–5 were Iraq, Afghanistan, Egypt, Sudan, Ethiopia, Jordan, and Colombia. (OECD DAC 2006a). This compares with the top seven of 1994–95: Israel, Egypt, Haiti, Jordan, Somalia, Palau, and Rwanda.

The new security imperatives figure strongly in US official development assistance. Yet more strongly, the new security imperatives dominate other kinds of US aid that do not qualify as development assistance, such as the Economic Support Fund, which permits the US to give assistance for priorities the first among which is "assistance to allies in the global war on terror"; and foreign military spending, where the US provides articles and services to support coalitions partners and states critical to the Global War on Terror (USAID 2007). For example, in 2006 actual development assistance to the Near East (which includes Lebanon, Morocco, and Middle East Regional) was just over US$10 million, as compared to more than US$6 billion disbursed through the economic support fund (US$2.881 billion) and foreign military spending (US$3.814 billion) (USAID 2007, pp. 92–99). In South and Central Asia (which includes Afghanistan, Bangladesh, India, Nepal, Pakistan, Sri Lanka, and South Asia Regional), development assistance spending in 2006 was US$259 million as compared with over a billion on economic support (US$831 million) and foreign military spending (US$305 million) (USAID 2007, pp. 92–99).

Much of the US War on Terror has been funded through supplemental appropriations requested by the President outside of the annual appropriations act. For example, in September 2003 the President requested US$87 billion as a supplemental appropriation to fund ongoing military operations in Iraq and Afghanistan (www.whitehouse.gov/omb/budget/amendments/supplemental_9_17_03.pdf). Even though flows to Iraq had been dramatically increased, a further US$2 billion was being requested in 2007 as a supplemental to the Economic Support Fund, and a further US$770 million as an emergency fund for 2008. It remains the case that extraordinary expenditures in Iraq place pressure on all foreign assistance spending by the United States.

Contemporaneously with the war in Iraq, the United States in 2004 launched a bold new initiative—the Millennium Challenge Account—that promised to safeguard at least some US aid from geostrategic goals. The new foreign aid program was designed to help low-income countries who are "ruling justly, investing in their people, and encouraging economic freedom." Fenced off from other sources of US aid, the MCA would give grants according to the results achieved by the governments of those countries rather than the promises made by them. The criteria for grants would be objective and development based. The MCA also promised recipients substantial control over the projects so financed instead of offering them money to meet donor priorities (Radelet and Herrling 2003).

Countries are eligible after the Millennium Challenge Corporation Board applies sixteen indicators to assess the policy performance of individual countries.[4] The early list of MCA-eligible countries included Armenia, Benin, Bolivia, Cape Verde, Georgia, Ghana, Honduras, Lesotho, the Malagasy Republic, Mali, Mongolia, Morocco, Mozambique, Nicaragua, Senegal, Sri Lanka, and Vanuatu. It was interesting because most of the countries declared eligible had *not* been major recipients of US funding in the past. For Benin, the Malagasy Republic, Mozambique, and Senegal, for example, France has traditionally been the largest donor. Indeed, the early list roughly approximated the set of countries currently being funded by major European donors, including Denmark, Luxembourg, Norway, and the Netherlands, which had already committed themselves to directing significant amounts of aid to countries with better policies and institutions.[5]

Some twenty countries have subsequently been declared eligible for the MCA. As yet, however, the MCA has as yet had little effect on aid. It has disbursed only 6.8 percent of appropriated funds available for programs: a total of US$382 million (see www.mcc.gov/countries/csr/all_CSR.pdf; Herrling and Rose 2007).

A further problem with the MCA is that it added yet another institution to an already crowded arena. The MCA may not have disbursed much development assistance; it did, however, send a strong signal that the United States intended to channel development assistance through its own newly created, unilaterally controlled institution; this even though the field was already crowded by USAID, the World Bank Group, the UN special agencies, the regional development banks, and the other institutions mentioned above. A new agency was sure to result in duplication of programs and increased program costs.

The MCA is not the only new mechanism for US aid delivery. The United States has also channelled its assistance to Iraq and the fight against HIV/AIDS through new mechanisms that eschew multilateral cooperation and the technical expertise and experience concentrated in existing aid-directing institutions.

Most US aid to Iraq has *not* been managed by USAID, the federal agency responsible for foreign aid. Initially, a special Program Management Office was created to manage assistance aimed at reconstructing Iraq's infrastructure. This became the Project and Contracting Office (PCO) attached to the Coalition Provisional Authority, and subsequently migrated to the new US embassy in Baghdad. The result of this new set of arrangements was that an institution that did not exist in 2002 was by 2006 managing more US aid than USAID.

The creation of a new institution to manage aid to Iraq did not address a number of key problems in delivering aid (leaving aside the intense debate about Halliburton's role in Iraq's reconstruction; go to www.publicintegrity .org/wow). The PCO was not able to spend quickly; as of January 2005 only $1.48 billion had been spent on work in place.[6] The US aid package almost certainly devoted too many resources to capital-intensive projects managed by foreign contractors and too little to labour-intensive projects that would have created jobs for Iraqis. Indeed, it was reported in June 2004 that the United States was using $2.5 billion in windfall gains from higher than expected revenues from the sale of Iraqi oil to provide fast-disbursing "walk-around money" for US commanders to spend on "quick-hitting" projects of the sort that would deliver a bigger impact on the ground.[7] Using Iraqi oil revenues in this way avoided the restrictions intrinsic in the budget process and implicitly recognized the difficulties encountered in the formal reconstruction effort.

In the global battle against HIV/AIDS, the United States has increased its total funding more rapidly than other industrialized countries. By 2006 the United States had committed US$2.6 billion and disbursed US$1.6 billion, a small part of which was channelled through multilaterals (Kates et al. 2007).

In governing this aid, the US administration has made it clear that it prefers its own program to existing multilateral ones.[8] Overall AIDS funding is being coordinated by a committee chaired by the State Department rather than by the Global Fund. The administration consistently requested only $100 million a year for the Global Fund through the foreign aid budget (and another $100 million from the health and human services budget)—a figure that Congress raised to around $250 million in 2003 and $400 million in 2004 (with an additional $100 to 150 million in the health and human services budget). In announcing his Emergency Plan for AIDS Relief in January 2003, the president pledged $15 billion for a new initiative—just $1 billion of which would go to the Global Fund, and even that conditional on the fund showing results.

Bush's special initiative for fighting HIV/AIDS followed rapidly on that of his predecessor, President William Clinton, whose administration created the Global Fund for HIV/AIDS, Tuberculosis, and Malaria. This fund augmented work being done on the same issue by the World Bank, the World Health Organization, and several private organizations. Indeed, when the Global Fund was created, its founders were well aware that health program duplication was a problem. For this reason, the Global Fund was set up purely to disburse funds. Country coordinating mechanisms (CCMS) were established in each recipient country whose purpose was to formulate and administer proposals.

However, these CCMs often do not work well. The Global Fund and other highly worthy initiatives all suffer from the proliferation of competing rather than cooperating or coordinated agencies and programs.

Overall, US aid is marked by two trends. First, new security imperatives have increased flows of US "development assistance" and other external assistance to countries of geostrategic importance. On a smaller scale, the United States has also increased funding for the fight against HIV/AIDS and pledged a total of $6 billion to the Millennium Challenge Account. These increases will be difficult to sustain, given the ballooning budget deficit of the United States and constant increases for many budget items. The second trend in US aid is toward even greater national control of aid and the potentially costly creation of new mechanisms for disbursing and delivering it.

## Japan:
## Less Aid, More Security, More Institutions

Unlike the United States and the United Kingdom, Japan has absorbed the new security imperatives in the context of a shrinking rather than an increasing external assistance budget. From 1991 to 2002, Japan was the world's largest single provider of official development assistance (ODA).[9] In 1997 the government began to reduce its ODA budget, which fell by 27 percent between 1997 and 2003.[10] The large cuts were driven in part by a fiscal crisis in Japan that led to across-the-board reductions in government spending.[11] They also reflected a degree of "aid fatigue" and the perception that the public was disaffected with the government's development assistance program.[12] The Japanese government amended its Development Assistance Charter in 2003 so that it focused more strongly on its foreign policy priorities: poverty reduction, sustainable growth, peace building, and what it vaguely called "global issues" (which include terrorism and epidemics).

The recipients of Japanese aid tend to be in Asia; between 1998 and 2002 almost three-quarters of Japanese ODA went to Asian recipients (Japan, Ministry of Foreign Affairs 2001). By the beginning of the new millennium, China and India had displaced Indonesia and Thailand as the top recipients of Japanese aid. In part, this reflected the receding impact of the Asian financial crisis in the latter two countries. Since then, aid to China has been sharply cut—by some 20 percent in 2003. Meanwhile, India has continued to gain; recently it has become the top recipient of Japanese aid, much of it in the form of infrastructure loans. Japan also continues to provide the financial muscle behind the Asian Development Bank, contributing half its US$20 billion in Asian Development Fund resources. This is part of the 28 percent or so of Japan's ODA that it channels through multilateral institutions.

Japan's ODA budget allocations have continued to decline (they fell again in 2004, by almost 5 percent). Even so, it has made extensive commitments to help with postwar reconstruction in Afghanistan and Iraq (ibid., chap. 2). In January 2002 Japan pledged ¥6.5 billion in aid to Afghanistan over two and a half years, following the US-led military operations in the country. In 2003 Japan pledged $1.5 billion in grants to help rebuild Iraq and a further $3.5 billion in loans. To meet some of these commitments, the Diet increased Emergency Grant Aid funds from ¥22.2 billion to ¥31.7 billion (an increase of about $100 million) for 2004—an increase significantly less than the allocation requested by the Ministry of Foreign Affairs.

Where will other funds for reconstruction come from? One source will be the Japan Fund for Poverty Reduction, established in the Asian Development Bank in 2003: some US$27 million of the $35 million fund administered by the bank will go to aid for Afghan reconstruction. At least some aid to Iraq has been in the form of new lending from the Japan Bank for International Cooperation (JBIC). Regarding the balance of Japan's pledges, they may either not be met (in view of the politics of Japan's aid cuts) or come out of other elements of Japan's aid budget, involving a further redistribution among recipients. This is presaged by the 2001 White Paper on Japanese ODA, the second chapter of which outlines Japan's intention to use its aid more strategically to promote peace and prosperity and to further Japan's broader foreign policy interests.

What mechanisms is Japan using to channel aid? It is often asserted that as the United States becomes more unilateral, Japan becomes more multilateral. Yet the available evidence does not bear this out. The Japanese government has long underscored its commitment to multilateralism and its desire to see foreign aid undertaken in a more coordinated and more coherent fashion around the globe. However, not unlike the United States, Japan's subsequent actions have revealed a strong and persistent impulse to retain control over this assistance.

As chair of the G8 in 2000, Japan announced the "Okinawa Infectious Diseases Initiative" and its intention to provide assistance of approximately $3 billion toward combating infectious diseases over five years. How has this been spent? A large proportion of Japan's aid in respect of HIV/AIDS has been spent on bilateral programs to combat the disease in countries such as Vietnam, Sri Lanka, Kenya, Congo, Haiti, and Zambia. Japan also began in 2001 to investigate joint projects with the United States in Tanzania, Zambia, Bangladesh, and Cambodia.

Japan is contributing directly to multilateral organizations such as the UN Population Fund, the International Planned Parenthood Federation (IPPF), and UNAIDS. At the same time, though, it has found ways to retain control over programs funded through such organizations. For example, it contributes to special trust funds such as the Japan Trust Fund for HIV/AIDS established in the IPPF, and to the Japan Special Fund in the Asian Development Bank. Japan has also undertaken "multi-bi" cooperation, whereby it acts jointly with international organizations such as WHO, UNICEF, and UNFPA.

In sum, in response to the war on terror, Japan, like the United States, is using supplementary appropriations to deliver contributions to the war in Afghanistan and the reconstruction of Iraq. It has also moved to recognize a broader range of security goals as a legitimate part of its aid mission. The risk is that Japan, like the United States, may increasingly use aid to serve its own security aims. Although Japan is an active "multilateralist," it continues to participate in multilateral aid on its own terms, using special arrangements to retain some degree of national control.

### The United Kingdom:
### More Aid, More Security; Whither Multilateralism?

Like the United States and Japan, the United Kingdom is among the world's largest development assistance donors. Since 1997 it has significantly increased its development assistance, casting its priorities in stone in 1997 with the creation of a full Department of International Development (DFID). The DFID has a Cabinet-level secretary of state, who is prohibited from directing assistance to any person or body unless "he is satisfied that the provision of the assistance is likely to contribute to a reduction in poverty." In addition, British aid is governed by a public service agreement with the Treasury, which for the period 2005–8 has set out goals that include the following: to ensure that the proportion of the DFID's bilateral program going to low-income countries (LICS) is at least 90 percent; to achieve a greater impact of EC external programs on poverty reduction; and to work for agreement to increase the proportion of EC official development assistance (ODA) to low-income countries (LICS) from its 2000 baseline figure of 38 percent to 70 percent by 2008.

Since its creation the DFID has been assigned a rising share of government expenditures. Its budget had grown to £3.8 billion by the fiscal year 2004–5, with the 2004 Spending Review confirming annual increases of 9.2 percent (the highest of any government department) through to 2007–8. UK official development assistance rose from £5.9 billion in 2005 to £6.8 billion in 2006 (DFID 2007 at www.dfid.gov.uk).

At the same time, the United Kingdom has rapidly expanded its security commitments, stepping in behind the United States as that country's most visible ally in both the War on Terror and the occupation of Iraq. Preliminary figures for the costs of the occupation of Iraq have been very significant. The Ministry of Defence spent £1 billion on additional costs of operations in Iraq in the year 2005–6. A further £200 million was spent on the additional costs of operations in Afghanistan (Ministry of Defence 2006, p. 201).

The DFID's direct expenditure in Iraq has risen dramatically. In 2002 it was 0.39 percent of the total net UK bilateral official development assistance. By 2005, Iraq was receiving 16.14 percent of the total net UK bilateral ODA (DFID 2007, p. 242). Iraq has also consumed a large share of multilateral assistance. The imputed UK share of multilateral net official development assistance to Iraq rose from 1.9 percent in 2002 to 18.6 percent in 2004, dropping to 4.5 percent in 2005 (DFID 2007, p. 263).

The strain on the DFID's resources and mandate to reduce poverty generated by the War on Terror and the war in Iraq had immediate effect even before the increments described above. Afghanistan, Iraq, and Pakistan shot to the top of the department's list of bilateral recipients by 2004. Commitments to Iraq made it harder in 2003–4 to pursue the pledge that 90 percent of country program resources, excluding humanitarian assistance, would be provided to LICS by 2005–6 (ibid.). To address this, spending in middle-income countries was reduced by around £100 million in 2004–5 and 2005–6.

Through what institutions does the United Kingdom deliver aid? It has retained a large bilateral aid program but has also long been committed to delivering a large portion of its aid budget through multilateral mechanisms. Between 1990 and 2001 over 40 percent of British ODA was channelled through multilateral institutions. This had declined to 28.8 percent by 2002 but rose again to 37.7 percent in 2003. In 2004 the DFID reported that 45 percent of its program expenditures were being channelled through multilateral organizations (DFID 2004b). By 2006 this had dropped back to 37 percent (DFID 2007, p. 140). The British also work closely with European aid agencies, channelling a significant proportion of their aid through the EC. Finally, the DFID has increased the degree to which it channels aid to partner governments for them to spend using their own management, procurement, and accountability systems. Since 2000 budget supports and other forms of program aid have accounted for about 15 percent of the DFID's bilateral aid program (DFID 2004a).

The British have also tried to make their aid policy more coherent throughout the government. Since 2000 the DFID has operated, jointly with the MOD and the Foreign and Commonwealth Office (FOC), two conflict prevention pools (CPPS): one for Africa, the other for the rest of the world. Continuing allocations to these were confirmed in the 2004 Spending Review; the budget for the Africa CPP rose modestly to £60 million per annum, and remained stable at £74 million for the global CPP. While it is generally agreed that conflict prevention is vital to creating conditions for development in fragile states, the nexus of conflict/security/development issues is a highly sensitive one, as demonstrated by the concern among development NGOS over recent proposals to review the definitions of ODA in the DAC (more on this below).

In sum, British aid and the government's focus on poverty reduction, including in middle-income countries, is undoubtedly being diverted by the new security imperatives. However, this effect is being mitigated by a rising overall aid budget and by multilateral lending to middle-income countries. Conversely, the high share of British aid channelled through the EU is increasingly being used to meet new security imperatives.

## The EU:
## More Security, More Aid; How Much Coordination?

The EU and its member states together provide the world's single largest bloc of bilateral and multilateral aid, amounting to 52.32 percent of worldwide official development assistance (European Commission 2006). Individually and collectively, its member states have committed themselves to the Millennium Development Goals declared at Monterrey in 2002. In 2004 the EU declared that it is "firmly on target" but emphasized the need for greater coordination and harmonization among European donors in order to make aid more effective.[13] These goals were reaffirmed in the EU Development Policy Statement signed on 20 December 2005 (European Commission 2006).

Coordination is a crucial issue within the EU, which presents a golden opportunity for aid policies to be coordinated at least among its members. Coordination has already succeeded in trade and political partnerships. The common External Trade Policy and single seat in the WTO work to pull European countries into the same positions alongside their EU political partnerships (Grimm with Woll 2004). However, on aid more generally the story is a different one.

Each of the fifteen older members of the EU has its own large bilateral program as well as its own position on multilateral agencies. In the past, members' aid together with the EU budget, priorities, and policies was diluted by trade-offs among competing priorities. Typically, the Nordic states, the Netherlands, and the United Kingdom argued for a focus on poverty in overall allocations and within programs (in other words, they see the budget primarily as a development assistance budget). Southern EU member states tended to argue for allocations on more political grounds, either to address domestic political concerns (e.g., migration from northern African states) or to pursue external political goals (e.g., strong relations with Latin America). The 2005 Policy Statement reflects greater coherence and commitment to the Millennium Development Goal Targets. This reflects in the regional distribution of EU official development assistance in 2005: 44 percent went to Africa and 18 percent to Asia (European Commission 2006, p. 154).

The new security imperatives have reshaped EU patterns of action beyond its borders. Traditionally, the EU's security policy has been separate from its development assistance. Security policy has been pursued by individual member states, with the costs even of shared actions such as the recent joint military interventions in Macedonia (Operation Concordia) and the Democratic Republic of Congo (Operation Artemis) being borne mainly by individual participating states. Development assistance, by contrast, has always been to some degree administered by the EU as a whole—mainly through the External Action budget, which amounted to some €5.18 billion (out of a total annual EU budget of €111.30 billion) in 2004.

In June 2003 significant changes became noticeable when a new EU security framework was adopted (General Affairs and External Relations Council 2003). The 2003 framework declared security as a "first condition for development"—although it did not mention the reverse possibility, that development may sometimes be a first condition for security. It proposed that the EU's security strategy pay heed to programs aimed at strengthening governance through conditionality, trade measures, and technical assistance. It emphasized the need to create synergy between security and development goals through a more coherent and comprehensive approach.

The 2003 EU strategy fits with a broader shift among donors toward the use of aid for security purposes. The guardian of what constitutes "official development assistance" (ODA) is the OECD DAC. This body generally restrains efforts by donor governments to broaden the definition of ODA. However, in April 2004 the DAC announced that it was adjusting and clarifying the definition of ODA as it related to preventing the recruitment of child soldiers, enhancing civil society's role in security, and promoting civilian oversight and democratic control of security expenditures (OECD DAC 2004). The result was to widen the categories of assistance that DAC counts as ODA.

Is EU aid becoming more subservient to security goals? The EU's efforts to enhance coherence in external relations have provoked concern among development agencies (both governmental and non-governmental) that this will happen. The European Commission sought early on to allay this fear.[14] Several factors need to be assessed in analyzing the current trend.

The EU has been streamlining the governance of its External Relations aid budget. In 2001 it began channelling its aid through one agency—EuropeAid—rather than through four different directorates, as previously. Broader constitutional changes are afoot. A high representative of the union for foreign affairs and security policy—some would say a European foreign minister—is being created and will sit on both the Council and the Commission. It has been proposed that aid and all other external action items be brought under the heading "The EU as a Global Partner," with "economic cooperation and development" and "security" instruments brought closer together within the Common Foreign and Security Policy funding (Mackie and Rossini 2004). Put simply, development assistance could soon find itself squarely under foreign policy leadership.

Great policy coherence has been sought since 2001, culminating in a commitment in the 2005 Development Policy Statement to "Policy Coherence for Development," which calls for agricultural policy, trade policy, research and development policies, and other policies all to be deployed coherently to contribute to the Millennium Development Goals objectives.

The EU has devoted significant resources to reconstruction in Iraq and Afghanistan. In Iraq, efforts have focused on providing humanitarian relief and political and financial support to launch the reconstruction process. Since 2003, in addition to individual members' assistance, the European Commission has provided assistance to Iraq for an amount of €518.5 million (http://ec.europa.eu/external_relations/iraq/intro/index.htm). In Afghanistan, for the period 2002–6, the European Commission has delivered more than €1 billion in reconstruction aid (http://ec.europa.eu/external_relations/afghanistan/intro/index.htm).

The EU has funded most of its initial contributions to the War on Terror through additional appropriations. It has also begun to debate security and to broaden the types of security goals in the service of which it is prepared to deploy development assistance. It has also begun to consider institutional reforms that would pull development and security goals more closely together— possibly under a European foreign minister. For some this indicates a positive shift toward greater policy coherence; for others it raises the risk that development goals will become subservient to overarching strategic security concerns.

## Conclusions

Development assistance that prioritizes human development goals is at risk. A rapid increase in aid has been channelled to new security imperatives. But with acute budgetary pressures besetting Japan, France, Germany, and the United States (among others), it is a virtual certainty that much of the new aid flow (generated largely to fund the War on Terror as defined by the United States) will dry up. Development agencies, with their more stable budgets, will then be urged to give priority to the development needs of countries at the front lines of the War on Terror.

Paradoxically, previously rational efforts to enhance coordination and coherence among donors may now in some instances be counterproductive. The case of the EU highlights the possibility that while greater European coordination and coherence could *in theory* direct very significant aid flows toward the shared commitments of the Millennium Development Goals, in practice, current institutional shifts and political pressures suggest that the common European agenda will instead be driven by foreign policy concerns. This is only one case where, in the name of coherence, a greater diversion of aid flows for geostrategic purposes may take place, and increased coordination would magnify that effect. This is the global security scenario for foreign aid.

An alternative scenario is one in which development agencies continue to prioritize human development and the achievement of the Millennium Development Goals, which include human security, leaving to other agencies preoccupations with counterterrorism and WMD. Instead of attempting greater "coordination and coherence" of foreign, aid, and security policies in general, this scenario calls for a stronger differentiation and allocation of goals at the global level. This would require a commitment by donors to use existing multilateral institutions instead of perpetuating the erosion of multilateralism evident at present in increasing bilateral aid budgets. It would also require some protection within donor governments of the development assistance remit, to prevent a return to the Cold War patterns of almost purely geostrategically led aid that so obstructed rather than facilitated human development.

The development-led scenario requires two further things from donors. First, the development assistance community must address the timescale and predictability of aid flows. Donors need to join together and develop a long-term financial compact between themselves and recipients. Volatile or unpredictable aid flows do little to bolster good governance, coherent government budgets, or the development of sound institutions of accountability in recipient countries. Yet in most developing countries aid is proving to be even more volatile than fiscal revenues (Bulir and Hamann 2003), despite evidence that shortfalls in aid produce poor policies (Gemmell and McGillivray 1998). The new security-driven aid flows are already proving to be volatile and short term. But in other sectors as well where new resources are being promised—such as the global fight against HIV/AIDS—there is little guarantee that new flows will be sustained in the long term, or that the multiplicity of donor institutions that are supposed to disburse the assistance will not change priorities. What is needed is specific donor coordination with a view to committing long-term, predictable flows of resources.

Second, donors must rationalize the demands they place on recipient governments. A recent study by major donors details the duplications and gaps that result when donors impose a plethora of financial audits on recipients. Most damningly, it concludes that though the "World Bank and IMF would continue to take the lead in conducting most assessments of public expenditure management," all other parties should have access to information and "the views of governments (and other local stakeholders)" should be taken into account (Allen, Schiavo-Campo, and Garrity 2004). That finding highlights the extent to which donors' efforts have enhanced auditing of their own loans but failed to build capacity and accountability in public finances within recipient countries. The broader aid picture reveals a multiplicity of donors, whose demands not only fail to strengthen governmental processes within countries but also probably even hinder their development. Amid a growing cacophony of donors, very little space is left for local agencies to build, coordinate among themselves, and strengthen local governance. Scarce resources are used up strengthening and maintaining external relations with donors and undertaking externally demanded actions, some of which are contradictory. The problem is likely to grow as the number of goals and institutions involved in development assistance increases. At the very least, what is needed here is sharply focused coordination among groups of donors—such as shared, streamlined reporting requirements, so as to lessen diversion of local resources to the management of donors (OECD DAC 2003a). These conclusions highlight serious challenges for donors attempting to export good governance.

## Notes

* This analysis draws on an earlier article, "The Shifting Politics of Aid," *International Affairs* 81, no. 2 (March 2005): 393–409.
1 Ulterior motives have long encouraged critics on the right and the left to argue against aid. See, for example, Bauer 1984; Hayter 1971.
2 These figures are from http://www.af/dad/index.html.
3 An initial OECD DAC study documented how Rwanda donors failed to coordinate even in setting policy, each instead following its own priorities, with disastrous results. See OECD DAC 1998. The Working Party is detailed in OECD DAC 2003a.
4 See http://www.mca.gov.
5 Figures and comparisons are provided in World Bank 2006a.
6 http://www.rebuilding-iraq.net.
7 Steven R. Weisman, "U.S. Is Quietly Spending $2.5 Billion from Iraqi Oil Revenues to Pay for Iraqi Projects," *New York Times*, 21 June 2004, 1.
8 For a description of the president's new plan, see http://www.whitehouse.gov/news/releases/2003/01/20030129–1.html. For the difficulties facing the Global

Fund, as well as a summary of the debate swirling around the restrictions on the use of US funds to purchase generic drugs that have not passed US safety tests, see Gautam Naik, Mark Schoofs, and Sarah Lueck, "In the Aids Fight, Ambitious Goals Meet Hard Realities," *Wall Street Journal*, July 1, 2004.

9  A large proportion of Japanese bilateral ODA is disbursed in the form of loans, which constituted nearly 55 percent of total bilateral aid in 2002, by far the highest proportion among OECD ODA members. These ODA loans are generally untied, except for the short-term, tied Special Yen Loan facility (1999–2002), which is designed to help countries affected by the Asian financial crisis. The proportion of grants to loans in Japanese ODA has remained roughly constant over the past five years, but the loan component is likely to rise in the immediate future as loans for Iraq reconstruction are disbursed (more on this below).

10  Figures from Japanese Ministry of Finance; see http://www.mof.go.jp/english.

11  The populist version of the argument is reported by Tim Large, "Cash-Strapped Japan Rethinks Foreign Aid," Reuters AlertNet, October 20, 2003. http://www .alertnet.org/thefacts/reliefresources/106665138683.htm.

12  See the debate between the government and the leading opposition party on this, reported in *Yomiuri Shimbun* and reproduced in translation by Financial Times Information, "Matter of Opinion," 11 April 2003.

13  EU progress toward the goals is reported in EC 2004a.

14  EU Development Commissioner Poul Nielson in a communication to British NGOs, "Letter to the British Overseas NGOs for Development," http://www.bond .org.uk.

▲

# 2

## FOCUSING AID ON GOOD GOVERNANCE:
## CAN IT WORK?

### Sue Unsworth

## I
## Introduction

Can foreign aid be used to enhance good governance in recipient countries? The prevailing view among donors is still that the quality of governance in developing countries is critical to achievement of the Millennium Development Goals. There has been an explosion in numbers of governance advisers and projects, covering a broad, increasingly ambitious range of interventions touching on virtually all aspects of the public sector. Thinking about governance is shaping donor approaches to aid delivery, through Poverty Reduction Strategy processes, budget support, and current debates on aid conditionality. However, the question of *whether* donors can be effective in promoting "good governance"—as opposed to the constant restless search for how to do it better—is hardly ever asked.

This may be, in part, because the question is unanswerable, at least in any definitive way, given the current state of our knowledge. There have been few systematic evaluations that offer good learning above the level of individual projects. The main actors have different, often vague definitions of what they mean by good governance, although the implicit model—embodied, for example, in governance assessment frameworks—is the reproduction of Weberian norms and democratic political systems as found in OECD countries. There is a lack of agreement about measurable indicators, and often no clearly articulated working hypothesis linking inputs with outputs and higher-level objectives. Donors come with different objectives: democracy builders see this as an end in its own right, while others pursue better governance as a means to promote growth and poverty reduction, or to counter the security risks posed by collapsed or fragile states.

Nevertheless some worthwhile learning has accumulated, based on the experience of practitioners and on evaluation studies. From this has emerged a new conventional wisdom about the importance of local demand and "ownership" of reform measures, the risks of overloading the agenda, and the need for realism about timescales and for better understanding of political economy constraints. The critical question is what donors will now do with these insights.

This chapter starts by taking a brief look at the history of donor efforts to strengthen public institutions in developing countries, and at how these have evolved in response to accumulated learning and changing interests and ideas. Section III takes a closer look at the findings of recent evaluations of governance interventions. Section IV considers the inferences that development practitioners are drawing from those evaluations. It suggests that without a fundamental reappraisal of underlying assumptions about governance, the impact of past learning will be at best marginal. In particular there is a risk that good intentions will get derailed under pressure to make large, rapid increases in spending to meet the timetable for achieving the Millennium Development Goals.

Section V looks at what a fundamental reappraisal would involve. Some donors are starting to take a serious interest in the relevant political science research. This is informing internal debates and informal discussions that increasingly recognize the scale of the challenge confronted by poor countries seeking to build more effective, legitimate public institutions; the fundamental lack of knowledge about the processes involved; and the limitations on what external actors can contribute. But these insights are only partly reflected in more formal policy statements. Donor rhetoric may recognize the importance of politics, but the reality is all too often continued adherence to a fairly conventional set of good governance interventions. Donors should be less afraid of confronting the uncomfortable implications of their increasingly sophisticated understanding of "governance." Greater realism need not induce pessimism: it could instead offer greater clarity about priorities, open up new opportunities, and suggest ways in which donors might—often indirectly—help strengthen local political processes that are indispensable to the search for more effective and accountable government. These issues are explored in sections VI and VII.

This chapter does not deal with collapsed states or states engulfed in conflict, where particular considerations apply and where priorities revolve around basic security and survival. It is concerned with a wide range of poor countries with functioning governments, but where major weaknesses in political legitimacy and administrative capacity act as significant constraints on economic and social development. Donors often employ the term "good governance" without defining it, but implicitly associate it with the development of more democratic political systems and Weberian public institutions. Section v suggests the need for a less normative approach, with the emphasis less on formal organizational structures and more on how they actually work.

Finally, in addressing the question of whether donor interventions can enhance good governance, the chapter assumes that—whether as an end in itself, or as a means to other ends—better governance has been a genuine objective. In practice, of course, donors often have to strike compromises with other parts of their own governments pursuing different, and possibly conflicting, objectives. This issue is specifically addressed in section VII.

## II
## Insights from History

Good governance came on to the donor agenda in the 1990s. But it was preceded by a long history of donor efforts to strengthen public institutions in developing countries. These included, in the 1950s and 1960s, interventions inspired by modernization theory, such as the Rule of Law movement supported by the US government. By the 1970s the focus had narrowed back to a preoccupation with identifying and meeting skills gaps, especially in the public service and the judiciary, with an emphasis on training and counterpart arrangements. For example, the UK's Ministry for Overseas Development supported hundreds of "supplemented" staff throughout the public service in the ex-colonies, conducting regular "manpower reviews" to assess needs. By the 1980s the focus had broadened to encompass the organizational context, including interventions in management restructuring and job evaluation. In the mid-1980s, with the advent of structural adjustment programs, the focus shifted again, to include broader public service restructuring, with an emphasis on cost reduction and the retrenchment of government from non-core functions. But the impact was modest, early gains proved difficult to sustain, and there was mounting concern that reforms were damaging already weak capacity. By the mid-1990s there was renewed concern with capacity building in the public sector as the key to improved service delivery, supported by interventions to decentralize functions, create more autonomous agencies, and improve incentives and pay as well as the wider work environment.

In parallel, and accelerating throughout the 1990s, was a new preoccupation with "good governance." The democracy building movement took off on a wave of optimism inspired by the end of the Cold War and political opening in Eastern Europe, the former Soviet Union, and many parts of the developing world. There was burgeoning support for civil society, linked both to democracy promotion efforts and to movements to empower poor people and encourage their participation in the design and implementation of projects. But there was also increasing concern that weak administrative capacity, systemic corruption, and lack of "political will" were impeding programs for poverty reduction, especially in highly indebted and aid-dependent countries. A growing list of governance reforms was advocated for inclusion in Poverty Reduction Strategy papers (Grindle 2002). There was increasing focus on the links between institutions and growth, based on the work of Douglass North and others. There was emphasis on the need for "ownership" of policy reform, and recognition that externally imposed conditionality was a very defective instrument for achieving it (Killick 1998). Toward the end of the decade concerns were being raised about the failure to take sufficient account of political and institutional factors, based partly on the experience of transition countries. These various trends are well reflected in a series of Target Strategy Papers published by the UK's Department for International Development between 1999 and 2001.

Why is any of this interesting in relation to the central question being addressed? Primarily because of what it tells us about the culture and political economy of donors. A positive interpretation would be that it shows serious professionals intent on learning lessons from past experience and responding to them, and there is a good deal of truth in this. But a more negative view would be of a constant, restless search for the next "fix": a rapid succession of new remedies, often poorly understood by harassed program managers, and dictated more by fashions or changing preoccupations in developed countries than by a good understanding of processes of change in developing countries. The agenda has been set by donors: structural adjustment, liberalization and privatization, good governance, even (arguably) poverty reduction. It has been shaped by thinking based on research and experience in developed countries: New Public Management, New Institutional Economics, the Rights Based Approach. Most striking, perhaps, is the way in which the governance agenda has expanded to incorporate a huge range of interests and concerns, with the result that it risks becoming diffuse, incoherent, and unmanageable (Grindle 2002).

## III
## Evaluation of Governance Interventions

All commentators bemoan the lack of systematic evaluation studies of governance interventions. However, there is material that provides at least a preliminary assessment of different components of donor support for improved governance. These include democracy building, civil society assistance, public sector reform including pay reform, and anti-corruption interventions. From a sample of studies, working papers, and meeting reports, some common themes emerge.

### Modest Impact, Huge Challenges

Overall, the impact of external assistance has been at best modest, and the challenges are recognized as huge. "What stands out about US rule of law assistance since the mid 1980s is how difficult and often disappointing such work is" (Carothers 1999, 170). A review of civil service reform projects implemented by the World Bank between 1987 and 1997 (World Bank 1999a) found that only 29 percent were "satisfactory." "The Bank has achieved only modest success so far in achieving durable outcomes [from anticorruption efforts] … the unusual complexity of the task in hand, and the magnitude of the challenge, account for the gap" (OED 2004, x). Particular doubts emerge regarding top-down attempts to transfer institutions from developed countries: a recent DAC paper on anticorruption, for example, acknowledges that importing institutional models from OECD countries (such as anticorruption commissions) has been successful in only very limited circumstances (DACb 2006, 7).

### Success at Project Level, Lack of Impact at Sector Level

An OED evaluation of World Bank country assistance programs (OED 2005, 4–5) finds relatively successful outcomes for public-sector management interventions at a project level, but lack of impact at a sector level. This is echoed in individual project evaluations—for example, of a long-running project supported by the UK in Bangladesh to implement reforms in budgeting and expenditure control (DFID 2001). This found evidence of tangible improvements at the output level in data quality and availability (budgeting, financial reporting), but a lack of demand that constrained its use in improving resource allocation and financial management more generally. A common finding for many donor-supported projects is that overoptimistic assumptions are made at the outset about the institutional environment to support project objectives at "purpose" level, with the consequence that objectives, or timescales for meeting them, often prove unrealistic.

## Importance of the Political and Institutional Environment

The importance of the political and institutional environment is highlighted in many studies, and parallels World Bank findings about economic aid having a positive impact where institutions and policies are supportive. Levy (2004) suggests that a principal reason for limited success of civil service reform and other capacity-building efforts in Africa is "the implicit assumption that the weakness of public administration was managerial" (2004, 11). Instead, he suggests, a central lesson of experience is that public administrators are embedded in a "complex, interdependent system" incorporating "political institutions and social, political and economic interests more broadly" (ibid., 11). Public-service reform has been relatively successful in Tanzania, which has a long history of external support based on government commitment and indeed innovation. It has been much more problematic in Zambia and Ghana (Stevens and Teggemann 2004). The politics of pay reform have proven especially challenging (Kiragu, Mukandala, and Morin 2004). Carothers (1999, 304) suggests that democracy assistance can help "speed up a moving train" where democratic forces are already at work, but that it doesn't affect outcomes in decisive or significant ways. For example, democracy assistance seems to have played a modest but useful role in recent developments in Ghana (Booth et al. 2005). Donor assistance for the constitutional review process in Kenya in 2000–2 arguably contributed to the success of that movement (though the subsequent history showed the limits of donor influence once the local coalition for change fell apart). Conversely, Carothers has found that where democracy is stagnating or sliding backwards, aid has few chances of reversing the trend.

## Pattern of Early Unsustainable Success

A common pattern is of early success that is not sustained. For example, a DAC-sponsored review of public-service reform programs in five Anglophone African countries shows evidence of some success with "quick wins" of limited scope (e.g., in faster processing of business licences), but difficulty in sustaining broader structural reforms, especially as they relate to civil service pay (DAC 2002). The experience with autonomous revenue authorities is decidedly mixed. The case of Uganda is particularly poignant: it shows both how aid can have a significant positive effect where there is strong government ownership of a reform program, but also how vulnerable hard-won gains are to reversal when political conditions change.

## Intermediate Success Stories

On a brighter note, there are some intermediate success stories that should not be undervalued—notably, the development of better diagnostic tools and the encouragement of more open public debate about the negative effects of corruption; and the placing of poverty or rule-of-law issues on the political agenda through the Poverty Reduction Strategy process (PRSP) or through rule-of-law programs. Also, civil society assistance has achieved gains at the micro level, though it may have done little to encourage genuine pluralism or to support broader democratization objectives (Ottaway and Carothers 2000).

## Good Ideas: Relative Success of Home-Grown Reforms

Good ideas can catch on. For example, tax reform efforts in Latin America in the 1990s, inspired by the International Financial Institutions, have achieved improvements in tax administration and some policy reforms, including tax reductions on foreign trade and a lowering of marginal rates on upper incomes. Unsurprisingly, efforts to broaden the tax base have been less successful, and equity issues have not been addressed. The most striking development, perhaps, is the relative success of home-grown reforms that address local issues, including the political dimensions of tax reform (Lledo, Schneider, and Moore 2004). More generally, some of the most successful initiatives—such as the right to information movement in Rajasthan—have deliberately eschewed external support.

## IV
## The New Conventional Wisdom

The limited impact of many past reform efforts can be explained in part by the following: a lack of realism regarding higher-level objectives; inadequate investment of time and resources; poor project design and implementation; failure to take account of likely opposition; and poor sequencing. But most commentators point to more fundamental concerns. They underline that all governance interventions—and indeed, the broader poverty reduction agenda—are highly political, and that external interventions need to be much better informed by an understanding of local political factors. From this has emerged a new conventional wisdom, the main elements of which are as follows:

- **Donors need a better understanding of the political and institutional context**  Anticorruption strategies call for "an approach that views corruption in the context of the wider political economy of public sector governance in each country" (DACb 2006, 3). Donors need to understand the local political environment and to take into account the underlying interests and power relations in which institutions are embedded. "Democracy promoters have to challenge their own ideas about politics and come to terms with how much—or how little—they really know about political change in other societies" (Carothers 1999, 343). They also need a better understanding of the political economy of reforms. "Corruption is grounded in political contexts and social fragmentation over which the Bank has limited influence … a better understanding of social and political factors at a country level would enhance the quality and impact of Bank advice" (OED 2004, ix).

• **Donors need to nurture demand for improved governance**  There is a need to nurture demand for improved service delivery and to broaden the constituency for public-service reform (DAC 2002, 9). Improving governance calls for action both on the "supply" side (improving capabilities of public institutions) and the "demand" side (accountability arrangements) (World Bank 2006a, 10). Externally generated demand—for instance, through conditionality—seldom works: "We believe that it is inappropriate and has proven to be ineffective for donors to impose policies on developing countries" (DFID 2005, 4). There is a need to "deal with the demand dilemma" by fostering demand among a wide spectrum of stakeholders (OED 2005, 52).

• **Institutional development needs time and patience**  Donors need to recognize how fundamental the challenge is. Impatience with institution building is one of their "seven deadly sins" (Birdsall 2004, 5). Institutional reform and capacity building for effective governance are critical to successful outcomes, but this takes time (the 2005 OED country assistance evaluation suggests "several years"). Corruption is addressed most effectively through long-term institutional reforms (OED 2004, ix). "Development partners need to … engage on a long-term basis.… It took many years for durable governance institutions to emerge in today's industrial countries" (World Bank 2006a, 16).

• **Donors are a big part of the problem**  This finding is reflected in an extensive literature on the "aid business" as a whole (see, for example, van de Walle 2001). The dysfunctional effects of donor-funded projects on local institutions and accountability mechanisms highlight the case for moving from projects to budget support. A DAC-sponsored evaluation of public service reform in Africa (2002) suggested that donor interests are too often dominant—they make heavy and competing demands on governments, which are difficult to fulfil. Donors are said to be guilty of misguided optimism, proliferation and fragmentation of effort, and stingy and unpredictable funding (Birdsall 2004).

All of this has become part of the conventional wisdom in the sense that it is not seriously contested within donor agencies. Virtually everyone pays lip service to it. It provides the rationale for much mainstream donor policy and practice: to improve donor harmonization; to nurture country ownership of poverty reduction programs; to strengthen country recipient control over planning, budgeting, and procurement arrangements for aid; to apply conditionality in a more selective and nuanced way; and to carry out better political and institutional analysis. As discussed by de Renzio and Mulley later in this book, these principles are now enshrined in an ambitious, high-profile Declaration on Aid Effectiveness signed by officials from developed and developing countries in Paris in March 2005. It calls for partner country ownership and leadership, alignment of donor support with national development strategies, harmonization of donor procedures, and management for results and "mutual accountability."

How much difference is this really going to make? It would be unfair to dismiss the "new conventional wisdom" as mere rhetoric. It clearly is influencing donor policy and practice—up to a point. But donors have not come to terms with the radical implications of recognizing that the local political process is central to both governance and development. What many of them have done is take the insights derived from past attempts to promote governance reform and incorporate them into an existing frame of reference. This essentially means retaining the (often unspoken) assumption that getting better governance involves supporting civil society; promoting the "right" policies; fostering "political will"; and strengthening public institutions by providing resources and well-designed technical assistance—but adding to all of this the need for more patience and more local "ownership." So understanding the political and institutional context is seen as important in order to better overcome obstacles to a poverty reduction or good governance agenda and to market the reforms designed to promote it. The risk is that political economy analysis will become the next "fix," tied to what is still a donor-driven agenda. The benefits are likely to be marginal—and difficult to sustain—without a more honest reappraisal of the governance challenge. Without that, donors are at risk of getting captured by their own rhetoric.

The other problem with building on the conventional wisdom without a fundamental reappraisal of the underlying assumptions is that good intentions can easily be derailed. Mounting concern about continuing poverty in sub-Saharan Africa, dismay about the social and economic consequences of HIV/AIDS, and the prospect that many countries will fail to meet the Millennium Development Goals are all adding to pressure for a large and rapid increase in aid, coupled with demands for redoubling efforts to improve governance. The list of things to be promoted includes the rule of law, political and social rights, accountable and efficient public administration, and sound economic policies (UN Millennium Development Project 2005)—all things that have proved remarkably problematic over the past forty years or more. The risk is that, given the pressure for action, hard-won lessons from past experience will be overridden.

These unresolved tensions are reflected in several recent high-profile statements from donors. For example, the British government's White Paper "Making Governance Work for the Poor." asserts that building better governance takes time and has to come from within each country: outsiders cannot impose models. Good governance is about how citizens, leaders, and public institutions relate to one another to make change happen. The role of politics in governance and development is emphasized: "Politics determines how resources are used and policies are made. And politics determines who benefits. In short, good governance is about good politics" (ibid.). Yet at the same time there is still surprising faith in the power of the aid relationship to change behaviour. Commitments to increased aid in 2005 were underpinned by an explicit "deal": increased aid and debt relief were offered in return for a commitment to better governance. This commitment (which extends to upholding human rights and other international obligations, improving financial management, and fighting corruption) will be regularly evaluated in a "quality of governance assessment" and can, it is suggested, be reinforced by programs of technical assistance for capacity building, coupled with support for grassroots civil society and the media to help hold governments to account. The role of aid conditionality is implied but not explicitly discussed (DFID 2006, 19–31).

The Paris Declaration makes a welcome acknowledgment of the negative impact of donor behaviour on the capacity of partner countries to use aid effectively. It commits donors to important changes that are challenging but feasible: harmonizing procedures, rationalizing activities, untying aid, increasing the predictability and transparency of funding. By contrast, it commits developing countries—many with weak administrations, unstable politics, and limited policy capacity—to what past experience would suggest is an impossibly ambitious agenda, including developing and implementing results-driven development strategies; ensuring that administrative arrangements for managing aid are effective, accountable, and transparent; undertaking public management reform; and creating an enabling environment for public and private investment. The unspoken assumption is that donors and their "partners" have shared objectives that will be reflected in national development strategies and that additional resources, commitment and capacity building will allow them to accelerate the pace of change.

The World Bank's 2006 Global Monitoring Report (2006a) offers important insights on governance, including the role of informal institutions; the need to take account of the diversity of individual country experience and the historical factors that shape different governance trajectories; and the need for a long-term perspective. But—like the British government's White Paper and the Paris Declaration—it is primarily concerned with governance as an essential element in scaling up aid and achieving the Millennium Development Goals. So the strong temptation is to gloss over the evidence from past experience that shows how hard it is to use aid to buy good behaviour or to devise effective interventions to strengthen governance directly. Essentially, the World Bank's message is that everyone must try harder, by instituting a "systematic and disciplined approach" to address the challenges that poor governance and corruption pose for poverty reduction and to "align the incentives of [local] state officials" with a reform agenda (World Bank 2006b, 23).

All of these donor statements understate the challenge involved in translating aspirations of partnership and developing country ownership of reform into practical reality. They place a lot of faith in supporting local reformers and building demand for change, while underplaying the local political pressures on partners to respond to different agendas. They also ignore one highly significant factor that is changing the context for foreign aid, especially in Africa— namely, the rapidly growing Chinese influence. China is offering investment, training opportunities, and very cheap loans and making it clear that their interest is in oil, various minerals, and markets for their manufactured products, not in poverty reduction or good government. This could prove an attractive alternative to more demanding "partnership" deals with donors (Moore and Unsworth 2006).

However, all of these recent donor statements do represent an important advance, in two respects. The first—exemplified by the Paris Declaration—is recognition that donors' behaviour has the potential to undermine the often fragile capacity of their developing country partners. The second—particularly prominent in the White Paper and the Global Monitoring Report—is a new awareness of the complicity of global actors (both public and private) in contributing to bad governance. "The global milieu has powerful influences on governance systems in developing countries. Global markets can be a source of virulent, corrosive corruption or a powerful disciplining device" (World Bank 2006a, 122). Furthermore, "incentives for good governance are heavily influenced by the international economy, the behaviour of other governments and the private sector" (DFID 2006, 33). Sections v and vi below pick up this theme and suggest ways in which more rigorous action by wealthy countries to curb the negative effects of their actions on poor countries could offer a powerful, if indirect, way of contributing to better governance.

## V
### Rethinking Governance

The new conventional wisdom recognizes that getting better governance involves a local political process, not just strengthening institutions transferred from OECD countries. Increasing numbers of donors are exploring the relevant political science literature, and this is informing internal debate and out-of-hours discussions. The initial impact is uncomfortable: it means coming to terms with how little is really known about key causal linkages—between institutions and growth, growth and corruption, democracy and poverty reduction—and about which reforms to prioritize in different country circumstances. It means being open to different ways of thinking about institutions. Work by Dani Rodrik and others, for example, has shown how China achieved phenomenal growth in spite of weak systems of formal property rights. This suggests that transitional, unorthodox, bitty arrangements that target local constraints in politically compelling ways may be more effective than trying to build on institutional models from wealthy countries (Rodrik 2003). Scholars taking a historical approach (Chang 2002) have questioned the "governance first" model of economic development and shown how institutions in now developed countries grew in a piecemeal way in response to felt needs. Others have pointed out that normative approaches that seek to eliminate corruption may be ineffective or counterproductive—the challenge is to understand both the root causes and the impact of corruption in different country circumstances (Khan 2002).

Donors have started to commission more in-depth country-level analyses of political and institutional contexts. Examples are DFID's initiative on Drivers of Change, Sida's "power analysis" studies, and the World Bank's political economy work. Together with a growing body of research directly commissioned by donors, analyses are helping illuminate the underlying causes of bad governance as well as providing alternative ideas about how more effective, accountable public authority might be constructed. These narratives are still tentative and contested, but in different ways they are helping to explain why local political processes and "ownership" matter so fundamentally.

For example, research commissioned by DFID—and widely known within the organization—suggests that achieving better governance involves striking a balance between the need for effective state control and capacity to act, and the need for holders of state power to be accountable for their actions. Constructing more effective, accountable public authority involves a political process of engagement between holders of state power and organized groups in society. For this to result in institutions that are legitimate and sustainable, the process needs, over time, to deliver positive-sum outcomes—arrangements that are valued and that become "institutionalized" because they are seen as serving the common interests of those involved. An example from the history of Western Europe is the long process of (often violent) bargaining between rulers and citizens that resulted in the creation of civil, political, and economic rights in return for recognition of obligations to pay tax. This process of institution building is inherently messy, conflict ridden, incremental, uncertain, and long term (IDS 2005).

Developing countries today face a huge challenge: they must engage in basic state building while simultaneously developing a range of economic, social, and political institutions that will allow them to function in an increasingly globalizing world. For many countries in sub-Saharan Africa and elsewhere, the experience of state formation has left an especially difficult legacy. State power was forged by an outside authority, often supported by little sense of political community, and was handed over at independence to a small elite, which was not confronted by broadly based interest groups able to counter the private use of public power. Moreover, the current global environment, in which very poor countries coexist and interact with very rich countries, has created unprecedented problems for governance. Political elites in poor countries often have access to huge rents from controlling the supply of oil, mineral resources, and narcotics to rich countries, as well as access to generous amounts of aid. This weakens the requirement for states to engage in bargaining with taxpayers or other organized groups and to build state capacity to collect and administer revenues. Both political elites and rebel groups have access to sophisticated military technology and external support, and this further undermines the prospects for even-handed engagement between states and citizens (Moore 2004). Political mobilization is often along ethnic lines rather than around economic or other interests of the sort that would facilitate compromise over time and provide incentives for political actors to respond. The fact that poor people, even in democracies, are often not organizing around common interests in poverty reduction is clearly problematic from the point of view of gaining support for a pro-poor agenda.

All of this is illuminating in a negative way. The governance reforms that donors commonly push—improving public expenditure management, tackling corruption, strengthening the bureaucracy—require collective action by state and societal actors. This is difficult in any circumstances—essentially because it means people must surrender tangible, short-term, private gains for the more uncertain prospect of sharing in wider public goods (growth, better services) (Brautigam 2000). Getting this kind of collective action is particularly problematic where governments have not established legitimacy and built capacity through negotiated relationships with organized groups in society, but instead operate on the basis of highly personalized, patronage-based networks. This helps explain why so much donor assistance to support capacity building or to strengthen the voices of service providers is ineffective. When the basis of public accountability is an expectation that politicians will deliver highly direct, tangible benefits on a personal basis to their supporters, citizens have few incentives to organize to demand that services be provided on the basis of universal rights. When MPs are not elected in the expectation that they will be watchdogs for taxpayers, the Public Accounts Committee and the Audit Commission will lack teeth, however much they receive in resources and technical assistance.

This is all very challenging for donors. It exposes the limits of their influence—indeed, it exposes their capacity to make a bad situation worse. It unearths the huge gap between the highly personalized, patronage-based systems found in many developing countries, and the Weberian ideal of institutionalized, rules-based, autonomous public institutions that underpins the traditional governance agenda. If, as seems likely, it is not possible in most situations to "skip straight to Weber" (Pritchett's telling phrase), donors may well be left feeling at a loss as they confront a scene of huge complexity and diversity, and hear themselves being told to look for locally driven, country-specific solutions without any clear road map or indeed destination in view. This risks becoming unmanageable.

## VI
### So What Could Donors Do about Governance?

The good news is that donors need not succumb to undue pessimism (about the intractability of deeply entrenched political culture), nor to unwarranted optimism (about their ability to achieve change through aid partnerships). Their capacity directly to promote better governance may be limited, but donors and the international community more generally could do much more to influence the behaviour of political actors in poor countries by helping change institutional incentives.

One clear starting point is to prioritize those actions over which policymakers in rich countries do have some control. These include a range of interventions that have been on the agenda for some time and that have been given much more prominence in recent statements on donor policy. The list in the British government's White Paper is ambitious: it includes regulating the behaviour of transnational companies; tackling international money laundering; cleaning up illegal trade in natural resources; strengthening safeguards by national export credit guarantee agencies against corruption; placing better controls on trade in conventional arms; and extending the principles underpinning the Extractive Industries Transparency Initiative to public procurement in health, defence, and construction. The single most important thing that donors could do to improve the prospects for better governance in poor countries is secure agreement within their own governments to give these issues real weight. There may also be scope to increase the range of issues tackled, by appealing to the reputational concerns of the private sector—for example, by enlisting the cooperation of major pharmaceutical companies to help control corruption in the procurement of drugs. There is also scope to extend to other sectors measures (such as the Forest Law Enforcement, Governance and Trade Regulation [FLEGT]) that capitalize on the EU's diplomatic and economic bargaining power to change the incentives facing governments and business in poorer countries. Action at an international level could be complemented by donors at a country level—for instance, by helping timber-exporting countries develop monitoring and licensing systems to comply with the FLEGT. This could be a much more effective way of improving governance—albeit indirectly—than funding an anticorruption commission (Moore and Unsworth 2006).

Donors need to get serious about "harmonization"—not just by improving coordination, but through much more radical rationalization of their programs so as to limit the number of donors that are operating in any given country and making demands on its hard-pressed government. This could be done relatively quickly and could make a significant difference, not just by reducing transaction costs, but by increasing the coherence and consistency of donors' behaviour, and changing perceptions in recipient countries regarding their motives. The perceived legitimacy of donor activity matters.

Donors could also have an indirect effect on governance by doing more to improve the enabling environment for growth. Specifically, they could attach much greater urgency to action (already on the international agenda) to reduce agricultural subsidies and to remove barriers that prevent poor countries from benefiting from trade and investment opportunities. Moreover, a range of traditional donor interventions to build human skills, enhance livelihoods, and improve communications and access to information and services could all do much to foster a more conducive environment for groups—including groups of poor people—to organize public action. In some countries road building would do more to improve governance than direct assistance to strengthen institutions. Instead of starting with a particular economic or social policy agenda and viewing weak governance as an obstacle to be overcome, it may be more productive to think about better governance as a long-term endeavour closely linked to economic and social change. That implies taking a less normative view of what constitutes good governance and, instead of frontally assaulting the symptoms of poor governance, looking for more indirect ways for donors to support (and not undermine) local processes of change. It also means looking for (often small, incremental) ways to nurture growth or improve services in spite of poor governance (IDS 2005).

### Aid Modalities

Given the potential for aid to distort local priorities and to weaken incentives for collective action, a very high priority for donors must be to understand the impact of different aid modalities on local institutions and political processes. This has underpinned much of the thinking on the move from projects to budget support—thinking often accompanied by heroic assumptions about the scope for the latter to strengthen domestic accountability and local management of public expenditures. The risk is that the failure to achieve quick results will lead to the abandonment of these mechanisms before they have had a chance to work. Alternatively, such mechanisms may get captured by donors and, far from strengthening government accountability to local stakeholders, be used instead to increase donor influence over spending priorities.

What more can donors do to adjust their aid modalities with a view to their impact on local political process? Here are some ideas:

- Take a more hands-off approach to preparing national development strategies, reducing the list of donor requirements, increasing transparency of the whole process, allowing for much more local variation, and encouraging open discussion of priorities for economic and social development. Don't think of "dialogue" as something that is always donor-led. Take a longer-term view and live with the implication that the results in the short term may be less directly pro-poor.

- Get serious about predictable funding, and make it a higher priority in setting and managing conditions for financial aid. Predictability can cut both ways: it can increase the moral hazard problem, but it can also provide the basis for a more objective planning process based on needs and rights rather than ad hoc patronage benefits, if people believe they can plan for the longer term. This could be important, and not just as a way to increase efficiency of resource use—it could also help make it worthwhile for user groups to organize, and in the longer term it can contribute to more issues-based politics.

- Make much more country-specific judgments about the likely effect of volumes and types of aid—including budget support—on local institutions and political processes, including their impact on fragile democratic processes. Keep a focus on process: Could a more institutionalized, rules-based process of budget formulation and monitoring, and more accessible public information, provide entry points and incentives for collective action by stakeholders—including MPs, taxpayers, and business groups as well as civil society organizations?

- Consider linking the availability of budget support to a dialogue about tax reform and local revenue raising, with a view to gradually replacing aid with tax revenue. (It is striking that the mechanisms embraced by donors, including national poverty reduction strategies and budget support, focus on spending and beneficiaries to the exclusion of revenue raising and taxpayers.) This would have to be handled with care, given the risk that fiscal targets could provoke more oppressive methods of revenue raising, but it is hard to see how domestic accountability can be strengthened without more public debate linking sources of revenue with spending and with more broadly based, less arbitrary and coercive tax administration. Think about whether, in the shorter term, aid could be designed to look more like tax revenue—for example, through a trust fund arrangement subject to rules enshrined in local legislation.

- Think about how the design of projects and sector programs might provide incentives for bureaucrats and beneficiaries, as well as entry points for different groups of stakeholders to take collective action to improve services. Preventive health programs in northeastern Brazil (Tendler 1997), and the Employment Guarantee Scheme in Maharashtra (recently extended in a modified form to other Indian states), are well-known examples of how the institutional design of public programs can affect incentives. Donors tend to think of support for civil society in terms of increasing pressure on the state for more accountability—but the state itself has an important role to play in shaping opportunities and motivations for different groups to organize (IDS 2005). It is important not to lose sight of these local dynamics in the enthusiasm for a move to budget support.

- Be prepared for a radical rethink of donor language. By framing the agenda (poverty reduction and good governance) in a particular way, donors risk failing to engage with powerful groups of people—business, religious and traditional leaders, professional associations, elected politicians, social movements—who may have objectives that coincide or overlap with those of donors, but who are not inspired by the language of Millennium Development Goals or liberal democracy. Other things, including reputation, national security, prosperity, fear of social unrest or ethnic violence, and ideological or religious values, may have much greater salience. Historically, poor people have almost always made progress in alliance with more powerful groups, and finding a basis for accommodating different interests is critical to the democratic process. When donors insist on continuing to frame the agenda and set policy prescriptions in ways that resonate with them, they miss out on opportunities to find common ground with local power holders and opinion formers. They could start by trying to talk in more accessible language to private business people.

• There is, however, scope for societies to learn from one another. One thing that external actors can do is provide access to experience—and resources—from elsewhere. This could be done much less intrusively, with the emphasis on responding to local demands, supporting local capacity for policy analysis, and helping generate and disseminate more reliable, accessible data. Examples include the multidonor governance partnership in Indonesia and DFID's Enabling State Programme in Nepal. There have been problems with both these mechanisms; even so, it is worth persevering with this concept.

• Where the local environment is not too unpromising, a case can be made for continuing with more traditional capacity-building efforts, with realistic objectives and a willingness to stay engaged over the long haul. Priorities should include public financial management and procurement systems. This is an area where good practice is fairly well agreed upon, where a number of countries have made good progress, and where donors have some legitimacy to engage.

The important point underlying all of these ideas for changing donor practices is to make the local context the starting point for shaping a reform agenda, rather than setting off with preconceived policies and looking to "manage" the politics. Donors tend to look at governance reform as a means of promoting growth and poverty reduction, or with a normative agenda of democratic change in mind. So they restrict themselves to a rather limited menu of options and look for direct interventions to strengthen formal institutions, all the while supporting "demand side" pressures for change. Rethinking governance suggests that more indirect, incremental approaches may often be necessary; but it also reveals that a whole range of seemingly technical measures (such as tax reform) have governance implications. While this means much more realism regarding short-term reform objectives, it also considerably expands the potential scope of interventions for changing the institutional incentives for political and economic elites in poor countries.

## VII
## Can Any of This Really Be Done?

Quite a lot of the above would be doable if policy actors in wealthy countries really believed it mattered. Above all, they could get serious about changing the negative impact of their own behaviour on poor countries, by restricting access to rents and improving the global environment for trade and investment. Donors could get serious about rationalizing country coverage, improving their understanding of political and institutional contexts, trying to engage more effectively with local processes of change, and watching their language. Some of this is already happening. The importance of "rethinking governance" is that it explains what lies behind the conventional wisdom about the need for "ownership" of policies and programs and for better understanding of the local political environment. Without that, the sense of urgency about changing donor behaviour will be lost, and the temptation to overload the agenda will be hard to resist.

However, there are more fundamental difficulties. Donors face a whole range of bureaucratic pressures: to meet spending targets, to comply with the latest intellectual fashion or political preoccupation, to launch initiatives, to demonstrate short-term success, and to be seen to be "doing something" about the vast and intractable challenges facing developing countries. These pressures have an impact at the level of the organization, but they also affect the career progression of individuals. They make it very difficult to defend long-term, locally driven strategies for incremental change. The internal organization of donor agencies tends to value technical or bureaucratic skills over in-depth country knowledge. There is still surprisingly little interest in historical perspectives.

There are tensions—in some countries, deep tensions—between the objectives of donor agencies and the preoccupation of other parts of government with conflicting objectives. These tensions relate to short-term fiscal management, national security, specific foreign-policy goals, and commercial considerations. Such tensions are inevitable but they can be negotiated: perceptions regarding what best serves the national interest can and do change. Conflicts among competing objectives might be easier to manage if the opposing parties at least had a common understanding of how the world really works. An important potential benefit of DFID's Drivers of Change and Sida's "power analysis" studies is a better shared understanding with other government departments of the complex realities each of them confronts.

But the most difficult challenge arises from the fact that donors "own" the money they supply in aid and are accountable for it to their own taxpayers. This means they must respond to the demands and expectations of organized groups in their own society, which may be in tension with local realities and expectations in recipient countries. Especially difficult issues arise in relation to conditionalities that link financial aid to the observance of human rights by recipient governments (for a thoughtful discussion of this thorny topic, see Uvin 2004).

So is there a better way of managing these tensions? There is no overall formula for doing so. But if donors confronted the challenges more honestly, they might be able to manage the trade-offs differently. The need for some measure of conditionality attached to donor funds would not disappear, but it could be managed in a less intrusive way provided that donors embraced longer time horizons and more realistic starting expectations, better appreciated the constraints under which their "partners" were operating, and were willing to settle for second-best outcomes in a far from ideal situation. They could manage the trade-offs between predictability of funding and conditionality differently if they really believed in the value of predictable funding. They might have to settle for achievements in limited areas rather than across-the-board improvements. They could value a more genuine political process for national development strategies over a donor-driven, more directly pro-poor agenda. They could do more to educate their own taxpayers about the depth of the challenges faced by many poor countries. If they operated in a smaller number of countries, they might stand a better chance of building relationships with broader groups in society and of spotting opportunities to support locally driven change. If they could get better at separating their own foreign-policy objectives from their aspirations to help poor countries achieve development goals, they might be able to increase their perceived legitimacy. They might even be surprised at how quickly things could move in some areas if they could find ways of linking the development agenda more closely with the interests and concerns of local groups that have some political clout.

They could do this if they really believed that local political processes matter. And cumulatively, over time, they could make a difference.

▲

# 3

## BOY SCOUTS AND FEARFUL ANGELS:
## THE EVOLUTION OF CANADA'S INTERNATIONAL
## GOOD GOVERNANCE AGENDA

### Ian Smillie

*Fools rush in where angels fear to tread.*
—Alexander Pope, *An Essay on Criticism*, 1711

### Introduction

Canadian foreign policy has been bipolar for as long as anyone working in the Pearson Building can remember. So says Allan Gottlieb, former Under-Secretary of State for External Affairs and former Canadian Ambassador to the United States. He observes that "one pole ties us to hard reality, *realpolitik* if you will, and makes us want our governments to protect the national interests when it deals with other states. Canadians, when they think this way, talk in terms of sovereignty, security, territory, trade, economic growth and prosperity" (Gottlieb 2004, 1).

In contrast, the other pole takes a visionary, even romantic approach to the world: "The vision changes from time to time, but at its most expansive, it is based on a mission to create a more just world, promote democracy, reduce inequities among nations, protect victims of injustice, and alleviate the conditions of the poor and the oppressed" (ibid.). These competing themes, Gottlieb says, have rarely been reconciled, creating confusion and incoherence in Canadian foreign policy. Gottlieb has little time for the "romantic" side of the Canadian persona, describing it in terms of do-gooders and Boy Scoutism. Canada alone, he believes, can have little impact on transforming state behaviour elsewhere, and the romantic approach will accomplish little, apart from making its proponents feel good.

This chapter is about the part of Canadian foreign policy that Gottlieb rather inaccurately describes as "romantic"—Canada's mission, as perceived by governments over the past three decades, to create a more just world, to promote democracy stability and security, to reduce inequities among nations, and to protect victims of injustice.

The chapter examines the evolution of the "good governance" agenda, beginning with early thinking about human rights and the implications for both foreign policy and aid programming of taking such issues seriously. It then reviews the evolution of thinking about economic governance in the 1980s, before the end of the Cold War. The journey then moves into the post-1989 period, when policy-makers dared at last to speak the name that had so long been kept behind closed doors: *democracy*. Today, the good governance agenda, at least in Canada, covers all of these areas and more—including the role of civil society, and competent, transparent, and responsible administration of government. When the term "*good* governance" is used in this chapter, it usually refers to this collection of ideas and norms as they are understood today, although a final section of the chapter discusses the possibility that they should perhaps not be conflated, at least not until a great deal more is known about them.

In the early summer of 2005, Michael Ignatieff, then a respected Harvard human rights professor and a frequent contributor to the *New York Times*, wrote a lengthy article about US efforts to spread democracy. It was titled "Who Are Americans to Think That Freedom Is Theirs to Spread?" (Ignatieff 2005a). He described the historical contradictions in American thinking about freedom and democracy, quoting Thomas Jefferson's final letter, written on the occasion of the fiftieth anniversary of American independence. The slave-owning third president, who a half-century earlier had penned the immortal words, "all men are created equal," said he believed that democracy's worldwide triumph was assured. Despite the obvious contradictions, Ignatieff wrote, "if Jefferson's vision were only an ideology of self-congratulation, it would never have inspired Americans to do the hard work of reducing the gap between dream and reality."

Ignatieff's view of America's worldwide effort to promote democracy would be immaterial to this chapter had he not used several paragraphs to criticize Germany, France, and Canada for their timid efforts at spreading democracy:

Never have there been more democracies. Never has America been more alone in spreading democracy's promise. Ask the Canadians why they aren't joining the crusade to spread democracy and you get this from their government's recent [2005] foreign-policy review: "Canadians hold their values dear, but are not keen to see them imposed on others. This is not the Canadian way." (ibid.)

Rewind less than four months to the March 2005 national convention of the Liberal Party of Canada, where Ignatieff gave a keynote address:

South of us, they talk about "life, liberty and the pursuit of happiness." They want to export freedom and democracy to the world. Canadians tend to be skeptical about such dreams. But we have a dream too. We are the people of "peace, order and good government." From Sri Lanka to Iraq, from South Africa to Ukraine, we can help promote democratic federalism for multi-ethnic, multi-lingual states. Exporting peace, order and good government should be the core of a disciplined foreign policy that concentrates on what we do best and shares the Canadian dream with the rest of the world. (Ignatieff 2005b)

It may be that Ignatieff, in using the imperative tense in March, was attempting to influence the government's as yet unreleased International Policy Statement (IPS). Having reviewed that statement after its April release, however, and safely back at Harvard, he could take a stick to it. Things change, of course, and Ignatieff did not long remain at Harvard. In January 2006 he was elected to Parliament as a Liberal, coincident with the defeat of the Liberal government. As an Opposition backbencher and a failed contender for the leadership of the Liberal Party, he now had considerable opportunity to berate the new Canadian government and to help reshape the thinking of Liberals on how best to spread democracy.

Until the defeat of the Liberal government, the IPS was the most important public document on Canada's foreign policy. With Stephen Harper's election, that was destined to change, but the IPS remains an important benchmark in many ways, not least on the subject of governance. The IPS devoted two pages to the issue of "promoting good governance," stating that "Canada will assist countries to build the conditions for secure, equitable development by promoting good governance, focussing Canadian efforts on democratization, human rights, the rule of law, public sector capacity building, and conflict prevention" (Canada 2005a). The CIDA estimates for 2005–6 included $565 million for governance, 12.8 percent of total ODA; in contrast, USAID planned to spend only US$208 million from its development assistance budget on democracy, conflict prevention, and human rights. As might be imagined, the numbers were not strictly comparable, with much depending on how subjects were coded in budget documents (about which, more later). That said, to the Canadian amount could be added $119 million for a Peace and Security

Program managed by the Department of Foreign Affairs, and to the US numbers could be added another US$840 million, which although undisaggregated, included funding for Egypt and Israel as well as balance-of-payments support for Turkey and the Andean Counterdrug Initiative, along with monies for a wide range of democratic institution-building programs in developing and transition countries. This would bring total Canadian spending on governance to $684 million (or about US$570 million) against US$1,048 million by the United States. In other words, Canada, with a population and economy one-tenth that of the United States, planned to spend 54 percent of what the latter country did in real terms on governance. Another way of putting it is to say that in per capita terms, Canada planned to spend five times more than the United States on democracy and governance-related issues.

Michael Ignatieff might have been more accurate if instead of saying, "Never has America been more alone in spreading democracy's promise," he had said, "Never has America been more alone in *talking* about spreading democracy's promise."

## Good Governance:
## The Evolution of Understanding

### In the Beginning

The term "governance" is as elastic as the word "downtown," and the idea of promoting "good governance" has evolved dramatically over time. It is essentially about building effective institutions and rules imbued with predictability, accountability, transparency, and the rule of law. It is about relations between institutions and processes, governmental and otherwise. A UNDP report (2002, 52) states: "It is also about protecting human rights, promoting wider participation in the institutions and rules that affect people's lives and achieving more equitable economic and social outcomes.... Governance for human development must be democratic in substance and in form."

The government's 2005 IPS acknowledged that "governance is a broad field" and declared that the government (soon to be defeated at the polls) would be developing programs in governance around five main pillars:

- **Democratization:** electoral democracy; strengthening democratic institutions and practices, including electoral and legislative systems, citizen engagement (particularly with women), and the role of civil society in the political process;
- **Human rights:** support for the promotion and implementation of human rights, including the rights of women and of children, particularly those affected by conflict, gender-based violence, and natural disasters;

- **Rule of law:** legal/judicial reform with a focus on institutions, including strengthening the judiciary, the Bar, and legal-aid systems;
- **Public sector institution and capacity building:** Canadian-supported programming will help build core institutions and technical and managerial competencies, including oversight, accountability, and anti-corruption measures;
- **Conflict prevention, peacebuilding, and security-sector reform:** programming will include integrating conflict indicators and early warning systems; demobilization of former combatants; truth and reconciliation commissions; small-arms collection programs; and policing, transparency and oversight of security organs. (Canada 2005a)

In the 1960s, during the "first development decade," the word governance was nowhere to be found in the development lexicon of any Western donor nation. At that time, overseas development assistance (ODA) focused more on the tangibles of development: health, education, infrastructure, and economic growth. The 1969 *Partners in Development: The Report of the Commission on International Development,* known more familiarly as the Pearson Report, touched on political issues in an oblique manner, speaking of the need to break restrictions of class and caste and of the need for land reform: "There must be administrative reform to make the government machinery more responsive to popular need and more effective in implementing development plans" (Pearson 1969, 54). This is a component of today's idea of governance, but only one, and beyond a single paragraph, the report had little more to say on the subject.

At the time, human rights—a key part of most modern governance programs—were only vaguely understood as something aid programmers might consider. Such rights were seen in much the way Jefferson understood all men to be equal—that is, in a somewhat selective manner. *Foreign Policy for Canadians,* published in 1970, was an effort by the young Trudeau government, transitioning from the Pearsonian idea of Canada as "helpful fixer," to establish a fresh set of principles and priorities for Canada's foreign and defence policies. One of its six themes was the promotion of social justice, although this referred almost exclusively to the economic development of Africa, Asia, and Latin America. Nowhere was there any mention of human rights. Even in a retrospective 1995 memoir by Trudeau and his Special Assistant Ivan Head, there is no discussion of human rights as a prominent issue (Head and Trudeau 1995).

Human rights *were* at times considered—for example, in the suspension of aid to Idi Amin's Uganda in 1973 and to Pol Pot's Cambodia in 1977. But as a clear focus for CIDA programming, human rights were again given a miss in the government's 1975 *Strategy for International Cooperation 1975–80*, and they were not mentioned in a critique of that policy by the North-South Institute in 1980 (North-South Institute 1980). By then, however, changes internationally were at least being noticed in Canada. The 1975 Helsinki Accord, a diplomatic agreement among thirty-five states, was beginning to influence Communist signatories in the field of human rights. The Carter administration had emphasized human rights in its aid allocations—albeit somewhat selectively— and Norway and the Netherlands had introduced human rights into their development programs. In 1979, during the brief Clark government, Foreign Minister Flora MacDonald announced that Canada would begin to take human rights into account in its international relations. This created a stir in the media—and in the Pearson Building. But the Clark government did not last, and in the report of the 1980 Parliamentary Task Force on North-South Relations, human rights were again passed over.

Nevertheless, during the 1980s, human rights crept inexorably up the international agenda, and gradually the issue came to be addressed more often and more forthrightly by Canada. During the 1980s, aid to a number of countries was suspended on the basis of human rights violations, albeit sometimes only briefly or selectively (Guyana, El Salvador, Guatemala, Suriname, Fiji). Canada cut off part of its aid to Sri Lanka over the forced resettlement of Tamils in a controversial hydroelectric project, and in the late 1980s, it suspended aid to Haiti and Burma. A 1986 Department of Foreign Affairs Green Paper listed justice and democracy as one of six basic objectives for Canadian foreign policy. This objective was framed mainly in terms of aid and human rights, with the focus on key human rights flashpoints of the day: South Africa and Central America (Canada 1986). The same year a special Joint Committee of Parliament endorsed the idea of linking ODA with human rights performance and suggested that an "International Institute on Human Rights and Democratic Development" be established. Although it would take three more years to create what was finally called the International Centre for Human Rights and Democratic Development (ICHRDD), the Mulroney government accepted the recommendation almost immediately.

In 1987, CIDA published "Sharing Our Future: Canadian International Development Assistance," the most comprehensive statement on Canadian aid policies up to that point and the launch of the first major organizational shift to support governance-related objectives. Though it did not discuss democracy beyond a reaffirmation of the ICHRDD, it declared that the government was "firmly committed to integrating human rights fully into the broad sweep of Canada's external relations" (CIDA 1987). In cases of "systematic, gross and continuous" human rights abuses, aid would be reduced or denied. CIDA development officers were to receive special human rights training, and a unit was to be created within CIDA to ensure that all programs were consistent with the government's human rights concerns.

### Changes in the International Environment

Where the issue of democracy was concerned, political events during the 1980s began to overtake the normative discourse. The Cold War had cast a chill over any serious discussion of democratic development in a wide range of superpower client states, including Zaire, Liberia, Ethiopia, Afghanistan, Mozambique, Somalia, and Angola; other states such as Indonesia and China were excused from the discussion for strategic or commercial reasons. But winds of democratic change began to blow across Latin America during the 1980s, fuelled by debt crises that turned autocratic regimes to flight. Peru was the first to hold democratic elections in 1980, followed by Bolivia in 1982, Argentina in 1983, Brazil and Uruguay in 1985, Chile in 1988, and Paraguay in 1989. By the middle of the decade there were other changes. The Marcos dictatorship in the Philippines fell to a popular uprising, and in the Soviet Union, Mikhail Gorbachev startled his fellow citizens and the entire world with his new policies of *glasnost* and *perestroika*.

A variation on the governance theme, although not labelled as such at the time, was a rising concern among donor governments with economic management. A 1981 publication by the World Bank, "Accelerated Development in Sub-Saharan Africa: An Agenda for Action" (sometimes referred to as the Berg Report), is regarded as a watershed in the evolution of governance thinking at the Bank. In fact, the word *governance* never appears in the report, and neither does the word *democracy*. The report did, though, observe that political fragility in Africa had (and presumably this was a bad thing) "forced the post-independence leadership to give especially high priority to short-term political decisions" (World Bank 1981, 11). The same report provided a recipe for effective administrative reform: smaller government; more cost-effectiveness civil service, especially near the top; better definitions of accountability and incentives; "novel approaches to community involvement"; and, finally, high-quality analysis and prescription tailored to a country's specific needs.

The Berg Report emerged at a time that for many developing countries was as bad, economically speaking, as the Great Depression. The oil crisis of the 1970s, global recession, famine and drought, and commodity and debt crises forced one country after another into difficult stabilization agreements with the International Monetary Fund (IMF). Structural adjustment became the watchword of the decade, and governance—*economic* governance—became its handmaid. During the 1970s the IMF had engaged in about 10 stabilization programs a year. In 1980 the number rose to 28, and by 1985 there had been 129. Typically, adjustment programs had three components: expenditure reduction; expenditure switching (exchange rate devaluation as well as reduced subsidies, import controls, and taxes); and institutional and policy reforms (trade liberalization, privatization, fiscal reform, and less state involvement in the economy). This cocktail, developed during the self-assured conservatism of the Reagan/Thatcher/Mulroney era, reflected an orthodoxy that would soon become known as the "Washington Consensus." By the late 1980s, however, the side effects of this economic chemotherapy were often proving worse than the disease. In 1987, UNICEF produced an influential review of the experience thus far and concluded that "overall, prevailing adjustment programs tend to increase aggregate poverty, or in other words the number of people—and of children—living below the poverty line" (Cornia et al. 1987, 66). For most donors, however, the governance issue would remain, and it would remain largely fixed on economic governance.

CIDA's *Annual Report* for 1985–86 stated hopefully that "economic stabilization programs negotiated with the IMF are beginning to bear fruit" (1986, 11). Two years later, the minister responsible for CIDA reported on a UN Special Session on Africa at which "Africans pledged reform, and the international community promised more support" (CIDA 1988, 5). ODA was about to enter a decade-long decline; "reform"—in the shape of more structural adjustment— was not. In its 1989–90 *Annual Report*, CIDA still had economic reform and structural adjustment at the top of its list of priorities (CIDA 1990a, 15).

## 1989: Twelve Months That Shook the World

The year 1989 was a seminal one in world history. More autocratic governments were overturned in the name of democracy than at any time since the antimonarchist revolutions of 1848. In 1989 the Berlin Wall fell, a wave of independence surged across a dozen Soviet vassal states, and the Cold War whimpered to an end. At a more mundane level, serious questions were being asked in developing countries about the past decade of high-handed donor demands and about whether conditionality squared with democratic governance. In a trenchant critique of aid conditionality—thinly disguised as "policy dialogue" and donor "advice"—development economist Tony Killick said that the experiment with structural adjustment had gone too far. He warned against simplistic, single-solution responses to complex problems and economic systems. He told donors to "beware the temptation of exaggerating the appropriateness of policy prescriptions derived from mainstream theory, and the overconfident advocacy of those prescriptions which such exaggeration can cause" (1989, 63). He warned about the political pitfalls of economic policy reform:

"By the act of laying down policy conditions aid donors willy-nilly become active players in the domestic politics of the recipient country," where their ability to bring about change is heavily circumscribed and where serious unanticipated risks are borne by others (ibid.).

Conventional wisdom had long held that authoritarian governments were more likely than democracies to carry out unpopular adjustment polices. This might explain why, throughout the 1980s, the World Bank had restricted its interest in governance to economic management. In 1989, however, the Washington-based Overseas Development Council (ODC) published a series of articles under the title *Fragile Coalitions: The Politics of Economic Adjustment.* The ODC found that while there were no easy solutions to the economic problems of developing countries, "constitutional governments have done as well as authoritarian regimes in managing fiscal and monetary policy during the 1980s" (Haggard and Kaufman 1989, 74). The OECD went even further in its 1989 DAC report: "Now that the word 'democracy' has become an acceptable word to use in development circles, we are also hearing more often concerns about 'corruption'.... We are even beginning to hear that one-party systems do not work" (OEDC DAC 1989, 16). It added that "There is a vital connection, now more widely appreciated, between open, democratic and accountable political systems, individual rights and the effective and equitable operation of economic systems" (ibid., ii).

The change in thinking can be seen in differences between Robert Cassen and Associates' 1985 *Does Aid Work? Report to an Intergovernmental Task Force*, and the second edition nine years later: "A new issue had entered into the aid discussion for the 1990s—that of governance. It was as if the donors were going up the ladder of causality, from projects to policies to the way in which countries were governed" (1994, 82). In *The Other Path*, Hernando de Soto demonstrated the cost of a badly functioning government to the economy of Peru. Inefficiencies and weak legal systems had caused small entrepreneurs to avoid the formal sector of the economy entirely—a phenomenon common to this day in much (if not most) of the developing world (De Soto 1989).

Although structural adjustment would continue, the accompanying dogmatism of the past was now muted. "Adjustment programs should continue to evolve," said the Bank, and furthermore, those programs would have to "take fuller account of the social impact of reforms" (1989, 14). Although the Bank still had a hard time writing down the word *democracy*, its thinking on governance was now reaching cautiously beyond economic management. There would not be much external help from donors, it said, "unless governance in Africa improves. Leaders must become more accountable to their peoples" (ibid., 1). And as with the OECD, the C-word was out of the bag. The report discussed corruption and patronage in detail and spoke of the need for "plural-istic institutional structures...a determination to respect the rule of law, and vigorous protection of the freedom of the press and human rights" (ibid., 61)

In its 1989–90 *Annual Report*, CIDA acknowledged that "the wave of democ-racy sweeping Eastern European countries is shaking some African nations, whose people are calling for more democracy." But this did not appear to impinge on CIDA's approach to programming, where macroeconomic rectitude remained the number one priority. "In 1989–90, Canada was steadfast in its sup-port for structural adjustment programs," the report stated without qualifi-cation (1990a, 21). Meanwhile, on the human rights front there was little for-ward movement. Although human rights had featured prominently in *Sharing Our Future* two years before, CIDA Minister Monique Landry admitted in June 1989 that human rights had so far not yet been factored into recommendations to Cabinet on aid distribution (Morrison 1998, 322).

By 1989, confidence in the old approaches had only started to wobble within the aid establishment. Outside, however, criticism was raging. Graham Han-cock's 1989 *Lords of Poverty* was subtitled "The Power, Prestige and Corrup-tion of the International Aid Business." Although Hancock overstated his case against official aid, every chapter dripped with well-documented stories of incompetent aid delivery and corruption in developing countries. A more credible aid critic, and one less easy to dismiss, is Joseph Stiglitz, former chief economist and vice-president of the World Bank. Stiglitz, who worked at the Bank between 1997 and 2000, soon afterwards wrote that "those who valued democratic processes saw how 'conditionality'—the conditions that interna-tional lenders imposed in return for their assistance—undermined national sovereignty" (2002, 7). The net effect of the policies set by the Washington Consensus "has all too often been to benefit the few at the expense of the many, the well-off at the expense of the poor. In many cases, commercial interests and values have superseded concern for the environment, democracy, human rights, and social justice" (ibid., 20). In fact, in their inability to hear and respond to criticism, the World Bank and the IMF themselves provide useful case studies in questionable governance.

### Words and Deeds: China, South Africa, and Indonesia

Canadian supporters of human rights and democracy found an unexpected champion in the conservative international political climate of the late 1980s and early 1990s: Prime Minister Brian Mulroney. The Mulroney government took strong, principled stands on three issues: the Tiananmen Square mas-sacre, apartheid South Africa, and Indonesian human rights abuse in East Timor.

In the immediate aftermath of the Chinese government's suppression of the pro-democracy movement in June 1989, Foreign Minister Joe Clark announced the suspension of five aid projects budgeted at $61 million. Although Canada would not jeopardize long-standing links between Canadian and Chinese institutions, it halted any support that might strengthen the Chinese government's repressive capacities, and three projects were eventually cancelled.

Canada had been slow to enunciate and even slower to enact a general human rights policy in its aid programs during the late 1980s—with one major exception: South Africa. In a speech to the UN General Assembly in October 1985, Mulroney declared: "Canada is ready, if there are no fundamental changes in South Africa, to invoke total sanctions against that country and its repressive regime. More than that, if there is no progress in the dismantling of apartheid, relations with South Africa may have to be severed absolutely (in Freeman 1997, 149)."

This was followed by a series of measures, including aid to victims of apartheid as well as a number of political and economic sanctions—the first ever by Canada—against South Africa. Canada actually had very little trade with South Africa, but symbolically the sanctions were important in Canada and South Africa as well as throughout the Commonwealth. In the process, Mulroney personally confronted Margaret Thatcher, the British prime minister, arguing that in the twenty-five years since John Diefenbaker initiated South Africa's expulsion from the Commonwealth, enough time had passed to demonstrate the ineffectuality of other efforts at persuasion. While Canada may not have made a great deal of difference to the outcome of events in South Africa, it is noteworthy that the Conservative Mulroney government, with its strong corporate constituency, pursued a Southern Africa policy that was radically different from that of the Trudeau government and of Britain, assuming a kind of moral leadership on this issue within the Commonwealth.[1]

In October 1991, Mulroney, speaking at a Commonwealth Heads of Government Meeting, said that nothing was more important in international relations than respect for individual freedoms and human rights: "For Canada, the future course is clear: we shall be increasingly channelling our development assistance to those countries that show respect for the fundamental rights and individual freedoms of their people. Canada will not subsidize repression and the stifling of democracy."

A month later, when Indonesian troops opened fire on independence demonstrators in East Timor, the Mulroney government was true to its word—sort of. New aid projects to Indonesia were frozen, although ongoing aid programs were not affected. At about $35 million a year, Indonesia remained one of Canada's largest aid recipients throughout the 1990s. That figure was dwarfed, however, by two-way trade of $1.6 billion in 1997 and by Canadian arms sales to Indonesia of $420 million between 1993 and 1997. Meanwhile, despite the cutbacks in China, that country actually remained the second-largest recipient of Canadian government assistance, courtesy of CIDA and EDC concessional loans.[2]

## Canada's Pursuit of Good Governance

### A Fifteen-Year Retrospective

Since 1990 much has changed both globally and domestically in thinking about good governance and international relations. An internal CIDA document prepared in February 1990 considered the environment that was likely to develop over the coming decade. CIDA did not foresee—it could not have foreseen—the collapse of the Soviet Union, two Gulf Wars, the disintegration of Yugoslavia, conflicts in the Caucasus, Central Asia, and Africa, or the 9/11 attacks on the United States. But as the last of four issues under the heading "Recent Geo-Political Developments," it discussed what it called "The Fight for Democracy," noting that many authoritarian regimes had crumbled during the 1980s and that "accountability of governments and participation from the people are key ingredients for economic growth" (1990a, 14) The same paper stated that "one of the challenges of the 90s will be to support governments of developing countries to achieve more democratic, open, transparent, accountable and efficient decision-making process[es] in both resource allocation and economic regulation."

On closer reading, this seemingly clear endorsement of democratic institutions is actually quite narrow. Whether deliberate or not, it limits CIDA's possible interest in democratic processes to "resource allocation and economic regulation" rather than extending that interest to democracy writ large.

Nevertheless, with government funding, the ICHRDD—often referred to as "Rights and Democracy"—opened its doors that year under the leadership of former federal NDP leader Ed Broadbent. The following year CIDA suspended aid to Zaire on multiple grounds of human rights abuses, corruption, and all-round bad governance. Prior to the Canadian election of 1993, the Liberal Party had highlighted human rights as an issue, stating in its Red Book election platform that it would be publishing "report cards" on human rights abuses and political repression, and that it would begin seeking "to lead the international community in a revitalization of the concept of human rights as a principle for action" (Sallot 1995). Once the Liberals gained office, however, this plan changed. Soon after the October election the government created a

Special Joint Committee of the Senate and the House of Commons to examine Canada's entire foreign policy, a reflection of the enormous changes that
had taken place in the world since the last exercise under the Conservatives in
1986. After an extensive series of hearings, the committee released its report in
November 1994. In a document of 88 pages, human rights and democracy
occupied only half of one page.

The committee affirmed, however, that "human rights, good governance
and democratic development are universal values that should find central
expression in Canadian foreign policy." Canada, it said, should seek to promote the global respect of these values through a wide range of instruments
(Canada 1994). But the "wide range of instruments" was not spelled out, and
the report's handling of these issues was dismissed by critics at the time as little more than a series of platitudes (CCIC 1995).

The following year the government released a new foreign policy statement
that was more fulsome if not any more specific. *Canada in the World* listed
"the projection of Canadian values and culture" as one of three key objectives.
The application of values, it said, "—respect for democracy, the rule of law,
human rights and the environment—will be critical to the struggle for international security in the face of new threats to stability" (Canada 1995, 11). Foreign Minister André Ouellet, speaking at a meeting of ASEAN foreign ministers in May the same year, expressed a slightly different view. He told that
group that trade was the best way to promote democratic development: "Canada
has expressed, through this new government, our desire to vigorously pursue
a series of [trade] initiatives in a number of countries *irrespective of their
human rights records*" (emphasis added) (Scharfe 1996, 29).

So there was to be no linkage between Canada's trade policies and human
rights. On the other hand, not long after Lloyd Axworthy replaced Ouellet as
foreign minister, the government did announce a policy for CIDA on "Human
Rights, Democratization, and Good Governance." That policy—released at the
end of 1996—is still on CIDA's website as of this writing, well into the tenure
of the Conservative Harper government (CIDA 1996a). Given the revolving
door in the CIDA minister's office in 1996, the policy probably reflects as much
Axworthy's views as those of anyone else in government.[3] And given the evolving nature of the subject and the changeability of aid policies, this is something
of a record in consistency and longevity. The policy is also unusually discursive. With respect to the development cooperation program administered by
CIDA, it says that "the Government's policy is to enhance the will and capacity of developing country societies to respect the rights of children, women
and men, and to govern effectively and in a democratic manner." CIDA, it says,
"will seek to strengthen:

- the role and capacity of civil society in developing countries in order to increase popular participation in decision making;
- democratic institutions in order to develop and sustain responsible government;
- the competence of the public sector in order to promote the effective, honest and accountable exercise of power;
- the capacity of organizations that protect and promote human rights in order to enhance each society's ability to address rights concerns and strengthen the security of the individual; and
- the will of leaders to respect rights, rule democratically and govern effectively."

The policy is frank about the limits of knowledge regarding the successful promotion of good governance: "Development agencies active in this field agree that there are few formulas for success. As the importance of rights, democracy and governance for sustainable development comes to be recognized, it is important for CIDA and others to test approaches, monitor and evaluate initiatives, and build this learning into future policy and programming." However, in contrast to earlier documents that showed ambiguity in their understanding of democracy, here there was a definition:

> By democratization we mean strengthening popular participation in the exercise of power, building democratic institutions and practices, and deepening democratic values in society. Mechanisms for participation include formal processes such as elections and referenda. Participation also takes place less formally through a wide range of independent popular organizations (referred to collectively as "civil society") which serve to articulate and channel people's concerns. Democratic institutions include federal and provincial/state legislatures and municipal councils, and institutions such as the judiciary that are responsible for the rule of law.

During Lloyd Axworthy's tenure as foreign minister (January 1996 to September 2000), Canada ramped up its promotion of democracy, human rights, and good governance. This was a period of growing international certitude about the merits of such things, and Canada was not alone. In 1997, for example, the UNDP issued a policy document that stated unequivocally: "Governance and human development—the two are indivisible. Human development cannot be sustained without good governance. Governance cannot be sound unless it sustains human development" (1997a). And Canada's Department of Foreign Affairs and International Trade (DFAIT) began to develop a concept of "human security"—a term used in the past by the UNDP but now expanded in Ottawa. The government defined human security "as an approach to foreign policy that puts people—their rights, their safety and their lives—first." The objective was "to build a world where universal humanitarian standards and the rule of law protect all people; where those who violate these standards are held accountable; and where our international institutions are equipped to defend and enforce those standards. In short, a world where people can live in freedom from fear" (Canada 2000).

Because of the separation between the Department of Foreign Affairs and CIDA, the DFAIT articulation failed to mention freedom from want—historically a key pillar of good governance. But then CIDA's minister, Maria Minna, expressed a more rounded view, presented at an OAS meeting in June 2000: "Human security goes beyond the traditional concept of physical protection as a result of conflict. My definition includes the elimination of poverty; ensuring access to basic education and health services; the protection of children; the promotion and protection of human rights, including the rights of women, indigenous peoples, and marginalized groups; the eradication of disease; and the preservation of the environment."

Canada's human security agenda manifested itself in various ways. Canada took the lead among governments in promoting a Land Mines Treaty. It promoted the Statute of the International Criminal Court and advocated treaties to protect children and control small arms. It became an active member of the Kimberley Process, which aimed to end the traffic in "blood diamonds." The Kimberley Process eventually created a global international certification system for rough diamonds—certainly an exercise in international governance. Canada took the lead in creating an International Commission on Intervention and State Sovereignty, which in 2001 produced the a report titled *The Responsibility to Protect*, about which, more below. For its part, DFAIT established its own peacebuilding fund to promote conflict prevention and good governance, over and above what CIDA was funding in these areas. Although not directly tied to democracy, the concept of human security was very much related to human rights and good governance—and to some of the hard-security issues that the pre-9/11 world was confronting in the wars that raged across Africa, the Balkans, and the Caucasus.

As Axworthy put it in 2001: "In the time since I became Foreign Minister of Canada, a shift has occurred in what it means to be secure. Today, the language of foreign affairs includes protecting civilians, war-affected children, the threat posed by terrorism, drug trafficking and forced migration, not just states rights and national sovereignty" (in McRae and Hubert 2001, 3). And in 2005, Irwin Cotler, then Canada's justice minister, drew a direct line between human security and democratic institutions: "The best protection for human security is … the building of national justice systems as part of the building of an international justice system for the twenty-first century organized around democratic institutions and rights-protecting instruments, including Charters of Rights, protection of minorities, an independent judiciary, a free press, protection of human rights monitors, transparency, accountability, and responsible government."

## Too Soon Eureka

Unfortunately, or perhaps fortunately, as soon as something has been accepted as a truism, as soon as a policy has been enunciated, as soon as money is devoted to the new idea, doubt creeps in. An academic industry develops in support of an idea, and another grows to refute it. The following paragraphs highlight some of the current debate surrounding the promotion of good governance, and the challenges facing any donor country seeking to embed it in its aid programming.

DEMOCRATIZATION AND PEACEBUILDING  Many studies over the past fifteen years have made a direct link between the spread of democracy and reductions in armed conflict, thus supporting and encouraging donor involvement in these areas.[4] The UN has invested a decade, not just in the idea, but in holding elections and promoting democratic institutions from Cambodia to Sierra Leone, from East Timor to Burundi. Much of Canada's peacebuilding effort over the past decade has been predicated on the idea. NEPAD—the New Partnership for Africa's Development—widely endorsed by African governments and much beloved of donors, has as its first principle "good governance as a basic requirement for peace, security and sustainable political and socio-economic development" (n.d.). NEPAD does not hedge on the word *governance* as some donors do; for NEPAD, governance and democracy go hand in hand: "democracy *and* good, political economic and corporate governance."

The ink was barely dry on documents like these—some of which reached as far back as ancient Greece for inspiration—when new research began to find that "immature" democracies may actually have an increased tendency to go to war, and that the spread of market economies and democracy may widen group hatreds and ethnic violence. Jane Boulden, writing at Canada's Royal Military College, argues that a distinction is to be made between liberal and democratic values. She argues that "perhaps we should be giving more emphasis to liberal values relating to individual freedoms and the rule of law" in early post-conflict recovery, than to the building of democratic processes and institutions. She argues as well that donors and the UN need to develop a more nuanced understanding of democratization in post-conflict situations (2005, 45).

**DEMOCRATIZATION AND GROWTH/DEVELOPMENT/POVERTY**  David Gillies, an alumnus of the ICHRDD and CIDA, pours cold water on the correlation drawn between democracy and growth (a correlation strongly supported and variously articulated by the UN and a phalanx of donors). "As a whole," he writes, "the empirical evidence directly linking democracy and economic growth is ambiguous at best. There is no ironclad law defining the relationship between democracy and economic growth" (2005, 21). (It might be noted here that there is, in fact, no ironclad law defining the relationship between *anything* and economic growth.) All good things may not go together, Gillies says, and donors need to think about disaggregating governance, human rights, and democracy. "It is governance," he writes, "that has become the master value for some, if not most, official aid agencies" (2005, 21).

This idea is a reversion to where the World Bank was in the 1980s and may explain why the Bank has so assiduously steered clear of the word *democracy*. "The decisive ingredient of the East Asian miracle," Gillies writes, "seems to have been the quality of economic governance and institutional arrangements. These included a capable, merit-based civil service; effective public-private consultation and collaboration; and crucially, the effective implementation of policy." This is shorthand acknowledgment of the economically successful, yet authoritarian, governments of countries such as South Korea, Taiwan, Vietnam, China, and Singapore.

Legitimacy is an important part of effective governance, and higher standards of living can bestow a degree of legitimacy. Historically, there have been many forms of legitimacy; however, Francis Fukuyama (2004, 28) observes that "in today's world the only serious form of legitimacy is democracy." Government accountability is important but is unlikely to be enough if allegiance is owed more to donors and international financial institutions than to the citizenry. So it is possible to contest the relationship between development and democracy. The argument, though, could be stated another way. There is no correlation—and certainly no ironclad law—between authoritarian governance and economic growth, as countless dictators have demonstrated in recent years. Amartya Sen has demonstrated how a free press and accountable politicians can help avert famine: "No famine has ever taken place in the history of the world in a functioning democracy" (2000, 16). He adds that democracies are more likely than dictatorships to enjoy long-term political stability. And it is worth adding that in a democracy, a bad government can at least be defeated at the polls.

As a part of good governance, institutions do matter, of course, and aid agencies have been "building institutions" since day one. In the early years of development programming, however, institution building tended to focus narrowly on building management and technical capacity; such projects were not cast in a governance mode until very recently. The World Bank announced a new strategy in this regard in a 2000 paper, "Reforming Public Institutions and Strengthening Governance." That report stated clearly, however—perhaps in deference to the vexed nature of the discourse on democracy and governance—that certain issues of governance would be left to others, including parliaments and criminal justice systems. And even these were mentioned only in a passage in the report that excluded them from the Bank's purview.

Building institutions (whatever they may be), especially from the outside in or from the top down, is no easy matter. Culture, history, values, norms, money, pay scales, the nature of social capital, and the quality of human resources all play important roles. Fukuyama (2000) gives an example: "Many people speak of the "rule of law' as if it were a binary condition that is either on or off. In fact … establishing a rule of law involves extensive construction not just of laws but also of courts, judges, a bar, and enforcement systems across the entire country. Putting such a system in place is one of the most complex administrative tasks that state-builders need to accomplish" (59). He adds: "There is no legal system in the world that can be "fixed' by ten technocrats, no matter how bright" (84).

**HUMAN RIGHTS AND DEMOCRATIZATION**   John Humphrey, a Canadian, was one of the original drafters of the UN Universal Declaration of Human Rights in 1948. Although application of the Charter's provisions in Canada's international relations was patchy and inconsistent during the Cold War, funding for human rights promotion has long been provided through CIDA, mainly to NGOs. As already noted, during the 1970s and 1980s Canadian aid to a number of countries was suspended on the basis of human rights violations. Various parliamentary committees in the 1980s advocated a stronger human rights position for Canada, and the 1987 CIDA policy statement, "Sharing Our Future" (1987), explicitly called for aid to be tied to human rights performance (although the actual record—in places like Indonesia and China—is more than a little patchy). The creation of the ICHRDD in 1990 signalled a shift from reactive sanctions toward the promotion of human rights; but it was not until the 1995 publication of *Canada in the World* that the government made a similar shift explicit in its own foreign policy.

The linkages between democracy and human rights have been widely studied in academe, and donor agencies have made critical connections as well. The OECD's Development Assistance Committee (DAC), for example, says that "it has become increasingly apparent that there is a vital connection between open, democratic and accountable systems of governance and respect for human rights, and the ability to achieve sustained economic and social development" (OECD DAC 1993, 2). In all of its statements and policies, however, including its recent "International Policy Statement" (Canada 2005a), the Canadian government has compartmentalized human rights and democracy, placing them on the same page but never actually articulating a link. According to human rights analyst Nancy Thede (2005, 26), "both FAC (Foreign Affairs Canada) and CIDA use a shopping-list approach to democracy, positing that a series of characteristics or building blocks (democracy, respect for rights, accountability), are necessary. This approach does not allow for devising a strategy, because it provides no understanding of the dynamic relationships among the components." In fact, some argue that democracy, the rule of law, and human rights do not all fit together neatly and may even conflict.[5]

CIVIL SOCIETY  The term "civil society" entered the discourse on democratic governance among aid agencies in the early 1990s. The importance of civil society as an alternative to the state, or as a buffer, goes back to the writings of Tocqueville, Hegel, and Gramsci. Certainly NGOs and other civil society organizations—trade unions, educational institutions, and professional associations—had been programming actively in developing countries, usually with significant support from their home governments. But not until Robert Putnam published his study of governance in Italy did ideas about civil society's role in the promotion of democracy began to gel (Putnam 1993). Through a detailed analysis of five centuries of documented Italian history, Putnam showed that it was civic institutions and what he called "social capital" that explained why the north of Italy enjoyed democracy and good governance while the south of Italy did not.

Soon, books, studies, and tracts on civil society were flying off the printing presses of Europe and North America. Courses on civil society sprang up at the London School of Economics, Johns Hopkins University, Yale, and dozens of other universities. Definitions and descriptions proliferated. Alison Van Rooy (1998) sums up some of the mid-1990s literature, grouping civil society organizations into five conceptual clusters: civil society as a collective noun; civil society as a space for action; civil society as a historical moment; civil society as antihegemony; and civil society as an antidote to the state (1998, 6).

As with many Big New Things, however, the bloom was soon off the rose. By the end of the decade, discussion about civil society had become less fulsome. It was no longer touted as the answer to all problems, and in many developing countries the idea of building the capacities of civil society centred less on buffering against the state than on creating alternative service providers in countries where the state had been downsized and emasculated courtesy of the Washington Consensus. In situations like this, civil society was now being asked to pick up the pieces from failed experiments in just about everything.

**TAXATION**   The issue of taxation may seem like a stretch in a discussion of governance—something like taking the definition of "downtown" well into the suburbs. But recent studies by the Institute of Development Studies (IDS) show how taxation matters for accountability. As the IDS stated in one report: "The way states raise revenue has major implications for state formation. State–society bargaining over tax is central to building relations of accountability based on mutual rights and obligations, rather than on patronage. Recent changes in the fiscal environment, including a shift from indirect to more direct taxation, could encourage taxpayers to mobilise around broader, common interests, with potentially positive outcomes for governance" (IDS 2005).

The purpose in mentioning taxation so late in this chapter is actually to make another point entirely: most people in poor countries do not pay any direct taxes. A billion people, perhaps even two billion, do not earn enough money to be income taxable even when there are systems in place to make this possible. They live in informal economies, making lives for themselves that are almost completely outside the state's formal structure. This is not to say, though, that they do not understand concepts of good governance. Unlike the many donor governments that actively supported the criminalization of governance in Zaire, Liberia, Angola, and a dozen other places over three or four decades, most citizens of these countries could probably always tell the difference between a political right and a political wrong. Whenever they are given the opportunity, hundreds of thousands of illiterate and desperately poor people go to the polls in the hope of electing a better government. Even the poorest villager in Africa knows what corruption is, what a judge is supposed to do, and why there are police.[6]

The truth is that the intricacies of today's debate on governance have little relevance to the millions of people living in countries where the state has all but disappeared except as predator. The problem is not so much to teach those millions what good governance is, but how to promote, achieve, and sustain it. As Kofi Annan put it: "Obstacles to democracy have little to do with culture or religion, and much more to do with the desire of those in power to maintain their position at any cost. This is neither a new phenomenon nor one confined to any particular part of the world" (UNDP 2002, 14).

An even bigger possibility where democracy is concerned is stated with depressing if contentious clarity by economic and social historian Eric Hobsbawm (2004): "The campaign to spread democracy will not succeed. The 20th century demonstrated that states could not simply remake the world or abbreviate historical transformations. Nor can they easily affect social change by transferring institutions across borders" (2004, 41). But Niall Ferguson, apologist for empire and author of *Colossus: The Rise and Fall of the American Empire*, disagrees. In his view, the British Empire, for all its failings, gave (or imposed on) its colonies and dominions structure, accountable if not democratic institutions, the rule of law, *Pax Britannica*, and a safe climate for investment. This took many decades, a small army of educated and dedicated personnel, and serious financial resources—all of which are in conspicuously short supply among today's purveyors of good governance.

## Security and the Three D's

When Brian Mulroney committed Canadian forces to Operation Desert Storm in 1991, he started to draw Canada away from its traditional peacekeeping role toward one of peace*making*, and the more interventionist strategies that were to come in Kosovo and Afghanistan. Since 9/11, of course, security has become a much more tangible part of international aid programs, and there is growing concern about the diversion of long-term development and short-term relief assistance to the new agenda. Ngaire Woods (2005) observes that new security concerns "have rapidly come to dominate foreign policy since the terrorist attacks on the United States in September 2001. Inevitably they are spilling over into aid policy" (2005). Mark Duffield (2005), however, says that in many respects, "'development' has always represented forms of mobilization associated with order and security. While different strategies have come and gone, the general aim has remained that of a modernizing reconciliation of the inevitability of progress and the need for order" (2005, 207). Since its inception, he adds, it has singularly failed in this objective.

The paradigm did begin to change with the 1999 NATO intervention in Kosovo, which added the question of state sovereignty to more general issues of security. Canadian foreign minister Lloyd Axworthy, speaking at a meeting of G8 foreign ministers, stated that non-interference remained basic to peace and security and that Kosovo could not be used as a precedent to justify intervention "anywhere, at any time or for any reason." But, he added, "in cases of extreme abuse, the concept of national sovereignty cannot be absolute" (Axworthy 2004, 190). This became the guiding idea behind the Canadian government's commission to examine the intervention–sovereignty conundrum, whose December 2001 report, *The Responsibility to Protect* (International Commission on Intervention and State Sovereignty 2001), defined sovereignty not on the basis of the prerogatives of the state, but on the state's responsibility to protect its citizens. As Axworthy explained: "It is a way of coming both at the tyrants who hide behind the walls of sovereignty and at those states that can't or won't protect their citizens, without usurping the rights of those states that exercise their sovereign duty to care for their people" (ibid., 193).

Canada continued to support the endorsement and implementation of the "responsibility to protect" concept through the first half of the 2000s, and succeeded in having the idea—foreshortened among the cognoscenti to "R2P"—adopted at the landmark September 2005 UN General Assembly meeting of heads of government. The agreement on intervention specified cases of "genocide, war crimes, ethnic cleansing and crimes against humanity," but in the post–Cold War world, this covers a vast amount of territory. The remaining issue at the time of writing was whether the Security Council would endorse R2P, how it would be interpreted in the future, and whether—as in the case of Darfur—it would ever be implemented at all.

What this brief history of R2P indicates is that debates about state sovereignty and the responsibility to protect are far from over, and that many developing countries have significant misgivings about it. Without using either term, in 2004 Prime Minister Paul Martin brought the development and security issues together under a single roof: *governance*. "True security," he said, "is much more than simply defense against attack. It is a conviction that we will be more secure when citizens in all countries are able to participate fully in national life, when they can see clearly that their own well-being and freedom require a functioning state that listens to them and—ultimately—is accountable to them. They key ideas here are 'functional' and 'accountable'" (Martin 2004b).

Countries cannot work, Martin continued, unless they have institutions that work. "In Canada we refer to the three Ds—defense, diplomacy, and development. This means we are integrating our traditional foreign policy instruments more tightly—especially when responding to the needs of vulnerable states to build up their own capacity to govern themselves." Referring to Afghanistan, he argued that security and political stability go hand in hand and that the effort requires more than "some police training and a prison or two."

Addressing the UN General Assembly in September 2006, Canada's new prime minister, Stephen Harper, said something similar. Success in Afghanistan, he said, "cannot be assured by military means alone. This we all recognize. For success also requires a strong and unwavering civilian contribution: educators, engineers, elections advisors; direct aid and technical assistance. The list is lengthy, but the contributions essential.... That is why this spring we increased our development assistance, raising Canada's total contribution to nearly $1 billion over 10 years, to assist the people of Afghanistan. These two actions—rebuilding a shattered society and providing a stable security environment—go hand in glove" (Harper 2006a).

In its February 2005 budget the Liberal government announced the creation of a $100 million per year Global Peace and Security Fund (GPSF). Managed by the Department of Foreign Affairs, the fund would "support the renewal of the Human Security Program and provide security assistance to failed and failing states, as well as resources for post conflict stabilization and recovery" (Canada 2005b, 214). The fund, which survived the 2006 election, will be used in part for activities that do not fall under the ODA rubric. It is expected to be part of a broader Global Peace and Security Pool—not unlike Britain's Global Conflict Prevention Pool—that will encompass some CIDA programming. The budget was soon followed by the "International Policy Statement" (IPS; mentioned above), which was billed as Canada's "first comprehensive, integrated international policy framework." Bringing the three Ds together in a coordinated fashion, the IPS purports to embody the OECD's most oft repeated recommendation to its members: that policy be made to cohere across issues of aid, trade, and diplomacy. Indeed, around the same time as the IPS, the OECD published new DAC guidelines in "Security System Reform and Governance" (OECD DAC 2005). This report linked the two concepts much more clearly than ever before and explicitly added yet another issue to the heavily laden governance agenda.

What is especially interesting about the IPS is that the issue of weak and failing states gets more attention in the sections on defence than it does in the sections on development:

> Whether in Somalia, Afghanistan, Haiti or Sudan, the past 15 years have confronted us with the concept and consequences of failed and failing states. The inability of governments in these countries, and others like them, to maintain political authority, to provide security and other basic services, and to protect essential human rights has trapped millions of vulnerable civilians in a cycle of misery, poverty and violence.... Failed and failing states pose a dual challenge for Canada. In the first instance, the suffering that these situations create is an affront to Canadian values. Beyond this, they also plant the seeds of threats to regional and global security. They generate refugee flows that threaten the stability of their neighbours, and create new political problems for their regions. More ominously, the impotence of their governing structures makes them potential breeding grounds or safe havens for terrorism and organized crime. (Canada 2005a)

At the time of writing, the Department of Foreign Affairs was reorganizing itself, bringing a number of units under a newly formed Stabilization and Reconstruction Task Force (START), which aims for a more coherent government response to crises in relation to the GPSF. The "three Ds," START, and the new funds represent a move toward greater policy coherence. Whether they also represent new incursions by the Department of Foreign Affairs and the security agenda into the territories of good governance and long-term development is not yet clear. Many critics contend that the evidence points in that direction, citing Canada's massive contributions in Afghanistan and Iraq as confirmation. The IPS—crafted with difficulty over an inordinately long time— was disowned by Canada's new government in 2006. Even so, speeches by Prime Minister Harper and Chief of Defence Staff General Rick Hillier have repeatedly suggested that sentiments in this area remained unchanged.

## Programming for Good Governance

In recent years, as this book shows, CIDA has supported a wide range of governance initiatives. In Egypt it has supported civil service reform; in Ghana it has worked with the government on fiscal decentralization, and in South Africa, through the International Development Research Centre (IDRC), it has supported major public service reforms as part of the transition from apartheid. In Central Europe, CIDA has worked with several governments to develop local and municipal administrations; it has also worked in many countries on legal and judicial reform. In China it has worked with the Senior Judges Training Centre in support of a law promoting gender equality; in Brazil it has supported a Human Rights and Police Accountability Project; and in Haiti it has rebuilt court buildings and supported training programs in the Department of Justice. In addition to the "freedom from want" concept articulated by CIDA Minister Maria Minna in 2000, CIDA has also taken on board the security sector concerns of DFAIT.

A 1987 study on Canadian activities in the area of democracy, good governance, and human rights found that even that far back a wide variety of initiatives were under way, through CIDA, the Departments of Justice and Labour, the RCMP, Elections Canada, NGOs, and the IDRC (Côté-Harper 1987). The whole, however, was less than the sum of its parts—that is, something less than a coherent program. A subsequent in-house review of "lessons learned" found that CIDA was weak on analysis, that its staff lacked experience in human rights and democratic development, and that they were drawing on individual rather than corporate experience when designing new projects. The same report added that "it is essential to have a sophisticated understanding of the political context" in which interventions are being made (Brown 1995).

A decade later, Sue Unsworth, formerly Chief Governance Advisor in Britain's Department for International Development (DFID), was saying the same thing. In chapter 2 of this book she suggests—under the heading "rethinking governance"—that donors must "increase their understanding of political and institutional context.... [They must] increase their awareness of the impact of external interventions on local initiatives and capacity for action." A number of other needs she identifies will be familiar to donors in other settings: for donor coordination and harmonization; for predictable funding; for real meaning to be given to the idea of local ownership; for ways to find out what is working and why; and for realistic expectations.

Other scholars have written about the long, expanding, and overwhelming nature of the good governance agenda; about the lack of clarity regarding which programs are essential; and about the best sequencing of such initiatives. Merilee Grindle (2002) contends that if more attention were given to sorting out these kinds of issues, the end point of the good governance imperative might be recast as "good enough governance," that is, a condition of minimally acceptable government performance and civil society engagement that does not significantly hinder economic and political development and that permits poverty reduction initiatives to go forward (2002, 1). In the short and medium term, some improvements in governance may be less important than others in helping reduce poverty. Above all, she suggests, good governance—especially good enough governance—requires research and critical analysis (ibid., 27).

The case chapters in this book, especially those on Afghanistan and Haiti, point to the need for a comprehensive understanding of local conditions and of the history that has created them. Some speak of the need for an iterative approach to programming. "Iterative" means "repetitive." Repetition and replication are good where a positive lesson has been learned, but in the absence of blueprints and in the absence of a significant volume of learned (and useful) lessons, *emergent* strategies must certainly be a large part of the mix. "Emergent" does not mean lurching from one fad to another—a major failing of the global aid business; rather, it means building on experience, and it means exploiting good opportunities as they arise. The Afghanistan chapter describes Canada's approach there in recent years as opportunistic, although in the absence of knowledge, experience, and seasoned staff, this was perhaps the right approach. Certainly—even with the best talent in the world—there was, and there still is, no blueprint for those promoting good governance in Afghanistan. Nilima Gulrajani makes a similar point about opportunism in the chapter on Vietnam: "The drive for political accountability in Vietnam does not require more funding so much as slow, sustained, bitty, and transitional donor involvement exploiting key, if often unexpected, entry points for change."

This raises the question of what a good strategy of "aid for good governance" might actually look like. Management guru Henry Mintzberg (1994) distinguishes between intended strategies and those which actually emerge over time. Perfect realization of intended strategies, he says, "implies brilliant foresight, not to mention inflexibility, while no realization implies mindlessness. The real world inevitably involves some thinking ahead of time as well as some adaptation en route" (1994, 14). He draws a picture of real-life strategy development:

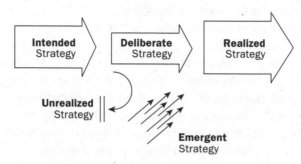

On the learning front, CIDA got off to a good start in the second half of the 1990s with a variety of studies aimed at building knowledge of what worked. There were studies of governance initiatives in South Africa, West Africa, and Sri Lanka, as well as the "lessons learned" study noted above. Studies were also produced relating to anticorruption programming, decentralization projects, and legal and judicial reform. Also, in 1996–97, CIDA produced a first annual report on its support for human rights and democratization. But then the studies and annual reports stopped. The website fell dormant around 2000, and there were no more reports. Then in 2006 the reports that had been compiled were removed from CIDA's website. Whether this reflected changing priorities or just flagging enthusiasm for studies and for website administration is not clear.

In CIDA, governance is a cross-cutting theme—a horizontal issue—whereas all programming is vested in vertical silos, arranged geographically. Governance is like other horizontal themes, including gender, health, and the environment. There are no proactive, central budgets for these issues. CIDA's "geographic" programs take them up based on experience and opportunity, and in line with whatever priority they have been given in the overall scheme of things. While CIDA has a well-informed governance unit in its Policy Branch, each of the geographic programs also has at least one person responsible for governance. Coordination and coherence across the agency is as good or as bad as it is on any cross-cutting issue. The Policy Branch people follow trends and issues, develop policy statements as required, and help establish Canada's position at the UN and the OECD, and in other international forums. To the extent

that geographic programmers need special expertise on governance, democracy, and human rights, they can consult the Policy Branch, but they are more
likely to hire specialized consultants in the area at hand. There is no central
clearing house for governance projects. More oddly, given its importance in
budgetary and political terms, there is no consistent reporting on CIDA's governance programming.

Even the amount of money spent on governance, democracy, and human
rights is uncertain. At the beginning of this chapter, the CIDA estimates for
2005–6 were cited to show that at $565 million budgeted for governance—
12.8 percent of total ODA—Canada was spending twice as much per capita on
governance, democratization, and human rights as the United States. The truth
is that the Canadian numbers (and the US numbers as well) are almost totally
unreliable as a guide to real spending.

Canada is now focusing its ODA on twenty-five "better performing" developing countries, but a huge proportion of the money coded as "governance"
is actually going to Afghanistan, Iraq, and Haiti, none of which is on the list
of twenty-five. Large, multifaceted programs, such as one in Ethiopia, are clus-
tered under the "governance" heading, although this one includes gender projects, electric power, food security, and assistance with the formulation of a
Poverty Reduction Strategy Paper. The companion chapter by Scott Gilmore
and Janan Mosazai on Afghanistan spells out the coding problem there in considerable detail. The actual amount of money spent by Canada on governance
programs in Afghanistan, they say, is elusive, as different layers in different
organizations all provide different numbers.

A large proportion of governance funding is spent through NGOs, although
there is no clarity on how much of this actually relates to governance. Much
of it might as easily be coded under "basic human needs," "gender," or half a
dozen other things. In any case, it is unlikely that much of this "civil society"
spending is aimed at supporting organizations as governance players in their
own right. Rather, their projects will be supported if they can project measurable outcomes in any one of several fields. This is not to say that the advocacy
and human rights efforts of civil society are not being supported by CIDA, but
they are more likely to be supported as discreet, short-term projects than as
organizing ideas around which an institution would receive a sustaining grant.

Regardless of coding, the truth is that none of the donors—not Canada,
and certainly not the United States (*pace* Michael Ignatieff)—is devoting the
time, attention, or resources required to transform much bad governance into
good. According to General Anthony Zinni (USMC ret.), who was commander-
in-chief of US Central Command in the Middle East between 1997 and 2000,
"we preach about values, democracy, human rights, but we haven't convinced

the American people to pony up. There's no leadership that steps up and says, 'This is the right thing to do'.... That's the basic problem.... We should believe that a stable world is a better place for us. If you had a policy and a forward-leaning strategy, the US would make a much greater difference to the world. It would intervene earlier and pick fights better" (in Priest 2003, 117).

Coding and volume aside, a further problem for CIDA in today's climate—one might say today's "fog"—of results-based programming relates to the need to demonstrate cause and effect—that is, to show that efforts aimed at democratization or improving human rights have actually had some results. The 1995 "lessons learned" survey found that staff "lack confidence and feel at risk operating in a high-risk sector within CIDA's risk-averse environment." This has not changed in the years since. There are several reasons why it is so difficult to demonstrate results. One is that for aid agencies, the democracy and good governance "business" is only fifteen years old and human rights programming is not much more mature than that. Given the enormous enthusiasm for democratization at the end of the Cold War, it is not surprising that expectations have been unrealistically high. It is even less surprising that short-term attributable results have been patchy.

## Conclusions

In Canada's 2005 "International Policy Statement," and in this chapter, "good governance" is taken to mean several things: democratization, human rights, the rule of law, and public-sector capacity building. Historically these have emerged as different streams in Canadian policy and programming, with different emphases at different times. Human rights has the longest record, perhaps because as a discipline it is well articulated internationally and has deep and honourable, if vexed, roots in Canada's domestic history (see, for example, Lambertson 2005). The international application of a human rights policy has been at times principled and at other times situational. Concerns about Indonesian human rights violations in East Timor, for example, were not allowed to interfere with sales of weapons and other commodities. But Canada took a principled position on South African apartheid in the mid-1980s, and while it may be argued that the political and economic cost of the approach was not high, it was a policy that put a conservative Canadian government at odds with its conservative counterparts in the United States and Britain.

As an explicit tool in the ODA arsenal, "governance" has a more recent provenance, emerging largely from structural adjustment programs in the 1980s and what became known as the "Washington Consensus." Canada was an eager member of this consensus, which emphasized cutbacks to the state in some areas without much thought to strengthening states in other areas where this was badly needed. Only in the past decade has the need to *build* state capacities been seen as an important part of governance—a position that Canada now strongly endorses.

The promotion of democracy and democratic processes emerged as the most recent part of Canada's good governance agenda in the mid-1990s. This, too, has been somewhat situational, although the ambiguities are not as striking as in US policies, where there are stark everyday trade-offs between, for example, the promotion of human rights and the detention of terrorist suspects at Guantánamo Bay, or between support for democracy and human rights and the desire for friends in countries such as oil and gas-rich Kazakhstan and Azerbaijan, both of which are running serious deficits in democracy and human rights.

Some critics of Canada's approach to governance lament the absence of coherent policies tying all aspects of the agenda together. A patchy, project-by-project approach with no obvious central policy and no central management, they say, is unlikely to yield coherent results. This may be true, but given the overwhelming size of the governance agenda and the limited track record in its promotion by any donor, healthy doses of humility and caution are warranted, along with a good set of brakes in the expectations department. Given the complexity of the challenge, a case can be made for selective interventions, made in concert with other donors, aimed at learning what works and what does not. The apparent absence in Canada, however, of a place where the lessons can be rolled up, spelled out, shared, and remembered, works against the learning that is so badly needed in this field.

It is perhaps worth adding a final comment on Canada's approach to governance. Canada Corps, an idea promoted by Prime Minister Martin in 2004, soon became a locus for policy discussions about good governance. Essentially a tool for mobilizing and dispatching Canadians, Canada Corps was described in the IPS as a "vehicle to strengthen Canada's contribution to human rights, democracy and good governance internationally." "*Particularly* through Canada Corps," Canada would promote "democratization, human rights, the rule of law, public sector capacity building and conflict prevention" (Martin 2004, 12). Given what is known about the complexities of good governance, the idea of technical assistance as a prominent delivery mechanism, significantly predicated on volunteerism and youth, is little short of bizarre.

Canada Corps nevertheless found enthusiastic supporters outside government, some of whom saw it as a horse to which they might hitch other wagons. Thomas Axworthy and others have been promoting the idea of a Canadian Centre for the Study of Democracy, along the lines of the US National

Democratic Institute (NDI), since 2004. It was proposed in 2005 that this Democracy Canada Institute might find a welcoming home "as a core institute of the Canada Corps," taking $20 million of a suggested $100 million budget for the whole shooting match (Axworthy, Campbell, and Donovan 2005). A Democracy Canada Institute modelled on the National Endowment for Democracy (which serves as an umbrella funding mechanism for governance initiatives of US political actors—including business, labour, and the NDI) could well be an important way to involve parliamentarians, political parties, and others in democratization programs. It could also be a way to bring coherence, discipline, and learning to the Canadian discourse on good governance, although there are questions. One might ask why the International Centre for Human Rights and Democratic Development, a creation of the Canadian government and accountable directly to Parliament, has never received more than $5 million a year in government subventions, and why a new institute is now required at four times the price. One might also ask why a Democracy Institute would have even the slightest interest in being a subsidiary of an untried volunteer-sending operation. The answer is as speculative as the question is rhetorical, because by the end of 2006, "Canada Corps" was quietly bifurcating into an "Office of Democratic Governance" and a more traditional personnel-sending operation.

This little debate is emblematic of the yin and the yang of Canada's foreign policy: the push of the "realism" school and the pull of the "romantic" one. These two themes were identified by Gottlieb at the outset of this chapter. We can conclude that increasing clarity in the articulation of human rights policy has been offset by realpolitik in its application. Lloyd Axworthy's human security initiative seemed to fade somewhat after his departure, and the views of "I Branch"—FAC's International Security Branch, which deals inter alia with international security, the military, police, and intelligence—looked to be on the ascendant. On the other hand, what Gottlieb disdainfully called "Boy Scoutism" in Canadian foreign policy alive and well, as evidenced by the newly forged link between Canada's good governance policy and the Canada Corps—a kind of governance-related Outward Bound for the new century with "Boy Scout" written all over it.

But maybe it is not that simple. Perhaps life at the Pearson Building and Place du Portage should not be all about one thing or the other; perhaps there is a real and important role for Canada in the world beyond concerns about its trade, its oceans, and its neighbour to the south. Perhaps the boy scouts of the past had an idea that war and collapsing states in Asia and Africa would inevitably have a real and significant impact on Canada, in much the way that war and collapsing European states did in the 1930s. If so, they were correct. The world of 2007 is considerably more fraught with the outcomes of bad governance than anyone might have imagined in 1989. The question today is not so much whether Canada should be promoting an international good governance agenda, as whether Canada knows enough yet to do it well, and whether it will commit adequate resources in the future to do more, once lessons have been well and truly learned.

This chapter, then, does not end with a long list of what should now be done. In the face of governance disasters in Haiti, Afghanistan, and two dozen other "failed" and "fragile" states, humility and caution are important watchwords for outsiders. So this chapter ends, rather, with the following admonitions, which are found in all thoughtful critiques on governance: good governance does not drop from the sky; it is not a gift; it cannot be imposed. Good governance is unlikely to flow from a collection of disparate, time-bound projects offered by a dozen ill-coordinated donors. It cannot be transferred holus-bolus like pizza from a delivery truck. It must be earned and learned, not just by those for whom it is intended, but by those who would help them. Effective application of the full governance agenda as we now understand it is still pretty much undocumented, untested, and uncoordinated. And it is far too young for dogmatism and certainty.

It *is* old enough, however, that mistakes should not be repeated. And it is important enough that lessons, both positive and negative, should be documented, learned, remembered, and applied. Aid agencies have a problem with this sequence, in almost everything they do. But for democratic governments that want to encourage some of their values elsewhere, doing this well is a test of their own understanding of, and commitment to, principles of democratic good governance.

## Notes

1   For a discussion of Canada's South Africa policy, see Adam and Moodley 1992; Freeman 1997.
2   Total Canadian aid and EDC loans to China in 1991–2: $66.02 million; in 1992–3: $54.9 million. See Morrison 1998, 349.
3   Ouellet managed both foreign affairs and CIDA. After his departure early in 1996, the recently elected Pierre Pettigrew was appointed minister for CIDA, but he was succeeded before the end of the year by Don Boudria, who also lasted only a few months.
4   For example, Diamond 2002; Weart 1998; Windsor 2003.
5   In *At Home in the World*, Jennifer Welsh (2004, 195–98) reviews some of the arguments against combining democracy, human rights, and the rule of law in a single approach to good governance.
6   For a discussion about local perceptions, see Donini, Minear, and Smillie 2005.

▲

# II
## CASE STUDIES
▼

# 4

## SUPPORTING THE STATE THROUGH AID?
## THE CASE OF VIETNAM

### Nilima Gulrajani

### I
### Introduction

When Vietnam finally opened its doors to the world in 1986 through an economic "renovation" policy known as *Doi Moi*, interest in this Communist nation peaked among the international development community. Bilateral donor involvement in Vietnam dates no earlier than 1990, when normal diplomatic relations were restored with most Western countries apart from Sweden and Finland.[1] Relations between Canada and Vietnam blossomed in 1994 with a visit by a Canadian trade delegation led by then Prime Minister Jean Chrétien and the formulation of the Canadian International Development Agency's first Country Development Program Framework (CDPF) for Vietnam.

This chapter traces the contribution that CIDA has made in advancing good governance during this decade or so of involvement in Vietnam. It assesses the overall approach that CIDA chose to adopt and the consequences that strategy had for its good-governance aims. Inductive, qualitative methods are used to conduct this assessment. These include documentary analysis that traces the official *and* unofficial record of CIDA's interventions in Vietnam, examination of scholarly work on Vietnam's political economy, and structured interviews with relevant stakeholders both within and outside CIDA. Based on the rich contextual understanding these methods foster, an appraisal is then made of CIDA's effectiveness in advancing good governance in Vietnam.

But what is good governance? Good governance entails, first and foremost, "improving the capacity, commitment and quality of government administration, of developing an effective developmental state" (White 1998, 25). The historical record of the transition to capitalism has shown that strong, if undemocratic, states are necessary in order to steer industrialization, navigate market liberalization, and arbitrate global competitive forces (Centre for the Future State 2005; Chang 2002; Watts 1998, 454; White 1998). In other words, the market alone is an insufficient condition for the transition to capitalism. Developmental states, however, must carefully balance being effective (or autonomous) with being accountable (or embedded); and the balance that is struck has a strong influence on their long-run democratic potential (Centre for the Future State 2005; Cheema 2005; Evans 1995). As Unsworth writes in this book: "Getting better governance involves striking a balance between the need for effective state control and capacity to act, and the need for holders of state power to be accountable for their actions." This chapter adopts this two-pronged definition of good governance, suggesting that the desire for good governance is a desire for the twin plans of an autonomous and embedded state. This assessment of CIDA's good-governance work in Vietnam thus focuses largely on the ways its program fosters a developmental Vietnamese state that balances these countervailing imperatives, with an eye on its prospects for evolving into a modern democratic polity.

In section II of this chapter, a brief development and political profile of Vietnam is provided. Section III presents CIDA's overall priorities and financial commitments for good governance in Vietnam and outlines the nature of CIDA's current operational work in good governance in terms of two aid modalities: stand-alone technical assistance projects and multidonor financing arrangements. In section IV, the distinctive attributes of CIDA's efforts as a bilateral donor in Vietnam are analyzed. Finally, section V examines possible intended and unintended effects of CIDA's governance interventions for the autonomy and embeddedness of the Vietnamese state.

## II
## The Backdrop for Aid in Vietnam

Prior to 1988, Vietnam was largely isolated from the international aid community (Conway 2004). It received only small amounts of assistance from a handful of friendly OECD nations and UN agencies. This changed drastically in 1986 with the election of the reform-minded Nguyen Van Linh as Secretary General of the Communist Party. Linh initiated a process of economic liberalization—*Doi Moi*—that improved almost all aspects of citizen well-being.

Vietnam has been viewed as an economic success story since the launch of *Doi Moi*. Gross national income (GNI) per capita increased from $114 in 1990 to $480 in 2005 (all figures in USD unless specified). Adjusting for purchasing power parity, this qualifies Vietnam as a low-income country and thus makes it eligible for concessional lending from the International Development Association (IDA). Vietnam is perceived to have weathered the 1997 East Asian financial crisis well; between 1990 and 2002 its annual GDP growth averaged 7.1 percent. The production of export goods also increased dramatically during the same years: seafood exports rose from $239 million to $2 billion, rice exports from 1.6 to 3.2 million tonnes, coffee from 93,000 to 713,000 tonnes, coal from 800,000 to 5,600,000 tonnes, and garments from $214 million to $2.7 billion. Annual capital investment increased from $1.4 million in 1990 to $11 billion in 2002. (For an overview of Vietnam's impressive economic success, see Saumier 2003).

Vietnam is a casebook example of the impact that sustained and equitably distributed economic growth can have on poverty reduction. The number of poor as percentage of the population fell from 75 percent in 1990 to 32 percent in 2000. During this same period, primary school enrolments rose from 80 percent to 94 percent, infant mortality declined from 50 deaths per 1,000 live births to 29, and under-five mortality dropped to 38 per 1,000 from 54. The *Human Development Report 2005* (UNDP 2005b) ranks Vietnam in 108th place among 177 nations on the basis of its human development index (HDI). Overall, Vietnam suffers from less income inequality than the United States, a positive legacy of Communist rule. It looks poised to attain many of the UN's Millennium Development Goals, and has thus given itself additional targets to meet by 2015, including many that relate to governance—for example, the implementation of grassroots democracy, the enhancement of budget transparency, and the advancement of an agenda for legal reform. A set of worldwide indicators on governance designed by the World Bank has ranked Vietnam relatively low in terms of the state's accountability to its citizenry but relatively high in terms of its autonomy and effectiveness (Table 1). Overall, there do seem to be small positive improvements in the state's political and social embeddedness over the 1998–2004 period.

Given Vietnam's apparent dynamism and development success, one must consider why it continues to draw so much donor interest. If anything, Vietnam's experience points to the irrelevance of external financing for development and to the paramount importance of a strong state. Yet for better or for worse, Vietnam continues to attract donor attention and resources. Indeed, Vietnam actually has a surfeit of Official Development Assistance (ODA) funding. In 2005 it was the World Bank's second-largest concessional borrower

TABLE 1

Select Governance Indicators for Vietnam (2005)

| Governance indicator | Year | Percentile rank[a] | Number of surveys/ surveys polls[b] |
|---|---|---|---|
| Voice and accountability | 2004 | 7.3 | 10 |
|  | 1998 | 4.2 | 4 |
| Political stability | 2004 | 51.9 | 10 |
|  | 1998 | 69.1 | 6 |
| Government effectiveness | 2004 | 44.2 | 12 |
|  | 1998 | 49.2 | 6 |
| Regulatory quality | 2004 | 27.6 | 10 |
|  | 1998 | 24.5 | 5 |
| Rule of law | 2004 | 35.7 | 15 |
|  | 1998 | 20.5 | 9 |
| Control of corruption | 2004 | 27.1 | 13 |
|  | 1998 | 29.5 | 8 |

*Source*: World Bank 2005a.

[a] Percentile rank indicates the percentage of countries worldwide that rate below Vietnam (subject to margin of error).
[b] Percentile ranks reflect the statistical compilation of responses on the quality of governance by citizen and expert survey respondents.

after India and the largest IDA-only borrower in the world. Commitments to Vietnam totalled $700 million, up from $368.1 million in 2003. Vietnam's absorptive capacity for ODA is limited largely by donors' concerns with perceived problems of governance—problems that jeopardize the effective use of external resources for developmental purposes. As such, state capacity building provides an important, if often implicit, rationale for donor involvement in Vietnam. This involvement is justified by the relatively widespread importance assigned to quickening disbursements to Vietnam, advancing the use of program instruments, and deepening democratic impulses in the country.[2] Nevertheless, donors continue to justify their interventions in Vietnam on the basis of poverty levels. To some extent this is correct, for many Vietnamese live only marginally above the poverty line despite decades of socialist rule. Pockets of extreme poverty still exist in rural areas (especially in the highland provinces) and among ethnic minorities. Vietnam's recent accession to the WTO, in November 2006, also suggests that growing inequality between rich and poor may worsen before it improves.

In terms of the political backdrop for aid to Vietnam, the Vietnamese Communist Party (VCP) still dominates the landscape. The party's small size (2.5 mil-

lion members, or 3 percent of the population) belies its near monopoly of
coercive powers over both government and state (Abuza 2001, 9). Power is
concentrated in the vcp's Central Committee, members of which are selected
by the party. From this committee, members of an exclusive Politburo are
chosen. The Politburo is the pinnacle of the vcp, with its chairman acting as
the vcp's secretary-general. In the relatively recent transition to market socialism, the vcp has fought to preserve its power monopoly, looking to China as
its role model. Yet it must be said that Vietnam has liberalized far more quickly
and moved faster and further than any other comparable state socialist economy with a large agricultural base, including China (Watts 1998). Nonetheless,
a key consideration in all governmental policy and program debates remains
the extent to which the nature and timing of individual reform measures might
threaten or compromise the party's hegemony (Saumier 2003, 6).

The Vietnamese National Assembly has long been nothing more than a
rubber stamp for the vcp, although increasingly since the late 1990s it has
exercised greater assertiveness (Abuza 2001, 20).[3] The assembly sits for only two
months of the year, its powers devolving to a powerful Standing Committee
in the interim. The Government of Vietnam is composed of bureaucrats appointed on a de facto presidential model. The National Assembly appoints the
prime minister, although there is only ever one candidate, who is pre-selected
by the Politburo. There is no overarching coordinating body, such as the Cabinet found in Westminster Parliamentary systems, and the prime minister is
typically involved in the minutiae of government administration, though also
a member of the Politburo (Saumier 2003). He does obtain some support from
the Office of Government (the elite wing of the Vietnamese public service);
however, that office's reputation for ineffectiveness has compelled successive
prime ministers to appoint small and personalized advisory and analysis bodies. Generally, the government operates in a highly opaque and secretive environment. All senior officials are thought to be subject to special surveillance
by the vcp, government policy statements are never published, and the ratio-
nales for policy decisions are never made public, nor are they requested by
the state-controlled media.

Vietnam has sixty-four provinces and municipalities; districts and communes report to these (Conway 2004, 5). Communes are the lowest level in the
hierarchy, but villages are recognized as local representative units and interact with commune administrations. At each level in the hierarchy there are
People's Councils (the local legislature) and People's Committees (the local
executive, selected from within the People's Council). National–provincial dialogue takes the form of annual meetings between provincial/municipal chairs
and the prime minister. Also, senior official in central ministries are rotated into

senior posts in the provinces, and informal provincial delegations attend the National Assembly. The provinces do enjoy some discretion in implementing national policies and spending budgetary resources; that said, formal authority in Vietnam remains heavily centralized.

## III
## Canada's Governance Priorities and Commitments in Vietnam

### The Vietnamese Context

The values and objectives of Canadian aid are highly susceptible to both international trends and domestic political pressures. The rise of good governance as an area of programming in Canadian development policy is no exception to this. The first manifestation of this agenda arose from the heated debate over the role of Canadian aid to regimes that violated human rights, spent excessively on their militaries, or evidenced persistent problems of corruption (Schmitz, Pistor, and Furi 2003). In response to a sweeping foreign policy review in the mid-1990s, Canada endorsed human rights, democracy, and good governance as key program priorities. It is fair to say that good governance has captured both political and bureaucratic interest to the point where it is now a flagship item for Canadian aid policy.

Good governance has always been one of CIDA's explicit objectives in its relatively young aid program to Vietnam, albeit within an overall program that privileges poverty reduction.[4] This is in line with Vietnam's Comprehensive Poverty Reduction and Growth Strategy (C-PRGS), in which governance is one of three critical priorities. CIDA's priorities for good governance in Vietnam have largely been defined in terms of facilitating the country's transition from a centrally planned economic system to a market economy. This focus on improving economic governance is shared with the bulk of the donor community operating in Vietnam and is driven by the Communist government's reluctance to address uncomfortable questions about political reform, as well as by the international development community's professed desire for country "ownership." Demand by Vietnam for donor assistance in the area of governance is, however, strictly limited to maximizing the gains from poverty reduction through its capitalist transition and protecting the economy from the harmful residual effects of liberalization. Questions of political reform are generally sidelined except where they may directly benefit Vietnam's ongoing financial and economic liberalization. Thus, in parallel and often in concert with other donors, CIDA has defined its governance priorities in Vietnam in terms of formal legislative and regulative institution building, as well as less formalized initiatives for transferring knowledge and skills through capacity building of the sort that can foster equitable economic growth. This has not precluded CIDA's interest in improving the state's embeddedness in and accountability to society. That said, CIDA has framed its aspirations for enhanced political governance first and foremost by pointing to its benefits for the ongoing transition to market socialism:

> Governance programming will be designed to improve the policy environment and *strengthen the institutional capacity of the Government of Vietnam to facilitate Vietnam's economic transition* and at the same time contribute to more transparent and accountable governance.... In the view of CIDA and donors generally, the collective effort of reforming and implementing the legislative and regulatory regimes surrounding Vietnam's ongoing economic transformation *can also* have a positive impact on government and corporate transparency and accountability, democratic decision-making processes and, potentially, human rights. (CIDA 2004a, 22; emphasis added)

Since 1999, CIDA's bilateral program in Vietnam has aimed 40 percent of its ODA disbursements directly at governance, although it has fallen short of this goal for most of this period (Table 2). Canada's increasing financial commitment to governance-related activities in Vietnam is part of a visible trend among all donors. Demonstrating this through data on external resource inflows is a challenge, however, as there is no universally accepted operational definition for what constitutes sector programming in good governance. For example, the United Nations Development Programme (UNDP) groups external aid flows into Vietnam into one of six categories[5]: (1) major infrastructure, (2) policy and institutional support, (3) rural development, (4) human development, (5) natural resources, and (6) emergency and relief (UNDP 2005a, 23). Given that most donors define their activities in good governance in Vietnam in terms of policy and institutional supports for equitable economic growth, there are grounds for taking this category as a proxy for total ODA expenditures on governance.[6] Policy and institutional support accounted for 26 percent of total disbursements in Vietnam in 2003, the second-largest ODA category after infrastructure. The value of ODA within this category had increased by $533 million since 2002, a 226 percent increase (UNDP 2005a, 25). This suggests that among the community of donors operating in Vietnam, governance is an area of growing interest and commitment.

TABLE 2

CIDA Good-Governance Disbursements in Vietnam

| Fiscal | 2000–1 | 2001–2 | 2002–3 | 2003–4 | 2004–5 | 2005–6 | (projected) 2006–7 |
|---|---|---|---|---|---|---|---|
| Governance expenditures (in c$ millions) | 5.9 | 5.6 | 5.3 | 7.0 | 7.3 | 14.3 | 13.5 |
| As a % of total CIDA bilateral disbursements in-country | 36.1 | 24 | 22.9 | 33.2 | 25.7 | 46.8 | 47.6 |

Source: CIDA, in-house.

## CIDA's Involvement and Interlocutors in Vietnam

Over 2003–4, twenty-five bilateral donors reported ODA disbursements in Vietnam totalling $967.7 million (CIDA 2005a, 51). Canada provided 2.4 percent of this total assistance package (approximately $23 million), making it Vietnam's ninth-largest bilateral donor. This percentage belies both the country's importance in Canada's aid program—Vietnam is Canada's tenth-largest bilateral aid recipient and one of twenty-five priority countries identified in its *International Policy Statement* (CIDA 2005b, 33)—and the size of CIDA's influence among the Vietnamese donor community.

As of this writing, CIDA's bilateral involvement in specific governance-related activities in Vietnam takes two main forms. First, CIDA subsidizes the transfer of knowledge and expertise in specific technical projects. The second aid modality involves donors pooling financial resources in multidonor interventions.

One could cast the net wider to look at projects in other sectors that have an effect on improving governance in Vietnam. We do not do so here, which points to a dilemma involved in analyzing aid for good governance—a dilemma addressed by the editors of this book. The decision to examine CIDA's bilateral activities with explicit governance objectives is motivated by the belief that the linkages between operations and outcomes within these will be both more obvious and more direct, thus making an assessment of their impact on governance somewhat easier to discern. Furthermore, given the need to restrict the scope of this research, the examination of activities designated as governance projects seems appropriate. As such, while other areas of CIDA's bilateral programming—for example, decentralized rural development—may have outcomes for governance, this chapter limits itself to those bilateral operations which identify governance as a primary objective. Those operations falling within this category, current as of September 2005, are outlined in Appendices I and II of this chapter.

The first observation to make about CIDA's bilateral involvement in Vietnam is how many different activities are subsumed under the label "governance." Thus, technical assistance activities touch on areas ranging from legal reform to banking reform, judicial training, pollution management, policy formulation, language training, training for women, and flooding prevention. CIDA's multidonor contributions toward governance range from the harmonization of donor aid processes to support for financial management modernization and public administration reform and the World Bank's Poverty Reduction Support Credit (PRSC).[7] This diversity suggests that donors believe that creating an effective developmental state is a complex problem that can be attacked on many fronts. Nevertheless, this complexity and multidimensionality add to the difficulties of assessing the sum total of CIDA's programming impact for governance.

Second, CIDA channels the bulk of its programming for good governance through bilateral technical assistance. Its total operational project budget at the time of writing was approximately C$74.3 million, of which C$54.4 million or 73 percent was channelled through bilateral technical assistance. The remaining 17 percent of its activities is invested in multidonor governance arrangements, the bulk of which (97 percent) is invested in the PRSC. The balance struck between CIDA's bilateral and multidonor interventions raises important questions about whether this is the most appropriate resource allocation for strategically advancing good governance. Detractors suggest that governance is better achieved multilaterally by funding sectors with positive spillovers for governance—for example, through the strengthening of fiscal management systems. But ploughing monies into multilateral funds raises awkward questions about the rationale for bilateral agency engagement at the country level.

Interestingly, only a handful of CIDA's bilateral projects in governance are budgeted at less than C$1 million. This suggests that CIDA has capped projects that fall below a minimum threshold level, in line with thinking that effective development requires that assistance be focused on fewer, better-funded activities (Canada 2005a). It also potentially indicates that there is a consensus that good governance is best advanced through larger investments.

Another feature of Canada's bilateral aid program is the degree to which it advances opportunities for Canadian consultants, private-sector and civil-society actors, and members of the academic community. In a significant number of good-governance projects, the implementing agencies are purposely Canadian, albeit working in collaboration with the Vietnamese government. Yet recent initiatives such as the Paris Declaration on Aid Effectiveness (OECD

2005b) stress the value of untied aid and coordinated technical cooperation rooted in country-led implementation units. Notwithstanding this, there are good examples of Canadian counterparts maintaining exceptional responsiveness to government priorities. One is the Policy Implementation Assistance Project (PIAP). But this is not to deny the broader need for CIDA to critically examine the nature of Canadian partner involvement in bilateral projects in order to make sure it is not unintentionally substituting for the capacity it is supposedly seeking to foster locally.

Finally, it is noteworthy that most of CIDA's local partners are government agencies, ranging from the Prime Minister's Research Commission to the Ministry of Planning and Investment and the Ministry of Justice. This state-centred approach reflects CIDA's concern that pursuing programming with local non-state actors could provoke a strong negative reaction from the Vietnamese government. It also partly reflects CIDA's optimism that political reforms can emerge in Vietnam from within a one-party state. Yet, as will be highlighted later, this state-centred approach may be impeding the advancement of good governance in Vietnam.

## IV
### Canada's Distinctiveness in Vietnam

Given the number of active donors in Vietnam and the overabundance of ODA, there remain few *unique* contributions to be made by any single external actor. Indeed, Canada's distinctiveness as a donor in Vietnam probably derives more from its comparative advantage in particular professional fields. There is some indication that Canada's dual civil and common law traditions have made its advice on the design of a nascent legal system within the PIAP program highly valued, with Quebec's Civil Code informing and influencing Vietnam's Civil Code and Code of Civil Procedure. Canadian experience and expertise could also be drawn from in an upcoming judicial training project, which will be working to foster a better-managed court system and a more independent and accountable judiciary. Other areas where Canada could exercise leverage over both the Vietnamese government and other donors derive from its experience as a decentralized federation, as a result of which it has expertise in organizing and implementing public programs across political jusrisdictions (e.g., in the field of taxation). These sources of comparative advantage could be exploited more strategically in its diverse portfolio of technical assistance projects.

One must still ask whether CIDA's technical assistance programs provide it with greater leverage in advancing good governance objectives than its multi-donor interventions. This is not to question the success of many of CIDA's stand-alone technical assistance projects[8] but rather to consider whether such mechanisms are the best way to advance broader governance objectives. CIDA officials generally agree that the unique influence their governance programs enjoy in Vietnam is mainly the consequence of bilateral technical assistance activities, or at least from dual delivery mechanisms. In other words, CIDA's technical assistance programs in governance are a major source of its credibility and effectiveness and also justify Canada's involvement in multidonor arrangements such as the Like-Minded Donor Group (LMDG), with the former informing CIDA's participation in and contributions to the latter.

Yet it is interesting to compare this view with that of a larger and more influential bilateral donor in Vietnam—the UK's Department for International Development (DFID). For DFID, working through multidonor channels and through programmatic mechanisms is a way to foster aid effectiveness; doing so also places greater responsibility on the Vietnamese government for development results, besides permitting greater leverage for the policy reform agenda. The DFID office in Hanoi employs more than twenty people and has an annual budget of around £55 million, yet its portfolio consists of just one or two traditional bilateral technical assistance projects representing a small percentage of total allocations. While a few of its projects involve collaborations with other donors, most of its funds are channelled through programmatic and multidonor financing instruments. It can be argued that this shift to programmatic approaches has provided some of the momentum behind the success of the LMDG, which in turn has been an important influence on the growing size and credibility of CIDA in multidonor interventions in Vietnam.[9]

One thing is certain: CIDA's seat at the table of multidonor coordination bodies has allowed it to wield greater influence on the Vietnamese state than its relatively small portfolio would otherwise grant it.[10] Through its membership in the LMDG, CIDA has acquired agenda-setting powers and acted as an important interlocutor with the state. The LMDG also provides CIDA with enhanced opportunities for exercising moral leadership, further cementing its reputation as a bilateral donor committed to the new normative context of aid that privileges organizational partnerships and collaborative work. Canada's position as chair of the LMDG in 2005, the leadership role it has played in LMDG priority areas such as the PRSC and procurement reform, and its position as one of only two LMDG members of the Partnership Group on Aid Effectiveness, all lend support to this claim. Multidonor arrangements are important vehicles for developing leverage in core governance reforms;[11] they do so by uniting donors behind a common agenda with unified procedural requirements. The decision by CIDA to channel 73 percent of its good-governance programming through bilateral technical assistance should be considered against this evidence and experience.

Certainly, one impediment to CIDA's participation in multidonor aid programs has been its own particular organizational constraints. In 2002 an OECD peer review of CIDA described it as one of the most centralized bilateral donor agencies (DAC 2002b). This perception of Canada as a slow and cumbersome bilateral donor impeded CIDA's initial request to join the LMDG. This was surmounted only after CIDA country officials reiterated their commitment to play an active role that would not reduce the group's overall speed and effectiveness.

The perception that CIDA is inefficient is not unsubstantiated. For example, CIDA's country-based managers and Ottawa-based directors, and even its vice-presidents, have limited authority to contract for new projects (selection approval) or to disburse aid funds compared to their counterparts in other bilateral agencies. Amounts above the ceilings listed in Table 3 must be approved by the Minister of Development Cooperation, with projects over $20 million requiring approval of the Treasury Board Secretariat in Ottawa.[12] Meanwhile, a number of highly publicized government-related corruption scandals in Canada have greatly increased the pressure on CIDA to become more accountable to both central government agencies and their political masters. Yet in the drive to create more accountable government, complex, cumbersome, and sometimes even contradictory strategic performance management systems have been introduced to an organization that is already viewed as far too centralized and risk averse (Goldfarb and Tapp 2006). The result has been a further reduction of CIDA's speed, flexibility, and responsiveness. This is limiting possibilities for action within multidonor bodies such as the LMDG and is channelling Canadian involvement into positions of reactive/moral rather than proactive/financial leadership. Ultimately, it is sure to undermine its capacity to capitalize on small, emergent, and transitional spaces for advancing good governance. CIDA recognizes these organizational limitations and to its credit is engaging in innovations to overcome them. For example, it lobbied for raising the ceiling on the approval authority of vice-presidents within the LMDG

TABLE 3
Maximum Project and Selection Authority
for Three Levels of CIDA Staff (C$)

|  | Country manager | Director | Vice-president |
|---|---|---|---|
| Project approval (disbursal) | $50,000 | $500,000 | $5 million |
| Selection approval (new projects) | 0 | $ 50,000 | $100,000 |

*Source*: CIDA, in-house.

initiative, and decentralized greater authority to the field in its Africa program. What is now needed is greater political will both within and beyond CIDA to engage in organizational reforms that will ensure that Canada's development agency remains as effective as it can be in the field while preserving its accountability to Ottawa.

## V
## Assessing Effectiveness:
## A Final Note

In the introduction to this chapter the term good governance was equated with an effective and embedded developmental state—that is, a state that possesses the capacity to act while remaining accountable for its actions. Examining CIDA's overall bilateral program in good governance, one is left with the impression of a strongly state-centred portfolio that prioritizes effectiveness over embeddedness. This can be broadly attributed to CIDA's reluctance to antagonize Vietnam's established political order. Vigorous donor demands for political reform would violate the current international consensus on the importance of recipient country "ownership" and rooted principles of state sovereignty and donor neutrality. It could also undermine CIDA's relationship with Vietnamese officialdom, thereby jeopardizing Canada's place and position as a bilateral donor.

In this climate, a state-centred approach is the only feasible option for CIDA. In Vietnam this approach takes two principal forms. First, within its technical assistance projects, CIDA has focused on attaining its economic governance goals by enhancing formal institutions and officials' capacity to act within and through these. CIDA is engaged in organization building, knowledge transfer, and skill development in highly specialized areas such as legal system reform and environmental management, with newer technical assistance projects involving banking reform and judicial training poised to build on this earlier work. Second, CIDA's involvement in multidonor arrangements relating to public administration reform, procurement reform, and public financial management have given it important influence within a core set of governance activities. Using this two-pronged approach to aid delivery, CIDA is undoubtedly succeeding in fostering formal institutions, enhancing professional conduct, and improving managerial competencies within the official state apparatus.

This state-centred focus, however, seems to have at least two possible unintentional consequences. First, the privileging of the state as CIDA's primary interlocutor and the desire to avoid sensitive discussions on political reform have meant that Vietnamese societal forces are usually a secondary consideration in CIDA programs. While the role of social movements and CSOs is of concern to CIDA, it is generally separated from strategic discussions on the implications for accountability relationships between the Vietnamese state and society. Instead, societal forces become salient only as state substitutes in relatively uncontroversial areas such as language training, disaster planning, environmental planning, and gender equality. As Smillie notes elsewhere in this book, CIDA's efforts in advancing governance through civil society do not support these organizations as governance players in their own right; rather, the agency engages more often than not in discreet, short-term projects that seek to achieve specific sectoral outcomes. The common belief is that there are fewer benefits to be accrued in supporting non-state groups because of their limited policy influence and relatively continuous identity with the Vietnamese government and state. Yet this ignores the fact that fostering embeddedness does not require a programmatic "choice" between state and society. State embeddedness in a dense network of societal ties provides an alternative source of intelligence, as well as channels of implementation that can enhance the state's competence (Evans 1995, 248). Donors need to recognize that fostering good governance requires prioritizing actions that enhance reciprocities and mutual dependencies within state–society interactions and that consider societal actors as vehicles of governance in their own right.

A second possible unintentional outcome of state-focused development programming may arise from the ways a state-centred approach limits the possibilities for nascent opposition movements in Vietnam that are striving for greater embeddedness. There remains considerable uncertainty regarding whether, and through what generative mechanisms, the focus on formal state institutions and officials translates into a more effective *and* embedded developmental state. While CIDA officials largely reject this potential unintentional consequence of their program, it makes sense to at least consider the possibility. Obviously, a state-centred focus does not per se prove that CIDA's program—or any other donor's, for that matter—is undermining indigenous reform movements by strengthening state autonomy to the detriment of its embeddedness. Nonetheless, one might suggest that this state-centred approach may be reinforcing conservative trends, if only by channelling vast resources to support formal Vietnamese state institutions at a time when nascent civil society organizations, political opposition, and social movements are increasingly trying to test it (Fforde 2005). There are important limitations on CIDA's ability to champion political reform in Vietnam and work closely with non-state actors; that said, opportunities to renegotiate state–society relations appear to be lost in Vietnam as donors fall into line behind the development aid "dogmas" of multilateral agencies. This may unintentionally silence the few critical voices asking uncomfortable questions about even the most minor political reforms in Vietnam (Fforde and Porter 1995, 14). Indirect *étatization* by donors aligned behind a "harmonized agenda" may be particularly unfortunate given the relatively small number of local change agents and intrasocietal alliances in Vietnam—forces that have proven pivotal in the history of democratization elsewhere (Abuza 2001, 9; Ferguson 1994). As Unsworth argues in her contribution to this book, external assistance has always been better at nurturing local social movements than at creating them from scratch.

Yet there are some examples of best practice by CIDA occurring in Vietnam. For instance, CIDA has limited its aid program's demands on government by engaging in multidonor financing approaches; many of these arrangements involve harmonizing aid policies and procedures. The sincerity of Canada's efforts in this area is a promising basis for an honest and constructive relationship with the Vietnamese state that may go some length toward altering domestic incentive structures in favour of improved governance. One outcome of the success of multidonor cooperation in Vietnam, however, has been the increasing popularity of governance programming among all bilateral donors. Increasing numbers of bilateral donors seek a foothold in Vietnam in formal institution and capacity building, even though many donors already operate in this sector and even though the ODA account is relatively bountiful. One can only ask whether Vietnam is attracting aid for governance that might be better spent in low-income countries where state capacity may be far less but the possibilities for enhancing state embeddedness are more obvious.

An effective and embedded developmental state *is* within Vietnam's grasp in the medium to long term. But the drive for political accountability and reform in Vietnam does not require more funding so much as small-scale, slow, and sustained donor involvement, where interventions exploit key if often unexpected and fleeting entry points for change (Centre for the Future State 2005, 44). It also requires donors to focus their interventions on improving interactions and accountabilities between state and society. For bilateral donor agencies willing to engage in highly organic, politically sensitive, and frustratingly unpredictable processes, the gains from governance programming are likely to be enormous.

▼

## Appendix I:
## Current CIDA Bilateral Investments for
## Good Governance in Vietnam

CIDA's bilateral involvement in governance-related activities in Vietnam largely takes two forms.[15] This appendix provides an overview of operational CIDA governance activities that rely on both technical assistance and multidonor interventions. It examines the purpose, value, duration, and key Canadian and Vietnamese interlocutors of current bilateral interventions in order to appreciate the variety of operations, approaches, and sectors associated with CIDA's good governance agenda. All data and figures were supplied and verified by CIDA at the time of writing (September 2005).

### Technical Assistance Projects

Legal Reform Assistance Project (LERP)
    CIDA contribution: C$5 million
    Duration: 2001–2007
    Canadian implementing agencies: Bearing Point, Centre for Asia-Pacific
        Initiative, University of Victoria
    Local partner: Vietnam Ministry of Justice

This project develops mechanisms to improve the application of the law in order to promote sound economic development. It also informs and educates Vietnamese citizens on the nature of the law and improves their access to and utilization of the justice system. CIDA has sought to build local capacity in comparative law analysis for the purpose of supporting government reviews of current legislation and help the ministry comply with wto trading regime regulations. There are tentative plans to contribute an additional C$10 million toward a second phase of this legal reform project beginning in 2007.

Vietnam Banking Legislative Review
    CIDA contribution: C$225,000
    Duration: June 2003–December 2005
    Canadian implementing agencies: Canadian Embassy, Hanoi
    Local partner: State Bank of Vietnam

The Government of Vietnam places a high priority on banking reforms that can create a stable macroeconomic environment, develop local capital markets, and support growth of the private sector. This project was intended to provide short and punctual assistance to the State Bank of Vietnam in reviewing banking legislation, specifically the Law on the State Bank of Vietnam and the Law on Credit Institutions. At the end of the review, the National Assembly passed a revised Law on Credit Institutions.

## Banking Reform Project

CIDA contribution: c$9.175 million
Duration: 2002–2009
Canadian implementing agencies: DevPar/Gowlings/IBM
Local partner: State Bank of Vietnam

Following on from the Vietnam Banking Legislative Review, this project aims to improve the State Bank's overall organization and management. Its focus is on banking supervision functions and prudential management and compliance standards at state-owned commercial banks and private shareholding banks.

## Policy Implementation Assistance Project (PIAP II)

CIDA contribution: c$10 million
Duration: 2000–2006
Canadian implementing agencies: Experco-Stikeman Elliott International
Local partners: Prime Minister's Research Commission (PMRC), Prime
    Minister's Research Group on External Economic Relations (GEER),
    National Assembly Standing Committees on Laws and Social Affairs

This project supports the knowledge needs of high-level decision makers in the Vietnamese government as they navigate the uncertainties and challenges of transforming Vietnam's planned economy. It follows from PIAP I, which had a budget of c$10.2 million to promote economic and administrative reform by building government-desired knowledge of and capacity for policy formulation, assessment, and implementation. A PIAP III phase is expected to begin in 2006 with an expected budget of approximately c$10 million.

## Judicial Development and Grassroots Engagement Project (JUDGE)

CIDA contribution: c$12 million
Duration: 2005–2010
Local partners: Supreme People's Court, the Ministry of Justice, select civil
    society organizations

This project builds competencies within the legal–judicial sector by improving the quality of administering justice and increasing access to the legal system by disadvantaged groups. The focus is on developing judicial training institutions, assisting the Supreme Court in reforming the court system, and improving dispute resolution mechanisms for target populations.

## Vietnam–Canada Environment Project (VCEP II)

CIDA contribution: c$12.3 million
Duration: 1999–2005
Canadian implementing agencies: ESSA Technologies and SNC Lavalin
Local partners: Ministry of Natural Resources, Department of National
    Resources

The Government of Vietnam has been reluctant to engage in environmental mitigation efforts where such efforts might jeopardize industrial and employment expansion. As such, CIDA has attempted in this project to improve environmental capacity, transparency, and accountability of organizations and institutions in order to implement environmental mandates. CIDA will contribute another C$10 million to implement Phase III of VCEP, which begins in 2006.

### Young Canadian Volunteers in Vietnam

CIDA contribution: C$3.5 million
Duration: 1998–2006
Canadian implementing agency: World University Service of Canada

This project provides English and French training for the purpose of enhancing socio-economic development and facilitating the transition to a market economy.

### Vietnam–Canada Social and Women's Initiative Fund Phase II

CIDA contribution: C$1 million
Canadian implementing agency: Canada Fund

This fund follows from an earlier project that sought to improve the political, entrepreneurial, and managerial skills of Vietnamese women and to heighten gender-equality awareness.

### Capacity Building for Adaptation to Climate Change

CIDA contribution: C$1.2 million
Duration: 2002–2005
Canadian implementing agency: Canadian Centre for International Studies and Cooperation

This recently concluded project sought to reduce social and economic vulnerabilities deriving from climate change, particularly from flooding in Central Vietnam.

## Multidonor Interventions

### Vietnam Harmonization of ODA Procedures

CIDA contribution: C$384,000
Duration: 2004–2006
Fund contributors: Like-Minded Donor Group (Canada, Aus AID, UK, Finland, Netherlands, Switzerland); Japan, World Bank
Primary local partner: Ministry of Planning and Investment

This project is an outgrowth of efforts among the Like Minded Donor Group (LMDG), Japan, and the World Bank to increase donor harmonization and improve government capacity in project and program management. CIDA has budgeted a further C$10 million toward a harmonization facility that will provide funds to multidonor initiatives within the LMDG to be dispensed by 2010, either through pooled funding or multilateral co-financing/basket-funding instruments. The facility will be used to support governance activities and promote aid effectiveness. The harmonization facility overcomes bureaucratic procedures within CIDA by giving vice-presidents the power to select projects valued up to C$2 million.

## Multidonor Support for Financial Management Modernization

CIDA contribution: C$350,000
Duration: 2002–2005
Implementing organization: World Bank
Fund contributors: Like-Minded Donor Group (Denmark, Netherlands,
    Norway, Sweden, UK, Canada, Switzerland)
Local partner: Ministry of Finance

The purpose of this initiative is to harmonize donor efforts in supporting the development and implementation of the Government of Vietnam's Public Financial Management Reform Initiative. This project is expected to improve fiscal management processes and provide a stronger fiduciary basis for donors seeking to provide greater budget support to Vietnam. The implementation of this fund is through two jointly financed funds supervised by the World Bank.[16] The project is held to be a working example of donor coordination.

## Poverty Reduction Support Credit Contribution (PRSC)

CIDA contribution: C$19 million
Duration: 2002–2007
Implementing organization: World Bank
Fund contributors: Under aegis of LMDG (Denmark, Netherlands, Sweden,
    Britain, Canada); other co-financiers (European Commission, Asian
    Development Bank, Japan)

The PRSC is an aid instrument created by the World Bank to provide budget support for countries implementing their Poverty Reduction Strategy Paper (or in Vietnam's case, the C-PRGS). Disbursements depend on the success Vietnam makes in advancing the main objectives of the C-PRGS, including actions relating to public financial management, legal reform, and anticorruption. The PRSC is co-managed by the World Bank and the Government of Vietnam, although it is becoming the single most important mechanism for donor harmonization through co-financing arrangements with LMDG members. CIDA has provided its contribution under the aegis of the LMDG in order to reduce transaction costs and exercise greater influence on government. CIDA has taken an interest in the environmental and educational components of the PRSC, assuming the position of sector leader in the working group dealing with the former. It is expected that CIDA will contribute another C$19 million toward the next PRSC over the 2007–2010 period.

## Other

## Vietnam Multidonor Governance Reform Project

CIDA contribution: C$1.1 million
Duration: 2001–2010
Implementing organization: UNDP
Fund contributors: Canada, Netherlands, Norway, Sweden, Switzerland

While this intervention is not listed in Appendix II, interviewees often referred to it as representing a substantial Canadian contribution to a UNDP-led initiative in public administration reform in Vietnam. This contribution is part of a larger, pooled basket fund totalling US$18.4 million.

▼

## Appendix II

### Current CIDA Operations in Governance in Vietnam with Projected Disbursements (C$)

| | Project Budget | Historical Disbursements | FY 05/06 | FY 06/07 | FY 07/08 | FY 08/09 | FY 09/10 | Total |
|---|---|---|---|---|---|---|---|---|
| **GOVERNANCE PROJECTS—OPERATIONAL** | | | | | | | | |
| *Technical assistance projects* | | | | | | | | |
| A Legal Reform Assistance Project (A-019065) | 4,995,000 | 2,366,892 | 850,000 | 1,000,000 | 778,108 | 0 | 0 | 4,995,000 |
| B Vietnam Banking Legislative Review (A-032094) | 225,000 | 121,834 | 103,166 | 0 | 0 | 0 | 0 | 225,000 |
| C Banking Reform Project (A-031629-002) | 9,175,000 | 369,335 | 1,680,665 | 2,220,000 | 2,240,000 | 1,910,000 | 755,000 | 9,175,000 |
| D Policy Implementation Assistance Project (A-019865) | 10,000,000 | 6,661,677 | 1,800,000 | 1,538,323 | 0 | 0 | 0 | 10,000,000 |
| E JUDGE-Legal-Judicial Reform Project (A-032113) | 12,000,000 | 10,898 | 800,000 | 2,400,000 | 2,400,000 | 2,400,000 | 2,400,000 | 10,410,898 |
| F Vietnam–Canada Environment Project II (A-019588) | 12,300,000 | 10,226,028 | 2,073,972 | 0 | 0 | 0 | 0 | 12,300,000 |
| G Young Canadian Volunteers in Vietnam (A-020976) | 3,500,000 | 3,121,843 | 378,157 | 0 | 0 | 0 | 0 | 3,500,000 |
| H Vietnam–Canada Social and Women's Initiatives Fund Phase II (A-021595) | 1,000,000 | 755,342 | 244,658 | 0 | 0 | 0 | 0 | 1,000,000 |
| I Capacity Building Adaptation to Climate Change (A-031297) | 1,205,000 | 1,030,388 | 174,612 | | | | 0 | 1,205,000 |

Appendix 11, *continued*

| | Project Budget | Historical Disbursements | FY 05/06 | FY 06/07 | FY 07/08 | FY 08/09 | FY 09/10 | Total |
|---|---|---|---|---|---|---|---|---|
| **Multi-donor interventions** | | | | | | | | |
| J Vietnam Harmonization of ODA Procedures (A-031833) | 384,000 | 89,446 | 294,554 | 0 | 0 | 0 | 0 | 384,000 |
| K Multi-Donor Support for Financial Management Modernization (A-31903) | 350,000 | 145,165 | 204,835 | 0 | 0 | 0 | 0 | 350,000 |
| L Poverty Reduction Support Credit Contribution Project (A-032271) | 19,200,000 | 7,000,000 | 6,100,000 | 6,100,000 | 0 | 0 | 0 | 19,200,000 |
| Total (Operational) | 74,334,000 | 31,898,848 | 14,704,619 | 13,258,323 | 5,418,108 | 4,310,000 | 3,155,000 | 72,744,898 |
| Total (Tentative) | 57,000,000 | 0 | 1,000,000 | 6,000,000 | 13,000,000 | 14,000,000 | 14,000,000 | 48,000,000 |
| Total (Operational and Tentative) | 131,334,000 | 31,898,848 | 15,704,619 | 19,258,323 | 18,418,108 | 18,310,000 | 17,155,000 | 120,744,858 |

*Source:* in-house, CIDA.

# Notes

1 The United States was one notable exception; only in 1994 did it remove its trade embargo against Vietnam.

2 Program-based arrangements are a way of engaging in development based on principles of coordinated donor support. Typically these arrangements involve a single comprehensive program and budget framework to which donors subscribe collectively. They are meant to reflect support for local strategies that use local systems of design, implementation, and financial management.

3 The VCP, however, still controls membership in the assembly.

4 In its most recent Country Development Program Framework (CDPF), CIDA adopted the overarching goal of reducing the percentage of poor and hungry households in Vietnam. In addition to governance, the 2004–9 CDPF outlined two additional priority areas: the improvement of rural livelihoods through support for agriculture and rural development; and enhanced access to quality basic education, particularly for disadvantaged children.

5 The UNDP's 2005 *Development Cooperation Report* for Vietnam (2005a) aggregates and refines the ODA taxonomy provided by the Development Cooperation Assistance System (DCAS). DCAS groups aid into seventeen sectors and more than eighty subsectors.

6 The policy and institutional support category includes contributions toward activities relating to economic management, development administration, and international and domestic trade.

7 The PRSC is an aid instrument created by the World Bank to provide programmatic budget support (in the form of concessional loans) in annual tranches for countries implementing their Poverty Reduction Strategy Paper (or in Vietnam's case, the C-PRGS).

8 Common examples cited as successful technical assistance projects include the PIAP program, which has achieved substantial leverage with high-ranking government officials and resulted in often unexpected policy outcomes, such as the promulgation in November 2004 of a competition law. Similarly, CIDA's environment project has been praised for strengthening the knowledge base of industrial pollution management control at subnational levels, for improving provincial/national collaboration, and for strengthening environmental protection laws.

9 The LMDG was the creation of the Utstein group of donors (the UK, the Netherlands, Germany, and Norway) in 1999; Canada joined in 2002. It now comprises those five members as well as Sweden, Denmark, Finland, Australia, and Switzerland. Historically, the share of ODA disbursed by the LMDG has accounted for between 12 and 17 percent of total ODA in Vietnam. The LMDG focuses on small projects; in 2003, 83 percent reported disbursements below $1 million and only six projects involved disbursements up to $10 million. In 2003 the group disbursed approximately $270 million—16 percent of total ODA to Vietnam (UNDP 2004a).

10 Among the ten members of the LMDG, Canada is the fourth-smallest contributor, ahead of only Finland, Norway, and Switzerland (UNDP, 2005: 53–54).

11  By core governance reforms, CIDA means public management, public administration reform, anticorruption, and procurement.

12  The Treasury Board Secretariat is a central government agency of Canada in charge of public expenditure management.

13  This review does not examine governance programs that operate through the Canadian Partnership Branch, which funds involvement in Vietnam by Canadian organizations (universities, professional associations, NGOs) and the Multilateral Programs Branch, which is responsible for CIDA's relationship with the international institutions.

14  CIDA's financial contribution represents less than 6 percent of the total value of each fund.

▲

# 5

## ASSISTING CIVIL SOCIETY THROUGH AID:
## THE CASE OF BANGLADESH

Fahimul Quadir

## I
## Introduction

A consensus seems to have emerged among official aid agencies, key global interstate organizations, academics, and development practitioners that "economic development" is inseparably linked with the notion of "political development." Even those global macroeconomic institutions that once refused to acknowledge the role of politics in the development process now argue that economic development cannot succeed unless it addresses the challenges of governance. At the heart of this new understanding of development is the belief that greater democratization[1] of the entire decision-making process is a necessary condition for economic development (Islam and Morrison 1995; Leftwich 1993, 603). A considerable amount of aid is thus directed toward civil society as well as toward democracy promotion programs designed to foster a culture of pluralism in the economic and political arenas (Ottaway and Carothers 2000). All major bilateral and multilateral aid agencies, including the World Bank, the IMF, the UN system, the US Agency for International Development (USAID), the Canadian International Development Agency (CIDA), and the Japan International Cooperation Agency (JICA), are now moving away from their traditional focus on "economic development" toward a new emphasis on "good governance" as the instrument for enhancing human rights, democracy, civil society, and market-oriented economic reforms. Interestingly, this new aid paradigm is increasing opportunities for collaboration among states, NGOs, and global decision-making organizations, and hence for the involvement of non-state actors on more positive terms than in the past.

Critics, however, see good governance as a framework for creating a homogenous world based on the Western, especially the American, model of capitalist development (Moore 1993; Schmitz 1995, 68). Some authors also argue that the technocratic language of good governance is enabling national elites to apply the concept of good governance for their own political and economic ends (Orlandini 2003). Other critics raise ethical questions regarding donors' current policy of using good-governance conditionality to promote democracy, civil society, and human rights. They argue that the widespread use of aid conditionality not only generates serious tensions between conditionality and the right to self-determination, but also raises serious questions as to the intentions of donors' democratization initiatives, as many multilateral organizations themselves lack a democratic political culture. The critics demand greater democratization of the donor community, especially with regard to the international financial institutions (IFIS) (Collingwood 2003).

Given this lively debate over good governance, this chapter analyzes Canada's development assistance programs in Bangladesh, especially those relating to good governance. While good governance means different things to different people, democratization is often a key part of the definition. So the analysis here will pay particular attention to initiatives aimed at improving democratic governance. This chapter comprises six sections, including this introduction. Section II of this chapter offers a brief overview of the present state of human development in Bangladesh and identifies the reasons why donors view governance as a priority in their development programs. Section III offers a historical account of Canada's development assistance programs, including a discussion of how its priorities have shifted away from support for relief and rehabilitation toward the fostering of an enabling environment for economic growth and human security. Section IV identifies recent trends in Canada's governance programs in Bangladesh, which appear to revolve around three strategically important areas: environmental governance, democracy promotion, and gender equality. It also looks at how social development, governance, and private-sector development are all connected. CIDA's governance programs are assessed in section V. Finally, section VI discusses prospects for good governance in Bangladesh that CIDA might consider in the near future.

## II
## Bangladesh's Development Profile:
## Why Governance Matters

Recent studies conducted by official aid agencies, including CIDA, the United Nations Development Programme (UNDP), the World Bank, and the UK Department for International Development (DFID), state that Bangladesh has made tangible progress in improving its economic and financial governance. Boosted mainly by expansion in both domestic and external demand, Bangladesh's economy has been growing at an average annual rate of 5 percent or more for the past few years. Despite frequent natural disasters, the agriculture sector—which employs 63 percent of the country's labor force—has experienced moderate growth over the past decade. Industrial growth has remained robust at about 7 percent annually; exports have shown a strong upward trend; and the service sector has grown at an average annual rate of 6 percent in the past few years. Inflation has been around 4 percent (i.e., moderate) in recent years (ADB 2004; 2005).[2]

The country has also taken strides in food production, public health, family planning, and universal education. In addition, it has managed to make significant progress in improving its overall policy environment since the mid-1980s. On the political front, Bangladesh has undergone a successful transition from military rule to constitutional democracy over the past decade. Three fair and democratic elections since 1991 have opened up opportunities for people to elect their leaders.

More important, perhaps, is that both rural and urban poverty dropped during the 1990s. On the basis of a national head count index, the Bangladesh Planning Commission reported in 2005 that the percentage of Bangladeshis living in poverty declined from 58.8 percent in 1991–92 to 49.8 percent in 2000. The same report also suggested that the poverty gap ratio dropped from 17.2 to 12.9 percent over the same period. The UNDP's human poverty index (HPI)[3] points to a similar trend in Bangladesh's efforts to reduce poverty. The 2005 *Human Development Report* indicates that the country's HPI declined from 61 percent in 1981–83 to 44.1 percent in 2004.[4] Though rural poverty remained much higher than urban poverty throughout the 1990s, empirical studies provide evidence of declining poverty in rural areas. A World Bank study suggests that while urban poverty decreased from 44.9 percent in 1991–92 to 36.6 percent in 2000, rural poverty remains a major concern for both policy-makers and development practitioners. Some 53 percent of rural Bangladeshis was living in poverty at the start of the new millennium (World Bank 2002a). Furthermore, growing inequalities pose a serious challenge to Bangladesh's poverty

reduction efforts. Both the donor community and the Bangladesh government acknowledge the apparent failure of current policies to address a significant rise in inequality in the 1990s. The Gini index of inequality increased
from 0.259 in 1991–92 to 0.306 in 2000 (Bangladesh Planning Commission
2005; World Bank 2002a).

As Table 1 indicates, Bangladesh's human development record also improved
significantly in the 1990s. Its human development index (HDI) rose from only
0.189 to 0.509 between 1990 and 2004. Remarkable progress has also been
made in reducing child malnutrition and the under-five child mortality rate
(which is now 95 per thousand live births). Impressive advances have been
made in adult literacy, which had risen to 61 percent by 1999. These tangible
social gains have impressed the international donor community, including
the World Bank and the UN. The UNDP, for instance, now recognizes Bangladesh as a medium human development country (UNDP 2005b).

Despite these significant improvements in Bangladesh's social and economic conditions, the country continues to face serious policy and structural
challenges that could negatively affect its prospects for democracy and human
development. A recent Asian Development Bank (ADB) commentary cautions

TABLE 1

Human Development Indicators over Time

| Year | Life expectancy at birth (years) | Adult literacy rate (%) | Real GDP per capita (US$) | Human development index | Human development rank |
|------|------|------|------|------|------|
| 1990 | 51.8 | 35.3 | 872 | 0.189 | 147 (out of 173 countries) |
| 1992 | 52.2 | 36.6 | 1,160 | 0.309 | 146 (out of 173 countries) |
| 1994 | 56.4 | 37.3 | 1,331 | 0.368 | 144 (out of 175 countries) |
| 1998 | 58.6 | 40.1 | 1,361 | 0.461 | 146 (out of 174 countries) |
| 2002 | 59.4 | 41.3 | 1,602 | 0.478 | 145 (out of 173 countries) |
| 2004 | 61.1 | 41.5 | 1,700 | 0.509 | 138 (out of 177 countries) |

Source: UNDP, Human Development Reports, 1993, 1994, 1997, 2000, 2002, and 2005.

that the termination of the Multi-fiber Agreement (MFA), further increases in food and oil prices, and the possible escalation of confrontational politics[5] could undermine the country's medium-term economic prospects. The report warns that Bangladesh's economy is likely to plunge into crisis unless the government makes serious efforts to "diversify the exports base, enhance competitiveness, remove structural impediments, encourage foreign direct investment, and upgrade infrastructure" (ADB 2005).

Recently published studies by the World Bank, the US Department of State, and the UNDP echo the concern that Bangladesh still confronts major challenges to attaining all of its Millennium Development Goals (MDGs). These reports indicate that poverty remains widespread in the country, with half the population still living below the poverty line.[6] Even though the child and infant mortality rate has been halved over the past ten years and maternal mortality has fallen, the country has one of the highest rates of child malnutrition and maternal mortality in the developing world outside of Sub-Saharan Africa. Even now, one-quarter of a million of Bangladeshi children die each year before their fifth birthday. Bangladesh is unlikely to succeed in reducing the maternal mortality rate from 320 to 400 per thousand live births (in 2001) to 143 by 2015. A large number of people lack basic services, including access to education and health care, and experience violations of human rights and security on a daily basis. The country's progress in ensuring environmental sustainability remains uncertain as it has not yet been able to mobilize its financial and institutional resources to address crucial issues such as deforestation, energy efficiency, and desertification. More worryingly, Bangladeshis are losing confidence in their country's administrative institutions, which are perceived as lacking integrity and efficiency (World Bank 2005). Official aid agencies contend that the country's social and economic progress has been slowed by Bangladesh's confrontational political culture and growing corruption at all levels of government as well as by the state's reluctance to introduce comprehensive economic and political reforms. Progress has also been halted by the politicization of the civil bureaucracy—a popular topic of discussion in the media. Instead of maintaining their autonomy, civil servants—especially at the senior level—are increasingly involving themselves in petty partisan politics. This is negatively affecting the country's institutional governance (Ali 2004).

The country's legal system is antiquated and understaffed. Its current civil justice system forces long and (usually) unnecessary delays in delivering justice. Also, Bangladesh lacks mechanisms for settling disputes through mediation. In addition, a deterioration in law and order has complicated the task of achieving the MDGs. Growing crime and the lack of law enforcement are discouraging local and foreign investors to explore investment possibilities (US Department of State 2003; World Bank 2002a).

A recent World Bank publication confirms that good governance in Bangladesh has deteriorated over the past decade. As Table 2 shows, the report paints a dismal picture of Bangladesh in all six selected areas of good governance. Other reports cast profound doubts as to the future of creating an accountable, transparent structure of both economic and political governance. Unanimously, donor agencies blame "poor governance" for the country's failure to promote sustainable human development in the new millennium. CIDA's Bangladesh Country Development Programming Framework (CDPF) offers a well-considered overview of Bangladesh's current state of development. That report declares poor governance to be the main obstacle to "pro-poor" economic growth. It goes on to say that a dysfunctional Parliament, high levels of corruption, precarious law and order, lack of accountability, and violence against women are all hindering Bangladesh's prospects for democracy and development in the new century (CIDA 2003a).

Similarly, a DFID-sponsored study published in 2002 contends that Bangladesh's ability to meet its MDGs by 2015 will depend on its ability to

TABLE 2

Bangladesh's Good-Governance Record, 1996–2004

| Governance dimension[a] | Year | Bangladesh's percentile rank[b] | South Asian regional average[c] |
|---|---|---|---|
| Voice and accountability | 2004 | 28.6 | 25.4 |
| | 1996 | 41.9 | 32.5 |
| Political stability | 2004 | 11.7 | 26.4 |
| | 1996 | 26.8 | 26.4 |
| Government effectiveness | 2004 | 26.4 | 38.5 |
| | 1996 | 22.3 | 47.5 |
| Regulatory quality | 2004 | 13.3 | 30.8 |
| | 1996 | 26.5 | 30.8 |
| Rule of law | 2004 | 22.2 | 34.2 |
| | 1996 | 27.1 | 35.5 |
| Control of corruption | 2004 | 10.3 | 37.9 |
| | 1996 | 35.3 | 37.9 |

*Source*: World Bank (2005).

[a] The World Bank in its 2005 report provides an aggregate governance performance record for 209 countries in six selected areas of governance.

[b] This value refers to the percentage of countries that are lagging behind Bangladesh in the selected area of governance. Higher percentages imply a better record of governance.

[c] The Bank's list of South Asian countries includes Afghanistan, Bangladesh, Bhutan, India, Maldives, Nepal, Pakistan, and Sri Lanka.

improve its quality of governance (Duncan et al. 2002). Both the UN and the ADB state that Bangladesh's major challenge in the twenty-first century will be to reform public institutions so "that [they] work openly and transparently, based less on the exercise of power and patronage and more on clear systems of control and accountability" (ADB 2005).

In other words, donor agencies, government officials, development practitioners, and mainstream political analysts concur that poor governance is threatening the poverty reduction targets outlined in the country's own Interim Poverty Reduction Strategy Paper (IPRSP).[7] The IPRSP calls for a substantial reduction in chronic poverty and for the invigoration of social development. Its findings focus on the following: pro-poor economic growth in order to raise incomes and create employment; human development through education, health, nutrition, and social programs; gender equity; social safety nets for the poor; and participatory governance so as to strengthen the voice of the poor. What is interesting about the IPRSP is that it amounts to an official declaration that unless Bangladesh improves its governance, its poverty reduction programs may well fail. So it calls for broad-based reforms, including the restructuring of the public sector, and for a redefinition of the state's role in reducing poverty.

## III
### Canada's Development Priorities in Bangladesh

Canada's development assistance to Bangladesh began in 1971, almost immediately after independence. During the early years, CIDA's support consisted mainly of food aid, humanitarian assistance, relief and rehabilitation work, and projects to rebuild basic infrastructure, which had been almost totally destroyed during the liberation war of 1971.[8] CIDA's development programs for Bangladesh, like those of so many other donors, are influenced strongly by Canada's ODA guidelines, which change over time. CIDA's CDPF for Bangladesh is based on the priorities set out in Canada's 2005 International Policy Statement (IPS; Canada 2005b) and is intended to address the country's principal development concerns.[9] Although the CDPF identifies Bangladesh's major development challenges, its programs have often focused on a handful of areas where Canada believes it can have an impact. For instance, the first CDPF (approved in May 1999) focused on two strategic areas: basic human needs, and good governance. In practice, however, CIDA has directed most of its resources toward improving the living conditions of the poor in areas such as health, education, water, and sanitation.

This focus on poverty reduction is consistent with Canada's past record in Bangladesh. In concert with local and international partners, Canada has helped the country raise its citizens out of both absolute and relative poverty over the past thirty years. Key areas of Canadian development support have included the following: food production; primary health care; family planning; literacy and primary education; income-generating activities and/or microcredit programs; water management as it relates to irrigation, fisheries development, flood control, agriculture, and environmental quality; and infrastructure services, including energy development and rural electrification (Bangladesh Economic Relations Division 1998; CIDA 1999b). The general objective of these CIDA-supported programs has been to reduce poverty; CIDA has, however, paid particular attention to gender equality—that is, to improving the status of women in Bangladesh's male-dominated society. Indeed, close to 80 percent of the beneficiaries of Canada's poverty reduction programs in Bangladesh have been women (CIDA 2003d, 10).

CIDA continues to emphasize social development and poverty reduction. Recently, though, it has also begun to address Bangladesh's governance challenges. Much of its programming in good governance is organized around a rather broad understanding of governance. Unlike the World Bank, its governance activities aim at increasing the sustainability of various NGOs engaged in promoting human development at the grassroots level (CIDA 1999a, 1). In recognition of the need to strengthen organizations for the poor, CIDA has taken a close interest in heightening the impact of popular organizations on development. A number of projects have been undertaken to help NGOs design, implement, and evaluate development programs (details below). Clearly, CIDA's aid to Bangladesh acknowledges the voluntary sector, including NGOs and civil associations, as key actors in development.

This might seem a natural course for donors to take today. Yet CIDA's decision to work closely with NGOs represented a unique approach to development and poverty reduction in the early 1970s. During those years, most official aid agencies focused on working directly with the state. CIDA officials in Bangladesh departed from this development praxis when they started supporting the activities of NGOs such as Proshika Manobik Kendra and the Bangladesh Rural Advancement Committee (BRAC). Part of this shift in strategy arose from CIDA's disappointment with the Bangladeshi state, which sharply suffered from a constant crisis of legitimacy. Local CIDA officials set out to create alternative service delivery mechanisms by strengthening organizations of the poor that were capable of promoting grassroots development. Since the early 1970s, CIDA has continued to help NGOs strengthen their institutional capacities so that they can play a greater role in achieving the broader goals of sustainable human development.

CIDA's goal of giving Bangladesh's popular sector a strong voice in development is also reflected in its latest country policy framework (CDPF), established in 2003, which focuses on the following three broad yet interrelated aspects of governance and human development:

- *Social development.* To improve the quality and delivery of services in health and education appropriate to the needs of the poor, in particular women and children, and to increase their access to those services.
- *Governance.* To improve policy development and regulatory reform of selected public and private institutions and link governance more directly to poverty reduction.
- *Private sector.* To address constraints in the development of small- and medium-sized enterprises by increasing their access to financial and capacity building services and by improving their regulatory environment (CIDA 2003 d, 14).

While Bangladesh[10] continues to be one of the largest recipients of Canadian ODA,[11] Canada's total disbursements have declined since 1990–91. As seen in Table 3, Canadian aid to Bangladesh fell from c$152.1 million in 1988–89 to $87.14 million in 2001–2 and $86.36 million in 2003–4. This marked a major change from the period 1971–72 to 1997–98, when Canada ranked fifth among twenty major donors, including multilateral organizations such as the World Bank and the EU. In 2000, Canada ranked ninth among multilateral and bilateral donors, who together contributed about US$2 billion per year to bridge Bangladesh's financing gap and to implement its poverty reduction strategies (Bangladesh Development Forum 2004). Canadian aid to Bangladesh now accounts for less than 5 percent of its total aid.

TABLE 3

CIDA Disbursements in Bangladesh in C$ Million (1999–2004)

| | 1997–98 | 1998–99 | 1999–2000 | 2000–1 | 2001–2 | 2002–3 | 2003–4 | 2004–5 |
|---|---|---|---|---|---|---|---|---|
| Bilateral | 36.92 | 34.47 | 35.55 | 34.34 | 36.88 | 35.89 | 53.25 | 50.00 |
| Partnership[a] | 2.56 | 3.04 | 3.92 | 3.86 | 2.78 | 3.04 | 2.89 | b |
| Food aid | 35.98 | 19.67 | 16.6 | 0 | 13.21 | 10.00 | 10.00 | b |
| Multilateral | 0.35 | 0.9 | 0.25 | 0.78 | 0.36 | 0.40 | 0 | b |
| IDRC | 0.23 | 0.42 | 0.34 | 0.55 | 0.43 | 0.30 | 0.17 | b |
| Subtotal | 76.04 | 58.5 | 56.66 | 39.53 | 53.66 | 49.63 | 66.31 | b |
| IFIS | 24.09 | 40.06 | 25.63 | 29.13 | 33.38 | 21.44 | 20.05 | b |
| Total | 100.13 | 98.56 | 82.29 | 68.66 | 87.04 | 71.07 | 86.36 | 50.00 |

*Source*: CIDA, Bangladesh Program Desk.

[a] Partnership refers to disbursements to Canadian voluntary-sector organizations and private-sector firms through CIDA's Canadian Partnership Branch.

[b] Disbursement data for these categories are not available.

The identification of Bangladesh as a "new investment target country" by the Minister of International Cooperation in 2002 has placed Bangladesh back on Canada's ODA priority list. The Bangladesh program desk at CIDA expects that Canada's bilateral aid will double by 2008 (CIDA 2003a, 5), which will make Canada one of the top bilateral donors in the country.[12]

Canada's ongoing emphasis on poverty reduction and social development is reflected in its current distribution of aid. As seen in Figure 1, almost two-thirds of its resources have gone into social development issues and concerns, which are divided into two main categories: health and education. While less than 10 percent of Canadian aid is allocated for programs[13] directly aiming at substantially improving governance, it could be argued that many of its social development programs also, albeit indirectly, address issues of power, management, politics, and democracy.

FIGURE 1
CIDA–Bangladesh

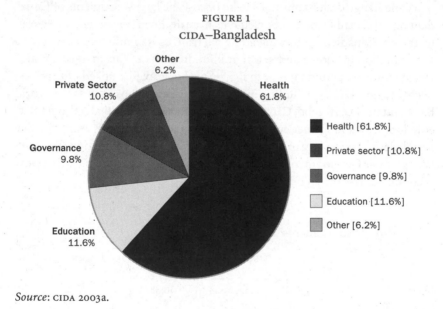

*Source*: CIDA 2003a.

IV

## CIDA's Governance Programs and Interlocutors in Bangladesh

As noted in its recent International Policy Statement (2005b), Canada takes an integrated approach to development in which good governance is viewed as a precondition for peace, security, and sustainable political and socio-economic development. Identifying the synergies among these sectors, the IPS seeks to vigorously promote "democracy, human rights, the rule of law, public-sector capacity-building, and conflict prevention" through its governance programs (ibid.). This understanding of governance is also reflected in CIDA's recent CDPF for Bangladesh, which highlights a combination of measures to help Bangladesh address its development challenges. Recognizing the conceptual and practical linkages between social development, governance, and private-sector development, it aims at reducing poverty, improving the quality of governance, and strengthening the role of the private sector in national economic development.

The CDPF links governance, market reform, and poverty reduction, but it also singles out governance as a priority for Canadian development assistance in Bangladesh. Canada's current governance activities in the country focus on legal reform, capacity building for both public institutions and civil society, and the promotion of human rights (especially women's and children's rights). The specific good-governance programs that support this overall objective fall into the following three broad categories: environmental governance; democracy promotion; and gender equality.

## Environmental Governance

One of the key objectives of CIDA's governance program is to help Bangladesh reduce its environmental vulnerability. All four of the environmental projects that CIDA is currently implementing are intended to build the local capacity to balance environmental sustainability with economic activity in decision making. For instance, the Bangladesh Environmental Management Project, with a Canadian contribution of C$12.61 million, aims to strengthen the institutional capacity of the Bangladesh government in environmental planning, management, and monitoring. In partnership with KPMG, Resource Futures International, Dalhousie University, and the Department of Environment (DOE),[14] the project seeks to turn the DOE into a more effective public institution capable of enforcing environmental rules and procedures.

The Environmental Monitoring Information Network (EMIN) project, with a Canadian contribution of $4.4 million, seeks to strengthen Bangladesh's water management. Two Bangladeshi organizations, the Water Resources Planning Organization (WARPO) and the Centre for Environmental Geographic Information Systems (CEGIS), are working with the Canadian partner RADAR-SAT International to develop a more effective early warning system capable of preventing the negative effects of flooding and erosion. Besides addressing the needs of the Bangladesh government, this project seeks to increase the capacity of NGOs and community organizations to deal with flooding. The project hopes to establish new forecasting mechanisms designed to coordinate and monitor data for areas that are often hit hard by flooding and river erosion.

CIDA's third environmental project, Reducing Vulnerability to Climate Change, involves NGOs—both Canadian and local[15]—in creating an ecologically balanced society in which national and local institutions can work together to engage the public in policy making. Specifically, this project (to which CIDA has allocated $3 million) targets 4,300 low-income households and community-based networks and seeks to build their awareness of the negative effects of global climate change on the lives and livelihoods of local people.

A fourth environmental project aims to strengthen the governance capacity of the Ministry of Water Resources in areas such as planning, budgeting, accounting, and auditing.[16] Canada's particular role is to help the financial divisions of the Bangladesh Water Development Board (BWDB) develop a computerized accounting system.

### Democracy Promotion

With other development agencies, Canada is making an effort to establish a system of governance in Bangladesh that is open, predictable, accountable, and corruption-free. Three of CIDA's current projects focus on ways for the country to eliminate obvious abuses of power; to replace the current patronage-based politics with the rule of law; and to allow civil society associations a central role in holding the state accountable and protecting the interests of marginalized communities, including women and ethnic and religious minorities.

The Legal Reform Project, jointly funded by CIDA, the World Bank, and the Danish government, is supporting the creation of a rules-based, accountable, transparent, and predictable legal framework in Bangladesh. It is offering assistance to the Ministry of Laws in restructuring the country's legal system, especially in the area of criminal justice. A second aim of the project is to support relevant initiatives undertaken by local NGOs and advocacy groups on behalf of the most vulnerable sectors of society.[17] CIDA is also helping develop better election mechanisms—and more broadly, a stronger democratic political culture—through its Fair Election and Institutional Reforms Project (FEIRP). This initiative is encouraging civic engagement in developing a broad-based consensus on necessary electoral and political reforms. It is also creating opportunities for civil society groups to play a more effective role in maintaining a free and fair electoral process and holding elected representatives accountable for their actions. Ultimately, the FEIRP is expected to help the Bangladesh Election Commission develop and strengthen its capacity to manage transparent, accountable, and participatory elections.[18]

Finally, in collaboration with the World Bank Group, Canada is helping Bangladesh Bank (the country's central bank) build up its research capacity. The goal here is to enable the Bank's Research Department to offer credible information that can be used to devise appropriate poverty reduction strategies.

## Gender Equality

CIDA's governance activities in Bangladesh pay close attention to gender equality. In collaboration with Bangladeshi organizations and other donor agencies, CIDA is seeking to transform existing relations through gender "mainstreaming" and gender awareness raising and by identifying the sources of gender discrimination. Two of its current projects address the subordinate position of women in Bangladeshi society. For example, the second phase of the Policy Leadership and Advocacy for Gender Equality (PLAGE)[19] project is seeking to increase the capacity of the Ministry of Women's and Children's Affairs (MWCA) to integrate gender into its planning and policy cycles. In partnership with civil society groups, the project expects to develop specific interventions capable of responding to practical and strategic gender needs, identifying target groups, and raising gender awareness within planning processes.

The Gender Fund[20] (phase three) project also addresses gender equality and empowerment. By supporting the initiatives of relevant local NGOs and advocacy groups, it aims to improve the conditions of women and girls in Bangladesh. Unlike most other CIDA projects, it offers a space for the Canadian High Commission in Dhaka to work with women's organizations and to test ideas for changing social and cultural patterns and practices that produce and perpetuate gender inequalities.

# V
## Assessing the Impact of Canada's
## Good-Governance Initiatives

CIDA's governance programs in Bangladesh are consistent with the general framework of governance adopted by the donor community, which emphasizes fostering a democratic political culture by improving the efficiency, transparency, and accountability of public institutions. The assumption driving CIDA's programs is that for an economy to be open, it must be supported by a free political process (Austin 2001). Drawing on this popular thesis, CIDA's good-governance initiatives make a clear effort to identify the missing link between economic and political development within the changing development realities of Bangladesh. Besides helping the country manage its economic activities more effectively at the macro level, most of CIDA's governance projects encourage the Bangladeshi government to enhance the accountability and responsiveness of public institutions, reform the legal system, and develop an efficient and professional civil service. This approach is driven by the recognition that the Bangladeshi government has failed so far to pursue a pro-poor reform agenda that is capable of accelerating economic growth and redistributing wealth and resources. CIDA's governance initiatives in such areas as free and fair elections, financial management, environmental sustainability, and gender equality are aimed at helping Bangladeshi officials strike a fine balance between these objectives and at addressing some of the country's deep-rooted institutional problems.

While its program decisions are influenced by Canada's international priorities as well as by budget realities, CIDA's governance and other development assistance programs are undertaken primarily in partnership with various bilateral and multilateral donor agencies, the government of Bangladesh, and local and international NGOs. The country's well-functioning aid coordination mechanisms—which include the Local Consultative Group (LCG), the Bangladesh Development Forum (BDF),[21] and the Like-Minded Donor Group (LMDG)—provide a framework for Canada to pursue its agenda for poverty reduction, good governance, and private-sector development. With its relatively small budget for Bangladesh, Canada uses these coordination structures, especially the LCG—the most important forum for coordination among major funding agencies—not only to ensure the most effective utilization of its resources but also to promote its distinct development agenda. The LCG comprises thirty-two Bangladesh-based representatives of bilateral and multilateral donors and the Secretary of the Economic Relations Division (who represents the Government of Bangladesh). It facilitates dialogue and collaboration among its members on specific sectors or thematic areas through its twenty-three subgroups.[22] Canada is currently chairing LCG subgroups on education and environment.

Canada also draws strength from its historical ties with a small group of donor countries in the LMCG, which includes Denmark, the Netherlands, Norway, and Sweden. The group made its first official appearance in 1984 when it published a report prepared by the North-South Institute titled *Rural Poverty in Bangladesh* (1985). Despite its small size, this group has managed to broaden the development agenda for donors by shifting the focus of development cooperation in Bangladesh away from traditional macroeconomic concerns toward human development (Blair 1986). The group has taken on a greater role in reducing poverty and promoting gender, human rights, and civil society. As a core member of the group, Canada has continued to use the LMCG's influence to assert its role in promoting good governance in Bangladesh.

What is more distinct is Canada's ongoing emphasis on strengthening the strategic capacities of Bangladesh's dynamic yet complex NGO sector. Given the weak implementation capacity and inefficiencies of public institutions in Bangladesh, CIDA sees NGOs as important, alternative development actors capable of more actively and effectively influencing the country's development process. It works very closely with development NGOs, especially intermediary NGOs, to ensure that these local bodies strengthen the local population's capacity for self-governance. CIDA's governance and other development assistance programs often create opportunities for NGOs to represent the voices of marginalized communities such as women, ethnic and religious minorities, and the rural poor when decisions are being made. They also involve a special set of NGOs directly in the implementation of various development activities and provide financial assistance to NGOs and civil society groups that are seeking to increase the participation and decision-making power of vulnerable communities. CIDA seems to pay particular attention to those NGOs which are either engaged in policy research on the dynamics of poverty and social change or involved in empowering women. It is important to note that while CIDA often works directly with local NGOs, its financial assistance is also channelled through Canadian NGOs, including CUSO, Aga Khan Foundation Canada (AKFC), the South Asian Partnership, and Inter Pares.

CIDA's assistance appears to have succeeded in strengthening the institutional capabilities of a group of selected NGOs, namely, the Bangladesh Rural Advancement Committee (BRAC),[23] Proshika, the Centre for Policy Dialogue (CPD), the Association for Development Agencies in Bangladesh (ADAB), *Nijera Kori*, and UBINIG, which are widely known for their success in providing greater democratic input by the people into the country's development process. The representatives of a few Bangladeshi NGOs, including BRAC, *Nijera Kori*, UBINIG, and ADAB, told this author that CIDA's support gave them greater recognition as development actors and enabled them to serve as democratic institutions. Many are now globally acclaimed for their innovative development strategies, which focus on group-based mobilization, beneficiary participation, micro-enterprises, and the involvement of women in various income-generating activities.

Unlike the World Bank or USAID, Canada has adopted a dual approach to good governance in its operations in Bangladesh. The former organizations tend to focus on financial and economic management, public-sector reform, private-sector infrastructure development, and the strengthening of the rule of law through democracy promotion; by contrast, CIDA attempts to establish links between governance and social development. Put another way, CIDA's governance activities are not undertaken in isolation. In addition to making public institutions more accountable, efficient, and transparent, Canadian governance initiatives in Bangladesh aim to build capacity for NGOs and to promote gender equity and human rights.

While this approach has been effective in creating an enabling environment for pro-poor activities and human development, it does not pay adequate attention to improving Bangladesh's institutional structures of governance. Currently, Canada's initiatives deal with only a few areas of intervention, albeit important ones. Part of the reason why Canada remains highly selective and why the scope of its current governance programs is fairly limited is its relatively small development budget for Bangladesh. The $50 million in annual bilateral ODA is not nearly enough for CIDA to vigorously promote good governance in Bangladesh. Current allocation practices also prevent Canada from undertaking a comprehensive program on good governance.

## VI
## Conclusions:
## Can Canada Do Better?

If good governance is a precondition for pro-poor economic growth and human development, one would expect Canada's development programs to pay more attention to improving Bangladesh's quality of governance. Funding agencies, civil society leaders, mainstream scholars, and development practitioners clearly agree that if Bangladesh hopes to meet its MDGs, it will need to thoroughly reform its public sector, strengthen the rule of law, combat corruption at all levels of government, and improve law and order. In light of this, Canada could consider rethinking and restructuring its governance initiatives to help Bangladesh meet these governance challenges.

Nowhere is the need for governance reform more obvious than in public institutions. A few donor agencies such as the UNDP and DFID are already pursuing a public-sector reform agenda; even so, Bangladesh requires much more outside support if it is to develop an efficient and professional civil service capable of realizing the country's full potential in a highly competitive global market. CIDA's governance program could be (re)designed to address this pressing challenge. In particular, CIDA could focus on redefining the role played by the civil service in human development by redesigning the programs of a few influential public-sector training institutions—specifically, the Bangladesh Public Administration Training Centre (BPATC), the Bangladesh Civil Service Training Academy, the Planning and Development Academy, and the Bangladesh Institute of Administrative Management (BIAM). Some Canadian universities are already offering public-service training programs; CIDA could partner with them to help these key public-service training institutions shift their activities away from routine courses on bureaucratic management toward issues such as participation, accountability, and transparency in governance. These training programs could also increase the level of civic engagement in public policy making.

The separation of the judiciary from the executive is another key area where Bangladesh needs immediate assistance and where CIDA could successfully intervene. Although the Bangladeshi government has shown some interest in

recent years in drafting legislation that would give the judiciary greater autonomy vis-à-vis the executive, nothing concrete has yet been done to realize this
important goal of good governance. Canadian legal experts drawn from a few
prestigious law schools and/or private organizations could help Bangladesh
develop legislation and strengthen the newly formed Judicial Service Commission (JSC).[24] These interventions would allow the government of Bangladesh to move forward with its stated aim of establishing a "rule-of-law culture"
in the country.

Reducing corruption at all levels of government should also be a priority
for CIDA in Bangladesh. In partnership with USAID, which is currently providing some assistance in combating corruption, CIDA could invest in strengthening the newly formed Anti-Corruption Commission.[25] The Canadian Auditor General's Office could consider providing Bangladesh with expertise to
streamline its auditing and accounting practices, which have often been ineffective in preventing government officials from routinely misusing public
money. CIDA's support could focus on the creation of performance-based
audits; this would involve restructuring the Comptroller and Auditor General's (CAG) Office and helping the government of Bangladesh separate the
auditing and accounting functions.

These crucial development interventions would certainly require CIDA to
allocate more of its ODA directly to governance activities in Bangladesh. The
current disbursement of roughly 10 percent to governance projects is unlikely
to be enough to make a dent in Bangladesh's development management problems. Given the country's governance challenges, a figure of 25 percent (which,
using current figures, would represent approximately $12.5 million annually)
would be more appropriate. But while such a major shift in funding would
scale up governance interventions, Canada's individual commitment would still
be inadequate to improve the prospects for good governance in Bangladesh.
Canada would also need to collaborate more effectively with other major funding agencies to promote a transparent, accountable, and responsive government
in the country. In other words, Canada would have to play a decisive role in
Bangladesh's formal aid coordination forums, which include LMCs, the LMCG,
and the BDF. The LMCG would likely to be the most effective mechanism for
Canada to mobilize its support and exert its influence over the entire process
of aid coordination.

Finally, besides reprioritizing its programs, CIDA may need to transform its
whole approach to good governance assistance, so as to move it beyond the discourse of formal democracy and a market economy. CIDA's current approach
to governance is effective in identifying and solving deep-rooted institutional
problems of the sort that so often undermine the Bangladeshi government's

development performance, but that approach does not always encourage popular participation in policy making. Here, the concept of "participatory governance," as used in critical development studies,[26] could help CIDA encourage donors to focus on broader and more diverse means of governance—especially those which enable people's *self*-development. Participatory governance can create and strengthen the political spaces where state and civil society associations work together to promote human development, representing the concerns of gender, age, caste, ethnicity, wealth, and class. It can also support an autonomous space for civil society, free from co-optation by either the state or the market. Above all, participatory governance can foster accountable and self-determined institutions based on the voices of ordinary citizens in decision making.

## Notes

1 Donors seem to rely on the widely held assumption that democratic governments are likely to make better political and economic decisions as they are held accountable for all of their actions (Ottaway and Carothers 2000, 5).

2 The inflation rate is probably much higher, about 7 percent, in 2005–6 owing to a significant increase in food and oil prices.

3 The HPI is calculated based on deprivations in health, education, and income. It focuses on the proportion of people below a threshold level in the three key aspects of human development, namely life expectancy, standard of living, and education.

4 Some studies, however, caution that despite some tangible progress in poverty reduction efforts, poverty rates were still higher in 1995 than the rates in 1985. Between 1985 and 1995 the number of absolute poor increased by 1.2 percent annually (Mahbub ul Haq Human Development Centre 1999, 13–14). What remains a puzzle for many is that some 83 percent of Bangladeshis live on less than two dollars a day (Bangladesh Bureau of Statistics 2004).

5 Growing conflicts of political interest between the ruling Bangladesh National Party (BNP) and the opposition, led by the Awami League, coupled with the resort to violence by competing political forces as means to achieve their conflicting political goals, have fostered a precarious situation in Bangladesh, where the future of democracy and development is becoming increasingly uncertain. These two mainstream political parties, which dominate Bangladesh's political landscape, promote very different views of governance relating to the role of religion in politics and how a national political identity should be constructed. The unwillingness of these parties' leaders to come to terms with democratic values has led to the development of a highly confrontational state–society relationship in which rival groups often rely on violence and non-constitutional means to advance their political goals. For a detailed discussion of the country's inability to foster a democratic political culture, see Quadir (2004).

6 A recent World Bank study contends that "Bangladesh still has the highest incidence of poverty in South Asia and the third highest number of poor people living in a single country after India and China" (World Bank 2005).

7 Also known as the *National Strategy for Economic Growth, Poverty Reduction and Social Development.*

8 During the early years, two-thirds of bilateral aid was in food or commodities; recently, though, the emphasis has shifted from food aid to development more broadly. By one estimate, development projects now account for 60 to 80 percent of CIDA's total ODA.

9 The IPS identifies Bangladesh as one of the twenty-five "core development partners" that will draw special attention from Canada.

10 It is important to mention that ODA is still a vital component of Bangladesh's development initiatives. As of June 30, 2005, the country has received a total of US $43.26 billion of external assistance in the forms of food aid, commodity aid, and project aid. While bilateral aid accounted for some 75.4 percent of the total aid in the 1970s, the country has witnessed a significant decline in bilateral aid in recent years. In 2005, bilateral aid was only 43.8 percent of the total aid the country received. In other words, the focus of ODA in Bangladesh seems to have shifted away from bilateral aid toward multilateral assistance owing to the declining share of "grant." Instead of allocating grants, multilateral aid agencies are currently more interested in offering loans, which now constitute more than 73.6 percent of Bangladesh's total ODA (Bangladesh Economic Relations Division 2006).

11 Excluding Afghanistan, Bangladesh is the largest traditional recipient of bilateral Canadian ODA in Asia.

12 Precise details on future levels of spending were unavailable from CIDA at the time of writing.

13 In other words, CIDA claims that governance is a top priority for its activities in Bangladesh, but its current budgetary allocation does not support such a claim.

14 The DOE is a Bangladeshi partner that represents the government's key environmental agency—the Ministry of Environment and Forests.

15 A number of international NGOs, including CARE Canada and CARE Bangladesh, as well as local NGOs, are working together as partners on this project.

16 CIDA has committed C$4 million to this project, which involves Cowater and Corporate Renaissance Group of Canada and Bangladesh's Ministry of Water Resources (MWR) as partners.

17 This important governance project involves a Canadian contribution of CDN $15 million, and brings together the Department of Justice, the Canadian Bar Association, and IBM. The local Bangladeshi partners are the Ministry of Laws, Justice and Parliamentary Affairs, the Ministry of Social Affairs, and a variety of local NGOs.

18 Canada has committed C$5 million to this project.

19 This relatively large project (cost C$11 million) has established a consortium of Cowater International Inc., Carleton University's Pauline Jewett Institute of Women's Studies, and Bangladesh's Ministry of Women's and Children's Affairs (MWCA).

20  Various Bangladeshi feminist organizations are working with CIDA on this low-budget project, in which Canada's contribution is some C$2.5 million.

21  The Bangladesh Development Forum, previously known as the Annual Aid Consortium, coordinates donor policies and regularly reviews the country's state of economic and social development. Under the direction of the World Bank, the Aid Consortium was established in 1974 to meet annually both to review the performance of Bangladesh's economy and to pledge ODA. Canada has been an active member of the Forum since 1974.

22  Currently there are twelve sectoral subgroups, which address the following: agriculture; food security and nutrition; fisheries; water management; water supply and sanitation; education; health and population; energy; transport; urban sector; rural infrastructure; and finance. There are nine thematic subgroups; they address poverty; women's advancement and gender equality; governance; NGOs; private-sector development; environment; project implementation issues; macroeconomic developments and technical assistance; and disasters and emergency response. There is also one region-specific subgroup for addressing development issues in the Chittagong Hill Tracts.

23  BRAC is now the largest NGO in the world.

24  There are precedents in this area. For example, Canada has recently helped Iraq draft its first democratic constitution.

25  This independent commission was established in February 2004 to combat corruption.

26  The notion of participatory governance focuses on bottom-up participation of all stakeholders, especially the poor, in the development process at the grassroots level in the context of both poverty reduction and human development (Bickerstaff and Walker 2001; Grote and Gbikpi 2002).

▲

# 6

## THE BENEFITS OF AN INDIRECT APPROACH:
## THE CASE OF GHANA

### Peter Arthur and David Black

### Introduction

Since it embarked on the transition to democratic rule in 1992, Ghana has been widely perceived in the international community as one of Africa's success stories in terms of the promotion of good governance.[1] Most significantly, it has been able to hold successive elections that have been perceived as free and fair, despite some anomalies, and that have resulted in an orderly change in governing parties. Yet substantial challenges remain for both governance effectiveness and democratic accountability. This chapter therefore analyzes the role of the donor community in the process of promoting good governance in Ghana. In particular, it focuses on the nature and priorities of Canada's governance assistance. In general, Ghana emerges (as it has regularly over the past couple of decades) as an important "test case" for the new approach taken by the donor community (including CIDA), with its pivotal focus on good-governance reforms. The results of that approach to date reflect a combination of progress, promise, and uncertainty.

The case of Ghana shows how, broadly speaking, good-governance reforms involve two distinct priorities. First, there are more technocratic reforms, which are concerned mainly with the "machinery of government," including its ability to establish and implement policy priorities, particularly (albeit not exclusively) in the domain of economic policy. These sorts of reforms are the primary emphasis of the international financial institutions (IFIs), among others. Second, there are more political reforms, the purpose of which is to deepen democratic openings and processes by reinforcing structures of accountability within core political institutions (such as Parliament and the courts) as well as between the state and civil society (by supporting the capacity of the media and other non-state actors to scrutinize and pressure government officials and political leaders). Like many other donors, CIDA has tended to emphasize the former, more technocratic side of governance reforms, and to this end has focused on "good economic governance" as defined by a broad-based donor consensus; relatively speaking, it has given less weight to more political reforms aimed at deepening democratic accountability. Yet aspects of both are almost certainly necessary for sustained development and poverty reduction in Ghana; indeed the two are arguably codependent. Thus, failure to pay more attention to the latter compromises prospects for the former. In other words, better governance in the "machinery of government" sense is likely to depend on more robust democratic accountability, even if the results of this deepening of democracy are indirect and less neatly consonant with donor preferences.

This chapter begins by outlining the development situation in Ghana that necessitated the adoption of economic and political reforms. It briefly reviews the achievements of governance reforms in Ghana as well as the ongoing challenges such reforms present there. This is followed by a discussion of the assistance Canada has provided in support of Ghana's governance agenda since the adoption of the last Country Programming Framework in 1999, highlighting the substantial changes that have taken place over the past several years as Ghana has emerged as a "core bilateral partner." The final section looks at key lessons to be learned from efforts to achieve the goals of good governance in Ghana. The emphasis here is on the need to pay closer attention to the indirect impact of democratic deepening as a key requirement for sustainable "technocratic" governance reforms.

## Ghana's Development Profile

The severe economic decline that Ghana experienced in the 1970s (see Aryeetey, Harrigan, and Nissanke 2000; Boafo-Arthur 1999; Hutchful 1989, 2002) resulted in the J.J. Rawlings–led Provisional National Defence Council's (PNDC) seizure of power through a military coup on December 31, 1981. After failing to resolve the crisis through "people's power," the PNDC embarked on a neoliberal structural adjustment program (SAP) in 1983 (Hutchful 1989, 102; 2002). Ghana initially chalked up impressive rates of economic growth under structural adjustment, but behind this initial economic "miracle" lay an "economic mirage" (Aryeetey, Harrigan, and Nissanke 2000). In governance terms, the SAP fostered and relied on a narrowly based, bureaucratic, and highly personalized policy process, driven architecturally by the International Monetary Fund (IMF) and the World Bank. Briefly stated, structural adjustment effectively undermined the foundations for improved governance beyond a highly concentrated policy elite.

Economic hardships and political alienation persisted. After 1984, public dissent sparked by urban-based groups and associations such as the Ghana Bar Association (GBA), the National Union of Ghana Students (NUGS), the Trade Unions Congress (TUC), and church-associated organizations such as the Christian Council of Ghana and the Catholic Bishops Conference led to rising demands for a return to constitutional rule (Hutchful 2002, 197–98). In a bid to legitimize its rule and to rebuild grassroots support while fending off domestic and international pressure for political liberalization, the PNDC government introduced a new decentralization program in 1988. Indeed, while Ghanaian governments had made intermittent efforts to decentralize authority through some form of district-focused public administrative system since independence in 1957, it was not until 1988 that the PNDC government embarked on a new and comprehensive decentralization program. Specifically, it established District Assemblies (DAs) on a "no party" basis. The PNDC sought to make the DAs the basis of the country's new political system; it saw decentralization as a means to stabilize a political system in crisis and to secure some of its own political objectives (Ayee 1994; 1997a, 88; Hutchful 2002).

Despite the adoption of these measures, domestic political opposition continued to grow. In 1992, with donors pushing for political as well as economic liberalization, the PNDC government finally embarked on a transition toward constitutional, multiparty democratic rule. Hence, while institutions such as the IMF and the World Bank insisted on good economic governance, with some of the country's top technocrats and neoclassical economists in the lead (Hutchful 2002, 36–37), the push for good political governance and democratic rights came primarily from Ghanaians, reinforced by key bilateral donors and the UN. Indeed, Whitfield (2003, 382) points out that international donors went to great lengths to secure Ghana's transition to democracy and ensure "free and fair" elections.

Since 1992, Ghana has made significant strides toward good political and democratic governance. Most strikingly, it has held three successive multiparty elections since 1992 that were essentially free and fair and devoid of violence. Indeed, the 2000 elections marked a milestone in the country's political history when the incumbent National Democratic Congress (NDC)—Rawlings's party—was defeated and power was peacefully transferred to John Kufuor and the New Patriotic Party (NPP) (Tettey et al. 2003, 2). Moreover, the

World Bank's new governance indicators show that Ghana scored above the median in all categories, especially in the areas of Government Effectiveness and Voice and Accountability, compared to other countries with similar socio-economic and development profiles (World Bank 2005a).

Some progress has also been made in the area of political decentralization. For example, the 110 (now 138) DAs, established as part of the decentralization process in 1988–89, not only survived the drafting of Ghana's new 1992 Constitution, but were empowered with revenue-generating and development-planning functions. Also, a District Assemblies Common Fund (DACF)[2] was established to provide the decentralized authorities with the resources necessary to implement their development plans (CIDA 1999c).

Yet substantial challenges remain. At the broadest level, challenges persist in consolidating a democratic culture as well as institutional structures based on tolerance and accountability. Some of these challenges revolve around core representative institutions, including Ghana's still relatively new multiparty Parliament as well as the DAs, which continue to deviate from principles of democratic representation. For example, little progress has been made on fiscal decentralization. DAs have only limited discretion over the use of the DACF: half the fund is earmarked by the central government, mainly for capital projects, while the remaining half is generally used as a matching fund for donor projects and to cover the administrative expenses of the DAs themselves. Other challenges to the consolidation of democratic principles and good governance revolve around judicial and quasi-judicial institutions, which many regard as an especially weak link in Ghana (see, for example, Hammerstad 2004; also Crawford 2004, 9–13). Ghana's vibrant, independent, and often courageous media are crucial for accountability and transparency; nevertheless, they have been weakened by tendencies toward "irresponsible journalism" and "reporting on rumour." These tendencies reflect, in part, limitations in both training and pay (CIDA interview August 24, 2005; Sandbrook 2000, 40–46).

In this connection, there is little doubt that structural problems such as the continued high incidence of poverty in Ghana have done much to undermine the country's efforts to promote good governance. Data show that the proportion of Ghana's population living below the national poverty line fell from about 60 percent in 1987–88 to under 40 percent in 1999. But this progress needs to be kept in perspective: when poverty is defined as living on less than one dollar a day, being "lifted out" of it falls far short of achieving basic human security. Moreover, progress in poverty reduction has been uneven; poverty is actually rising among urban dwellers and on the northern savannah (Booth et al. 2004; UNDP 2005b). Thus, although Ghana has made aggregate gains in poverty alleviation, millions of Ghanaians still face difficulties meeting their basic needs, with these millions concentrated unevenly in the country's cities and regions. Indeed, in 2005 Ghana ranked 138th out of 177 in the UNDP's Human Development Index: that year, the country's life expectancy at birth was 56.8 years, and its combined gross enrolment percentage for primary, secondary, and tertiary schools was only 46 percent (UNDP 2005b). In these conditions, tendencies toward corruption have been reinforced. Meanwhile, the relatively poor and marginalized majority has found it difficult to hold Ghana's elites accountable.

Finally, there is a widely recognized need to reform the country's public service and public finance management. Necessary in this regard are clearer policy- and decision-making procedures, greater transparency and accountability, and a strengthened capacity to track expenditures, reduce corruption, and implement policies. Thus, while the World Bank's new governance indicators point to significant improvements in Ghana since 1996 in the areas of Voice and Accountability, Government Effectiveness, and Control of Corruption, the country's scores and indices on Economic and Regulatory Quality, which measure trade and fiscal policies, and its overall effectiveness with regard to market-friendly policies, have been relatively low (World Bank 2005a). Indeed, as Crawford (2004) notes, public service and public finance reforms have consistently been a principal preoccupation (along with decentralization) among Ghana's donor community (2004, 36–38). The fact that these prodigious efforts have not met with greater success raises the obvious question of why this should be so, and more particularly how these types of governance reforms relate to broader efforts to strengthen democratic institutions and governance.

## Canada's Governance Priorities and Role in Ghana

### Context

Ghana and Canada have a long history in development cooperation. Indeed, Ghana is CIDA's longest-running program and has been a core recipient of Canadian development assistance since independence in 1957. In its last programming framework, CIDA (1999c) noted that by 2000, Canada would have contributed C$1 billion to Ghana's development efforts through all channels. The same report also estimated that Canada would be contributing more than $100 million in official development assistance (ODA) to Ghana between 2000 and 2003. It should be pointed out, however, that Canada's aid program in Ghana generally—and its programming on good governance in particular—has grown and changed significantly since the last framework was issued in 1999 (a new framework will soon be released). This makes many judgments concerning the effects of Canadian programming preliminary, in that some of the largest and most important initiatives are less than three years old. The difficulty of isolating the impact of CIDA programming is compounded by the fact that the agency is a medium-sized bilateral donor that accounts for only a small share of Ghana's overall aid income. According to World Bank data, CIDA's projected 2005 disbursements of US$38.04 million placed it seventh among bilateral donors—eleventh if key multilateral agencies were included—accounting for under 4 percent of US$1,135.76 million in total ODA.

CIDA's renewed commitment to Ghana is nested within a broader renewal of interest in and support for Africa as a whole. At the 2002 G8 meeting hosted by Canada at Kananaskis, for example, not only did former prime minister Jean Chrétien make Africa a principal focus of discussion but he also announced an extraordinary C$500 million Canada Fund for Africa in the context of the G8 Africa Action Plan (see Black 2004; Fowler 2003). Prior to this, at the Monterrey Conference on Financing for Development in March 2002, Chrétien had committed Canada to doubling its international assistance by 2010 through annual aid increases of 8 percent, with aid to Africa to be doubled by 2008–9. While the government was widely criticized in the context of the "Make Poverty History" campaign of 2005 for refusing to commit to a timetable for reaching the aid target of 0.7 percent of GDP, Canada's 2005 International Policy Statement reiterated Ottawa's Monterrey commitments. Finally, at the 2005 G8 finance ministers' meeting in London, Canada and other G8 members agreed that eighteen developing countries that had met minimum standards of "good governance" (including Ghana) would have their foreign debts cancelled. By then, Canada had already agreed (in 2000) to cancel the debt owed it by heavily indebted poor countries (HIPCs). Thus, the overall context for Canada's aid programming in Ghana has been a significant process of increasing and refocusing development assistance, especially in Africa.[3]

### The Ghana Program Prior to 2003

As noted above, CIDA's post-1999 aid policies in Ghana built on a long history of bilateral links. After 1999, CIDA's program in Ghana remained broadly focused on the provision of basic human needs and the promotion of good governance (both economic and political), along with cross-cutting themes such as HIV/AIDS, gender equality, and environmental protection. Within the provision of basic human needs (BHNS), which were projected in 1999 to account for 60 to 70 percent of CIDA's program resources to Ghana by 2002–3, the emphasis was on increasing food security, improving quality of life for poor groups, and increasing access to sustainable water supplies (CIDA 1999c). In particular, CIDA built on a twenty-five-year commitment to the water sector in northern Ghana to launch a number of water projects throughout the country (ibid., 10). In governance, the focus of Canadian aid policy was defined not only as improving the capacity of local and central governments in Ghana to plan and deliver poverty reduction programs, but also as increasing accountability, transparency, and participation in local and central government activities (ibid., 15–16). In addition, Canada announced its intention to focus on District Assembly capacity building and fiscal decentralization, and also to help strengthen the capacity of villages and towns to manage their own development, with the stated aim of consolidating improved governance and democracy (ibid., 16). In the context of the Government of Ghana's (GoG's) long-standing but slow-moving process of decentralization, the Canadian government sought to influence this process through a variety of means, including bilateral consultations with the GoG, the maintenance of agreed-on performance standards, and the fostering of coordination among donors (ibid.). Geographically, CIDA intended to focus mainly though not exclusively on northern Ghana in general and on three of the country's poorest regions in particular—the Upper West, the Upper East, and the North. It was anticipated that governance activities would account for 10 to 30 percent of CIDA expenditures by 2002–3—a strikingly imprecise commitment. Moreover, the precision of these estimates is further brought into question by the figures in Table 1, which indicate that in 2006 CIDA placed the governance share of bilateral expenditures for 2001 to 2003 at over 50 percent. While there is no clear explanation for the discrepancy between the 1999 governance projections and the 2006 ex post figures for much the same portfolio of projects, this was likely a result of simply reclassifying a substantial portion of program activities *from* BHNS *to* governance, underscoring the loose nature of these categories.

Overall, even though CIDA's program remained quite wide ranging, and even though the priorities of BHNS and governance are highly malleable, one

TABLE 1

Actual and Projected CIDA Disbursements for Good Governance in Ghana

| Governance expenditures | FY 01 | FY 02 | FY 03 | FY 04 | FY 05 | FY 06 | FY 07 |
|---|---|---|---|---|---|---|---|
| In millions | 7.17 | 6.99 | 7.16 | 19.55 | 15.46 | 23.02 | 34.51 |
| As a % of total CIDA disbursements | 53.4 | 53 | 51.5 | 50.2 | 37.5 | 40.7 | 38 |

*Source*: Ghana IPS Disbursements and Budgets, CIDA 2006-02-13.

can see in the 1999 Framework an attempt to focus on certain programming "niches" in both thematic and geographic terms. This was a natural and, in policy terms, sensible response to the period of fiscal restraint and cutbacks that preceded it. Moreover, many specific governance commitments—for example, on economic governance ($5 million, 1998–2002), fiscal decentralization ($2 million, 1998–2001), and parliamentary committee strengthening ($0.5 million, 1998–2002) were small in scale, representing a relatively low-risk but also low-reward strategy.

## 2003 Onwards: Ghana as a "Country of Concentration"

Since 2003, CIDA's Ghana program has grown and changed, building on but extending beyond these core focuses. The trigger for this process has been Ghana's designation in late 2002 as one of nine "enhanced partnership countries" (in the language of the G8's Africa Action Plan)—that is, countries judged by CIDA to be "good performers." This status was confirmed and reinforced in the 2005 International Policy Statement, in which CIDA designated Ghana as one of fourteen core bilateral partners in Africa and one of twenty-five overall. The Canadian government also pledged to invest about C$55 million annually in Ghana as long as the country continued on its path toward promoting good governance as well as achieving the Millennium Development Goals (MDGS). Indeed, bilateral expenditures are currently projected to peak at just over $90 million in fiscal year 2007. Much of the overall thrust of the changes that have occurred has been firmly in line with core elements of the consensus on "best practices" that has taken shape within the international aid regime since the late 1990s, as well as the CIDA programming reforms for "strengthening aid effectiveness" adopted as agency policy in 2002 (see de Renzio and Mulley in this volume; CIDA 2002; Therien and Lloyd 2000). Thus, steps have been taken to make longer-term and more predictable financial commitments, to increase donor collaboration and coordination ("harmonization and alignment"), and to foster closer "partnerships" and local and national "ownership" around national Poverty Reduction Strategy Papers (in Ghana's case the Ghana Poverty Reduction Strategy; GPRS).[4]

There has also been an effort to, in effect, integrate and thus blur the distinctions between the thematic priorities of BHNs and governance so that governance programs are designed to facilitate BHN objectives ("oiling the wheels to help government do its job better," in the words of a CIDA informant). As a comparison of the more limited list of bilateral projects in Table 2 with the longer list of projects in the chapter appendix indicates, for example, CIDA officials will include both more and less expansive lists of projects within the ambit of governance programming, depending on how strictly they are inter-

TABLE 2

Current CIDA Bilateral Governance Operations in Ghana (c$)

| Project number | Project Name | Disbursements projected to 2005–6 | Disbursements projected for 2005–6 | Disbursements projected for 2006–7 | Disbursements projected for 2007–8 | Disbursements projected for 2008–9 |
|---|---|---|---|---|---|---|
| A-015929 | Central Governance Project | 3,919,378 | 778,230 | 380,471 | | |
| A-031898 | Land Administration | | | 400,000 | 400,000 | 700,000 |
| A-031899 | District-Wide Assistance Project | 5,960,508 | 3,767,704 | 3,695,533 | 1,573,173 | |
| A-032034 | GPRS-BS (general budget support) | 22,750,000 | 24,743,000 | 17,007,000 | 17,000,000 | 11,500,000 |
| A-032089 | Parliamentary Committee Support | 485,441 | 660,688 | 946,563 | 835,000 | 550,337 |
| A-032297 | Research and Advocacy Project | 0 | 534,479 | 805,521 | 660,000 | |
| A-033154 | Promotion of Women in Local Governance | 0 | 90,000 | 10,000 | | |

*Source:* CIDA, 2006.

preting this focus. In terms of programs that have built on past initiatives, the District Capacity Building Project (DISCAP—$7.7 million, 2000–6; see appendix) has built on CIDA's twenty-five years of water programming in northern Ghana to strengthen local government capacities for managing potable water and sanitation resources, in collaboration with NGO and private-sector stakeholders. Part of this program has involved establishing gender desk officers in sixteen district offices. As informed observers and CIDA officers concur, early efforts in the water sector experienced some failures and setbacks, based partly on an inadequate understanding of the challenges of building capacity and fostering conditions for sustainability. However, CIDA also took from this experience the lesson that water projects can have organizational spinoffs that enhance the capacity of a community to manage and communicate in other areas; and also that these projects can form the basis for promoting gender equality and enhanced participation of women and other community members in decision processes. Thus, DISCAP reflects a concerted effort to build outwards from a long accumulation of lessons learned, political and cultural linkages, and well-established counterpart relationships. It has drawn on the agency's achievements in the provision of BHNs (clean water) to pursue broader objectives relating to governance and management capacity at the village, town, and district levels as well as in terms of gender empowerment. At the same time, the project is designed to help ensure the sustainability of past achievements in clean water provision. In short, DISCAP seems to illustrate the benefits of continuity, long-term commitments, and adaptability in the face of setbacks as well as successes in the provision of aid. It is not surprising, then, that CIDA is now attempting to leverage this experience, not only in terms of its own district-level programming (see below), but also by taking the lessons learned at the northern District level and bringing them into the national dialogue, with the objective of establishing similar systems on a wider basis (interview with CIDA officer, August 25, 2005). It remains to be seen how effective this effort will be.

Similarly, the Ghana Parliamentary Committee Support Project implemented by the Parliamentary Centre in Ottawa, which in its first phase focused on the Ghanaian Public Accounts and Finance Committees, has been extended in its second phase to include the Special Committee on the Ghana Poverty Reduction Strategy (GPRS), the Committee on Local Government and Rural Development, the Gender and Children Committee, and the Government Assurances Committee. The focus, in other words, has been broadened to encompass all those committees with particular responsibility for poverty reduction policy monitoring and evaluation, through ongoing scrutiny of the GPRS. This focus was apparently adopted at the request of the Ghanaian parliamentarians with whom the second phase was negotiated, and could help ensure that the executive branch of the Ghanaian government is held more accountable for its poverty reduction strategy, which is widely regarded as less participatory and broadly "owned" than the rhetoric surrounding PRSP's implies.

More expansively and controversially, CIDA has moved to embrace budgetary support programs, both in its established "niche" at the district level and at the sectoral and central government levels. Thus, in March 2004 it initiated a $15 million District-Wide Assistance Project (DWAP) to provide support through the Ministry of Finance and Economic Planning to thirty-four Northern District assemblies for the implementation of district development plans to reduce poverty. This district-level initiative is the first of its kind and, according to a CIDA official, is being watched with interest by other donors. In addition, also in March 2004, CIDA launched a five-year, $85 million Food and Agriculture Budgetary Support (FABS) program to provide budgetary support to the Ministry of Food and Agriculture for its Food and Agriculture Sector Development Policy. In this way, it has arguably built on the emphasis on food security set out in the 1999 programming framework in a way that aims to simultaneously fulfill governance objectives. Finally, it has joined nine other donors in the Ghana Poverty Reduction Strategy–Budget Support (GPRS-BS) program. This major initiative, of which CIDA's share for 2004–9 is to be $93 million, directly supports the GoG. With GPRS-BS, CIDA has contributed to a program initiative that not only is comparatively large, and aimed toward facilitating dialogue and "ownership" of poverty reduction policies, but also embodies an unprecedented level of donor coordination through the negotiation (reportedly for the first time in Ghana) of a common programming matrix and evaluation framework among seven bilateral donors, the African Development Bank, the EU, and the World Bank (the largest contributor, at 40 percent of the total commitment).[5]

Much stock has been placed in these budgetary support initiatives. For one thing, as noted above, they are seen by donors as combining the promotion of governance reforms with the pursuit of BHN and poverty alleviation objectives. They now account for about 70 percent of CIDA's bilateral program to Ghana and thus, depending on how they are "scored," represent a major increase in the agency's financial commitment to governance efforts. They are seen as a potentially effective means of combining accountability (to donors as well as Ghanaian stakeholders) with the fostering of local ownership, since they are premised on district, sectoral, and central government authorities applying the resources committed to their own policy priorities, and then accounting for their performance in implementing these priorities.

The process of negotiating these arrangements, it should be noted, has not been easy for many of the Ghanaian institutions in question. For example, according to a CIDA informant, it took the Ministry of Food and Agriculture several months of back-and-forth discussions to arrive at their programming priorities for the FABS program. The underlying issue, in his view, was that ministry officials were so used to operating on the basis of bilateral project funding that they weren't organized to set and implement their *own* programming priorities in their dealings with donor "partners." Indeed, the degree to which years of project-based funding have undermined the capacity for autonomous priority setting within recipient governments is a major governance concern. An additional, perhaps alternative, explanation is that budgetary support involves donors insinuating themselves far more deeply into the governance processes of recipient institutions in ways that can be highly demanding for these institutions, and which can hold up the provision of both initial and subsequent performance-based "tranches" (see Tomlinson and Foster 2004). This also raises issues of "ownership," to which we will return.

At the district level, the DWAP program (Appendix; Table 2) has several objectives, stated and unstated. Like other budgetary support programs, it aims to provide a predictable and timely flow of funds to enable DAs and administrations to implement projects arising from their own annual action plans. These have generally focused on infrastructure in the education, health, public security, water, and sanitation sectors. The districts are then accountable for their performance in meeting these objectives. The funds are disbursed through the GoG's District Common Fund Administration, thereby enabling district authorities to gain experience and build capacity and (theoretically at least) trust in managing their relations with central government authorities.

In this connection, the program also aims to provide support and impetus to the GoG's protracted decentralization policy, something that is widely regarded by donors as essential for effective poverty alleviation activities. Despite the formal process of decentralization that has been in motion since 1988–89, far less has been accomplished in terms of decentralizing *real* fiscal capacity and authority than would have been hoped for or expected,[6] owing to powerful resistance from several sources (Booth et al. 2004, 28). The GoG tends to cite concerns over the capacity of district authorities as justification for their reluctance to devolve more real authority to the districts. Yet especially considering the level from which the current decentralization process began in 1988–89, some real progress has been made in the devolution of authority to the DAs. Not only have they been given the power to award contracts up to $100,000 on the advice of the District Tender Boards, but they have also improved revenue mobilization and collection from sources such as market tolls, licences, fees, stool land revenues, and special levies (Ayee 1997a, 95). Furthermore, they are responsible for the construction and maintenance of streets, parks, cemeteries, and other public utilities. Indeed, the DAs have undertaken development projects such as the construction and maintenance of feeder roads, school classroom blocks, clinics, and places of convenience as well as the provision of water and electricity (Ayee 1997b, 39).

Therefore, part of what the DWAP program seeks to do is to demonstrate to the central government that the districts are stronger and more able than has been assumed or asserted, and to get the two levels of government more used to working with and trusting each other—thereby moving the decentralization process forward. This seems an admirably subtle strategic objective. The question remains, however: Is the central government genuinely open to ceding more authority and funds to the district level? Does the political logic of the Ghanaian system militate decisively against surrendering control over resources seen as essential to political success to other administrative levels, as the DFID "Drivers of Change" study on Ghana suggests (Booth et al. 2004)?

More broadly, budgetary support is a controversial strategy, within and beyond CIDA. Some see this approach in general, and multidonor budget support in particular, as the most promising way yet of fostering Ghanaian ownership in governance reform processes. CIDA interviewees cited encouraging evidence of the GoG being increasingly able and willing to "push back" in exchanges with donor agencies and to play a leadership role on policy priorities—a dynamic that is facilitated, in principle at least, by collaborative donor arrangements that allow it to engage one donor collective rather than multiple institutional "partners" across a wide front. Others see the effective implementation of this type of program as dependent on long-awaited public service and public finance reforms at the central government level, as well as on effective decentralization. In the absence of such reforms, some doubt the ability of the GoG to implement effectively the poverty reduction policies it has chosen to prioritize and to track the large infusions of funds that budgetary support programs entail. Thus, another CIDA interviewee expressed scepticism over whether the central government has the infrastructure, the courage, and the means to implement the reforms it "needs to undertake." In a similar vein, the authors of the DFID "Drivers of Change" study doubted that the historical and structural conditions currently prevailing within the Ghanaian political economy would allow its government to "skip straight to Weber" (Unsworth 2005, 11, following Pritchett) through the implementation of ideal-typical public service and finance reforms. They therefore advised against further emphasis on budgetary support, arguing that the "MDBS package already agreed goes beyond what seems wise under current conditions" (Booth et al. 2004, 62).

Finally, civil society and academic critics mount a deeper critique of budgetary support and other similar program-based approaches (PBAS). They argue

that the widely endorsed "good" of donor coordination can in fact significantly *reduce* effective recipient ownership. In part, this is because on the donor
side of the "bargain," effective harmonization and alignment can be enor-
mously difficult to achieve. According to Mulley and de Renzio (in this volume),
domestic political pressures for visibility, institutional rigidity, resistance to
change in policies and procedures, and the fact that some donors remain
unconvinced of the usefulness of this new approach, have all contributed to
a lack of commitment by some donors to deliver on commitments to coordination and local ownership. More broadly, multidonor budget support is usually premised on policy and governance priorities and modalities emanating
principally from the World Bank and IMF, which risk-averse medium-sized
donors like CIDA may be especially inclined to rally behind. The effect, in some
instances, has been the adoption of donor-coordinated policies that are inappropriate to the country context, thereby undermining the good governance
cause. From this perspective, collectively imposed conditionalities are the most
powerful of all (an argument that may be understood by analogy with the
challenges of negotiating with collectives like the European Union[7]). Such
critics take little comfort from the fact that budgetary support is tied to nationally "owned" PRSPs, because they regard the breadth and quality of participation in the negotiation of these vital "gatekeeping" documents as highly limited (for elaboration, see Tomlinson and Foster 2004). These are powerful
arguments that place issues of ownership and accountability into sharp relief.
We will return to them below.

The controversy over budgetary support also highlights the importance of
the most recent initiative to formulate a thoroughgoing package of public
service reforms within Ghana and, in this context, CIDA's Central Governance
Project ($5 million; 1999–2008). This has been a highly regarded project within
CIDA, in large part because of the quality of the work of the Canadian implementing organization (the Institute for Public Administration in Canada;
IPAC) and its effective cooperation with very able Ghanaian counterparts in the
Office of the President (CIDA interview, August 25, 2005). The project focuses
on "formalizing, strengthening, and systematizing the policy management
processes within the executive branch of the Government as well as the Central Management Agencies, Ministries, Departments and Agencies tasked with
either developing policies or translating policies articulated by the political
leadership into operational programs" (CIDA 2005d). The core problem, according to an IPAC official, is that "accountabilities are all mixed up," with two or
three parallel policy-planning processes in play and no clear procedures for
adjudicating between them. The project has produced a framework document
outlining much-improved policy decision-making procedures. Behind this

framework, more fundamental reforms to the decision-making process are implied. This is therefore a highly strategic and politically sensitive project, with limited results to date. One CIDA interviewee noted that while the project principals had done a good job of outlining practical proposals for moving the policy process forward, it had taken the GoG a year to even *respond to* these proposals. This was partly because of the December 2004 elections, which effectively suspended progress on politically sensitive governance reforms (IPAC interview, September 15, 2005). The project's efforts may, by the time this book is in print, have passed a crucial decision point, and CIDA officials have negotiated an eighteen-month project extension (to January 2008) to allow more time for the necessary consultations and decisions.

If the latest efforts to catalyze public service reform come to fruition, the project could have a highly significant impact on the work of government (CIDA interview, August 25, 2005). It remains to be seen, however, whether the political obstacles that have stymied such reform initiatives in the past can be overcome this time around. If they are not, or even if they are, it is likely that more attention needs to be paid to the broader context of democratization in Ghana, beyond direct, technocratic attempts to "skip straight to Weber." Without effective political impetus, embedded in the wider political process, technocratic reforms—no matter how well conceived—often falter. This is a theme we address further in the conclusion.

In terms of support for democratizing reforms, the one CIDA initiative that has been targeted directly at core democratic institutions has been the two-phased Parliamentary Committee Support project, noted above and projected to run through May 2008. It is conceived as complementary to the West Africa regional Parliamentary Strengthening Project ($9 million over five years), which is funded through the Canada Fund for Africa. CIDA officials see the Parliamentary Committee project as having had a markedly positive impact on the quality of the work done by the targeted committees in terms of what they discuss and how they discuss it—a trend reflected in the quality of parliamentary debates as well. CIDA sees this as a step toward more robust structures of democratic oversight and accountability between Parliament and the Executive, and thus also as "a risk mitigation factor for CIDA's budgetary support programming" (CIDA 2005d). The project aims to train committee members on how to analyze the budget, communicate with NGOs, monitor the implementation of the GPRS, and establish better links with the communities that are supposed to be its focus. The project has also fostered greater understanding and communication between key parliamentary committees and civil society groups, especially in Ghana's North, as well as a much greater awareness of gender issues. An unanticipated outcome was that by enhancing the national profile of these parliamentary committees, and particularly the credibility of then-opposition MPs through their leadership of the Public Affairs Committee, the project may have helped strengthen democratic choice by enhancing the electoral prospects of the NPP.

In a highly executive-centred institutional system, however, the sustainability of this project's achievements remains a significant concern. In the absence of durable systemic reforms, including ongoing structures for the provision of policy analyses needed for effective committee work, can the positive effects on individual MPs and the operations of committees in the "here and now" be sustained beyond the life of the project?

In sum, it is too soon to tell what the impact of many of CIDA's largest and most important governance programming initiatives will be. It can also be difficult to discern the effects of individual donor initiatives, particularly those of relatively smaller donors, in the somewhat amorphous governance domain. If the effectiveness and democratic legitimacy of the District Assemblies increase, for example, how much of this will be attributable to the work of the DWAP project? This difficulty may grow as donor collaboration increases, since it can be very hard to isolate the roles and contributions of donors such as CIDA through their "seat at the table" of formidable groupings such as the GPRS-BS project. This is why donors will sometimes be reluctant to collaborate and why, within CIDA, there is ongoing discussion about how much to be concerned over clear attribution of "CIDA results," versus effective "contributions" to collaborative donor efforts. One key test of governance programming is long-term sustainability. This test requires follow-up analysis over time of initiatives such as the DISCAP and parliamentary committee projects.

Nevertheless, there have been a number of significant and largely positive developments in CIDA's governance programming in Ghana over the past several years. Most importantly, the agency has made much larger and more stable financial commitments, linked (though perhaps not as firmly as they could be, especially beyond the district level) to tangible objectives in support of enhanced BHNs. It is to be hoped that this long-term commitment to Ghana and other core bilateral partners will help reduce the rapid turnover of project officers and the time-consuming, cumbersome approval and reporting procedures noted by some implementing partners. These frustrations can perhaps be understood as a function of the agency's fiscally induced difficulties and uncertainties during the 1990s, from which it has only recently emerged. Some real progress has been made in terms of donor coordination, not only in the highly formalized context of the flagship GPRS-BS initiative but also in sectoral and/or more informal contexts (e.g., around decentralization, with the Germans and the Danes; through monthly lunches of heads of development assistance programs; and through information sharing of agencies involved in parliamentary support work). However, CIDA officials acknowledge that considerably more remains to be done on this front, notably in the agency's core geographic focus area of the North. Efforts to coordinate and share information, and to avoid overlap and duplication, need to be improved. Some burden-sharing arrangements have been worked out in water programming, with different donors agreeing to focus on certain districts. But even in this context, challenges remain in terms of effective cooperation with NGOs.

More broadly, there are important questions concerning the sustainability of CIDA programming and, in this connection, the pivotal issue of Ghana's "ownership" of its own reform and poverty reduction efforts and the broader process of democratization within which they are embedded. It is to these key contextual issues that we turn in concluding.

## Conclusion:
## Lessons and Remaining Challenges

While Canada's foreign aid, together with that of other donors, has contributed to a wide variety of development projects and programs, helped alleviate the impacts of poverty, provided basic human needs such as safe water to substantial numbers of Ghanaians, and promoted good governance in Ghana, there is no denying that the goals and standards CIDA has set for itself have yet to be realized. Efforts have been hampered by a number of problems. First, there is the critical issue of "ownership." Everyone agrees in principle that fostering "genuine ownership and leadership on the part of the people you are working with" (CIDA interview, August 25, 2005) is essential for the success of governance reforms as well as other aid initiatives. It is much less clear how this can be achieved, especially in a context of the results-based management system (discussed by Wood later in this volume) and the imperatives of accountability to the Parliament and taxpayers of Canada. The latest answer is the move to a heavy emphasis on budgetary support anchored, at the national level, in the GPRS. There is also a presumption by some officials, at least, that budgetary support can only succeed in the context of a far-reaching program of donor-promoted public service and public finance reforms. Does this context foster "ownership"? Who is doing the owning, and with what consequences in terms of MDG objectives of poverty alleviation? Do GoG officials "tell donors what they want to hear" in order to secure donor resources? Or, if priorities are truly those of the political/NPP elite, are they really "pro-poor" in conception or effect? And even if budgetary support does seem in principle to encourage national, sectoral, and district priority setting and accountability, are its intentions likely to be undermined by its potential to reinforce deeply entrenched tendencies toward clientelistic strategies of political mobilization and dispensation?

There are no simple answers to these questions, but there are grounds for concern. As noted above, for example, it is doubtful that the GPRS truly reflects a broadly consultative/democratic process—or indeed, that it could realistically have been expected to do so. It is also not clear that Ghanaian political elites share the commitment embodied in the donor and MDG discourse to *generalized* poverty reduction. In the DFID "Drivers of Change" report on Ghana, the authors argue that "the character of local politics leads to expectations that the rich and the powerful will help the poor in their *own* communities. The boundaries of community may be more or less broadly defined, but would not normally include the whole national society. So poverty reduction, implying generally redistributive policies, is not at the forefront of anybody's political agenda" (Booth et al. 2004, 58). This should hardly be surprising; where, after all, is the generalized well-being of the poor a dominant political priority *in practice* of those who are relatively wealthy and privileged?

There are also grounds for suspicion when recipient country representatives articulate their needs in language that echoes the clearly expressed priorities of the donor community. One CIDA official acknowledged that, in discussing GPRS-BS priorities with GoG officials, one can never be entirely sure whether the latter are giving voice to their *own* priorities or those of the largest donors in the enterprise, such as the World Bank and the DFID. This has been referred to as "the politics of the mirror" in donor–recipient relations, in which sophisticated recipient governments become adept at absorbing and reflecting back donor priorities. This helps explain, for example, the remarkable similarities among various "nationally owned" PRSPs (see Tomlinson and Foster 2004).[8]

Finally, it is not clear that far-reaching public service and public finance reforms can be successfully implemented and sustained on the country's current political terrain—certainly in the absence of sustained domestic political pressure for greater transparency and accountability. It is therefore necessary to look *beyond* budgetary support for sustainable "ownership" and poverty reduction, though without discounting or dismantling these important large-scale initiatives. There must also be greater willingness to accommodate developing countries' choice of strategies and policies, and use of language, that diverges from the orthodoxy preferred by the donor community. This would seem to be a likely effect of more robust democratic institutions and political processes. In short, technocratic governance reforms cannot be expected to succeed, in the Ghanaian context at least, without sustained deepening of democratic accountability.

Thus, there is a need to focus considerably more attention on supporting the broader process of and context for democratization in Ghana, which has achieved so much already and holds the promise, however fragile, of fostering stronger dynamics of accountability, responsiveness, poverty alleviation, and, ultimately, "ownership." Indeed, since 1999 the World Bank's Comprehensive Development Framework—a three-pronged strategy for promoting overall social and economic development and reducing poverty—has assigned a key role to civil society participation and to the broader development community and stakeholders.[9] In particular, support to civil society organizations such as the media and voluntary associations to enhance their capacity for participation, monitoring, and advocacy of good governance and far-reaching policies for poverty reduction would be a very positive step. Since citizen access to information increases significantly through the activities of the media and other CSOs (Booth et al. 2004), support for civil society activities is one area where CIDA could usefully expand its governance agenda. While "home town" development associations and other socially rooted civil society organizations can affect wider political developments in Ghana, independent media have the ability to ensure the free flow of uncensored information and keep government in check. Indeed, Booth and colleagues (2004) note that Ghana's vibrant media have begun to raise the political costs associated with corruption and the more blatant forms of patronage politics. They have also moderated the advantages of incumbency and increased the probability that political leaders will be rewarded by voters for better management of the macroeconomy. These, then, are instances of how "indirect" dynamics and pressures can critically reinforce prospects for improved governance.

CIDA is providing some support to civil society organizations through its participation in the collaborative, US$7.62 million Ghana Research and Advocacy Program along with the DFID, DANIDA, and the Dutch Embassy (CIDA's contribution is to be C$2 million for 2005–7; see Table 1). This program touches very few organizations, however (twelve at present, of eighty that applied for funding in a competitive process). Given the potential importance of Ghana's relatively robust and diverse civil society in collectively strengthening dynamics of democratization, this seems insufficient. Similarly, Ghana's vigorous but underdeveloped (and underpaid) mass media would benefit from capacity building and training programs that would in turn better enable them to hold the government accountable in terms of anticorruption, transparency, and poverty alleviation. CIDA supports no such programs at present.

Moreover, if the government of Ghana is to attain the goals of decentralization, including the devolution of real authority and accountability, CIDA should encourage the GoG to build stronger support structures and to enhance the capacity of existing ones so that they can deliver on its decentralization programs. The goals of decentralization cannot be realized when local government structures are not properly resourced and remain heavily dependent on central government prerogatives. The political will to promote decentralized governance must be translated into devolution of power and the provision of financial, logistical, and human resource supports for local governments. It is appropriate, then, that engagement with district institutional structures and development programs remains a key CIDA priority.

There are certainly other areas where CIDA could usefully focus its governance efforts, including the country's still relatively weak judicial and quasi-judicial institutions. Clearly, however, the agency must decide where to focus its energies, given the financial and administrative constraints it faces. Much of its protracted push to strengthen aid effectiveness has been concerned with this process of making choices. In the Ghanaian case, as we have shown, these choices have tended to privilege efforts in support of technocratic governance reforms, linked to the GPRS and related donor-approved poverty reduction priorities, in collaboration with state-based interlocutors. For these efforts to become more fully effective, however, and in order to enhance the legitimacy and "ownership" of donor programming, including CIDA's, broader support for more robust dynamics of accountability will be required within both state–civil society relationships and core democratic institutions.

▼

## Appendix:
## CIDA in Ghana—Programming Overview

### Bilateral Program Projects

All of CIDA's bilateral aid interventions are provided in support of Ghana's Poverty Reduction Strategy (GPRS). Current program priorities in Ghana are food security/agriculture; water; and governance—all critical elements of the GPRS.

### Good Governance

#### Ghana Poverty Reduction Strategy—Budget Support (GPRS-BS) Project
CIDA contribution: $93,000,000
Duration: January 2004–March 2009

Ghana has a good chance of meeting some of its Millennium Development Goals, specifically those related to eradicating poverty and achieving universal education and access to safe water. The GoG's Poverty Reduction Strategy is the key development framework for pursuing the goals via growth and poverty reduction. The program provides the opportunity for the GoG and donors to discuss priorities for poverty reduction and growth, and to determine methods of assessing growth and setting targets.

#### Food and Agriculture Budgetary Support (FABS)
CIDA contribution: $85,000,000
Duration: March 2004–March 2009

The Food and Agriculture Budgetary Support project (FABS) is CIDA's contribution to the food and agriculture component of Ghana's Poverty Reduction Strategy. FABS provides budgetary support to Ghana's Ministry of Food and Agriculture (MoFA) to implement Ghana's Food and Agriculture Sector Development Policy (FASDEP).

#### District-Wide Assistance Project (DWAP)
CIDA contribution: $15,000,000
Duration: March 2004–September 2009

The five-year DWAP provides support through the Ministry of Finance and Economic Planning directly to the budgets of all thirty-four District Assemblies in northern Ghana for the implementation of District Development Plans (DDPS) to reduce poverty. Much of CIDA's investment to the project is supporting the construction of health clinics and centres, and school classroom blocks for community use.

#### District Capacity Building Project (DISCAP)
CIDA contribution: $7,700,000
Duration: November 2000–March 2006

The goal of DISCAP is to strengthen local government capacities in the Upper East,

Upper West, and Northern Regions of Ghana to manage, in collaboration with NGO and private-sector stakeholders, potable water and sanitation resources.

### Central Governance Project

CIDA contribution: $5,000,000
Duration: July 1999–April 2007

This project aims to strengthen the policy management capacity of, and to improve coordination between, the Office of the President, the Cabinet Secretariat, the Policy Planning, Monitoring, and Evaluation Directorates, the Ministry of Finance, and the National Development Planning Commission.

### Ghana Program Support Unit Phase IV

CIDA contribution: $4,900,000
Duration: January 2005–2010

The goal is to maximize the efficiency and effectiveness of the development assistance program in Ghana. The PSU supports cida and Ghana in planning, implementing, and monitoring CIDA's development assistance program in the context of the GPRS, donor harmonization, and Ghanaian ownership of the country's development agenda.

### Ghana Advisory Services Project

CIDA contribution: $4,500,000
Duration: November 2004–June 2008

The Ghana Advisory Services Project acts as a framework for program-level advisory services and knowledge-building activities in the Ghana program. It will provide a flexible, fast-acting, and proactive tool capable of responding to evolving program needs, and of supporting and identifying development needs and strategies.

### Ghana Parliamentary Committee Support Phase II

CIDA contribution: $3,325,000
Duration: February 2004–November 2008

This project works to strengthen accountability, transparency, and participation in the parliamentary governance of Ghana, with particular attention to achieving more effective poverty reduction efforts in the country.

### Developing Rural Entrepreneurs—NSAC

CIDA contribution: $2,180,000
Duration: March 2004–March 2008

Working with a range of educational institutions, government organizations, and ngos in northern Ghana, the project will develop the human resource capacity of educational institutions to address the needs of rural entrepreneurs. Ultimately, the project will enhance the ability of northern Ghanaians, especially women and youth, to start and sustain micro-enterprises and small businesses.

Ghana Research and Advocacy Project (G-RAP)

CIDA contribution: $2,000,000

Duration: 2005–2007

G-RAP is a multidonor initiative supporting the development of research and advocacy organizations (RAOs) in Ghana. It aims to enhance the capacity of RAOs to carry out evidence-based research on various issues, enabling them to make independent contributions to policy process.

Strategic Information Management Program Participants Ghana (SIMP)

CIDA contribution: $282,000

Duration: September 2003–January 2010

This program was developed to facilitate Strategic Information Management Program (SIMP) participation. The SIMP provides technical training and ongoing support for Ghanaian government partners in information management and information technology tools.

*Source*: CIDA 2005.

# Notes

1 As described in the Introduction, the good political governance agenda refers to how the rules, institutions and systems of the state—the executive, judiciary and legislature—operate at central and local levels, and how the state relates to individual citizens, civil society, and the private sector (Unsworth 2005, 3). It involves not only the promotion of the rule of law, increased information flows between the government and civil society, and the participation of civil society in political decision making, but also the creation of public structures and institutions that are legitimate, responsible, efficient, transparent and accountable to the general public, who are supposed to be the beneficiaries of government programs (Woods 2000). Finally, good governance is about improving the capacity, commitment, and quality of government administration as well as developing an effective developmental state (White 1998, 25).

2 Under Section 252 of the 1992 Constitution, not less than 5 percent of the total revenues of the Ghanaian government are to be allocated to the DAs for development. These moneys are paid into the DACF in quarterly installments (Ayee 1997a, 96).

3 Although there are signs of retreat from this emphasis on Africa under the new Conservative government of Stephen Harper.

4 These terms and trends are controversial, most fundamentally because they tend to obfuscate the fundamental power asymmetries within aid relationships but also because the processes of consultation by which "ownership" is supposed to be secured are, in practice, limited and selective. See Tomlinson and Foster 2004.

5 The other bilateral donors are Denmark, Germany, France, the Netherlands, Switzerland, and the UK.

6  For example, a previous CIDA project on fiscal decentralization ($2 million, 1998–2001) was not a success, producing a series of guidelines and reports on how to go about fiscal decentralization but no real commitment to effectively decentralize. Interview with CIDA officer, August 25, 2005.

7  See also Rogerson (2005a) on the hazards of "cartelization" in the aid industry.

8  Another example concerns CIDA's Food and Agriculture Budgetary Support (FABS) Project, in which the Ministry of Food and Agriculture ultimately prioritized increased production of raw materials for industry, increased production of agricultural commodities for exports, enhanced input supply and distribution systems, and enhanced output marketing systems. While these may all be worthwhile objectives, they are also clearly reflective of neoliberal priorities and are at best indirectly related to enhanced food security for the poor.

9  Although it is doubtful whether the Bank has in mind the kind of unfettered civil society activity and advocacy work that a more fully democratic politics would imply.

▲

# 7

## DEFENCE, DEVELOPMENT, AND DIPLOMACY: THE CASE OF AFGHANISTAN, 2001–2005

### Scott Gilmore and Janan Mosazai

## Introduction

This case study examines the Canadian experience in Afghanistan from 2001 to 2005, when Afghanistan became Canada's largest bilateral aid recipient in history.[1] Although governance projects represented a large and important part of the Canadian assistance package, Canada did not play a significant role in developing the governance strategy presented in the overarching Afghan National Development Framework (NDF). Nor did CIDA pursue a systematic strategy for implementing governance projects within Canada's own aid program. Rather, governance programming was delivered within the framework of the Afghan government's priorities; in this context most funding decisions were taken based on the individual merits of proposals and as opportunities arose. The program was not tailored to fit any specific Canadian capability, nor was it used specifically to leverage broader Canadian interests. It was recipient country preferences, rather than Canadian capabilities or interests, that guided governance initiatives.*

These projects were highly diverse in both nature and impact, and at the time of writing it is still difficult to gauge accurately the benefits of individual initiatives or the overall effectiveness of the governance program. Nonetheless, it is clear that the unusually active efforts of key Canadians on the ground, including the ambassador, the military commander, and CIDA's staff, gave Canada a higher profile and influence than the size or focus of its governance assistance would otherwise have provided.

We argue that while the "harmonization and alignment" agenda, discussed by de Renzio and Mulley elsewhere in this book, is a critical element for improving the effectiveness of aid on the ground, it is only one side of the coin. From the standpoint of donor governments, which are first and foremost responsible to their voters, the "effectiveness" of aid is also measured in terms of how it supports the donor's domestic agenda. For example, does giving aid to country A instead of country B make the donor nation more secure? Or would a development program focused on economic governance lay the seeds of a useful and stable bilateral relationship? These considerations are occasionally dismissed as irrelevant or counterproductive by some within the development community; nonetheless, they are a key concern for ministers and senior-level decision makers, who ultimately decide where and how much aid money to send to recipient countries. This is particularly the case for so-called failed or failing states, where security and development are linked in complex ways. In this regard, we conclude that the overall Canadian engagement in Afghanistan would have been improved had decision makers in Ottawa initially identified specific Canadian interests in the region and within the coalition. Determining those would have allowed officials to craft a more unified interdepartmental strategy, which in turn would have led to more effective coordination of the defence, diplomatic, and development initiatives on the ground, including the governance projects.

This case study reviews Canada's governance program from a "3D" perspective, encompassing the combined objectives of not only CIDA but also the Department of National Defence (DND) and the Department of Foreign Affairs and International Trade (DFAIT). Therefore, in examining the impact of initiatives in Afghanistan, Afghan as well as Canadian outcomes will be considered.

## Afghanistan's Development and Security Profile

Afghanistan has seen very little development, particularly over the past twenty-five years. Little infrastructure work was undertaken during the country's occupation by the Soviet Union, and much of what was built—including silos, roads, hydroelectric dams, and some factories—was of poor quality and degraded quickly. By the time of the Soviet withdrawal, these development initiatives had not added up to much, and the ensuing civil war (1992 to 1996) destroyed much of the remaining infrastructure. The theocratic Taliban rule (1996 to 2001) created further setbacks by discouraging foreign aid and by hobbling the emergence of a national government capable of managing reconstruction.

Current development needs are overwhelming. Many provinces in Afghanistan do not have a single kilometre of paved road. There are severe shortages of hospitals, health clinics, schools, and universities. The countryside is heavily mined, and many Afghans remain refugees in neighbouring countries. The list of sectors needing significant international assistance is long, including but not limited to the security sector, the judiciary, and the administrative, education, and health care systems. Governance issues cut across all sectors, playing an important role in Afghanistan's National Development Framework (NDF).

In all reconstruction and development efforts in Afghanistan, the re-emergence of the narco-economy is a central consideration. Afghanistan is now the world's largest producer of opium. The trade in illicit drugs accounts for roughly two-thirds of the national GDP. Poppies are a reliable and valuable crop, and opium production is perhaps the most dangerous challenge to the creation of stable, transparent, and accountable state institutions. Most observers agree that its continued production could once again plunge the whole country into chronic disorder and criminality (Ward and Byrd 2004).

In most of Afghanistan, the physical and state infrastructure has been partially destroyed, including roads, hospitals, schools, and public transport. Until very recently, NGOs acted as the de facto institutions of state delivering most basic services. A lack of state control resulted in the felling of thousands of acres of timber forests—an important source of revenue for the central government—as well as the destruction of most of the pistachio forests along the Hindu Kush. There is also a thriving trade in black market gems and semiprecious stones. Most of the profits generated from natural resources have gone into the pockets of local warlords, further undermining state-building efforts.

The presence of the international community in Afghanistan today is a direct response to the threat of terrorism. The goal of ensuring that Afghanistan never again becomes a sanctuary for terrorists underpins the entire development effort. This is particularly the case with governance projects, which are generally intended to support the government of President Hamid Karzai and to facilitate a stable transition to democracy. Decisions made by major donors regarding the scope and focus of aid and reconstruction tend to include as their goals stabilizing the provinces, reinforcing the central government, and undermining the warlords. To illustrate this point, consider the significant energy and money spent on developing rural livelihoods. These programs have been aimed straight at the heart of the narco-economy, which is widely viewed as funding the local warlords, who in turn support the Taliban and Al-Qaeda.

## The Challenge of Governance in Afghanistan

### Political Impediments to Reform

For many years, many state institutions in Afghanistan have existed only in name. The governance challenges facing the country cannot be exaggerated, notably in light of three major political impediments: the centre–periphery divide, ethnic conflicts, and foreign interference.

Because of the centre–periphery divide, regional and local officials are able to exercise power beyond their political mandates. The result has been the rise of regional strongmen. Given the historic divide between Kabul and the provinces, patronage politics has been the norm rather than the exception throughout the country. The central government has tended to appoint officials in their areas of origin, in order to win their allegiance and to appease local ethnic factions. This, however, is not viewed as a blessing by those—of whom there are many—who would prefer competent authorities.

The patron–client relationship is even stronger at local (i.e., provincial and district) levels. The central government can rarely appoint officials to local government positions without the consent of the respective regional warlords, who maintain their own informal patron–client networks within and outside formal state institutions. As a result, non-professional, illiterate individuals are often appointed to professional positions. There are numerous examples of this—for example, of former combatants with no formal education running provincial departments of education, or information and culture. Favours are granted based on various allegiances, most prominently factional, family, and tribal ones.

For many long decades it was the Pashtuns who controlled the levers of political power in Afghanistan. As a consequence, efforts to build and strengthen state institutions have been undermined by ethnic misunderstandings and grievances, and this has estranged many Afghans across the ethnic spectrum. These conflicts were exacerbated during the civil war and also during the removal of the Taliban. Smaller ethnic groups such as the Panjshiris, who dominated the US-supported Northern Alliance, usurped other, larger ethnic groups in Karzai's government. Due to historical ethnic divides, any decisions on developing governance in modern Afghanistan must take into account a complicated web of ethnic and tribal politics.

Afghanistan's strategic location between Central Asia, South Asia, and the Middle East has been a curse on the country's development, both politically and economically. Afghanistan has been a battleground for powerful empires, and its neighbours have often interfered with its internal affairs. The British and the Soviet empires tried their luck in the nineteenth and twentieth centuries respectively. Neither succeeded in colonizing the country; their invasions, however, did foster ethnic and tribal differences. With the defeat of the Soviet Union, Afghanistan once again became a competitive arena for its neighbours, notably Pakistan, Iran, Russia, Uzbekistan, and India, each of which supported its own ethnic, religious, or political favourites. Given the political and military developments since December 2001, there is hope that much of this interference will diminish. This is hard to predict, though, because of persistent instability in the region bordering Pakistan and the re-emergence of the Taliban.

## Cultural Implications of Reform

In Afghanistan, the central issue concerning good governance is not whether people aspire to it, but rather how it should be delivered. Overall, Afghans are extremely politically aware and know what they want: competent state institutions as well as impartial officials whose main concern is to provide services to the public. Related to this are a desire to avoid reverting to the bloody political competition of the recent past and a general distrust of political parties.

Traditional politics are based on *shuras* (councils) and *jirgas* (assemblies);[2] these are key mechanisms for conflict resolution and civic engagement in matters of social and community concern. These bodies address every issue, from land and water disputes to marriages and crimes. In some parts of Afghanistan, *jirgas* also serve as courts, and strictly enforce punishments—some of them extremely harsh—to ensure order. Although effective in maintaining community stability, many of the practices of such *jirgas*, especially in family matters, are biased against women. At present, village *shuras* are an important counterpart for national programs such as the National Solidarity Program, which addresses rural development with maximum grassroots participation. Villages elect their representatives to *shuras* so that they can set out collective priorities for the community in consultation with their peers.

The challenge with these institutions relates to the propensity for small groups of individuals at the top to use coercion, most often in the form of intimidation and the threat of public shame and/or punishment. This was evident in a few cases in southeastern Afghanistan during the presidential elections of October 2004, when voters were told to cast their ballots for a particular candidate or face the prospect of having their houses burned down. However, this is not the case across the entire country. In the June 2002 elections for the Emergency Loya Jirga, for example, Burhanuddin Rabbani, a former president, was not elected in his own district in Badakhshan despite considerable intimidation and bribery.

Before and during the Soviet occupation, many Afghans—mostly in rural areas—did their best to keep their children away from schools out of fear of the possible secular influence. Today the situation is almost completely reversed.

Afghans now list education as one of their top priorities. This change is due in part to the influence of returning refugees, who saw the benefits of education while in Pakistan or Iran.

Women play an integral part in raising families and looking after the community. In the countryside they also take on many of the same agricultural duties as men. However, Afghanistan's patriarchal social system has worked strongly against political, social, and economic participation for Afghan women. Even though Afghans now crave education for their children, they are reluctant to send their daughters and sisters to school. Even in urban centres, many girls are prevented from attending school after they reach puberty.

At the same time, many Afghan men are sensitive about "foreigners" attempting to liberate Afghan women. There is a common view among the local population that international organizations and foreign countries place too much emphasis on women's rights, usually to the detriment of what many consider more important issues, such as combating corruption (which is endemic) and developing sustainable livelihoods. Donors consider it irrefutable that empowering women benefits society as whole, and local arguments to the contrary rarely persuade them otherwise. Nonetheless, cultural sensitivities like this one need to be factored in when development choices are being explained to "partners" in a recipient country. At the very least, an awareness of different cultural perspectives should guide the information campaigns that donors pursue in support of their programming.

## Creating the Governance Strategy

### Early Post-Conflict Phase

The reconstruction efforts in post-Taliban Afghanistan began with an unprecedented level of donor coordination and consultation that resulted in an overall development strategy, the NDF. Unlike in previous international aid efforts, such as in East Timor and Cambodia, the lead donors made a conscious effort to avoid overlap and to ensure Afghan participation in setting priorities. Canada participated in almost every stage of this process, but the officials involved in this conceded that they never significantly influenced the final outcome of any specific elements of these early consultations, including governance. In part, this was because Afghanistan had not been a traditional country of focus for Canada (as Haiti was, for example). But it was also due to the lack of a clear set of objectives on the part of officials in Ottawa—objectives that could have guided Canada's participation in multilateral discussions. In the case of governance, CIDA's strategy paper on the issue (discussed below) was almost ten years out of date and was unknown to the Canadian officials who attended the Afghan consultations. Among the donors, the most influential player was widely considered to be the United States. This was mainly a function of realpolitik: the Americans had led the fight against the Taliban and had managed much of the early diplomatic manoeuvring that resulted in Karzai's appointment. American influence was perhaps inevitable, given the larger diplomatic and aid presence the US government had in Kabul. There were simply more bodies on the ground and in attendance at critical meetings.

The donor consultations began in November 2001, before fighting had ended, in Bonn, Germany. Donors, international agencies, Afghan warlords, and members of the diaspora came together for the first time to consider the daunting reconstruction task ahead. Canada did not send a delegation from Ottawa but was represented by the Canadian Ambassador to Germany, who participated as an observer with the objective of demonstrating support for the multilateral approach. Canada was not considered a key international player,[3] nor did it try to assert itself as one. The view among senior officials in Ottawa was that Canada should be seen to be "doing its fair share" but only in the context of a broader multilateral effort. An oft-heard phrase at that time was that "Canada should not get ahead of the like-minded." As a result, Canadian officials did not pursue any specific priorities beyond the general goals of many Western countries, such as human rights and gender equality.

The immediate task of the Afghan leaders and the major donors in Bonn was to distinguish urgent, short-term needs from long-term ones. At the same time, the conference was intended to fill the power vacuum left behind by the Taliban and to ensure immediate security in Kabul. The resulting political agreement, brokered by UN Special Representative Lakhdar Brahimi with vital support from the United States, served as a road map for broad governance objectives in Afghanistan, including the next steps for the Emergency Loya Jirga and the Constitutional Loya Jirga. It also laid down plans to re-establish a judiciary, reform the civil service, empower civil society, and foster civic participation, human rights, and a free press.

The Bonn meeting was followed by a series of senior official meetings in Washington and elsewhere. These were dominated by a core group of like-minded nations that included the United States, Japan, Saudi Arabia, and several EU states. This group commissioned the World Bank, the United Nations Development Programme (UNDP), and the Asian Development Bank (ADB) to conduct a needs assessment and develop a coordinated strategy for delivering donor aid. Canada did participate in some of these meetings, either by sending mid- to low-level officials from Ottawa or by asking the resident diplomats to attend and report back. In either case, Canadian input in this process was minimal.

The resulting grand blueprint for Afghanistan's reconstruction was endorsed by the principal donors (such as the United States, Britain, Germany, and Japan) at a conference in Tokyo in January 2002. In the three years following, those key players have been reluctant to renegotiate the NDF, though considerable fine tuning and adjustments have taken place in response to events unfolding on the ground.[4] Canada did not play a substantive role in setting out this road map, though it would eventually contribute to its execution, and it was not invited to join the core group driving the initial agenda. Its level of participation in the donor conferences gradually increased, culminating in the attendance of then–CIDA minister Aileen Carroll at the Berlin conference, but by that time the NDF had been well established.

### Agreed Objectives

A clear set of priorities emerged from the donor consultation process. They are reflected in the NDF's three pillars and twelve development programs as listed below (Table 1). In the context of the NDF's twelve priority programs, governance itself was not identified as a specific objective. It was, however, a cross-cutting issue throughout the three pillars. In particular, there was significant emphasis on governance in public administration reform and security and rule of law. Regarding these, the Afghan government and core donors identified three broad areas they viewed as critical to the success of development efforts: judicial reform, civil service reform, and elections.

TABLE 1

Afghanistan's National Development Framework Priorities

| PILLAR 1<br>Human Capital and<br>Social Protection | PILLAR 2<br>Physical<br>Infrastructure | PILLAR 3<br>Trade and Investment,<br>Public Administration, and<br>the Rule of Law/Security |
|---|---|---|
| 1 Refugee and IDP Return | 1 Transport | 1 Trade and Investment |
| 2 Educational and Vocational Training | 2 Energy, Mining, and Telecommunications | 2 Public Administration |
| 3 Health and Nutrition | 3 Natural Resource Management | 3 Security and Rule of Law |
| 4 Livelihoods and Social Protection | 4 Urban Management | |
| 5 Cultural Heritage, Media, and Sports | | |

*Source*: "Afghanistan National Development Strategy: An Interim Strategy for Security Governance, Economic Growth, and Poverty Reduction" (30 January 2006), Presidential Oversight Committee, Islamic Republic of Afghanistan.

## Canada's Role in Assisting Afghanistan

### Phases of Involvement

Historically, Canada has had very limited relations with Afghanistan. In 2002, even though it was home to a sizable Afghan immigrant community, Canada had no embassy in the country, and its aid contributions were limited to humanitarian assistance delivered through multilateral agencies such as the UNDP. There was no traditional foreign policy agenda for Afghanistan as existed with countries in the Caribbean, the Middle East, and Europe. The events of September 11, 2001, changed this situation dramatically, but not overnight.

Canada quickly contributed military resources to the US-led Operation Enduring Freedom (OEF) against the Taliban government in Kabul. Most notably, the Princess Patricia's Canadian Light Infantry Battle Group participated in the hunt for Al-Qaeda and Taliban insurgents near Kandahar in February 2002. However, this deployment was short lived, and Canadian combat troops were repatriated in July of the same year.

Canada had yet to establish an embassy, choosing to cover events in Kabul from the High Commission in Islamabad. Nonetheless, CIDA pledged more than $350 million in aid after the January 2002 Bonn Conference.[5] This made Afghanistan the single largest recipient of bilateral aid in Canadian history. Belying the size of this commitment, there were no CIDA officials in the country, although a subcontracted project support unit (PSU) was established. Much of the larger part of Canadian development assistance was funnelled through trust funds or multilateral agencies. While this pooled approach has become standard among OECD donors, Canadian officials are split on its merits. Those in favour argue that this is a more efficient means to deliver assistance. It facilitates harmonization, eliminates overlapping programs, and in theory reduces administrative overheads. Also, by pooling funds with other donors, Canada can achieve economies of scale in ways that would not be possible if the money were spent on smaller bilateral projects. The opposing view maintains that the recipient agencies such as the UNDP are in fact *less* responsive and *more* bureaucratic. In the case of Afghanistan, Canada's funding commitment was large enough to stand on its own and would not necessarily have benefited from pooling. Furthermore, as we illustrate below, individual country contributions cannot be disaggregated from overall agency spending; it therefore becomes a challenge for donors to track the impact and effectiveness of their aid. With respect to Afghanistan, the question was moot: Canada had a small staff covering Afghanistan from Islamabad in Pakistan, and thus did not have the capacity to disburse its largest aid program in history in any other way than through multilateral organizations.

There was no pressure from either the government or the bureaucracy to increase Canada's participation in international efforts, until the unexpected decision by Canada's Cabinet in February 2003 to contribute a battalion group and brigade headquarters to the UN-authorized International Security Assistance Force (ISAF). Almost in the same breath, Cabinet decided to match its military commitment with a diplomatic one: a Canadian embassy would open as soon as possible. Until that moment, officials were only examining the possibility of contributing a much smaller provincial reconstruction team (PRT) to Afghanistan. The decision to send an entire battalion left bureaucrats scrambling to develop a broader strategy of engagement.

In September 2003 the Canadian embassy opened and Canada's role in Afghanistan jumped to a new level. With a large and highly visible military presence, a considerable aid program, high-level visits from Ottawa, an energetic ambassador, and extraordinarily active embassy staff, Canada suddenly emerged as a significant player in Kabul. Contributing to this were key aid initiatives that leveraged the new-found influence to raise the Canadian profile even higher. These included the decision to be the first country to fund the voter registration process, allowing it to start on time and thus setting the stage for Afghanistan's presidential elections. Equally important, and as a result of the efforts of Ambassador Christopher Alexander and the Canadian commander of Task Force Kabul, Major-General Andrew Leslie, Canada played a key role in the cantonment of heavy weapons in Kabul. This defused tensions among the various warlords in the Afghan Cabinet—an essential precondition for peaceful elections.

Canada's role in Afghanistan evolved yet again in mid-2005 with Operation Archer, the launch of a Canadian PRT in Kandahar. Aid then levelled off to amounts more consistent with those of other bilateral programs, and there was an expectation that the embassy would be "temporary" and remain open for only a few years. As of December 2006, General Leslie was speculating that the Canadian Forces could remain in Afghanistan for twenty more years. Officials in Ottawa began moving away from an ad hoc approach, of the sort to be expected from a bureaucracy faced with an unexpected shift in priorities, toward a more measured and planned strategy. The Canadian government's overall attitude toward Afghanistan in 2005 became more long term than it was between 2001 and 2004.

## Measuring Aid

Using the OECD's Development Assistance Committee (DAC) statistics for consistent comparison, in 2003–4 net official development assistance (ODA) for Afghanistan was US$1.6 billion. Canada ranked ninth among donors, contributing $65 million of that amount. Over the same time period, however, Afghanistan ranked first among bilateral recipients of Canadian aid.[6]

While CIDA, FAC, and DND all provide developmental assistance in one form or another, CIDA's assistance is by far the largest component of the overall Canadian aid package, with C$616.5 million allocated from 2001 to 2009, excluding the cost of military operations.[7] CIDA's program focused on four priorities chosen from the Afghan government's NDF: rural livelihoods and social protection; security and the rule of law; natural resource management and agriculture; and budgetary support to the Afghan government (through the World Bank).

It is difficult to decisively measure how much CIDA spent in these four priority areas, and even more difficult to determine how much was spent specifically on governance programs. Under CIDA's internal accounting processes, projects can be "coded" against more than one priority. As an example, a project to support anticorruption measures in Afghanistan's Ministry of Agriculture could be classified as part of rural livelihoods, rule of law, and/or resource management. In particular, governance projects are often coded against different objectives. Further complicating matters, CIDA provides the vast majority of its assistance to Afghanistan through multilateral partners, who may then treat the funds as fungible. For example, Canada gave $4 million to the Law and Order Trust Fund (LOTFA), managed by the UNDP, earmarking it for salaries and training. Yet in practice, international agencies pool donor funds and it is impossible to determine with certainty where any particular donation goes. The timings of aid disbursements add to the confusion. Pledges are not delivered at once, and when the total amount of delivered aid is calculated, much depends on whether projects have been allocated, disbursed, or executed.[8]

Because of these difficulties, the actual amount of money spent by Canada on governance programs in Afghanistan is elusive. The CIDA office in Kabul, the Afghanistan desk officer in Ottawa, the governance unit at headquarters, the CIDA minister's office, and the CIDA website all provide different numbers for this period. The range is $18 million to $54 million per year. A CIDA press release dated September 14, 2005, stated that "since 2001 Canada has contributed over $33 million to assist the democratic process in Afghanistan." By another estimate, CIDA expenditures on human rights, democracy, and good governance represented more than half of total Canadian disbursements to Afghanistan over a three-year period, with $60 million in 2002, $57 million in 2003, and $53 million in 2004. A more detailed breakdown provided by the Afghanistan desk at CIDA suggests that these numbers are inclusive, casting a very broad net over projects that may be only tangentially linked to gover-

FIGURE 1
CIDA Disbursement as of January 2004 ($137m)

- Operating Budget Support to Government [49%]
- Governance [20%]
- Rural Livelihoods and Social Protection [20%]
- Security Sector Reform [10%]
- Natural Resource Management [1%]

*Source*: Calculated with data provided in correspondence with CIDA and Embassy staff, August 2005.

nance objectives. If one uses the official total disbursement figures of $266 million over thirty-one months beginning in September 2001, the low estimate of $18 million would represent 17 percent of Canada's aid package to Afghanistan.

Using January 2004 figures as an example, projects with an obvious relation to governance (voter registration, constitutional commission, government capacity building, etc.) comprise approximately 20 percent of Canada's disbursed funds. If one considers the central importance of funding the Afghan government's operating budget as a governance-related initiative, the proportion climbs to 69 percent[9] (see Figure 1). By any estimate, governance and related efforts represent one of the largest elements of the development "D" of the 3D approach.

### Explaining the Canadian Commitment

Given the scope of Canada's commitment to Afghanistan, there has been considerable speculation about the government's motives for making this unprecedented commitment of aid, military forces, and diplomatic capital. This deserves a brief examination as it may shed light on why the development assistance program is so large and so heavily focused on governance.

When Canada ramped up its efforts in Afghanistan in 2003, spokespersons from DND, CIDA, and DFAIT used closely synchronized talking points. Communications, unlike more operational elements of the government's response, were relatively well coordinated by the Prime Minister's Office and the Privy Council Office. According to official statements, Canada's largest overseas commitment since the Korean War was being undertaken for four reasons. First, to support Canada's traditional allies including the United Kingdom, the United States, and Germany (which was heavily committed to ISAF). Second, to contribute to the "War on Terror," as Afghanistan had been the safe haven of Al-Qaeda (this was to be Canada's key commitment in that war). Third, to address the "genuine needs of the Afghan people" after decades of conflict. Fourth, to assist in the peacebuilding efforts of the UN and NATO as a long-time supporter of the multilateral system. This last point received pride of place among the others, and it was implied that this was the foremost reason for the massive investment of troops, diplomats, and cash (Canada DND 2003).

Several officials interviewed for this chapter questioned this public rationale, given the timing of the Liberal Cabinet's decision to invest so unexpectedly in Afghanistan. In early 2003, Canada was under pressure from Washington and London to participate in the looming war in Iraq. At home there was significant opposition to this US-led campaign. Some believe that the governing Liberals wanted to demonstrate that Canada was carrying its weight in the "War on Terror," while at the same time supporting the "softer" side of the struggle: multilateral state building. If this is the case, it would explain the significant amount of money that was channelled through multilateral agencies and toward a large number of good-governance and rule-of-law projects designed to support Afghanistan's nascent government. As will be discussed later, however, it appears that systemic factors dictated the Canadian aid program and not political or strategic considerations.

In general, even the nominal strategic objectives in Canada were rather vague. It was difficult for those making planning and operational decisions at the bureaucratic level to fathom Canada's commitment to maximizing the benefit to "traditional allies." More important, the four reasons given for Canada's involvement did not draw a map of specific Canadian interests in Afghanistan, except insofar as they reflected an overly broad desire to avoid a NATO failure and to help improve the lot of Afghans. This lack of specificity hampered later efforts to focus Canada's development and reconstruction assistance.

### The 3D Approach

Canada's commitment to Afghanistan was intended to be a coordinated effort involving DFAIT, DND, and CIDA. Traditionally, interdepartmental coordination in Ottawa has been sporadic at best. In the case of the three principal internationally focused departments, cooperation has often been overshadowed by competition. This is not to say that coordination does not exist. As CIDA officials pointed out in the course of this research, departmental cooperation occurs frequently, figures prominently as a key principle in CIDA's 2002 Strengthening Aid Effectiveness policy, and was a cornerstone of Prime Minister Paul Martin's 2005 International Policy Statement (IPS). However, during the early stages of Canada's involvement in Afghanistan, the IPS remained incomplete and the vast majority of those interviewed for this paper agreed that cooperation was inconsistent and ad hoc.

In the case of Afghanistan, the Clerk of the Privy Council explicitly directed the three departments to work together under a unified strategy. Senior bureaucrats, working at the assistant deputy minister (ADM) level, repeatedly made it clear that a "Whole of Government Approach" was necessary, and officials were encouraged to find ways to cooperate across departmental lines. Setting an example, the ADMs took the unprecedented step of meeting weekly to review progress on the Afghanistan issue. At the working level, deputy directors were in daily contact to ensure, with varying degrees of success, that individual departmental initiatives were mutually supportive. This initiative was called "3D" after its principal component parts: defence, development, and diplomacy. Eventually other federal departments and agencies such as the RCMP and Justice Canada participated. The overlapping priorities of the three departments were limited, but there was agreement on the importance of supporting the emergence of a stable Afghan government.

Of all of CIDA's programming options, those which supported elections and institution building provided the most obvious common ground. Each department could draw a direct link between the establishment of a stable political environment in Kabul and the success of its specific departmental objectives. In reality, each department largely continued to follow its own priorities on the ground, even if Afghanistan marked the first time that any effort was made to ensure that officials knew about one other's activities and attempted to coordinate them as closely as possible. The 3D concept improved communication in Ottawa and in the field; it also fostered a new sense of common purpose among the often estranged military, diplomatic, and development branches of the Canadian government. But it is difficult to discern any example of a governance project that was instituted directly as a result of this new cooperation.

## Specific Canadian Governance Projects

Canada's governance projects in Afghanistan have been highly diverse, as illustrated by the three notable examples below.

**THE CONSTITUTIONAL COMMISSION**   Emerging from the Bonn Agreement was a political road map for holding national elections. One of the first and most important milestones was the drafting of a new constitution. Canada contributed $1,750,000 to support this process, which entailed the establishment of a Constitutional Drafting Commission consisting of nine legal scholars and jurists, including two women. The draft was completed in late 2003 and presented to the Constitutional Loya Jirga. Against the expectations of many, the constitution was accepted and was seen as relatively democratic and progressive. The commission's work in preparing a draft that addressed the contradictory aspirations of Afghan society has been hailed as one of the great successes of the post-Taliban period.

**VOTER REGISTRATION**   Another critical step toward meeting the objectives of the Bonn Agreement was the registration of Afghan voters prior to the presidential elections. Complicating the already daunting task of finding and registering 13.5 million voters in the midst of an Afghan winter was the fact that large parts of the countryside were still unstable and that security fears prevented international elections workers from moving freely. Canada was one of the first donors to support the voter registration by providing $10,450,000 to the International Foundation for Election Systems (IFES). That funding was used to procure registration equipment in time to begin work before the snow blocked access to the remote mountain regions. The process was considered a great success: 90 percent of eligible voters registered. This encouraged international donors and the Afghan government to pursue the Bonn timetable of elections unfazed by threats of disruption from the Taliban and disaffected warlords.

**STRATEGIC ADVISORY TEAM (DND SECONDMENT PROJECT)**   In 2005 the Department of National Defence quietly launched an interesting innovation that went well beyond the traditional role of the Canadian Forces in peacebuilding missions. Fifteen DND employees, including civilians, were seconded to the Afghan government to act as technical governance advisers. The advisers focused on assisting Afghan officials on governance as well as on social and economic development. This project included activities ranging from budget management to donor relations. The placements included the Office of President Karzai, where DND planners helped produce a strategy to coordinate donor projects. In September 2005 the initiative was renewed with the rotation of fifteen new Canadian staff into Kabul. The project has been funded through the DND budgetary envelope, separate from CIDA's governance spending.

The Strategic Advisory Team initiative was a remarkable deviation from normal practices. Prior to it, the Canadian Forces' forays into development assistance had been limited to Canadian Civil-Military Affairs projects (CIMICS). These are usually small infrastructure projects within the military's zone of operations and are designed largely to "win hearts and minds." Examples in Afghanistan include providing school tents, rehabilitating Kabul's fire department, and reconstructing a water reservoir and pump system. These projects are a regular point of friction between CIDA and DND because of conflicting mandates. CIDA's long-term approach to development decisions with a particular emphasis on sustainable development can clash with DND's short-term operational needs. The Canadian Forces may see a well-digging project on their patrol route as an expeditious way to build a working relationship with local leaders, while CIDA may question how it would fit into broader developmental priorities.

It is perhaps because of these conflicting objectives that DND chose not to seek funding or other assistance from CIDA when Canadian personnel were placed in strategic locations within the Afghan government. On the positive side, this permitted DND to address needs quickly soon after they were identified without going through CIDA's more time-consuming project approval procedures. It also stands as a good example of a governance project that helped the Afghan government while simultaneously supporting parallel Canadian objectives (in this case strengthening ISAF's strategic partner in key areas). Critics in other departments have argued that the DND officials seconded into the Afghan government are not trained in providing technical assistance and that this project's objectives may fall outside the agreed NDF. In this case, however, the former Afghan Finance Minister Ashraf Ghani has specifically singled out the Canadian Forces as one of the most effective organizations for delivering assistance and praised their ability to operate efficiently and smoothly within the priorities of the Afghan leadership (Ghani 2005).

As of 2005, it was too soon to measure the impact of this initiative, but senior officers within DND were optimistic. They were also impressed by the initial results (Capstick 2005). For example, the project's contribution to ensuring that individual departments coordinate their individual objectives within the broader NDF was widely hailed as an important one. It is likely that in future circumstances where Canada is engaged in post-conflict reconstruction, the Canadian Forces will use similar mechanisms to deliver strategically placed governance assistance.

## Assessing the Process

### Obstacles to Strategic Programming

For several reasons, CIDA did not begin with an overarching list of priorities for its governance assistance program in Afghanistan. First and foremost, there was no up-to-date governance policy to guide programming decisions. The last major policy paper on the topic had been written almost ten years previously; it was largely unknown at headquarters and had never been seen in Kabul. A 1997 paper commissioned by CIDA to examine its governance program listed the following four governance priorities for the Asia Branch:

- to strengthen the role and build the capacity of civil society and democratic institutions;
- to promote the effective and accountable exercise of power by the public sector;
- to support organizations that promote and protect human rights; and
- to strengthen the will of leaders to respect democratic rights. (CIDA 1997)

CIDA officials interviewed for this chapter stated that these priorities were not taken into account in programming decisions. Rather, it was CIDA's broader institutional objectives—to support the developmental priorities of the Afghan government (as outlined in the agreed NDF), and to avoid overlap with other donors—that were the foremost strategic considerations guiding its policy.

In the case of Afghanistan, Canada's governance programming appeared to be largely dictated by tactical realities. Foremost among these was the fact that the small Canadian embassy were extremely overburdened: there were only two CIDA officers[10] on the ground. Keeping in mind that Afghanistan was the largest aid recipient in Canadian history, the small CIDA unit in Kabul simply could not be expected to provide a sophisticated delivery strategy for particular components of the aid envelope. According to staff on the ground, most implementation decisions were necessarily taken in an ad hoc fashion, in response to proposals from the Afghan government or international agencies. Not surprisingly, this led to the consideration of proposals on short notice and on a rolling basis; frequently, funding opportunities could not be compared relative to one another.

Some Canadian domestic pressures do nevertheless influence governance programming decisions. Chief among these is the need to disburse the allocated funds within the fiscal year. This pressure naturally discourages a more measured approach to crafting a long-term *Canadian* governance strategy on the ground. In addition, in 2002–3 Ottawa was anxious to promote a 3D approach to funding decisions, which meant that DFAIT and DND priorities would also have to be taken into account, further complicating the task of crafting a consistent governance program.

## Canada's Interlocutors

Canadian officials in Kabul make programming decisions based on input from an unusually wide network of interlocutors. Due to the embassy's high profile in Kabul, the Canadian Ambassador and his staff enjoyed frequent access to key Afghan decision makers all the way up to the President. Initially, an important reason for this was that, compared to their British and American colleagues, Canadian diplomats were able to circulate more freely in Kabul due to lower threat levels against Canadian nationals. Unfortunately, as the Canadian profile rose, so did the threat level, and eventually the embassy staff found themselves equally hamstrung by security precautions.

The embassy's high profile also gave the ambassador and his staff a higher level of influence than anywhere else in the world at that time. This influence is reflected in the broad network of interlocutors, which stretches well beyond the Afghan Cabinet. The CIDA officer, for example, regularly talks to ISAF officers, relevant government officials, and the heads of the international agencies and significant NGOs. In this regard, governance programming decisions are taken within a broad context of opinions and collaborating information.

In terms of execution, CIDA's main interlocutors for delivering its governance programs were a small number of large international agencies. The UNDP office in Kabul has been its principal partner, most notably in the voter registration project. Following closely is the IFES, an American-based non-profit organization that specializes in delivering support for elections and rule-of-law projects.

## Determining Canada's Impact on Governance in Afghanistan

### Challenges in Measurement

There are a number of reasons why it is difficult to assess the overall impact of Canada's governance program in Afghanistan or the impact of specific projects. First, the donors and the Afghan government are attempting to build democratic institutions almost from scratch, and these are still early days. Progress is slow and incremental and will be measured over decades, not fiscal years. Similarly, the impact of Canada's governance projects will only be felt over time. While donors can point to the two successful Loya Jirgas and the presidential elections as important historic milestones, their success depended as much on a stable military environment as on particular governance projects.

Second, as suggested above, most of CIDA's governance funds were contributed as portions of larger projects. In these cases, the recipient agencies have treated the Canadian money as fungible, making it difficult to directly track the impact of specific contributions.

Third, due to the limited number of CIDA staff on the ground, it was extremely difficult—bordering on impossible—to closely track the impact of individual projects. For the most part, CIDA relied on assessments provided by recipient agencies, and in many cases these assessments have not yet been provided. Furthermore, project reports generally cover the overall impact of projects, not specific elements that may have been funded by Canadian contributions.

### Relationship with Other Donors

Canada's efforts in governance were not intended to be distinct from those of other donors. Instead of seeking to carve out a unique program that was clearly "Canadian," the embassy and CIDA officials in Ottawa opted to support multilateral initiatives that were already under way. The vast majority of Canadian money spent on governance was applied to parts of larger projects prioritized through the NDF. This approach is part of a broader strategy to bolster the coordinated multilateral efforts of the international community and to avoid duplicating the efforts of other donors. It is also relatively cost effective, since it means that Canada does not have to undertake its own needs assessments and can directly contribute funds to larger multilateral projects that do not require as much CIDA oversight. Furthermore, the lack of Canadian governance experts with experience in Afghanistan would have hampered the effectiveness of Canadian-branded stand-alone projects.

This collegial approach to donor funding, which sees Canada's contribution absorbed into a multilateral effort, does have its shortcomings. To begin with, in the case of Afghanistan, Canada did not play a significant role in determining the overall design of the NDF and therefore trusted many of its underlying assumptions to external players such as the US State Department and the Japanese International Cooperation Agency. There is also the issue of visibility and credit. Being a "good team player" means that the broader Afghan public and fellow donors are not as likely to recognize Canada's contribution. While this does not affect the impact of projects, it does undermine Canada's diplomatic and military interests in the region—a reality that Canadian development actors need to better understand. In Kabul, this has been mitigated by the very public and active role played by Ambassador Alexander and Generals Leslie and Hillier.

Finally, as we have suggested, a collaborative approach prevents the implementation of a coordinated Canadian strategy that takes Canadian strategic interests into account. These interests are not explicitly identified beyond the ex post facto list: supporting multilateral agencies, the "War on Terror," the

Afghan people, and the efforts of bilateral allies. If, as a hypothetical example, it had been determined in 2001 that Canada had a strategic interest in the development of the trans-Afghan pipeline, which would foster investment and provide commercial opportunities for the Canadian oil patch, a bilateral approach to governance funding would have permitted CIDA to support the development of the Afghan Ministry of Natural Resources. Or, to take another example, it is not clear to Canadian planners and managers whether achieving stability in one Afghan province is more important than achieving it in another. Because funds are being channelled through a multilateral framework, room for making these kinds of strategic calculations remains limited. It should be emphasized, however, that for a strategic approach to be useful, clear national and departmental interests need to be identified from the beginning; furthermore, they must be objective and obvious enough that civil servants can use them as guideposts for crafting a programmatic response.[11]

### Relative Size of Canada's Aid Program

The relative size of the Canadian governance effort during this period made it unlikely that the overall program would make a large impact, or one distinct from that of the international community at large. Governance is a cross-cutting issue, and for the reasons discussed above, it is very difficult to extract the precise amount spent on it by Canada—or by other donors, for that matter. If overall spending patterns are used as an indicator, Canada's contribution has been a drop in the bucket. Although it is the largest Canadian aid effort in history, it still ranked only ninth on disbursed aid among donors overall and tenth on pledged donations among donors overall. (See Figure 2.) This represents 3 percent of disbursed assistance and less than 1 percent of total aid pledged.

### Intended and Unintended Effects

Canada's overall impact on the reform and development of Afghanistan's government has been limited; even so, it has had several notable side effects. The main one is that it has enhanced Canada's diplomatic profile in Afghanistan, due largely to the timely support of the voter registration project, which was widely welcomed at the time. This improved the embassy's access to important government decision makers and helped Canada "sit at the table" among the other core donors as a key contributor. This project also facilitated broader coalition objectives at key moments when momentum was needed—a fact that was recognized and appreciated both at the UN and in the donor community.

## FIGURE 2
### Total Aid Pledges from Major Donors

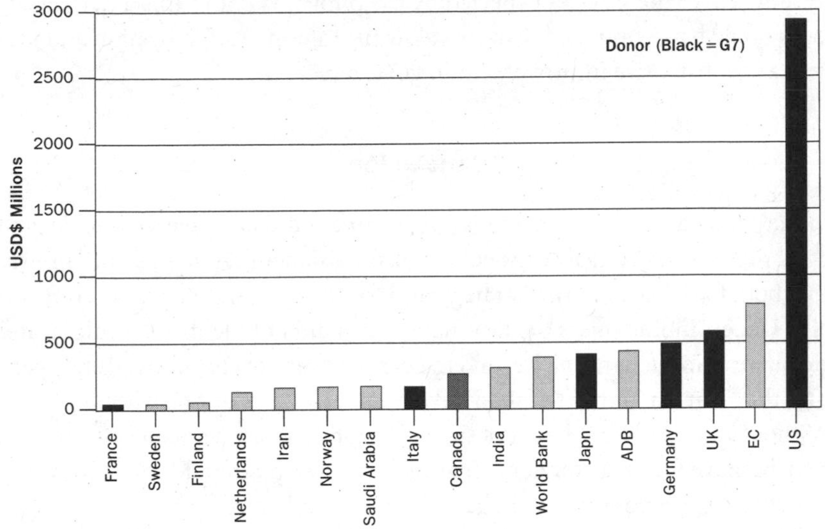

*Source*: Afghan Ministry of Finance, based on data available as of October 1, 2004.

The governance program has also provided access to nascent political parties, which are being nurtured by projects such as those executed by the National Democratic Institute (NDI). While this will not pay dividends right away, it has strengthened relations with future Afghan politicians and built up Canada's political capital in the country. In the coming years, these small investments may reap significant diplomatic rewards.

### The Governance Impact of Non-Governance Aid

In examining the case of Afghanistan, it is important to note that some of the Canadian-supported initiatives that would not normally be classified as governance projects have had a significant impact on governance objectives nonetheless. One example already discussed is the Afghanistan Reconstruction Trust Fund, which is intended to provide budgetary support for the operating costs of the fledgling government of President Karzai. As former finance minister Ashraf Ghani has frequently pointed out, donors cannot expect postconflict governments to develop effectively if many of the traditional tasks of central administration are being delivered through internationally funded NGOs. By giving the Afghan government budgetary support, CIDA has provided the new government with increased sovereignty and in the process enhanced the capacity of the bureaucracy to shoulder its expected duties.

In a similar vein, Canadian efforts in the cantonment of heavy weapons in Kabul had a direct impact on the new government's ability to extend its authority and deliver the services expected by the public. Without this aid, the warlords would have continued to overshadow the Interim Administration and prevent any substantive improvement in governance.

## Conclusion

In the period 2001 to 2005, Canada's government did not have a strategic plan or set of priorities for delivering governance assistance in Afghanistan. This was true both for CIDA's internal strategy and for that of the broader 3D community. Underpinning this is the fact that Ottawa did not identify specific strategic interests in Afghanistan beyond the baseline support for multilateral agencies, the "War on Terror," Afghan development, and relations with key allies. Without a clear understanding of Canadian interests, a governance plan would have been useful solely for coordinating efforts with other donors and would not effectively support or leverage strategic Canadian goals.

Ideally, before the initial decision to send troops and aid to Afghanistan, the Cabinet would have agreed on and articulated a set of Canadian interests in the region and within the coalition. From that, officials could have developed a more detailed 3D strategy that included a coordinated approach to governance assistance. That strategy, in turn, would have allowed Canadian officials in Bonn and elsewhere to help formulate the NDF. While Canada did participate in the process that established the NDF as an overarching strategic road map, it did not play a significant role in defining its priorities. A more coordinated approach would have made it easier for the development, diplomatic, and defence initiatives of the three departments to mutually support one another on the ground in Afghanistan.

Closer interdepartmental coordination implies a certain degree of compromise on the part of CIDA, DFAIT, and DND, with each department having to sacrifice some policy independence. Understandably, this makes some officials nervous. CIDA has an additional reason to be wary of further coordination, and that is the belief that closer cooperation with DND would compromise the agency's relatively neutral reputation in a volatile security environment. This concern is usually cited in relation to the PRTs, which partner small military teams with a small number of diplomats and development officers. In the context of Afghanistan, however, it is highly unlikely that the Taliban would see CIDA as a neutral party, regardless of its level of cooperation with DND.

From 2001 to 2005, Canadian officials on the ground were too few in number to implement effectively a coordinated governance strategy, given the scope of the combined tasks of delivering the 3D aid. As a result, Canada's governance projects were loosely based on recipient country needs; they were chosen largely according to individual project opportunities as they arose in order to fill the many gaps identified by the NDF. The needs listed in the NDF were broad enough that there were numerous opportunities to address Afghan and Canadian priorities simultaneously. But while using recipient nation priorities as a framework for tailoring aid programs is an important operating principle, it cannot substitute for a coherent aid strategy.

There was undoubtedly very good work being done in Kabul by Canadian officials on the ground. But the governance projects that were funded were highly diverse. While some were important successes, such as the voter registration process, overall there was no reliable way of consistently measuring the impact of individual donations or the cumulative impact of the Canadian governance program. Without an overarching strategic plan, it was difficult to coordinate governance initiatives in such a way as to leverage either Canada's additional value in particular areas of governance such as elections, or Canada's larger strategic interests in the region.

As a postscript, the period 2005 to 2007 saw a considerable evolution in Canada's 3D activities in Afghanistan. The Liberal government was replaced by the Conservative government of Prime Minister Stephen Harper, who immediately emphasized the central importance of Afghanistan to his foreign policy by travelling to Kandahar and stating that Canada would be there for the long haul and would not "cut and run" (Harper 2006b). With a new government came the renewed efforts of CIDA's president, Robert Greenhill, to modernize and improve the organization's impact and efficiency. As an example, the Afghan team at headquarters was increased approximately tenfold, to over seventy people. At Foreign Affairs, the Afghan task force also increased dramatically in size, and the Prime Minister appointed a senior diplomat, David Mulroney, to act as an Afghanistan "czar," coordinating the interdepartmental efforts.

In the field, the Canadian embassy country team was expanded, and with the deployment of troops to Kandahar, the entire Canadian focus shifted south. A PRT was deployed to Kandahar city, and included DFAIT and CIDA personnel. More CIDA money was pledged, over and above the previous large commitments made by the Martin government. In fiscal year 2006–7, $139 million was disbursed, and an additional $100 million per year was pledged through 2011, with an additional $200 million on top of that for 2007–8 (PM Harper Press Release February 26, 2007). During this expansion of Canada's efforts, governance has been given a new emphasis as one of CIDA's three priorities, with more explicit measurements for tracking progress. Unlike previous donor coordination exercises, Canada played a much larger role in the multilateral development of the Afghanistan Compact, which sets out detailed areas of focus for the donors and specific indicators of progress.

With these additional resources, and more people in Ottawa and Afghanistan to manage the assistance, it appears much more likely that Canada will be able to harmonize its governance assistance both with its partners and with Canada's own strategic agenda.

## Notes

\* This case study was researched and written in autumn 2005 and reflects statistics and policies current at that time.

1 In 2005 it was surpassed by Iraq.

2 *Shura* is Arabic for "council"; *jirga* is the much older Pashtu term for a similar mechanism.

3 A subjective term that in this case refers to the United States, the United Kingdom, Germany, Saudi Arabia, Japan, Pakistan, Iran, and the EU, in rough order of influence.

4 Particularly at the donor pledging conference in Berlin in March 2004.

5 This was pledged in two different tranches: $100M in Tokyo, and $250M in Brussels in April 2003.

6 OECD DAC 2004, Donor Aid Charts (http://www.oecd.org/dac). Note: These numbers differ from Government of Canada figures because the OECD uses different definitions of what constitutes assistance.

7 The total cost of the Canadian Forces deployment can be calculated in several ways, as many of the costs have been absorbed by existing budgets. At a minimum, the incremental cost for Operation Apollo was at least $900 million; the total cost, however, was significantly higher. (See "Budget 2005: Chapter 6 Meeting our Global Responsibilities," Department of Finance Canada; http://www.fin.gc.ca/budget05/bp/bpc6e.htm.)

8 The problem of how to accurately code projects and track disbursements accordingly is an important one. Without an accurate or consistent labelling system, decision makers are deprived of a fundamental tool for strategic planning. In the case of Afghanistan, it would be a crude approach to simply give each project one label. At a minimum, there should be consistent use of the coding so that every level of decision making from the field to the Minister's Office can work with the same numbers.

9 Some officials in CIDA have asserted that this is a very narrow view of what constitutes governance programming that fails to recognize the important governance aspects of initiatives such as demobilization and heavy weapons cantonment (in-

cluded under Security Sector Reform); work in the justice sector; or support to the Afghan government for program coherence and development. However, for the sake of clarity, the authors have chosen to focus on those projects which have a primary or significant secondary impact on governance objectives.

10  From the embassy's opening in 2002 until mid-2004, there was only one CIDA officer on the ground, supported by a Project Support Unit staffed by contracted employees. With the launch of the Canadian PRT, this was increased to two CIDA officers in Kabul and one in Kandahar. As of February 2006 there were three CIDA officers in Kabul.

11  Canada has since identified Kandahar as a strategically important province and has shifted its priorities accordingly.

▲

# 8

## THE PERILS OF CHANGING DONOR PRIORITIES IN FRAGILE STATES: THE CASE OF HAITI

### Robert Muggah

*Better governance within fragile, failing or failed states means building effective public institutions.... We saw this in Haiti. Almost 10 years ago Canada, the United States and some other countries intervened to help restore the then-democratically elected president back into office who had been overthrown in a coup.... The problem is that none of us, neither the States nor Canada nor France ... stayed long enough nor did we make the time and the effort that was required to build these institutions. So 10 years later, here we are, back with the same problem and the same mess, but this time, we have got to stay until the job is done properly.*

*—Paul Martin, July 7, 2004*

### Introduction

Building better—much less good—governance takes time and sustained commitment. Despite considerable investment, only meagre dividends have been realized in Haiti, a country that has experienced more than thirty military coups and twenty constitutions since independence in 1804. Even before the notorious Duvalier dictatorships came to an end in the mid-1980s, Haiti was described alternately as "failing," "failed," and "fragile" in international policy circles. By far the poorest country in the Western Hemisphere and rated the world's most corrupt, Haiti has the ignoble distinction of being categorized as both a "fragile state" and a "difficult partner" by Canada and many others in the international community. Canada's lengthy and troubled experience of promoting good governance in Haiti yields compelling insights into the real challenges accompanying sustained investment in failing states.

Following a historical overview of the country's governance crisis, this chapter traces out the endogenous and exogenous causes of Haiti's protracted fragility. It finds that failures in governance are frequently attributed to Haitians "from below" rather than as a result of external geopolitical manipulation and flawed prescriptions mandated "from above." Next, the chapter chronicles Canada's specific role and record in governance promotion between 1990 and 2006. Canada's approach has oscillated between reinforcing public institutions and more radical efforts that bypass the state altogether in order to strengthen "civil society." Though Canada has played a prominent role in promoting governance—particularly through multilateral intermediaries such as the UN, the Organization of American States (OAS), and a host of non-governmental organizations, its strategic approach has been heavily influenced by other donors. Weaknesses in its overall strategy include ambiguous and shifting definitions of governance, a simplistic understanding of the local context and appropriate "entry points," and difficulties in forging coherence with strategic partners. The chapter concludes with a number of reflections on how governance promotion might be strengthened in the context of fragile states and difficult partners.

### Chronicling State Failure

Though spectacular levels of violence have featured in media headlines since the ouster of President Jean-Bertrand Aristide in early 2004, Haiti has in fact suffered from a profound crisis of governance for decades. After the promulgation of a new constitution in 1987, the country was crippled by chronic political instability at the centre. Positive gains arising from the democratic transfer of power to President Aristide in 1990 were quickly reversed after his forced removal less than twelve months later by Lieutenant General Raoul Cédras of the Haitian Armed Forces (FADH). To pressure Cédras to reinstate Aristide, the UN, the OAS, and various major donors—including the United States, the European Union (EU), France, Canada, and the World Bank—applied mandatory and voluntary sanctions[1] and authorized a large-scale US-led intervention force and UN mission (UNMIH) between 1993 and 1996 (Muggah and Krause 2006).

After he was reinstated in 1994, Aristide promptly disbanded the FADH and by presidential decree re-formed the Haitian National Police (HNP) as the sole provider of state security. A limited US Army and USAID-led weapons buy-back and demobilization initiative was launched to return the FADH to civilian life. This effort was described as a "dismal failure" by American generals at the time because of how the weapons were merely recirculated and because command and control remained largely untouched. New elections in 1996 heralded in President René Préval, then a close ally of Aristide, and aid poured into the country for the next few years. But donors made only modest improvements to the country's re-established police force, and meanwhile, donor fatigue was mounting, with the UN coming under mounting pressure to phase out peacekeeping and civilian police (CIVPOL) operations completely.[2] By the end of 1997 the UN had ended many of its peacekeeping operations and only a small CIVPOL contingent remained. The Préval administration faced a succession of political deadlocks as well as popular discontent spurred on by civil society, notably pro-Lavalas groups and thugs.

The years 1998 to 2002 were especially dark. Widespread corruption—including within the HNP and the customs service—became increasingly difficult to conceal, and political violence once again escalated. By mid-1998 approximately US$340 million was held back by international financial institutions (IFIs) for reasons of "political instability, woefully poor governance and corruption" (World Bank 2002b). Meanwhile, Canada and the OAS continued to promote conventional "technical" governance activities—particularly the strengthening of key public-sector institutions (such as the Treasury), training for the judiciary, and human rights monitoring through NGOs, all of this with limited success. Multilateral and bilateral efforts to stimulate economic growth, promote social development, and strengthen the security sector came to a grinding halt following the hotly contested legislative elections and the re-election of Aristide in 2000. By 2001 the UN had almost entirely closed down its activities in the country: only essential UNDP staff working and representatives of a handful of operational agencies remained. The World Bank announced once again that it was suspending its loans.

In 2002 the country began to implode. A rash of cross-border massacres by "rebels"—in fact, they were paramilitary death squads and FADH soldiers—was tipping the country into chaos. Few actors, including the Caribbean community (CARICOM), were prepared to intervene beyond the usual expressions of concern and outrage. From this point on most donors, including Canada, along with the commercial elite and the Diaspora, became demonstrably uneasy with the president's autocratic style and use of armed militias, nicknamed the *chimère*. As will be discussed below in more detail, certain donors began indirectly supporting the recruitment and training of "opposition groups" (their euphemism for this was "governance activities") in the Dominican Republic, Chile, and Washington, DC.[3] In February 2004 the so-called rebels headed by a former police commissioner stormed the capital and Aristide was spirited away by a US aircraft, bound for Africa. He disembarked in the Central African Republic before pushing on to South Africa, where he currently resides.

In April 2004, almost exactly a decade after the last large-scale peacekeeping mission came to an end, the UN Security Council (UNSC) again sanctioned a Chapter VII intervention. UNSC resolutions 1529 and 1542 established the UN Stabilization Mission in Haiti (MINUSTAH) with an initial twelve-month mandate, later extended into 2007. Within weeks of Aristide's departure a caretaker government had been installed to prepare the country for legislative and presidential elections in November 2005. While the new interim government periodically demonstrated a will for genuine reform, it was hampered from the beginning by a marked inability to absorb funds, weak institutional capacity, and signs of flagrant corruption. The executive was undermined by the absence of a sitting, elected legislative body and could only legislate through executive decree.[4] What is more, the government's credibility had been eroded by its manifest inability to demonstrate gains in public security. Progress in promoting governance was painfully slow and an admittedly secondary priority among donors to ensuring safety and security on the ground.

A centralized funding mechanism—the Interim Cooperation Framework (ICF)—was established soon after the interim government was installed. The ICF combined a needs assessment with a mechanism for pooling pledges and harmonizing programs, with some allowance for earmarked contributions. The ICF promoted four pillars to guide recovery and reconstruction: political governance and national dialogue; economic governance and institutional development; economic recovery; and access to basic services. In July 2004 more than US$1.089 billion was pledged by over a dozen countries (with the United States and Canada spearheading the contributions).[5] The expectation was that the mechanism would ensure coherence of priorities between donors and the interim government. Many also expected that the ICF would serve as the basis for a future Poverty Reduction Strategy Paper (PRSP). Its mandate was eventually extended to September 2007.

But as has so often been the case in Haiti, expectations severely misjudged realities. Part of the problem was inherent to the multidonor ICF itself. For one thing, it lacked vertical and horizontal legitimacy. The mechanism had been hastily cobbled together over two months in mid-2004 by 26 bilateral and multilateral partners—including 250 national and international experts— and was to be jointly overseen by the World Bank, the UN, and the Inter-American Development Bank (IADB). As such, it was never "owned" in any meaningful sense by Haitians and the process was hardly "inclusive" beyond consultations in the capital of Port-au-Prince and to a lesser extent in the regions. Moreover, the ICF's objectives were overambitious, given the political and economic realities among donors and on the ground. Twelve months after its creation, it was reported that less than 10 percent of the earmarked funds had been disbursed.[6] Commitment to the ICF was erratic, and certain donors—notably the United States and France—were bypassing it completely before the ink had even dried on the agreement.[7] As so often happens with pooled funding mechanisms, pledged moneys failed to materialize despite a series of international conferences in 2004 and 2005 to shore up support.[8] What is more, the commitment of regional partners—especially countries like Brazil, Argentina, and Chile, which for the first time were directing a UN peacekeeping force—began to waver, as declared UNSC priorities were abandoned and their own domestic constituencies began asking uncomfortable questions about the mission's effectiveness. In 2005 and 2006, as a result of mounting international pressure—from senior UN policy-makers in New York and Port-au-Prince, as well as from human rights groups—MINUSTAH peacekeepers began adopting increasingly aggressive tactics to counter armed gangs in the shantytowns of urban centres. In late 2006 and early 2007, armed civilians were given an ultimatum: disarm or die.

## The Causes of Haiti's Governance Deficit

Haiti's governance crisis is often blamed on the Haitians. In other words, it is viewed as a consequence of weaknesses in Haitian society associated with political illegitimacy, rampant corruption, and structural underdevelopment.[9] Lip service is paid occasionally to the crippling effects of geopolitics on the country's political and economic development, though this is seldom reflected in the mainstream Western media, much less academic discourse. It is true that Haitians are partly responsible for the collapse of governance "from below." Few observers dispute the existence of deep political, social, and economic cleavages in Haitian society, which are a consequence of the country's legacy of authoritarianism between the 1950s and 1980s, as well as the militarized populist politics of the early 1990s. And no one disagrees that these political and social problems are compounded by systemic corruption at the centre and by poor macroeconomic planning.

Except for a brief interlude in the mid-1990s, the state appears to be reluctant to and incapable of sustaining and managing accountable, legitimate, and accessible public services for the vast majority of urban and rural Haitians. It can be argued that a poisonous cocktail of corruption, divisive politics, weak or predatory state services outside the capital, and a precarious economic environment has contributed to a series of violent outbursts over the past two decades. But as will be discussed next, exogenous factors have played an equally insidious role in shaping the contours of governance "from above."

### Endogenous Factors

For at least the past five decades, political power in Haiti has been concentrated within a small political and commercial elite. From the 1950s into the 1980s, Haiti was governed by brutal dictatorships that showed little interest in democratic or pro-poor policies.[10] As was typical of the Cold War era, donors were relatively content with the stability such dictatorships provided—especially given the proximity of nearby Communist Cuba—and with the visible order they imposed.

Following the meteoric rise of Jean-Bertrand Aristide and his Lavalas Party in the 1990s, a strong populist and pro-poor sentiment temporarily defined the political landscape. Aristide had come, after all, from the ghettos surrounding Port-au-Prince and claimed to know what poverty was all about. But in the turbulent 1990s, both Lavalas and mainstream opposition parties practised a highly personalized politics, one that focused on unseating individuals (or worse) and advancing personal agendas rather than propounding viable social platforms. The result was an increasingly polarized political space and the erosion of any predictability or stability; instead of forming coalitions, opposition parties and citizen movements contested power in a zero-sum, winner-take-all game.

A monumental obstacle to legitimate, predictable, and efficient governance in Haiti is corruption, which has been endemic there since the 1970s, long before the term crept into the international discourse on development and governance in the 1990s (see Smillie, this book). In 2004, Transparency International rated Haiti the most corrupt country in the world (out of 145), though its ranking seems to have improved since then.[11] Since the early 1990s, key donors—including the United States, Canada, the EU, and France—have repeatedly identified corruption as one of the primary factors corroding their bilateral relationships with Haiti's central authorities, regardless of the regime.[12] But corruption and the illegitimacy it fosters extend well beyond the ruling elite; it has burrowed deep into the security sector, the judiciary, and other line agencies. As a result, donors have adopted extremely cautious approaches in their dealings with Haiti's formal institutions.

Despite a succession of large-scale UN-led interventions and considerable inflows of aid to the country designed specifically to stimulate economic growth, the country's macroeconomic record is woeful, marked by persistently high inflation and intermittently negative growth (see Figure 1).[13] Accord-

FIGURE 1
Economic Indicators, 1990–2004

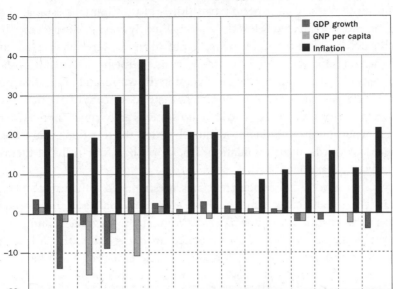

*Source*: http://www.worldbank.org/data.

ing to the World Bank, the structural conditions for rapid growth in Haiti were simply not present in the 1990s. The macroeconomic environment was then and still is characterized by a small export sector, the elites' monopoly on imports of basic goods and commodities, a massive informal sector dependent on subsistence agriculture and remittances, and a long-standing dependence on ODA to shore up government revenues. Haitians rely heavily on unsteady wages in the informal sector. National budgets are seldom issued, and the country's escalating deficit has repeatedly been financed by bonds issued by the National Bank. As a result of severe economic decline fuelled by multilateral and unilateral sanctions [14] as well as natural disasters throughout the 1990s, remittances from diaspora Haitians increased from US$256 to $931 million annually between 1997 and 2002 ($4 billion over the past decade). Today, remittances are the primary source of domestic revenue.[15] Because of prolific corruption and physical insecurity, direct foreign investment has fallen to the point that the World Bank, the IMF, and the IADB have repeatedly suspended loans over the past two decades and repeatedly downgraded the country.[16]

Because of the unstable macro- and micro-economic environment, the country's human development indices are well below comparator countries and among the lowest in the world. In 2003, Haiti ranked 153rd out of 177 countries on the UNDP's Human Development Index (UNDP 2004b). This actually represents a decline over the past decade; in 1992 the country ranked 148th out of 175. Over the same period, two-thirds of the country's estimated 8.4 million people remained below the poverty line. By 2004, life expectancy had declined to less than fifty-three years, half of all adults were still illiterate, and less than one-quarter of rural children were attending primary school. Infant mortality rates are today among the highest in the world, and under-five mortality is 118 per 1,000. What is more, less than 40 percent of Haitians have access to safe drinking water, and sanitary systems are virtually non-existent. These national indicators do not adequately reflect the situation in rural areas, where two-thirds of the population live, more than four-fifths of them in poverty (Montas 2003).

Systemic poverty and demographic pressures, coupled with inefficient farming practices that increase vulnerability to environmental disasters, have combined to make Haiti one of the most environmentally degraded countries on the planet. These conditions have remained unchanged since the early 1990s. Since the 1990s, NGOs have been funding and implementing a number of significant social programs to reduce poverty and improve public services; however, the effectiveness of these has been dramatically reduced since the late 1990s as a result of acute political instability and physical insecurity. No surprise, then, given the country's barren environmental and economic landscape, that the governance agenda has failed to take root.

### Exogenous Factors

However dismal Haiti's internal state, external factors have also done much to cripple its capacity to govern. Arms transfers, narco-trafficking, and the in-migration of criminal elements greatly undermined the country's security environment in the 1990s and severely hampered efforts to promote rules-based and predictable governance. For example, though "official" exports of small arms to Haiti have been comparatively modest over the past two decades (due to a variety of OAS, UN, and US arms sanctions and the limited needs of the armed forces), the covert and illegal arms trade is thriving. It is believed that throughout the late 1990s, besides supporting "governance activities," elements within the US government channelled military equipment and training covertly to various anti-Lavalas militant groups and disgruntled FADH soldiers in the Dominican Republic (Muggah 2005a). What is more, black market trading for weapons persists through an "ant trade" for weapons between Haiti and its neighbours. Source countries for illegal weapons since the early 1990s include the United States, Jamaica, Colombia, Brazil, and the Dominican Republic, as well as Central America (Carment 2005; Muggah 2005b).

Other important exogenous factors include multilateral/unilateral interventionism and conditionality. For example, in the lead-up to the disputed elections won by Aristide in 2000, the OAS—backed mainly by the United States and Canada—exerted considerable pressure on the president and his allies through a combination of threats, sanctions, and the withholding of ODA. This pressure did not yield its desired effect (of keeping Aristide from being re-elected) and in fact worsened an already bad situation.[17] The fractious relations between donors and Haitian authorities resulted in uneven and wasted investment to the extent that "of the roughly US$2 billion spent by the international community between 1994 and 1998, there is today virtually no legacy" (Hawrylak and Malone 2005, 35). As a measure of their discontent, donors began to bypass Haitian authorities altogether and to support civil society organizations directly.

In Haiti's highly politicized environment, donors found it exceedingly difficult to locate alternative entry points to the state. In the early 1990s, donors began to conclude that the costs of missteps in an environment where political negotiations between coalitions regularly turned violent were far too high. In the latter half of the 1990s, frustrated by the increasingly aggressive postures adopted by Aristide, certain donors—including the United States and France—began to provide under-the-table support to civil society groups (anti-Lavalas parties). This included assistance to the "Group of 184" by the National Endowment for Democracy and the International Republican Institute—funds earmarked by the US State Department.

Even in the best of circumstances, it is a challenge to identify and strengthen civil society groups, which aid experts view as fundamental components of the governance agenda. After considerable efforts to strengthen voluntary associations, cooperatives, trade unions, and NGOs as service providers in a fragile state—and as a political counterweight to Aristide—the World Bank (2002b) concluded pessimistically that "the country appears to have a weak civil society with limited capacity to challenge public authorities in order to enhance their performance and responsiveness to the citizenry." Some senior donor representatives in Haiti noted with despair that Haiti lacked a civil society altogether.

As the following section will make clear, Canada's efforts to promote governance between 1990 and 2004 persisted despite far poorer than expected returns. As noted above, many other IFIs and donor governments found it difficult to justify continued ODA with so few dividends to show for it. Diplomats were quietly describing the country as a "black hole." Canada, often after pressure from the United States and France, periodically suspended its lending and grant activities to Haitian government bodies. The EU also suspended direct support to the government in 2001, though it continued to route some funds to civil society groups. As noted, the World Bank and the IADB were bitterly disappointed with Haiti's record since the mid-1980s, to the extent that they terminated lending in 1997 and again in 2001.[18] While these tactics reflected more general changes in the strategic orientation of donors such as the World Bank and the Canadian government, notably the refocusing of attention on "good performers," they also represented something of an indictment of donor-driven agendas in the 1990s.

### Why Does Canada Promote Good Governance in Haiti?

Despite an avowed commitment to promoting governance in Haiti, Canada and other countries have struggled to define what "good governance" actually means. When asked by the author what "governance" implies institutionally and practically, a number of senior DFAIT and CIDA representatives referred to CIDA policy statements or DFAIT reports,[19] though they could not personally offer a substantive definition. Meanwhile, as DFAIT and CIDA policy analysts hammered out the conceptual and practical parameters of good governance in the Haitian context, the issue quickly glided up the foreign policy agenda. Former prime minister Paul Martin repeatedly described governance as a key plank of Canada's strategy in the country: "As we have seen in Haiti, all the aid in the world will have only a fleeting effect if a country does not have functioning public institutions. We must build countries' governance capacities and take the time to do it right" (Canada 2004). The Harper administration confirmed in 2006 that it would "follow the lead of his [Prime Minister Harper's] predecessor" in making governance a priority" (McGregor 2006).[20]

In the 1990s, governance promotion was a euphemism inclusive of everything from nation building and democracy building to preparing for elections, monitoring human rights, strengthening rule of law, and reforming the public sector. As Ian Smillie notes in his chapter of this book, security sector reform (SSR) has also recently been added to the Canadian government's agenda. All of these priorities have been described as legitimate aspects of governance, along with other closely related thematic priorities such as poverty reduction and social justice promotion. For the purposes of this chapter, and because of the "maximalist" approach adopted by FAC and CIDA, governance is defined broadly and refers to the rules, systems, and institutions of the state and how they relate to civilians, civil society, and the private sector (Unsworth 2005). In this way, good governance can be equated with democratic principles, Weberian bureaucracies, and the promotion of transparent, predictable, and equitable state–society transactions.

Notwithstanding the persistent definitional dilemma, Canada's official approach to promoting governance in Haiti over the past few years has also been motivated by the now commonsense wisdom of engaging "fragile states"[21] and "difficult partners."[22] Canada therefore offers two good reasons to invest in governance—on the one hand it is the appropriate and moral thing to do, while on the other, it is justified in order prevent regional instability, including the internationalization of crime and terrorism. While strategic engagement with Haiti remains the only option, many in international and domestic policy circles have begun to (privately) toy with the idea of setting up a temporary UN protectorate, similar to those established in East Timor, Cambodia, and Kosovo. However, it seems highly unlikely at present that the either the Canadian public or the UNSC has the stomach for such a radical step (Hawrylak and Malone 2005).

Canada has played a leading role in promoting good governance in Haiti since the early 1990s. In spite of daunting political and economic challenges—or precisely because of them—in 2004 Haiti earned the (un)enviable distinction of being Canada's "most important long-term development assistance beneficiary in the Americas." The same year, to emphasize Canada's deep commitment, Prime Minister Paul Martin appointed a Special Advisor for Haiti. Moreover, Michaëlle Jean, Canada's newly appointed governor general, who is Haitian-born, made her country of birth the site of her first official visit in 2006. Because of the history and complexity of Canada's relationship with Haiti, and the two countries' cultural links, Canada's motives for engaging with it are stronger than they are for other priority countries, including Ghana, Vietnam, Bangladesh, and even Afghanistan (see chapter 7).

Canada's involvement in Haiti goes back many decades: it has maintained uninterrupted diplomatic relations since 1954 and has been a core development donor since 1968. As a highly visible partner, Canada has long claimed a special relationship with the country. Both are members of the Francophonie, and there are robust cultural, linguistic, and economic links between the two, especially between Montreal and Port-au-Prince.[23] In part because of international and domestic pressures, but also informed by the moral imperative noted earlier, since 1990 Canada has repeatedly played a major role in UN or OAS-led international interventions; at various times it has provided financial, military, humanitarian, and development assistance. And while Canadian concerns coincide with the realpolitik interests of the United States and France (e.g., containing refugee flows and terrorism), the bulk of its support goes toward broader and decidedly softer priorities. While the two clusters of interests and strategies—containment and development—clearly overlap, our interest in this chapter is on the latter.

The main Canadian entity promoting good governance is CIDA, which has been active in Haiti since the late 1960s. Between 1968 and 2005, CIDA transferred more than C$780 million of ODA to Haiti.[24] This figure excludes military and policing support provided by FAC, the DND, and the RCMP. CIDA's preferred vectors for governance promotion in complex environments—as with relief and development more generally—include multilateral and non-governmental "implementing partners." A shortlist of these includes the OAS, the UNDP, UNICEF, the UN Population Fund (UNFPA), the Food and Agriculture Organization (FAO), the World Food Program (WFP), the Pan-American Health Organization (PAHO), the International Committee of the Red Cross (ICRC), and national Red Cross associations. Canadian NGOs are also principal agents for ODA; these include Oxfam-Québec, International Child Care, the Société de Cooperation pour le Développement International, Terre sans Frontières, Save the Children Fund–Canada, and the Centre d'étude et de coopération internationale.

The promotion of good governance in Haiti assumed priority status for CIDA in the early 1990s. Though an empirical and disaggregated treatment of investments in governance promotion is rendered difficult by complicated and non-standardized reporting procedures, it is possible to parse out general trends (see Annex 1). Specific investments intended to promote good governance, such as election support (e.g., voter registration and independent election monitoring), public-sector reform, and small-scale civil society projects focusing on human rights promotion and the media, have long been channelled through existing programs established by the OAS and the UNDP, by networks of Canadian tertiary education institutions, and by a vast assortment of Canadian and Haitian NGOs. In some cases this has coincided with broader strategic objectives. For example, after Canada joined the OAS in 1990, it observed that democracy promotion in Haiti was a stated goal of that group's newly minted Santiago Declaration. The OAS, together with Canada, envisioned Haiti as an early test case, with Canada acting as a steadfast supporter of the OAS and the UN as vehicles for addressing Haiti's challenges (Hawrylak and Malone 2005).

The overall outcomes of Canada's investment in governance since 1990 are harder to discern. Though a number of CIDA reports have detailed the many successes of governance promotion, it is in fact exceedingly difficult to measure the outcomes despite more than two decades of engagement (CIDA 2004b, c, and d; 2003b, c). There are few evidence-based evaluations of CIDA (or other) investments in this sector. Measurement is made especially difficult by the instability that has long plagued Haiti and by the absence of robust monitoring and evaluation systems. It is also hampered by Canada's restless conceptual approach to governance itself. Even so, by 2004, governance promotion was widely considered the main axis of Canadian intervention in Haiti, to the extent that then–foreign minister Pierre Pettigrew announced that "governance was the key to finding a viable solution" to that country's problems. Precisely what this "key" looked like remains strangely elusive.

### A Frustrating Period:
### Governance Promotion from 1990 to 2003

Canada's governance agenda in Haiti underwent several qualitative transformations between 1990 and 2005. The first phase can be described generally as *experimentation with democracy* (1994 to 1995), the second as *public sector reform* (1996 to 1999), and the third as the *promotion of civil society* (2000 to 2003). Each of these phases was accompanied by considerable investment by Canada in the security sector, especially in police and judicial reform. After 2004, engagement with Haiti entered a fourth period—a combination of *security-first approaches* with elements of all three aforementioned tactics. While CIDA undertook a number of internal evaluations to assess the merits of its conceptual and strategic approach to governance, it seems to have sidestepped the question of impacts and outcomes, intended or otherwise.

The first phase (1994 to 1995) sought to shore up incremental gains achieved after Aristide's reinstatement. It is important to recall that between 1991 and 1993, CIDA experienced what amounted to a three-year programming hiatus owing to economic and military sanctions in place at the time. Following the permissive entry of American, Canadian, and UN troops in 1994, however, Haiti's reconstruction and recovery needs were tremendous. Canada focused on emergency aid and reconstruction—including food relief through WFP, quick-impact projects (QIPS) to stimulate employment creation, and support for the training of civil servants through the UNDP—while simultaneously exploring entry points for the preparation of democratic elections with the OAS mission. CIDA (2004b) reports that it disbursed more than C$35 million over this period (see Table 1). Meanwhile, given the presence of extensive US military assets and the country's focus on downscaling the FADH, USAID undertook a limited demobilization and reintegration program (DRP). France assisted in constitutional and judicial reform—especially the training of judges and magistrates. Thus, from 1994 to 1995, activities focused primarily on security and judicial reforms, short-term humanitarian assistance, labour-intensive social and economic infrastructure development schemes, and preparations for democratic elections.

TABLE 1

Global vs. Canadian ODA Disbursement in Haiti, 1995–2005 (C$)*

| Year | Total ODA disbursed in Haiti | Total CIDA contribution to Haiti | Percent contributed contributed by CIDA to all ODA in Haiti |
|---|---|---|---|
| 1995 | 610,000,000 | 35,730,142 | 5.8 |
| 1996 | 420,000,000 | 33,064,226 | 7.8 |
| 1997 | 371,000,000 | 39,679,526 | 10.6 |
| 1998 | 330,000,000 | 44,908,795 | 13.6 |
| 1999 | 266,000,000 | 35,249,708 | 13.2 |
| 2000 | 189,000,000 | 39,029,902 | 20.6 |
| 2001 | NA | 27,344,516 | 13.6 est. |
| 2002 | NA | 18,693,430 | 9.0 est. |
| 2003 | NA | 22,323,985 | 11.1 est. |
| 2004 | NA | 26,284,629 | 13.1 est. |
| 2005 | 1,089,000,000 | 98,000,000 | 8.9 |

*Source*: Internal CIDA documents.

*This includes all ODA—including World Bank, IADB, and other loans and grants. Aggregate data from 2001 to 2004 were not available, though it is believed to have decreased to below C$200 million during this period. Estimates rendered from 2001 to 2004 should therefore be treated with caution.

The second phase (1996 to 1999) shifted from "recovery" to "development" with the aim of strengthening the capacity of public-sector institutions to deliver essential services. Governance strategies during this period included training civil servants in the justice, finance, and social welfare ministries, as well as public entities and line agencies, in the expectation that basic services could be extended to the poor and that the state's legitimacy could be consolidated. Many donors, including Canada, recognized (if only privately) that these agencies were themselves heavily politicized and riddled with corruption and incompetence. During this period, however, Canada's principal vehicle for strengthening the public sector was debt relief, in addition to modest judicial, policing, and public-sector reform (also declared priorities of France and the United States).[25] Total disbursements by CIDA and other Canadian partners between 1996 and 1999 reached some C$184 million. Intriguingly, while overall ODA was dramatically reduced by most donors during the period, Canadian funding actually appeared to increase (see Table 1). During the second phase, CIDA observed a marked disconnect between its stated policy prescriptions—

which anticipated stable institutions with rational bureaucratic execution and the promotion of absorptive capacity—and the realities on the ground. These years were also marred by escalating political violence perpetrated by rival militia factions, intractable corruption under Préval, and the likelihood of contested elections involving Aristide and his Lavalas Party. By the end of this phase, CIDA had decided to end the bulk of its support to public-sector reform, especially in the justice and security sectors. Predictably, many other donors were thinking along the same lines.

A third phase (2000 to 2003) followed on the heels of disputed legislative elections and witnessed a marked qualitative change in CIDA's approach. Instead of directing support toward state and public institutions, as had been the case over the previous four years, both good governance and developmental assistance were purposefully channelled toward an amalgam of international and national NGOs and community-based organizations. This shift coincided with plummeting donor confidence in Aristide, a new and more conservative US administration, and an emerging orthodoxy indicating that good governance depended not only on accountable state institutions, but also on a vibrant civil society. Most donors—particularly the United States, the EU, and Canada—felt that the deliberate exclusion of the Aristide regime and its supporters would send an unambiguous political signal to the president and his opponents to cooperate. The Americans actively solicited donors to apply strict conditions on all ODA to the Haitian government, ostensibly to induce more transparency, responsibility, and fiscal accountability within the new government (Haiti Democracy Project 2003). It was becoming abundantly clear, at least to the United States, the EU, France, and Canada, that Aristide had to go.

On the ground, CIDA made a concerted effort to decentralize assistance and strengthen the not-for-profit sector in order to enable the more efficient delivery of key services to beneficiaries. Harnessing the rhetoric of "improving efficiency" and "building capacity" at the grassroots, CIDA effectively bypassed the national public entities. In some situations it sought to work directly with local and municipal government agencies where feasible. Thus, between 2002 and 2003, some C$3.5 million in assistance was again provided to the OAS for its activities in relation to human rights monitoring, with smaller packages provided to literally hundreds of small-scale community-based organizations to enhance local governance. By 2004, CIDA was reporting that despite initial positive results from a scattering of small-scale community-based development projects, the aggregate impacts of those projects were somewhat meagre (CIDA 2004b). A corporate evaluation of 450 Canadian-funded development projects concluded that they were widely dispersed and highly differentiated and "did not seem to provide a critical mass of results" (CIDA 2004b, 12).[26] In

TABLE 2

CIDA Thematic Priorities and Disbursements, 2001–2005 (C$)

|  | 2001–2 | 2002–3 | 2003–4 | 2004–5 |
|---|---|---|---|---|
| Good governance | 3,492,591 | 5,104,566 | 3,442,384 | 35,538,128 |
| Basic human needs | 6,941,770 | 10,556,988 | 15,771,006 | 35,749,937 |
| Environment | 1,315,588 | 905,133 | 948,707 | 1,094,868 |
| Gender | 1,321,391 | 967,134 | 1,208,856 | 1,540,125 |
| Infrastructure | 1,610,472 | 907,245 | 819,620 | 12,486,977 |
| Misc. | 1,316,664 | 2,368,131 | 2,638,227 | 10,182,376 |
| Private sector | 2,667,190 | 1,496,866 | 1,672,183 | 1,547,097 |

Source: Internal CIDA documents.

fact, CIDA (2004b) reported that by the end of 2003, NGO actors (private and not-for-profit) accounted for almost 80 percent of all basic service delivery in the country. Far from improving efficiency, the decentralized approach seemed to be spurring a parallel service delivery system and raising the local costs of labour—effectively undermining the dilapidated services hitherto provided by the state. The question of "national ownership"—another supposed pillar of the good governance agenda—was moot.[27]

## A More Hopeful Chapter?
## 2004 and Beyond

After more than a decade of poor returns, CIDA undertook a major review of its internal and external functions and resorted to new thinking on the subject of "difficult partners." From 2004 onwards, revitalized strategic approaches to addressing governance in Haiti drew from conceptual frameworks advanced by the OECD DAC (2002), the World Bank,[28] and Canada's own "3D" strategy.[29] Early on, it was expected that the key mechanism for coordinating and implementing CIDA's new agenda in Haiti would be the Country Development Programming Framework (CPDF), a mechanism designed to bring about greater program coherence and better coordination with other departments. The approach that emerged was in fact appropriate, given the volatile circumstances that began to unfold in late 2003. Relatively conservative in its scope, this new strategy called for enhanced commitment to police reform, redoubled commitment to staying the course, a concerted effort to ensure policy coherence and donor coordination, investments in improved analysis and identifi-

TABLE 3

CIDA Governance Disbursement in Haiti, 2001–2007 (C$)

|  | CIDA governance disbursement in Haiti | % governance in Haiti as a proportion of all CIDA disbursement | CIDA governance global disbursement |
| --- | --- | --- | --- |
| 2000–1 | 4,869,098 | 1.32 | 369,312,905 |
| 2001–2 | 3,786,077 | 1.07 | 354,575,131 |
| 2002–3 | 5,374,585 | 1.45 | 370,192,974 |
| 2003–4 | 3,923,500 | 0.92 | 427,237,969 |
| 2004–5 | 33,825,780 | 5.76 | 587,048,871 |
| 2005–6 | 25,942,689 | 8 | 324,167,716 |
| 2005–6 (budgeted) | 45,322,911 | 8.52 | 532,104,550 |
| 2006–7 (budgeted) | 30,661,283 | 4.11 | 746,650,114 |

*Source*: Internal CIDA documents.

cation of "change drivers," a willingness to be more flexible and opportunistic, and renewed efforts to involve the Haitian diaspora in recovery. Governance was a central theme for CIDA's Haiti program, second only to poverty reduction (see Tables 2 and 3). The commitment to a governance-centred strategy for Haiti also reflected the general views held internally across the agency.[30]

In mid-2003, CIDA began to carefully review its own internal coherence in relation to programming in Haiti. A stated priority was to ensure that the lessons of the past three decades were effectively learned and applied. It was also expected that CIDA would eventually adopt an all-agency approach with common statements of objectives and strategic approaches, clear and unambiguous standards, and the maximization of synergies within the organization. Meanwhile, as debate heated up in Ottawa to decide the overall contours of the governance agenda, the situation in Haiti was rapidly unravelling. In late 2003 and early 2004, confronted with an extremely volatile and dynamic situation, the "governance promotion" agenda again found itself in a holding pattern. Given the precariousness of the security situation, short-term interventions such as disarmament, demobilization, and reintegration (DDR) and police recruitment and training was correctly identified as major priorities.

CIDA put its CPDF strategy into action. All program resources were to be directed toward the short-term goal of promoting security and ensuring elections and the long-term goal of "poverty reduction"—primarily through the formation of improved donor–host relationships based on aid-effectiveness principles (as discussed elsewhere in this book by Wood, de Renzio, and Mulley). Besides accepting more risk and uncertainty in its investments, and as befitted a crisis situation, the agency aimed to support rapid and decentralized decision making though rapid disbursement of relief. CIDA also sought to maintain political dialogue with the new Haitian authorities—in this case an interim government—while encouraging a rapprochement with national stakeholders—politicians, senators, and respected leaders—involved in governance-related activities.[31] Finally, CIDA aimed to strengthen cooperation and coherence among international donors, who time and again had proven both divided and confounded over what to do with this most difficult partner.

In the months following Aristide's second ouster in 2004, Canada adopted a "security first" perspective. In keeping with UNSC resolutions, Canada's immediate objectives during this period were to contribute to a secure and stable environment and to facilitate the delivery of humanitarian assistance, while simultaneously helping the Haitian National Police (HNP) and the coast guard maintain law and order. As outlined earlier in the chapter, FAC, DND, and the RCMP were heavily committed to this end.[32] At the UN's request, the Canadian Forces mission in Haiti was extended beyond its initial mandate to permit Task Force Haiti (TFH) to help expand the MIF to MINUSTAH in June 2004. Around 450 Canadian forces personnel remained in Haiti until mid-August 2004, and Canadian police continued to serve in CIVPOL (now renamed UNPOL). Between July and October of the same year, Canada also launched a "Plan stratégique de développement de la police nationale d'Haïti" to prepare the training of the police force. Surprisingly, by March 2005 Canada had also contributed C$500,000 toward disarmament, demobilization, and reintegration (which had been budgeted at US$18 million over two years). This, perhaps, was the first time CIDA had earmarked funds for such activities. By way of comparison, in addition to supporting the UN missions (i.e., MIF and MINUSTAH) in early 2004, the United States was pursuing a more aggressive and unilateral strategy of security sector reform—a strategy from which it would later back away (see Annex 1). Besides contributing to these and other operations, CIDA was providing support to multilateral agencies such as UNICEF and the WFP for food and livelihood assistance to violence- and disaster-affected populations, especially those outside the capital.

Along with the security-first approach highlighted above, the promotion of good governance was an important pillar of Canada's post-2004 strategy.[33] Here, "election support" was the single largest component of the governance portfolio. Monies for this included C$8 million in least three separate grants to the OAS, C$147,000 for a census administered by UNFPA, and C$17 million for administering the election and the UNDP in 2004.[34] Moneys for public-sector reform projects included the following: c$4.6 million toward a financial management centre; c$36,000 for trade union development (through the Centrale des syndicats du Québec); and c$15 million for debt repayment and restructuring. According to internal CIDA records, human rights support included c$3 million to create a justice and human rights fund (through René Mari) and c$34,000 for a human rights project executed by the Social Justice Committee. Finally, spending on "rule of law" totalled some c$1.5 million and was channelled to both the UNDP and the Ministry of Justice. Support for "political parties" included projects named "Appui politique et programmation BMG" (c$978,000) and "Renforcement des groupements pays" (c$73,000), both carried out by the Association Québécoise pour l'avancement des Nations Unies (see Annex 1).

CIDA's general strategy emphasized multilateral approaches to governance promotion, whether through multidonor trust funds or UN, OAS, and other international agencies, as well as small-scale support for civil society interventions. Overall, there appears to have been considerable emphasis on electoral and public-sector reform programs, with much smaller allocations to support NGOs in human rights, rule-of-law, and civil society development. Institutionally, besides supporting Canadian development organizations and academic centres, Canada announced that CIDA would support a three-year "Solidarité Canada-Haiti" project (c$7.5 million), which was expected to send some 250 Canadian volunteers (including diaspora Haitians) to the country with the aim of strengthening democratic institutions.[35] It was anticipated that this ambitious project, supported by Canada Corps, would help support public administration reform, strengthen the education system, increase the capacity of (Haitian) civil society organizations, support private-sector development, and improve the delivery of community services. All of these would have been challenging objectives even in a stable and secure environment.

CIDA's own reporting mechanisms make it difficult to determine trends in past and prospective funding. Very generally, CIDA has endorsed several broad priorities over the past five years of programming in Haiti (see Figure 2). The promotion of governance has either included or coincided with parallel priorities such as human rights and justice.[36] As in other fragile states where Canada is engaged—notably Afghanistan and Sudan—it is exceedingly difficult to discern from CIDA records (both public and in-house) what constitutes a good-governance program or project (as compared to human rights or justice promotion), much less how and to whom allocated funds are ultimately disbursed. In other words, it is impossible to track longitudinal trends because of the opaque manner in which budget items are coded and conflated. For example, available CIDA documents make it seem that well over c$33 million

FIGURE 2

Deconstructing Good Governance in Haiti:
Thematic Priorities 1994–2004

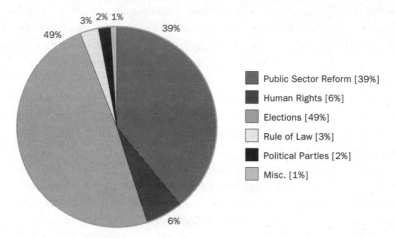

Legend:
- Public Sector Reform [39%]
- Human Rights [6%]
- Elections [49%]
- Rule of Law [3%]
- Political Parties [2%]
- Misc. [1%]

*Source*: Internal CIDA documents.

was budgeted in 2004–5 for governance—a huge increase over previous years (see Table 3). But when itemized spending is examined, it seems that less than c$9,000 was ultimately transferred as "support to non-governmental organizations" (read civil society)—in this case, the Haiti Media and Elections Training and Support Project, which was designed to improve awareness of and reporting on the impending elections. At the same time, in late 2005 Canada provided well over c$22 million to the OAS and UNDP (combined) to fund election preparations. It is unclear from available CIDA reports, however, whether these line items were draw-downs from the 2004–5 "human rights, justice, and governance" envelope.[37]

Canada massively increased its funding commitments to Haiti after Aristide's departure in 2004 and in the run-up to presidential and legislative elections anticipated for 2006. But raising funds for core priorities is one thing; getting them out the door is quite another. Donors are often criticized for not disbursing rapidly or flexibly in the context of political and natural disasters. But as noted above, CIDA disbursed emergency assistance comparatively rapidly: by March 2005 some c$96 million of more than c$180 million pledged for humanitarian and development ODA (fiscal years 2004–5 and 2005–6) had been disbursed. CIDA and the donor community also registered some important successes on the governance front, including the relatively free and fair election of René Préval in February 2006.

Even modest advances in governance were threatened by extreme levels of violence during the term of the interim administration (2004–6). Rates of homicide, victimization, and kidnapping increased severalfold between late 2004 and 2006. A controversial household survey revealed that during the twenty-two months of the interim government, 8,000 people were intentionally killed in the greater Port-au-Prince area alone (Kolbe and Hudson 2006). An estimated 35,000 women and girls were reportedly raped or sexually assaulted during this same period. Those responsible for these human rights abuses included the primary recipients of "security sector" assistance, including the HNP (Jiminez 2006; Muggah and Krause 2006).

Overall, if evaluated purely on the basis of disbursement and electoral outcomes in 2006, Canada's governance strategy performed comparatively well during the turbulent period 2004 to 2006 (Muggah 2005a). This is especially so when compared to the record for other donors such as the United States, the EU, and France, who have yet to make good on their original pledges. It is still far too early to tell whether Canada's recent investments in good governance have yielded a durable impact, though these short- to medium-term outcomes are grounds for cautious optimism.

## Conclusions

Canadian interpretations of and approaches to good governance in Haiti have undergone a series of transformations over the past decade. Globally, CIDA's approach to governance programming has remained relatively stable since 1996, when it announced the Human Rights, Democratization, and Good Governance policy. Bilaterally in Haiti, CIDA's approach to governance programming has been more erratic. Over the past fifteen years, changes in programming have been motivated as much by volatile conditions in Port-au-Prince as by shifting interests, prescriptions, and policy trends emanating from Ottawa, Paris, and Washington. Despite standard-setting initiatives from the OECD, the overall lack of donor coherence and coordination on strategic priorities in fragile states means it is difficult—and even disingenuous—to evaluate the practical outcomes of Canada's governance agenda in Haiti. All the more so when we recall that there is comparatively little evidence of a causal relationship between governance inputs and outcomes more generally, even with more promising partners such as Vietnam and Ghana. At the very least, the hubris that characterized the pro-democracy efforts of the 1990s has been replaced by a wary pragmatism.

If good governance means a functioning democratic political system and a Weberian-style bureaucratic order, then Canada's interventions in Haiti have yielded comparatively few gains. Despite years of investment, the country's problems appear to have grown *more* intractable, not less. But if governance is defined more concretely as a set of discrete interventions to strengthen specific forms of public-sector accountability and responsiveness, to create functioning electoral registration systems, to support the rule of law, to develop an accountable security sector and a reformed police service, and to promote human rights capacities among NGOS, then Canada's interventions, while not particularly successful, have yielded modest dividends. The very real challenges to promoting governance with difficult partners in fragile states must not be underestimated. Except for the elections in the mid-1990s and 2006 and a scattering of short-term successes, the situation in Haiti seems to have stumbled backwards: indicators of human development have actually dropped since 1990 and show signs of dropping further still.

A number of general patterns can be discerned from Canada's efforts to promote governance in Haiti during the 1990s. First, despite the frequent changes in strategic priorities, the vast majority of Canada's ODA *was channelled through multilateral agencies*—particularly the OAS and operational agencies such as the UNDP, the WFP, and UNICEF. Canada consistently invested in multilateral approaches and urged cooperation between donors and NGOS; as such, it aligned itself with enhanced harmonization and aid effectiveness (as described by other contributors to this book). Whether it was promoting election monitoring, human rights activities, or the rule of law, Canada carved out a niche for itself in the governance agenda befitting its multilateral instincts. Even so, despite Canada's commitment to multilateralism, it has not necessarily offered new or particularly innovative approaches to governance promotion on the ground.

Second, despite high-level political interest in governance, the application of overarching conceptual frameworks, and a growing emphasis on results-based management, Canada had difficulty *defining what precisely governance means and how it is to be measured and operationalized.* Definitions have changed over the decade from a proactive "democracy and elections" agenda in the early 1990s to a more tentative and risk-averse focus on "public-sector reform" and "change agents" today. Canada's changing definition of governance of course reflects geopolitical realities and the discursive zeitgeist; this in turn raises fundamental questions about accountability. It is exceedingly difficult to evaluate outcomes of good governance promotion if the goalposts are constantly being moved. It remains the case that agendas continue to be defined in Ottawa, Washington, and Paris, with comparatively few inputs from Haitians themselves. Canada would do well to reflect on local and differentiated interpretations of governance and how they might inform national strategies. Studies on elite and local perceptions of "poverty," for example, have found that many Haitians would welcome the return of a strong, authoritarian state— an aspiration that does not rest easily with the more progressive liberal expectations of certain donors (Reis and Moore 2002). Confirming this view, a Gallup poll conducted in August 2005 determined that the "Baby Doc" Duvalier dictatorship (1971–86) was rated "the most favourable" regime in the previous five decades.

Third, despite registering comparatively marginal gains, CIDA stands out for its *longevity*, *persistence*, and *commitment* when compared to other donors. Canada's engagement in Haiti has endured partly because of its history with the country and domestic pressures generated by an activist diaspora. Canada has long been a key donor to Haiti and between 2004 and 2006 was the second-largest bilateral contributor to the ICF, pledging more than C$180 million out of a total of US$1.085 billion. Canada also deliberately adopted the role of "consensus builder" among fractious donors. The difficulties of ensuring donor coherence and coordination—particularly in light of the unilateral tendencies of certain governments and the palatable frustrations of key donors—are very real.

Finally, it seems that CIDA *recognized the limitations of top-down agendas* and their poor "fit" with political realities on the ground. The agency has been convinced that better assessments of local political conditions are urgently required. Canada has learned a series of difficult lessons about its past approach to governance promotion with difficult partners and fragile states. For example, it has grasped—at least in theory—the importance of evidence-based diagnoses of the structural and institutional constraints on public-sector reform and civil society engagement in governance. It also recognizes the dangers associated with rapidly changing policy prescriptions, non-targeted sanctions, and heavily conditioned aid. This final section of the chapter closes with a sample of lessons drawn from the past decade of governance programming in the country. These include the importance of correctly identifying external and internal problems; moving beyond technical solutions toward political engagement; challenging generic labels; and devising a consistent and long-term strategy.

### External and Internal Problem Identification

Policy-makers and donors are regularly overwhelmed by the scale and magnitude of the challenges they confront in Haiti. This has resulted in rapid diagnoses and reactive approaches to targeting and administering aid. In the process, these governments have frequently adopted conflicting priorities, failed to consult one another, and in some cases withdrawn altogether. In the rush to provide assistance, donors have failed to prepare themselves with adequate or appropriate guidance to set priorities, execute programs, and monitor and measure results. This is partly because Haiti—its political realities, complex factions, shifting alliances, and rural economy—is not particularly *legible* to donors. Instead of adopting a deductive policy-formulation process that would respond to local realities, donors have devised governance agendas according to interests determined from above. The imposition of these agendas has eroded an already weak domestic policy-making capacity.

Political and social analyses of changing local circumstances are crucial—and sorely lacking in the Haitian context. Less than 1 percent of international policy-makers, country representatives, or UN practitioners even speak Creole, the lingua franca of the vast majority of Haitians. In her contribution to this book, Unsworth emphasized the importance of identifying and responding to local demand and ensuring "ownership" of governance reform measures. While no doubt good advice, donors in Haiti, including Canada, have had a hard time deciding who exactly should "own" reforms at all. To be sure, there are concrete dilemmas concerning how and with whom to engage. But external awareness must be complemented with internal reflection.

As the case of Haiti amply demonstrates, donor behaviour matters. The presence of too many donors with competing interests consumed the scarce time and energy of local policy-makers. Until recently, changes in donor policy in Haiti were shaped more by priorities determined from above than by local realities. It is now painfully obvious to most of CIDA's aid programmers that practical decisions on governance priorities and modalities must be sensitive and responsive to the local context, instead of catering disproportionately to visible political actors and geopolitical interests. Locally grounded knowledge will allow Canada to render more timely and effective support, and even more important, to know when to turn off the tap.

### Political Solutions over Technical Responses

Few in CIDA now wonder whether the governance deficit in Haiti is monocausal or amenable to quick fixes. There is now a keen sense that that deficit is deeply embedded, acutely political, and epiphenomenal. Canada has adopted a more cautious approach even while officially and publicly advocating opportunism and flexibility and applying diplomatic pressure at the highest levels. The scope for direct outside intervention and governance promotion with fragile states and difficult partners is more limited than once believed. This acknowledgment is important and calls for a certain humility in Canada's expectations in fragile states more generally. In some cases, Canada may find that the most appropriate course of action is to simply do nothing at all, however unpalatable this might first appear to politicians, interest groups, and human rights activists in Ottawa. To put it another way, donors such as Canada may need to redefine progress and accept "that in some instances, 'no change' is in fact an encouraging sign" (CIDA 2004b, 15).

Effective public institutions are created not by transposing models from wealthy to poor countries, but by a process of state–society bargaining. To be effective, such bargaining requires both state effectiveness and accountability *and* the identification and institutionalization of common interests between the state and civil society. In Haiti, the act of bargaining is especially tricky on account of the difficulties associated with defining agents and interests to begin with, the politicization of public institutions and their lack of accountability at the periphery, and the intentional violence that so often accompanies formal and informal state–civil society exchanges.

For these and other reasons, donors have encountered tremendous difficulties in facilitating meaningful state–civil society interactions. These challenges emerged when donors and UN agencies attempted to promote a "national dialogue"—a core feature of early UNSC resolutions. It was also apparent in the underhanded way that the US State Department supported oppositional groups in the late 1990s. In unpredictable environments, most donors preferred to craft and impose new aid frameworks, create new normative mechanisms, institutions, and organizations, and launch visionary strategies from foreign capitals or Port-au-Prince with comparatively little emphasis on engendering (or engineering) ownership at the municipal level—much less a participatory dialogue from below. With some notable exceptions, Canada is guilty on this count, with its fixation on formal electoral mechanisms and public sector reform on the one hand, and modest investments in NGOs at the expense of state institutions on the other.

One lesson is that "either/or" approaches to governance—alternately targeting political and public institutions and civil society—may well miss the point and could even do harm. Certainly the strategy adopted by Canada between 1994 and 2003—supporting the Haitian government and then alienating it in favour of civil society—yielded perverse outcomes (CIDA 2004b). There is a risk that by essentializing the "state" and "civil society"—that is, by treating one or the other as the *key* to unlocking good governance without a careful assessment of the structural power relations between them—outside agencies will foster power asymmetries and political pathologies.

Instead, governance strategies must explicitly consider the dynamic *relationships* between the two clusters of actors and build on the incentives for them to engage in collective action. Recall, however, that such a strategy is exceedingly risky in the context of fragile states. Here, as noted above, successful intervention depends on a sound grasp of the political and social context, which in turn depends on the recruitment of competent and relatively unbiased (ideally Creole-speaking) personnel—individuals in distressingly short supply. Moreover, it is difficult for meaningful state–society engagement to occur when the country in question lacks a neutral and non-politicized forum for public policy debate. In Haiti, the low levels of perceived legitimacy of the government, high levels of illiteracy, and weak systems of communication limit the possibilities for collective action.

## Beyond the Labels

Definitions matter. The careless application of labels can gloss over complexities—the understanding of which is essential to the promotion of good governance—in favour of simplistic technical solutions. There can be no doubt that Haiti is convulsed by a crisis—it is a failed state par excellence. And while security-first approaches are no doubt crucial, there is an urgent need to recognize the complex historical and nested interests that underlie the crisis and, it follows, point to the incentives and opportunities for altering them. Too often, positivist and apolitical labelling leads to formulaic interventions.

To be effective, good governance requires thinking differently about civil society. A key strategy for donors following Aristide's contested election win in 2000 was the redirection of assistance to a supposedly progressive civil society. This effectively bypassed what was widely regarded as a morally bankrupt state. CIDA's current strategy hinges on supporting change agents within civil society. But as donors have discovered in Haiti and elsewhere, there is nothing intrinsically benign about civil society—it is not an autonomous or undifferentiated sphere waiting to be strengthened. Having been stung by some poor returns, civil society is now either treated with suspicion or as a potentially dangerous entity not to be trusted—as alternately pro-Lavalas or against it. Again, this misreads the inherent complexities of civil society. The same goes for the elites, who are not simply a wealthy class of mulattoes in Pietonville, Jacmel, and Gonaive; they include various upper- and middle-class professionals, intellectuals, artists, and private citizens' groups and networks both within and outside the country.

CIDA is gradually recognizing the practical dangers of all-encompassing labels and is turning its attention away from reified definitions of civil society toward change agents (who are presumably "progressive" elements within the society). It appears that the agency is beginning to develop a less technical and normative understanding. It is beginning to conceive civil society as a heterogeneous constellation of interests that are by turns independent of and reliant on effective state institutions, which are similarly responsive to state action and inaction. Even more attention could be devoted to the relationships between particular state authorities and civil society actors, and to the design and support of representative institutions to facilitate political exchange and to (peacefully) channel grievances.

## A Long-Term Approach

There are no shortcuts for achieving governance in fragile states and with difficult partners. Donors must "know when to fold 'em,'" but they must also know when to adopt long-term visions—perspectives that challenge conventional aid cycles and short-term political horizons. Past efforts to shore up good governance in Haiti faltered not just because of endogenous factors such as insecurity, endemic corruption, and a legacy of militarized politics, but also as a result of geopolitical interests, uneven donor and UN commitment, and the placing of strict conditions on ODA. Though CIDA currently recognizes the principle of adopting a longer-term vision, together with the value of sustained funding and results-based management, there are no guarantees that the agency will not still be held hostage to the short-term imperatives of international and domestic politics. Even so, CIDA has taken some important steps in terms of improving its own internal organizational and policy coherence, and it has created a more positive and constructive environment in which to enact policy. So, while the content of what CIDA does has not changed greatly, at least the rules and mechanisms of engagement have.

Canada must proceed carefully with its governance agenda in Haiti. Security is of course a necessary precondition of good governance, and Canada's (admittedly controversial) focus on policing and security sector reform in the context of 3D is appropriate. In some cases, Canada's interests may well benefit from fewer projects and more attention to ensuring political coherence among donors, as has been emphasized in the past. Ultimately, if the good governance agenda is to be meaningfully advanced in the context of this most fragile and difficult partner, Canada must develop a real-time capacity to monitor and respond to evolving political and social realities. It must look beyond formal institutions and confront the complex, diverse, and often unpredictable informal relationships that underpin them. Finally, it must adopt a measure of humility with regard to what can be achieved. Above all, it must stay the course.

▼

## Annex 1

CIDA Programming on Governance: Historical and 2004–2008*

| Project name | Historical distribution | Distribution 2004–5 | Distribution 2005–6 | Budget 2005–6 | Budget 2006–7 | Budget 2007–8 | Total |
|---|---|---|---|---|---|---|---|
| *Bilateral* | | | | | | | |
| Agro-Forestry Project (Nippes) | 1,521,102 | 239,171 | 83,671 | 30,000 | 44,495 | 0 | 1,918,439 |
| Regional Human Resource Development Project | 196,308 | 87,517 | 1,732 | 0 | 0 | 0 | 285,557 |
| FEDEREC (civil reconstruction) | 1,427,304 | 76,851 | 153 | 0 | 0 | 0 | 1,504,307 |
| ACOOPECH Project | 1,436,994 | 350,917 | 275,182 | 84,256 | 211,053 | 0 | 2,358,402 |
| UPAZ Training Project | 128,128 | 572 | 0 | 0 | 0 | 0 | 128,700 |
| ACOOPECH III Project | 0 | 0 | 201,786 | 0 | 1,192,000 | 972,000 | 2,365,786 |
| Local Development Project (Nippes) | 0 | 0 | 0 | 74,443 | 350,000 | 387,500 | 811,943 |
| Media Support Project | −467,500 | 0 | 850,000 | 184,740 | 1,052,825 | 0 | 1,620,065 |
| Justice Sector Assistance Project | 0 | 0 | 336,950 | 363,050 | 2,500,000 | 1,360,000 | 4,560,000 |
| Voluntary Cooperative Support Program (Canadian Corp) | −250,000 | 0 | 500,000 | 0 | 1,665,930 | 1,790,954 | 3,706,884 |
| Police Advisers to MINUSTAH | 0 | 0 | 1,994,672 | 255,328 | 0 | 0 | 2,250,000 |
| Election Observers to Haiti | 0 | 0 | 479,679 | 2,159,272 | 0 | 0 | 2,638,950 |
| Logistical support for Management of the Voluntary Sector Project | 0 | 0 | 20,000 | 83,644 | 0 | 0 | 103,644 |
| Save the Children 2002–6— 3 Years Program | 0 | 0 | 0 | 0 | 0 | 0 | 0 |
| | 35,600 | 87,222 | 45,718 | 0 | 0 | 0 | 168,540** |

Annex 1, *continued*

| Project name | Historical distribution | Distribution 2004–5 | Distribution 2005–6 | Budget 2005–6 | Budget 2006–7 | Budget 2007–8 | Total |
|---|---|---|---|---|---|---|---|
| OCCDP Development Program (2004–2006) | –173,678 | 153,861 | 46,179 | 77,900 | 39,706 | 0 | 143,967 |
| Financing for pro-poor services project | 44,751 | 42,589 | 38,398 | 13,659 | 59,383 | 0 | 198,781 |
| Voluntary Cooperatives: 2004–9 (SUCO) | 0 | 61,382 | 37,219 | 1,762 | 51,975 | 51,975 | 204,313 |
| Human Rights Education Program: 2004–7 | –63,143 | 51,759 | 68,212 | 2,012 | 61,140 | 0 | 119,981 |
| International Cooperation Program (CTF) | 0 | 0 | 33,329 | 18,271 | 51,600 | 51,600 | 154,800 |
| Democratic Values Promotion Program | 0 | 0 | 44,501 | 44,501 | 97,214 | 0 | 186,216 |
| Organizational Capacity Building Program | 0 | 0 | 42,870 | 42,870 | 44,170 | 0 | 129,910 |
|  | 4,013,122 | 1,484,909 | 5,391,136 | 3,515,550 | 7,642,096 | 4,691,069 | 26,737,883 |
|  | 0 | 0 | 0 | 19,600 | 19,600 | 0 | 39,200 |
|  | 0 | 0 | 0 | 3,430 | 3,430 | 0 | 6,860 |
| Program Support (Save the Children Fund, 2006–11) | 0 | 0 | 0 | 0 | 54,888 | 54,888 | 109,776 |
| Planning Budgets | 0 | 0 | 0 | 24,010 | 79,878 | 54,888 | 158,776 |
| *Multilateral* | | | | | | | |
| CARICOM Capacity Development Project | –23,880 | 13,681 | 22,811 | 0 | 24,712 | 26,613 | 63,938 |
| Consolidation of the Rule of Law | 266,152 | 36,485 | 165,758 | 9,974 | 0 | 0 | 478,368 |
| Local Development Project (Marmelade) | 132,000 | 263,324 | 51,992 | 0 | 18,975 | 0 | 466,290 |
| Grant to the OAS Special Mission | 0 | 5,000,000 | 0 | 5,000,000 | 0 | 0 | 10,000,000 |
| Local Development Program in the Northeast | 0 | 0 | 231,000 | 115,500 | 231,000 | 231,000 | 808,500 |
| Electoral Support | 0 | 17,000,000 | 2,750,000 | 0 | 0 | 0 | 19,750,000 |

Annex 1, *continued*

| Project name | Historical distribution | Distribution 2004–5 | Distribution 2005–6 | Budget 2005–6 | Budget 2006–7 | Budget 2007–8 | Total |
|---|---|---|---|---|---|---|---|
| Rule of Law and Justice Sector Support (ICF) | 0 | 0 | 0 | 500,000 | 2,500,000 | 2,000,000 | 5,000,000 |
| CARTAC Phase II | 0 | 209,305 | 66,700 | 0 | 57,495 | 0 | 333,500 |
| UNDP support to DDR in Haiti | 0 | 500,000 | 0 | 0 | 0 | 0 | 500,000 |
| CDB SDF 6th Replenishment | –453,060 | 0 | 906,120 | 0 | 906,120 | 906,120 | 2,265,299 |
| | –17,942 | 23,039,512 | 4,548,960 | 5,795,069 | 4,083,776 | 3,508,033 | 40,957,408 |
| **Total Expenditures 2004–8** | 3,995,180 | 24,524,421 | 9,940,097 | 9,334,629 | 11,805,750 | 8,253,990 | 67,854,067 |

* All values are in C$. All distributions under C$100,000 are excluded.

** According to CIDA, Canada's total aid budget to Haiti for fiscal years 2004–5 and 2005–6 was C$180 million.

## Notes

1  The UN and the OAS implemented sanctions in 1993 on the importation of fuel and petroleum-related products, as well as temporary arms embargoes.

2  Hawrylak and Malone (2005) consider the geopolitical interests that have governed leadership on Haiti on the UN Security Council, with a particular focus on the United States and France.

3  These same opposition groups would later play a central role in the ousting of Aristide several years after the contested elections of 2000. See Bogdanovich and Nordberg (2006).

4  Cabinet members of the interim government pledged that they would not run for political office during the elections originally planned for November 2005. This preserved their integrity in the eyes of the international community, but also lessened their power over an entrenched civil service, which had long been dependent on systems of personal patronage.

5  According to the World Bank (2004c), bilateral pledges came from the United States, Canada, France, Germany, Japan, the Netherlands, Switzerland, Taiwan, Ireland, Mexico, Norway, and the EU, with additional commitments from the World Bank, IDA, IADB, and IMF as well as UN agencies.

6  According to the UNSC (2005c), "as of March 2005 disbursements amounted to only US$266 million. Seventy-two per cent of the disbursements were made in support of access to basic services, economic governance and institutional development; *22 per cent were allocated to political governance*, national dialogue and economic recovery; and 6 per cent were allocated for budgetary aid, arrears and unallocated funds" (emphasis added).

7  When the USAID director of the Americas Division was asked about US contributions to the ICF, he simply responded, "What's the ICF"? Interview, January 2005.

8  These include the Washington Conference (July 2004), the Cayenne Ministerial Conference (March 2005), and the Montreal Conference (June 2005).

9  CIDA (2004b) also observes additional sources of instability, including low-intensity violence, environmental deterioration, economic stagnation, and a history of slavery.

10  According to the UNDP (PNUD 2004), 1 percent of Haitians control about half the country's entire wealth. The upper class distinguishes itself along ethnic and linguistic lines. There is a modest middle class in Haiti's urban centres, though these groups are not well represented in government.

11  In 2003, Haiti ranked 131st out of 133, and in 2002 it was 89th out of 102. In 2004, Haiti's ranking had marginally improved, and it is currently tied with Bangladesh. See, for example, "corruption perceptions index" at http://www.transparency.org/surveys/html.

12  Following pressure from the United States, France, and the EU, as well as the IADB and the World Bank, some US$150 million was withheld from the Haitian authorities in 2001, despite being formally budgeted by Parliament and the international community. The World Bank (2002b, 21) noted that "if it resumes lending in Haiti,

the Bank will have to take into account the human resource constraints, the persistent budgetary shortages, and the risk that the lending itself can create opportunities for corruption."

13   See World Bank (2002b) and the IADB's reports on Haiti at http://www.iadb.org.

14   UNSC Resolution 841 (June 16, 1993) introduced a sanctions committee but lifted the embargo shortly after UNSC 861 of 1993. The arms embargo was restored again through UNSC 873 (1993) and finally lifted by UNSC 944 (1994), following the return of President Aristide. For a review of these and related sanctions consult Muggah (2005a, 2005b).

15   Haiti's main export and import partner is the United States, which accounts for some 81 percent of all exports and 53 percent of all imports. In 2003, Canada provided some 4.2 percent of all exports and 2.9 percent of all imports. Specifically, Canada imported some US$18.6 million in textiles, fish and seafood, twine, cocoa, fruit, and nuts. Canadian exports to Haiti totalled US$20.7 million over the same period, including dairy products, vegetables, paper, meat, fish, and seafood. Canada has included the country in the Least Developed Country Initiative, which means that tariffs and quota on most Haitian exports to Canada have been eliminated, except for certain agricultural products. See World Bank statistics at http://www.worldbank.org.

16   According to Gabriel Demombynes of the World Bank, "the bank's main approach to corruption has been to offer technical advice and some grant money for good governance." The World Bank is working with the current Powal administration to develop a PRSP for 2008."

17   Specifically, OAS resolutions 806, 822, and 1959 unintentionally deepened the crisis of governance by contributing to an expansion in corruption and illegal trade in various contraband—a fact now acknowledged with some regret by diplomats and national authorities in Port-au-Prince.

18   "The development impact of the Bank's assistance since 1986 has been negligible; new lending has been blocked since 1997 by the lack of a functioning parliament, and the few remaining projects have been cancelled. The outcome of the Bank's assistance program is rated 'unsatisfactory,' its institutional development impact is 'negligible,' and the sustainability of the few benefits is rated as 'unlikely.'" See World Bank (2002b, 43).

19   According to one such report, "good governance is achieved through promoting democratic institutions, supporting human rights commissions and supporting free and fair elections" (Canada, DFAIT 2005, 6). By way of comparison, a CIDA Canada statement (2005) observes that "programming in governance involves a wide range of activity areas: democracy, elections and parliaments, a fair and impartial judiciary, mechanisms to respect and protect human rights, an effective and transparent public sector, and a stable and reliable security system to protect people and resolve conflict fairly and peacefully. Good governance is also an integral component of private-sector development, creating an environment that enables economic growth."

20 According to Yves Petillon, Director of CIDA's Americas Branch, "the likely scenario is for Canada to continue channelling aid through multilateral agencies and NGOs, and not in the form of direct budgetary support to the Haitian government." Interview with author, January 2006.

21 According to CIDA (2004b), state "fragility" is determined according to a set of predetermined indicators, including declining socio-economic benchmarks that fall below a certain threshold, political instability and insecurity, weak or non-existent "social contracts," and low levels of trust between governments and their citizens. The OECD/DAC (2002c) has also elaborated an agenda to work with fragile states. Its Learning and Advisory Process in Difficult Partnerships (LAP) was established to this end.

22 According to OECD DAC (2002), a "difficult partnership is one in which the recipient state demonstrates neither the capacity, ownership nor commitment of development processes, resulting in a marked reluctance among donors to support relationships or provide assistance based on partner development frameworks." Thus, "difficult partnership" countries would technically not qualify for donor-supported Poverty Reduction Strategy Papers (PRSPS).

23 There are an estimated 100,000 Haitian families living in Canada (CIDA 2004b). Nearly 90 percent of Haitian immigrants to Canada since 1981 have settled in Montreal. Secondary destination points include Toronto and Quebec City.

24 By way of comparison, the United States provided over US$850 million in assistance between 1995 and 2003 alone. See, for example, Noriega (2004).

25 Canada's programming framework for Haiti was reportedly redesigned in 1997. The new approach was based on the assumption that security and development would flourish following Aristide's return in 1994 and the resumption of investment. As the anticipated scenario failed to emerge, and the inadequacies of its strategic engagement with Haiti became apparent, Canada reassessed its strategies in 2000. See CIDA (2004d).

26 CIDA reports that these were "funded on a very short-term basis, which inhibited continuity needed for significant change." The same report notes, however, that some decentralization efforts were more effective in "promoting good governance, human rights and social services where projects do not require such technical knowledge" (CIDA 2004b, 12).

27 According to CIDA (2004b, 13), "political instability and polarization, elite interests as well as aid volatility and donor-driven agendas seriously constrained the capacity of the Haitian government to develop ownership over the development process."

28 The World Bank applies the concept of "Low Income Countries Under Stress" or LICUS, as an indicator of GNI and the impact of external and internal stresses on a particular country. The LICUS Task Force applies a basic typology to characterize the situation of particular countries: (i) policy-poor but resource-rich countries, (ii) countries with exceptionally weak government capacity (e.g., Haiti), and (iii) countries emerging from conflict.

29  Baranyi (2004, 9) has outlined how since February 2004, Canada has sought to combine "diplomacy," "defence," and "development" in various ways, ranging from more active executive engagement in the country, to Operation Halo and increased aid commitments for 2004–6.

30  By 2003, some 16 percent of CIDA's total annual budget of more than C$2 billion was devoted to "strengthening governance" (CIDA 2003c, 18).

31  These are presumably the "change drivers" and "coalitions of key players" anticipated in earlier CIDA reviews.

32  Canada deployed 450 personnel and six CH-146 Griffon helicopters to assist a UN-sanctioned MIF over a ninety-day period from March 2004 (Operation HALO). By August 2004, sixty-six RCMP officers were also in country to support CIVPOL and training of HNP (Muggah 2005b).

33  Descriptive overviews of Canada's expenditures on "good governance" are provided in Figure 2 and Annex 1.

34  Canada deployed more than 106 election observers and 25 police offers for the February 2006 election. These observers and police also trained about half the 3,500 electoral guards manning polling stations.

35  The project includes the Canadian Centre for International Studies and Cooperation (CEI), World University Services of Canada (WUSC), the Paul Gérin-Lajoie Foundation (FPGL), and the Canadian Executive Service Organization (CESO).

36  Other sectors include the Canada fund for local initiatives (health and education); primary health care projects (HIV/AIDS and health service management training); basic and technical education (e.g., new school projects and education schemes); economic development (e.g., technical assistance for electricity, and assistance for agricultural cooperatives and savings and credit unions); environment and agriculture (veterinary, agroforestry, and local development projects); and regional programs.

37  In the meantime, some C$15.8 million was provided as debt relief to international creditors (described as meeting "basic human needs"), while C$17.7 million was spent on "emergency assistance and reconstruction."

▲

# 9

## ASTUTE GOVERNANCE PROMOTION VERSUS HISTORICAL CONDITIONS IN EXPLAINING GOOD GOVERNANCE: THE CASE OF MAURITIUS

### Richard Sandbrook

If good governance is, as CIDA defines it, "the exercise of power by various levels of government that is effective, honest, equitable, transparent and accountable" (CIDA 1996), then Mauritius has been characterized by exceptionally good governance during the past quarter-century. Why has Mauritius not succumbed to the ineffectual and often predatory neopatrimonial rule that is so common in sub-Saharan Africa? The reason cannot be effective aid programs, for aid to this tiny, middle-income developing country has been meagre since the advent of governance promotion in the early 1990s. There are two other possible keys to this country's governmental success: astute institutional design and capacity building, on the one hand, and/or unusual historical circumstances, on the other. Although it is impossible to be certain, the evidence suggests that unusual conditions constitute the key factor. If so, the Mauritian experience may suggest that governance promoters such as the Government of Canada should emphasize more the fostering of facilitative conditions for democratic governance and effective bureaucracy, and less the direct capacity building of the institutions themselves.[1]

### Mauritius as a Success Story

Since independence in 1968, Mauritius has made rapid socio-economic and political progress while other sub-Saharan countries have languished. Between 1983 and 2003 the economy expanded by almost 6 percent per annum[2]—albeit with periodic downturns caused by severe cyclones or droughts. With annual population growth at a low 1.2 percent, the average annual increase in real per capita GDP has been over 4 percent. Real income in Mauritius more than doubled in twenty years, to nearly US$4,000 per capita, whereas the comparable figure for sub-Saharan Africa as a whole was about US$450 (World Bank 2004). Moreover, growth has been accompanied by considerable diversification of an initially monocultural sugar economy, involving the successive development of a textile and clothing industry (in an Export Processing Zone—EPZ), high-end tourism, offshore banking and business services, and information and communications technology. Mauritian firms have even begun to invest in other African countries—textile and clothing manufacturing in Madagascar, sugar estates and factories in Mozambique, and joint ventures in information technology in Namibia and elsewhere. Although Mauritius has not matched East Asia's economic performance, its record has surpassed that of all other African countries except Botswana.[3]

Substantial social equity has accompanied this economic success. One indicator of the relative well-being of national populations is the United Nations Development Programme's (UNDP) annual ranking of countries according to a composite score, the human development index (HDI). Mauritius in recent years has ranked first or second among African countries on this index, thanks to its extensive welfare state. Life expectancy, adult literacy, school enrolment, and infant mortality rates approach those of the industrial countries. Also, income inequality has diminished since independence. The Gini co-efficient (where 1 signifies perfect inequality in income distribution, and 0 perfect equality) fell from 0.5 in 1962 to 0.37 in the mid-1980s, where it has remained, with minor oscillations, ever since.[4] Nonetheless, wealth remains concentrated, with 1 percent of the population, mostly whites, owning about half the land under cane cultivation and about 65 percent of the stock of productive assets (Mistry 1999, 554). Were it not for the tax-supported welfare state—with social spending accounting for 40 percent of public expenditures—this concentration of wealth might well have sabotaged democracy.[5]

The welfare state commands overwhelming public support.[6] Public pensions, originating in the 1950s, were expanded into a comprehensive scheme on the eve of the hard-fought 1976 election. This scheme included a universal Basic Retirement Pension (BRP) at age sixty (the equivalent of about $70 per month in early 2005), together with pensions for widows, invalids, and orphans. For workers, a National Pension Scheme based on compulsory contributions from employers and employees complements the basic pension. When the government announced in late 2004 its intention to restrict the BRP to those whose regular pension was less than 17,333 rupees ($630) per month, it was widely denounced as a stooge of the IMF (L'Express [Pt.-Louis] September 23, 2004).

Primary schooling, which has been free since colonial days, became compulsory in 1993. Governments extended free schooling to the secondary level in 1976 and to the tertiary level in 1988. The University of Mauritius, built just before independence, features a modern and well maintained campus and an enviable student–teacher ratio.

Comprehensive and free medical care is a major and cherished legacy of the country's first prime minister (and a medical doctor), Sir Seewoosegur Ramgoolam. In the 1970s and 1980s the government built health centres so that no citizen would be more than three miles from primary health care. Currently, 63 percent of medical doctors work in the public sector, with the remainder in private clinics, where the price of services is publicly regulated (Mauritius, Ministry of Health and Quality of Life 2001). The state has achieved remarkable success in controlling communicable diseases through the provision of clean water to all, the extension of a sewerage system begun in 1959, immunization campaigns, and the continuation of an antimalaria campaign introduced by the colonial government in the 1940s. Continuing subsidies of basic foodstuffs (white rice and flour) further improve overall health statistics by reducing malnutrition.

Other effectively administered public programs target particular disadvantaged groups. A Central Housing Authority started to build housing estates following a devastating cyclone in 1960. The Mauritius Housing Corporation (MHC) has been extending housing loans to middle-class families since 1963. Since the 1980s the MHC has been helping low-income families purchase housing through subsidized loans and grants. Widespread house ownership provides most people with a stake in the system.

There are also several targeted antipoverty programs, with contributions from various aid donors. These programs respond to the needs of those bypassed by the "miracle." A Presidential Educational Trust provides financial help to children in "deprived" areas from the age of three. A Trust Fund for the Social Integration of Vulnerable Groups, established in 1998, finances community development projects, microcredit schemes, loans to needy students, and free school meals. It had disbursed R107 million (US$3.7 million) by early 2003. The EU has provided the bulk of the funding (US$4 million) to A Nou Diboute Ensam (ANDE) since 1999. That organization acts as a funding agency to support microenterprises and community projects run by local NGOs. The state also provides social assistance to households whose income falls below a basic level as a result of natural disaster, loss of employment, or abandonment by the breadwinner. Although critics charge that applying for this benefit is a complex and humiliating process, such schemes do not even exist elsewhere in the region.

Finally, the government mounts employment and training schemes, whose importance has risen along with the unemployment rate (close to 10 percent by 2002) (see Mauritius, Central Statistics Office 2003, Table 5). These schemes upgrade skills, train people for employment in specific industries, and provide paid job experience to unemployed university and college graduates. Also, various subsidies and services promote small and medium-sized enterprises, which employ about 30 percent of the labour force.

In addition to these achievements, a centralized and regulated industrial relations system enhances the security and well-being of employees outside the Export Processing Zone (EPZ). This system derives from the Industrial Relations Act passed in 1973 by the Fabian-socialist Mauritian Labour Party, which at the time faced a Marxist-Leninist threat from militant trade unions allied to the Mouvement Militant Mauricien (MMM). Not surprisingly, this legislation makes it very difficult for unions to stage legal strikes. It also exempts employers in the incipient EPZ from regulations concerning overtime, maternity allowance, holiday work, night work for women, and termination of employment.[7] Such pro-capitalist measures were instituted in the context of a state of emergency that severely restricted protest activities. Nevertheless, the act (with later amendments) contains some important benefits for labour. Through tripartite (union–employer–government) wage negotiations and various labour tribunals, the state engages in a delicate balancing act: to reward workers with fair terms and conditions of employment while ensuring that improvements will not lower productivity or stoke inflation. Also, employers outside the EPZ are required by law to justify layoffs to a Termination of Contracts and Services Board on economic grounds—and compensate laid-off workers—before they can declare workers redundant. Unions have come to embrace these protections.

This socio-economic progress would probably not have occurred in the absence of good governance; democracy has reinforced the growth-with-equity strategy. The early years were not propitious: there was a state of emergency in 1971, and the first post-colonial elections were postponed by four years. Nevertheless, Mauritius has not deviated from the democratic path since the delayed election in 1976 (in which the radical MMM adopted the "electoral road" to power). The country has experienced seven hotly contested national elections, all of which observers deemed free, fair, and orderly, and four of which led to peaceful changes of government. Despite flaws (periodic corruption and nepotism, occasionally unstable coalitions), democracy in Mauritius has consolidated itself to a degree that is unique in Africa. In addition, an unusually effective public service has orchestrated investment and economic diversification and implemented the various social programs (as discussed below). Mauritius, in sum, satisfies the exacting criteria of a "democratic developmental state" (Sandbrook 2005).

Nonetheless, the country's record is far from flawless. Afro-Creoles, constituting about one-quarter of the population, have not shared equally in the rising prosperity. A range of subtle biases in the educational system, especially the importance placed on a mastery of English, impede Afro-Creoles in attaining the higher education and training needed to escape the unskilled and semi-skilled positions they predominantly hold (Bunwaree 2001). Politically, too, Afro-Creoles face hurdles in making their voices heard. Whereas other ethnic groups field their own associations to press their interests, Creoles have historically joined Roman Catholic associations—and rarely fill leadership positions (Laville 2000, 286). In addition, few black Creoles have sat in Parliament, where they might voice the aspirations and frustrations of this group. The result has been growing ethnic and class tensions, which exploded in three days of rioting in 1999.

As well, gender inequality persists in Mauritius (see Bunwaree 1999; Thacoor-Sidaya 1998). Until recently the country harboured a traditional, patriarchal society (or congeries of societies). Much has changed in the past twenty years, especially as a result of the academic success of women within a free educational system based on competitive examinations. However, women are still found disproportionately in the lowest-paid, least skilled, and most insecure jobs. At least two-thirds of those employed in the EPZ, whose firms are exempt from many of the country's labour protections and wage requirements, are women (Liang Lung Chong 1998; Uppiah 2000). In sum, though Mauritius has recorded notable achievements, it is not a paradise.

## The Role of Aid

Aid has played a minor role in Mauritius's governmental experience. Even at its peak in 1990, aid to Mauritius—as a share of gross national income (GNI)—was far below that for sub-Saharan Africa (SSA) as a whole or for Ghana—another African case considered in this book (see Table 1). Mauritius, a decade later, received negligible aid, whereas the region experienced a decrease of one-third relative to GNI and Ghana an increase. As the period since 1990 has been the era of governance assistance, and as overall aid to Mauritius by 1995 had already fallen to 1 percent of its GNI, we can conclude that governance assistance to the island has been of minor significance. This judgment is supported by OECD data for 2002–3: 74 percent of the minimal aid to Mauritius in that financial year was directed toward economic infrastructure and services, 12 percent to education, and 3 percent to production. Any governance assistance

TABLE 1
Aid as % of Gross National Income

|  | 1990 | 2000 |
|---|---|---|
| Mauritius | 4 (us$89 million) | 0.5 (us$20 million) |
| Ghana | 10 | 12 |
| Sub-Saharan Africa | 6 | 4 |

*Source*: World Bank, *World Development Indicators* (online).[8]

programming would have fallen within the remaining 11 percent of aid, which is identified as "program assistance" and "other/unspecified" (http://www.oecd .org/dataoecd/23/25/1882308.gif). In any event, Mauritius had achieved exemplary governance long before 1990.

Governance assistance been a minor aspect of aid in Mauritius; furthermore, CIDA has played a negligible role on this small island. Canada did not appear among the country's top ten donors in 2002–3; indeed, the EU and France alone accounted for about 38 percent of its official development assistance (ODA), with Japan a distant third (OECD data). Canada provided a total of C$1.9 million to Mauritius in a recent five-year period (2000–5), of which CIDA's Canadian Partnership Branch (CPB) accounted for 42 percent.[9] The remainder arrived in Mauritius through CIDA's support of regional programs (the African Union, the African Capacity Building Foundation [ACBF], the Southern African Development Community) and through multilateral channels. In fact, CIDA has had no bilateral programs in Mauritius. About one-quarter of CPB's limited funds have been targeted at "government and civil society" projects in Mauritius by way of various partners. The ACBF has received, directly or indirectly, three grants from CIDA since 1991 to support regional institution building. It is unclear, however, whether this foundation has supported any capacity building in Mauritius. Local government has been a focus of three CIDA-funded regional programs in which the partner was either the Federation of Canadian Municipalities, the Association Internationale des Maires Francophones (France), or the Commonwealth Local Government Forum in London. Other partners, such as the Canadian Bureau for International Education, have been involved in programs that may have had some tangential impact on governance on the island. All of these projects grew out of discussions with local actors.

Although aid cannot claim direct credit for this country's advanced governance, friendly foreign governments have made important indirect contributions. Healthy economic growth fortifies political institutions by building popular enthusiasm for them within emergent democracies. Preferential treatment of Mauritius in trade and credit agreements has assisted the island's economic development, thereby indirectly building democratic legitimacy. Three agreements in particular deserve mention. The EU boosted Mauritius's sugar exports through the sugar protocol in the Lomé Convention (1975), renewed in the Cotonou Agreement in 2000 (but soon to expire). The Multi-Fibre Agreement, phased out in 2006, has provided the country with relatively large textile quotas in Europe and the United States. (Textiles, clothing, and sugar accounted for about 63 percent of the country's exports in 2003.) Finally, India generously provided a line of credit of US$100 million to Mauritius in 2002 to use in creating a "Cyber Island." External assistance has therefore been important—but, unlike many other developing countries, Mauritius has been able to take advantage of its opportunities. This superior capacity requires explanation.

## Explaining Good Governance

The Mauritian experience sheds light on the knotty question of whether governance is more likely to be improved *directly* by institutional engineering or *indirectly* by fostering the conditions in which democratic institutions and disciplined bureaucracies can flourish. The "governance" school in international development, which emerged in the late 1980s, has assumed that "institutions matter" (in driving economic reform, market-based growth, and social development) and that appropriate institutions can be nurtured despite hostile conditions of poverty, corruption, and ethnic strife. Yet experts in the field would also acknowledge that particular institutional arrangements will work well only under certain conditions. But we cannot have it both ways: either we should focus our energies mainly on institutional capacity building or, accepting that unusual conditions produce exceptional governance, mainly on fostering those conditions. While no definitive resolution of this issue seems possible (Przeworski 2004), the Mauritian experience nevertheless allows us to reflect on the merits of each approach. Mauritius has benefited from astute institutional design; however, unusual conditions have underpinned the effectiveness of its political institutions.

### Astute Institutional Design

The first prime minister, Sir Seewoosegur Ramgoolam (1968–82), buttressed the institutional and policy foundations of an activist, democratic state. He adopted a conciliatory, non-communalistic, and issue-oriented approach to politics, rejecting a communal appeal to the Hindu majority. He adopted this approach both because his Labour Party had originated as a transethnic, anti-colonial movement and because the Hindus were too riven by caste and regional loyalties to succumb to such an appeal (see Teelock 2001, 378–82, 391–96). Consensus rested on a common social democratic outlook that Ramgoolam and most other leaders had imbibed in British and French universities and that accorded with the popular yearning for equity in this racially stratified former sugar colony. This moderately progressive outlook was challenged by the revolutionary-socialist MMM in the 1970s. Only when the MMM renounced its revolutionary message in favour of electoral competition and respect for property rights was the consensus restored (and a state of emergency lifted). Mauritius thus managed to avoid the familiar cul-de-sac of so many African countries: authoritarian leadership, communalism, and an issueless clientelism fuelled by state control of productive resources.

Institutional arrangements undercut communalism, which might otherwise have sabotaged the democratic state. First, the independence constitution mandates an electoral system that encourages all major parties to nominate candidates from minority as well as majority communities. The main island is divided into twenty constituencies of three members each, while Rodrigues (the second island of Mauritius) encompasses a single two-member constituency. These multimember constituencies penalize parties that appeal exclusively to a single ethnic group; when this happens, other ethnic communities respond by boycotting those parties' candidates to elect their own favourite son in one of the three slots. Second, the "best losers" system reassures all communities that they will not be deprived of representation; this was important during the first decade of independence (Mathur 1997). Under that system, an independent electoral commission appoints up to eight losing candidates to each new National Assembly to represent "underrepresented" ethnic groups.

A third innovation is an inclusive party system. Before independence, most parties had a distinct ethnic basis: Creoles, Muslims, and Hindus each dominated their own party or parties. However, caste, regional, and personal divisions among Hindus undercut their ability to use their majority status to impose Hindu domination of political life. Ramgoolam, after assuming leadership in 1956, continued to recruit candidates for the Labour Party[10] from all communities. Other parties, sooner or later, followed suit, and communal appeals became rare after independence. Also, governing has required the formation of coalitions, and this practice has further blurred ethnic divisions (Carroll and Carroll 2000, 136). Cabinets now routinely include ministers drawn from all communities. No ethnic group, with the major exception of the Afro-Creoles, need fear that democratic processes will ignore their interests.

The "civic network," as it was originally called, is another institution that political leaders use to accommodate diverse interests and to build policy consensus. This consultative tool originated in 1979, just prior to the adoption of a stringent structural adjustment program. To foster acquiescence to painful economic reforms, the government consulted a wide range of voluntary associations about the choices to be made. Since then, successive governments have regularized this consultative process. In the months leading up to a budget, the finance minister "makes the rounds of the country's major stakeholders, listening to their views, exchanging comments, accepting their written analyses. Each evening, these consultations are reported on the state-run television news: union members meet the minister one day; business associations another; and major social welfare NGOs and other groups have their days" (Brautigam 2004, 662). When the budget is presented, its details are widely disseminated by newspapers and the finance minister's website. Lively debate, both in and outside Parliament, ensues. As well, each ministry has developed a "consultations list" of organizations to be consulted on major policy issues. In 2002 the government formalized this innovation in the National Economic and Social Council, which brings together representatives from employers, unions, youth organizations, women's groups, senior citizens, NGOs, the universities, and experts in various fields. Although it is difficult to gauge the degree to which these consultations influence the budget and other legislation, they are apparently effective in building both public support for policies and public trust in government (Carroll and Carroll 1999b).

These institutions, together with the British-style bureaucracy inherited at independence, have proven resilient and strong. But would they have survived in the absence of Mauritius's historical circumstances?

### Unusual Historical Conditions

Although Mauritius after independence in 1968 shared many of the typical challenges facing other African countries, underneath the surface the country was quite atypical. In particular, an unusual colonial experience prepared the soil for democratic governance and effective bureaucracy. Consider first the shared problems:

- As with other countries in the region, Mauritius's history included servile labour, extreme racial inequality, and a monocultural economy. France, which controlled the island until 1810, forged a colonial society in which a small French oligarchy exploited African slaves on extensive landholdings. When the British took over, they employed incentives to convert these mixed estates into sugar plantations. The new colonial power abolished slavery in 1835 but replaced the slaves with indentured labourers from South Asia, a system that continued until 1910.

- Mauritius at independence suffered the rapid population growth and high unemployment that bedevilled other countries in the region. Unemployment ranged as high as 20 percent between independence and 1982 (Darga 1996, 80).

- Mauritius was typical both in its reliance on extensive state intervention in economic life and in its need to undertake structural adjustment to deal with an economic crisis in the early 1980s (Gulhati and Nallari 1990). Between 1979 and 1985 the island carried out a series of stabilization and adjustment programs with loans from the IMF and the World Bank. These measures were unusually successful: by 1983, Mauritius was well on the way to recovery.

- Mauritius is similar to many African countries in its extreme cultural diversity (Miles 1999). Hindus comprise just over half the population (52 percent). But Hindus do not constitute a unified voting bloc: they are divided by caste and regional/linguistic origins. Hindus predominate in the public service and some professions and are heavily engaged in agriculture as labourers and small planters. Muslims, also the descendants of indentured workers, form about one-sixth of the population. They are mainly involved in commerce in the towns and cities. Descendants of slaves, the Creoles account for 27 percent of Mauritians. Darker-skinned Creoles (often referred to as Afro-Creoles) constitute the bulk of this category. Afro-Creoles are disproportionately represented in low-paid, low-status employment, especially in the towns, and reside disproportionately in impoverished neighbourhoods (Laville 2000). The Chinese, though few in number (2 to 3 percent of the population), are economically influential as entrepreneurs and shopkeepers. Finally, Franco-Mauritians, a tiny but wealthy minority, have diversified from sugar cane production into manufacturing, tourism, and financial and business services.

- Mauritians, not atypically, tend to divide politically by ethnicity and religion, though here ethnicity, religion, and class overlap. Several instances of communal violence marred the island's transition to independence, just as "tribalism" marred decolonization in many mainland countries. The new state seemed headed for communal disaster. Confounding expectations, however, the country maintained social harmony for twenty-one years— until three days of unnerving riots and looting spearheaded by the Afro-Creole underclass in February 1999.

Yet in other ways, historical conditions in Mauritius are quite atypical, and account in large measure for the growth and survival of effective democratic governance. First, *Mauritius emerged from the beginning of colonial rule as a capitalist social formation* in which land and labour were treated as commodities. That Mauritius was uninhabited when the Dutch occupied it in the seventeenth century is key to understanding its unusual class structure. No potentially reactionary pre-capitalist classes—a landed aristocracy or poor peasantry—survived into the nineteenth and twentieth centuries, as they did elsewhere. Whereas other countries of the region comprised largely peasant societies that were inclined to clientelism and personal rule, Mauritius developed a powerful mercantile and agrarian bourgeoisie, a large class of small landowners and merchants, and a rural and urban proletariat. This class structure facilitated the formation of a disciplined capitalist state, while opening the possibility of an eventual social democratic class compromise.

An independent bourgeoisie emerged under French rule, with its roots in commerce and estate agriculture (see Allen 1999). This class transformed itself into a plantocracy when the British promoted Mauritius as a sugar colony following its takeover; its members depended largely on local resources to expand their holdings and productivity (ibid.). Local capital accumulation continued in the post-colonial era, when state incentives channelled the plantocracy's surplus into the EPZ and to a lesser degree into tourism and business services. Its cohesion enhanced by French culture, Catholic religion, and intermarriage, the business class remains well organized and powerful.

Labour, in contrast, has rarely acted as a united force. From the start, labour in the form of slaves and indentured workers was treated as a commodity. With the end of the indentured labour system in the 1920s, unions emerged to cater to the interests of a rural and urban proletariat (dockworkers and transport workers were particularly well organized). Yet no cohesive working class consciousness developed. Only in the late 1930s and early 1940s, in the context of general strikes and the formation of militant unions, and again in 1971–73 at the height of MMM's radical class appeal, did unions unite across ethnic lines to advance common interests (Oodiah 1991; Gokhool 1999). Otherwise, ethnic rivalries and suspicions pitted the largely Hindu agricultural workers against the largely Afro-Creole urban workers.

A variegated petty bourgeoisie also emerged in the nineteenth century. One fraction was composed of an educated and mainly Creole commercial and bureaucratic class ("les gens de couleur"), which remains prominent today. Another, much larger fraction was a Hindu yeomanry that purchased cane land, beginning in the 1870s, from Franco-Mauritian plantation owners forced to retrench in hard times. By 2002 almost 90 percent of the island's arable land was devoted to sugar cultivation, and small planters owned nearly half this total. (Seventeen large firms own the remaining cane fields, together with the sugar mills.) The 35,000 independent growers—whose families account for about 15 percent of Mauritians—own plots as large as 400 hectares, though 90 percent of the holdings are two hectares or less.[11] The larger of these independent farmers, by investing in their children's education, had engendered by the 1940s (together with government scholarships) a substantial Hindu professional and bureaucratic class that competed with the Creole elite in the colonial bureaucracy.[12] Muslim shopowners and Chinese entrepreneurs formed further ethnic fragments of the small and (later) large-scale business class.

Second, *the complex overlap of class and ethnic divisions facilitated a social democratic compromise by separating economic from political power.* At independence, economic power resided in a small Franco-Mauritian and Creole elite that owned and ran the sugar plantations. The colonial state depended on sugar revenues, yet British governors had rarely identified with the French-speaking elite, who held them at arm's length. Meanwhile, the educated offspring of the predominantly Hindu small planters, facing exclusion from the upper echelons of the sugar industry, sought advancement through the colonial state and independence movements, especially the Labour Party (formed in 1936). Politics and the state provided the majority Hindus with a way of countering the economic power of the plantocracy. Democratic politics would empower the Hindus in particular, for their leaders could tap the support of the majority, whose hostility to the plantocracy ran deep—a hostility deriving from a harsh history, from the fact that most small planters had family members who worked seasonally on the large plantations, and from an exclusionary and stratified racial system. The state, through its top posts and control of contracts, offered an alternative route to economic success. The plantocracy and the Creole elite opposed independence and majority rule for fear of Hindu domination; nonetheless, the British transferred power to a largely Hindu leadership in 1968.

The local capitalists who chose to remain in Mauritius (at least half) accepted an implicit bargain. They yielded their political dominance and accepted some redistribution in exchange for the legitimacy that a modest social democracy would generate, provided that social reform was limited to a tax-supported welfare state and excluded asset redistribution. This consensus has prevailed ever since; even the radical MMM acquiesced in 1982.[13] Hence, Fabian-socialist ideas, imbibed during lengthy stays in Britain, united the leaders of the major parties and provided the ideological basis for a welfare capitalism that drew support from the descendants of slaves and indentured labourers.

Third, *the patterns of governance established under British rule have positively influenced the formation of a democratic and developmental state.* The directive, developmental stance of this post-colonial state traces its origins to the first decades of British rule in the nineteenth century. The colonial state never pre-empted market forces; it did, however, forcefully intervene to mould these forces in accordance with a plan. Beginning in the mid-nineteenth century, the British orchestrated the transformation of Mauritius into a plantation economy based on sugar. The colonial power provided a range of incentives to planters, mobilized investment capital as needed, built the infrastructure of roads, railways, and port facilities, amended the legal code to establish limited-liability companies, and created a reliable labour force through the indentured labour system (Reddi 1997, 2–6). The strategy succeeded, establishing a tradition of an activist capitalist state.

Effective states are those in which the executive commands broad political authority and there is a disciplined and expert bureaucracy. Whereas other African states have disintegrated since independence, the Mauritian state has remained coherent and strong. Its authority and administrative capacity also derive from an unusual colonial experience. The dynamics of rule impelled the British authorities to extend political rights and to open the colonial bureaucracy to local talent at a much earlier stage than in other colonies. Tensions between the French plantocracy and British colonial officials motivated the latter to secure the support of local allies through legal and constitutional reforms. The British legal system, introduced in the 1830s, accorded a "technical equality" to all people, regardless of race. On many occasions in the nineteenth century, British judges ruled in favour of Indian indentured labourers in disputes with their employers (Reddi 1997, 9). Also, the colonial authorities tried to limit the Franco-Mauritian oligarchy's influence, and to maximize their own, by extending political rights, first to "Coloureds" (Creoles) and later, in 1885, to literate Indians. The oligarchy's demand for retrocession to France after the First World War accelerated this process. Although the era of mass politics dates only from the formation of the MLP in 1936 and the extensions of representative government in 1948 and 1959, the Indian vote had become significant in Legislative Council elections as early as 1921, by which time they formed 31 percent of the electorate (Reddi 1989, 10). Even those who were denied the franchise avidly followed political debates and attended campaign rallies from this early date (interview, S. Reddi, Réduit, May 16, 2003).

Equally conducive to democratic consolidation was the development of a robust, if ethnically fragmented, civil society during colonial rule. British rule accustomed people to a free press, in addition to regular elections and the rule of law (Dukhira 2002, 42; Reddi 1989). General strikes in 1937, 1938, and 1943, and the organization of trade unions, announced the arrival of the working class on the historical stage. It was to play an important role in pushing politics to the left in the revolutionary era of the early 1970s. In addition, the strong cooperative movement that exists today traces its roots to 1913–15. Fifteen cooperative credit societies emerged in that period under the tutelage of an expert contracted by the colonial government. By 1932 there were twenty-eight of these societies, most of which catered to small planters, with a total of 2,100 members. The postwar period saw an upsurge in cooperatives and their extension to workers, civil servants, entrepreneurs, consumers, and fishermen, as both colonial and post-colonial governments fostered their growth through advisers, training, and legislation. By 2000 more than one-tenth of Mauritians (156,000 people) belonged to 563 cooperative societies.[14] The island's tightly knit communities have spawned a variety of other civil associations over the years. The umbrella body of NGOs, the Mauritius Council of Social Services, estimates that five thousand voluntary organizations were operating in the country in 2000, though only about three hundred were well-structured and permanent organizations (interview, Ram Nookadee, Mauritius Council of Social Services, 2003). These trends help explain the unusual vitality of democracy in Mauritius. And with governments based on consent, political rulers have eschewed a standing army, thereby avoiding the debilitating military coups that afflict other African countries.

Bureaucratic independence, discipline, and esprit de corps—without which a developmental state would collapse into ineffectiveness and corruption— also emerged from unusual colonial circumstances.[15] Not only was this colonial state exceptionally well articulated, but it also employed a much higher proportion of indigenous personnel than elsewhere in the region. The weight of the colonial state prepared the ground for its developmental role; it had "four times the per capita state revenues, three times the number of police officers per capita, and ten times the number of magistrates and cases per capita" than other British colonial states in Africa (Lange 2003, 404). The British left a much deeper imprint on Mauritian governance than in its other African colonies, principally because, in the absence of traditional political institutions, the colonial power had to engage in direct rule. Elsewhere, as in Gold Coast, for example, colonial rule was less intensive, refracted as it was through traditional power structures in some version of indirect rule.

The colonial state also relied heavily on local employees. Even in the 1920s, Mauritians accounted for 93 percent of employees in the civil service, police, and judiciary, though Britons still filled the top positions. However, by 1932, 65 percent of officer-level positions were held by Mauritians (Lange 2003, 404). Indians entered the civil service as clerks in the 1920s, but discriminatory practices limited their rise into the higher posts. However, after 1936 the colonial authorities had to compete for the support of Creoles and Indians against the militant MLP. It did so partly by opening up opportunities for them in the public sector. The British fostered a local intelligentsia by awarding university scholarships to the top secondary school graduates—the number of annual scholarships eventually rose to 20. The Indians and Creoles who won most of these scholarships would typically join the civil service or judiciary on their return from Britain. It was members of this meritocratic elite who moved ahead as the public sector expanded after 1948 with the extensions of public education, health care, and welfare services. Hence, career bureaucrats developed an esprit de corps and managerial tradition decades before independence.

Meritocracy has continued, with the public service resisting the politicization that plagues other countries in the region (Carroll and Joypaul 1993, 434). An independent Public Service Commission, whose five members are appointed by the figurehead president of the republic in consultation with both the prime minister and the leader of the opposition, retains its constitutionally prescribed independence. The commission oversees recruitment, promotion, and disciplinary action within the public service. Although informed Mauritians acknowledge that civil servants are not immune to ethnic biases and corruption, the service retains considerable integrity. Public-sector employment continues to attract well-qualified applicants. In a country with limited secure employment, jobs that offer guaranteed employment with good benefits remain highly valued. Hence, "Mauritius has a senior public service which seems to be as competent, as ethical, and as committed to the goal of service to the public, as any public bureaucracy in the developed countries" (Carroll and Carroll 1999a, 187–88).

Thus, while Mauritius, on the surface, appeared to be a "typical" country of the region in the 1970s, its deeper historical and structural conditions were in fact quite atypical.

## Implications for Donor Policy

One implication of this study is that donors, to be effective, need to pay close attention to the specificities of each country's history in promoting good governance (as Sue Unsworth emphasizes in chapter 2). It was much more likely that effective, democratic governance would flourish in Mauritius than in other countries of the region because it (in contrast to most of the others) developed propitious conditions for political pluralism and, indeed, social democracy.

Mauritius has, in short, benefited not only from progressive leadership and astute institutional design, but also from four unusually favourable historical circumstances:

- It developed a wholly capitalist social formation in which an independent business class developed. In this way the island avoided a landlord class or a large peasantry that might have been open to a reactionary politics of, respectively, rigid oligarchy or neopatrimonial rule.
- There was a separation between economic power, largely in the hands of a Franco-Mauritian and Creole minority, and political power, controlled largely by Hindus. This separation was conducive to an equity-enhancing social democratic class compromise.
- The colonial experience of direct rule under the British implanted the rule of law, democratic institutions, robust civil associations, and bureaucratic esprit de corps from an early stage.
- A "growth with equity" strategy succeeded. Since the early 1980s that has meant a relatively advanced welfare state, a comparatively equitable distribution of income, and a contemporary per capita purchasing power (PPP) of US$10,000.

It is, in the nature of things, impossible to prove that these favourable conditions, rather than good leadership and astute institutional engineering, account for the comparatively advanced governance. The counterfactual is speculative: we cannot know with certainty what would have happened had the same institutional design and good leadership occurred under less positive circumstances. Yet it is highly doubtful that the same quality of institutional design and leadership would have underpinned a comparable level of governance in, for example, Haiti or Ghana (other case studies in this book), where the conditions were less favourable. Institutions matter, but appropriate conditions pave the way for strong institutions.

This conclusion accords with the predominant early theory of democratic development. It was initially thought that democracy is an *outgrowth* of socio-economic development, not its *cause*.[16] The revisionist view emerged in the late 1980s, when it was believed that poor governance was the principal cause of blighted socio-economic development. But this view overstates the independent causal significance of governance institutions. Governance is as much a dependent as an independent variable. Hence, governance promoters should aim to promote, not solely governance, but a coordinated and mutually reinforcing circle of economic, social, and political development.

These reflections suggest that a donor approach that focuses narrowly on building political and state institutions will rarely work.[17] This approach—which may aptly be designated "mainstream"—focuses on procedural democracy. It identifies democracy mainly with periodic and fair elections and the rule of law. It seeks to enhance the capabilities of democratic institutions (especially the electoral machinery, legislatures, judiciaries, political parties, and advocacy and human rights NGOs) and state bureaucracies (the civil service, tax administration, oversight commissions, and utilities in public hands). But this approach, when combined with market liberalizing policies, often *worsens* social and economic conditions and undermines democratic governance (Chua 2003). One major shortcoming is that procedural democracy provides elites with the scope to maintain or even extend their privileges—privileges that are widely regarded as unfair. ·

Consequently, the initial euphoria occasioned by democratic breakthroughs in developing countries is typically followed by disillusionment as democracy fails to bring the anticipated improvements. Persistent or deepening social inequalities, economic insecurity arising from volatile global markets, continuing mass poverty, and anemic and remote governance are the usual culprits. Popular disillusionment with such conditions is graphically revealed in a series of regional workshops—"Making Democracy Work for the Poor"—convened by Sweden's Institute for Democracy and Electoral Assistance (IDEA).[18] IDEA's South Asia workshop observed: "The trappings of democracy have allowed unrepresentative elites to hijack power, promote their own interests, and bypass the poor.... For most people elections have become irrelevant." The workshop on the Commonwealth of Independent States concluded that human rights have *deteriorated* since the break-up of the Soviet Union. Equal rights before the law is a chimera, it declared; the quality of public education and health care has fallen; no legal right to a job or basic sustenance survives; religious intolerance grows; and political rights are merely formal. Similar complaints surfaced in the Latin America and Africa workshops. Surveys such as the Latin American Barometer have found that democracy has lost legitimacy among a majority in most Latin American countries, mainly because the respondents believe that transitions have not diminished massive inequalities or improved living standards (Baviskar and Malone 2004). Elite power structures persist, manipulating procedural democracies to advance elite interests.

A broader approach to governance recognizes the futility of implanting and fostering political and state institutions without also building the requisite social, economic, and cultural foundations. People in poor countries overwhelmingly conceive of "real" democracy as a system that tackles poverty, inequality, and powerlessness. Such challenges often involve confronting entrenched power structures. That is the dilemma faced by donors such as Canada. Yet short of advocating revolution, there is much they can do (and sometimes are doing) to promote broad-based, incremental changes:

- Employ whatever influence they have to persuade entrenched elites that their own survival depends on their granting concessions in a renewed social contract to help alleviate the social deficit.

- Recognize that the combination of free-market reforms and democratization is often a lethal mixture in the global South, and thus refrain from penalizing governments that deviate from neoliberal thinking (as Mauritius often has done).
- Encourage a more equitable distribution of basic services by supporting free universal primary education and free basic health services.
- Advocate land reform in countries where land is highly concentrated.
- Emulate the experience of initially poor countries and states, such as Mauritius and Kerala (India) by providing basic social insurance even in straitened circumstances.
- Support independent foundations dedicated to the uplifting of socially and economically marginalized communities.
- Encourage the development of more participatory democratic processes on the models of the civic network in Mauritius, participatory budgeting in Brazilian cities, and local government in Kerala.

Effective democratic governance depends on giving voice, bread, and dignity to ordinary people. The Mauritian experience teaches one fundamental lesson: for procedural democracy to survive and thrive, it must move toward a more participatory and equity-enhancing democracy.

## Notes

1   This case study illustrates Sue Unsworth's main points (in chapter 2): that donors need to be better informed about the historical conditions of countries in which they promote governance, and that effective governance promotion involves fostering appropriate social and economic conditions. Note that my conflation of democracy with good governance follows the implicit or explicit identity of the two concepts in most governance thinking.
2   World Bank, "World Development Indicators," WDI Online at http://devdata.world bank.org/dataonline.
3   For the details, see Subramanian and Roy 2003.
4   For example, the most recent household budget survey (2001–2) records the Gini at 0.371, down from 0.387 in 1996–97. See Mauritius Central Statistical Office 2002.
5   That the state has actually been able to collect taxes from the wealthy distinguishes Mauritius from most other countries in the region.
6   A massive opinion poll in 2002 discovered that 88 percent of respondents proposed that the government spend more on social security; 78 percent recommended that government raise taxes on the rich to redistribute income to the poor. Centre for Applied Social Research 2003, 109.
7   At its height in the early 1990s, the EPZ employed almost one-third of the labour force.

8   Online at http://devdata.worldbank.org/dataonline/SMResult.asp.

9   Information from Murray Town, Acting Manager and Senior Country Analyst at CIDA.

10  The MLP was formed during the labour unrest in 1936 by Maurice Curé, a member of the Creole middle class. Only in the 1950s did Hindu leaders assume leadership.

11  These statistics on land ownership are drawn from Mauritius, Ministry of Environment 2002. Tea cultivation, with 680 hectares under cultivation in 2002, is overwhelmingly a smallholder crop, with only one of 1,350 planters cultivating more than 100 hectares. See the "Digest of Agricultural Statistics" at http://statsmauritius.gov.mu/report/natacc/agrico2.

12  This interpretation draws Allen 1999; Darga 1996; and Houbert 1982–83.

13  This interpretation draws on Houbert 1982–83; Meisenhelder 1999; Seegobin and Collen 1977.

14  This information is drawn from Mauritius, Ministry of Commerce and Co-operatives 2003.

15  This paragraph draws on the extensive historical research of S. Reddi (interview, May 19, 2003) as well as Lange 2003.

16  See, for example, the classic discussion of the structural requisites of democracy in Lipset 1981.

17  Indeed, some analysts argue that there is a *negative* correlation between the volume of aid as it is presently programmed and improvements in governance. See Brautigam and Knack 2004.

18  See IDEA 2000 for an overview. Each workshop was attended by a broad cross-section of activists and NGOs. Full workshop reports may be accessed at http://www.idea.int/2000df/dfreports.html.

▲

# III

## THE IMPLICATIONS

▼

# 10

## MANAGING CANADA'S GROWING DEVELOPMENT COOPERATION: OUT OF THE LABYRINTH

### Bernard Wood

*Foreign aid is taking money from poor people in rich countries to give it to rich people in poor countries.* —Traditional, 1950s

### Introduction

This chapter analyzes how Canada's foreign aid has been managed over the past four decades, with a particular focus on whether a more decentralized approach to management (attempted in the 1980s) would lead to greater effectiveness. The starting point is a recognition that the governance "system" at the Canadian end of the development cooperation chain decisively shapes the types and extent of cooperation Canada can provide, as well as the terms on which it does so. This system also determines Canada's ability to respond to the needs, resources, and obstacles within recipient countries.

This chapter examines and assesses the record of management in Canadian cooperation with an eye to the expected requirements for the next decade at least. Importantly and urgently, the context is one where promises have been made and expectations have been raised substantially, by Canada and others, in terms of the impact, quality, and volume of assistance; and also where standards and lessons of good practice are being more widely accepted and shared than ever before. The main argument advanced is that over the full history of Canadian development cooperation, the most important parameters and the most chronic weaknesses in management have consistently been found at the very foundations of the Canadian government's management process, where strategic directions are set for a basket of activities that can often barely be described as a "program."

## How Has Canada's Aid Been Managed?

In most assessments of a donor country's performance, the lion's share of interest quickly focuses on bilateral (country to country) long-term development assistance programs. This overlooks nearly half the total assistance effort (i.e., assistance delivered through alternative channels, such as multilateral institutions and NGOS) as well as the much larger potential for "non-aid" development cooperation. Thus it is important, as Table 1 indicates, to keep in view the full range of activities that an industrialized country can undertake with poor countries with the goal of advancing their development; to gauge the relative importance of these activities; and to assess the Canadian government's latitude and incentives to make particular choices within each major component. As the analysis shows, the development instruments available to the Canadian government are disparate in their nature, their relative importance for development, their predictability, the international and domestic incentives they engage, and the requirements for effective management. Given the available scope, I provide only a brief treatment of the overall management and governance of Canada's development cooperation, before focusing on those areas where it interacts most directly with governance in developing countries.

## The Approach Used

To administer long-term development assistance programs in difficult and far-flung countries is sufficiently challenging that a high proportion of analysis and action over the years has focused strongly on "technical" management arrangements. At the opposite end of the scale, other analysts have spent a good deal of time and energy trying to plumb the "grand political economy" of development assistance, with one extreme holding it to be a tool of conspiratorial capitalism, and the other viewing it as a folly of redistributive romanticism.

In fact, successive efforts over decades to improve Canada's performance in development cooperation have revealed a number of enduring constraints that, in the judgment of this author, fall below the level of grand forces of political economy, but on the other hand are of far greater consequence than mere administrative obstacles. The analysis in this chapter therefore aims at a different level, which I call "strategic management" (Wood 2001). It recognizes that the management of development cooperation operates within certain parameters of governance in a very broad sense. This means not only the

TABLE 1

## Canada's Development Cooperation Effort: Components and Choices

| Component | Size/ Importance* | Formal latitude of Canadian government | Political latitude of Canadian government | Principal actors |
|---|---|---|---|---|
| (1) Multilateral official development assistance (ODA)[a] | $608M (23% of ODA) | Wide, but major shares of multilateral aid are bound by statutory member contributions and multiyear pledges | Multilateral programs are often the first "entitlement" claims on ODA budgets, some funded as much as "dues" for Canada's standing in an area as for development impact. The 8% of ODA for the World Bank's IDA is locked in by a privileged position and ownership by the Minister of Finance. 5% of ODA is earmarked for Regional Banks, 8% for UN agencies. | Multilateral "burden sharing" systems, Department of Finance, CIDA, Foreign Affairs |
| (2) Bilateral ODA (apart from rows 3 and 4) | $1,509M (58% of ODA) Deducting a sum of $177M for first year resettlement costs of developing country refugees in Canada leaves $1,332M (51% of ODA) for bilateral spending on the ground[b] | Very wide, limited only by specific contractual undertakings | In practice, this has been the residual ODA budget. Government has fairly wide leeway internationally, but with pressure to give priority to countries in crisis; Africa; Francophonie countries; and traditional partners, with some regional balance. At home there are multiple, shifting political and bureaucratic pressures and constraints. | See Table 2 |
| (3) ODA to and through NGOS | (Approx.)[c] $187M (7% of ODA) Matched by $639M in grants by private voluntary agencies | Very wide, limited only by specific contractual undertakings | To date, has been limited. The laudable original intent of backing innovative action by a wide range of Canadian civil society groups has become increasingly difficult to balance against government objectives and conditions for support, given the autonomous nature of such groups, the sense of "entitlement" among some members, and their political access in Canada. | See Table 2 |

*Figures are in US$ and for 2004 unless otherwise noted.

*Continued on page 228.*

TABLE 1, *continued*

| Component | Size/ Importance | Formal latitude of Canadian government | Political latitude of Canadian government | Principal actors |
|---|---|---|---|---|
| (4) Emergency and distress relief | $295M (11% OF ODA) | Wide | Strong domestic and international pressures for Canada to provide "its share" of response to international disasters, or to be out in front. While some minimum levels of demand can be safely predicted, upper limits cannot (e.g., Asian Tsunami). | Media and NGOs in setting profile; Ministers (International Cooperation, Foreign Affairs) and Prime Minister's Office (PMO) in determining response; CIDA, multilateral and non-governmental relief agencies in delivering |
| (5) "Non-aid" policies and programs affecting developing countries (trade, investment, technology transfers, security and environmental policies, migration, etc.) | In aggregate, far more important than total ODA. For example, total two-way trade with developing countries was C$50B in 2001–2. In 2003 investment constituted $2,708M and remittances were estimated at $1,100M. | Mostly wide | Internationally, there are opportunities for leadership (e.g., debt relief, land mine ban, ICC, and trade access). Counteracting these are domestic interests, differing departmental mandates, international resistance, and concerns about "burden sharing." | PMO/Privy Council Office (PCO) in determining need for "Whole of Government" approach. CIDA (and ideally Foreign Affairs) in analyzing and defining priorities and strategies. Multiple ministers, departments, provinces, and constituencies in supporting or impeding responses. |

Sources: DAC, *Development Cooperation Report 2005*; North–South Institute Canadian Development Report 2004.

a  ODA refers to the activities of financial, technical, and commodity aid explicitly directed to promoting development and recognized as ODA according to the criteria of the OECD's DAC, accepted as the basic international standard.

b  In 2003–4, roughly 20 percent of this amount went to post-conflict reconstruction activities in Afghanistan and Iraq—as much as the next five aid recipients combined.

c  Canada's reporting on NGO funding has been marked by inconsistency in recent years. This table is derived from the DAC's International Development Statistics Online, from which more details are available than contained in *Development Cooperation Reports* (see Disbursements and Commitments of Official and Private Flows, Table 1).

arrangements in place for decision making, accountability, and legitimacy, but also the purposes, value, weight, and priority attributed to this work among the competing demands for attention and resources by the relevant actors in the larger governing environment of the donor country concerned.[1]

This chapter also analyzes the incentives at work in the Canadian system in order to identify problems and potential improvements. In this brief attempt to cover so much ground, I have adapted (and tested in a different country context) some of the frameworks from a very large-scale assessment in 2001 of the incentives at work in Swedish bilateral development cooperation (see Ostrom et al. 2002).

Since this study is concerned with the management of a program of the Government of Canada, it is important to take account of that government's own management standards and expectations, both as the most binding stated yardsticks of management performance and as a guide to the potential for improvement. The "Management Accountability Framework of the Government of Canada" (see http://www.tbs-sct.gc.ca/si-as/maf-crg/maf-crg_e.asp) succinctly charts all the key elements of the Canadian government's Integrated Modern Management (IMM) schema, which has been formalized over the past five years to capture the state of the art and key goals in good management, especially in public sector programs. The key elements of this framework are as follows: strategic leadership; clear accountability; shared values and ethics; mature risk management; integrated performance information; motivated people; and rigorous stewardship. These attributes provide a key checklist for appraising Canadian management of foreign aid.[2]

## Confused Strategic Direction and Governance

As I have argued elsewhere, the key choices and responsibilities relating to development cooperation rest with the Government of Canada as a whole, not just with CIDA. "The Agency has long had to struggle to execute its basic mandate in the demanding environments of developing countries, while at the same time responding to unrealistic and fickle direction from Government, and a voracious sense of entitlement from many interests in Canada, including other Government Departments. Caught in this crossfire, the reputations of the Agency and its staff have often been disparaged unfairly" (Wood 2004, 10). As this chapter suggests, Ottawa's central management processes represent both the key context for Canada's development policy and the source of that policy's main limitations. Weaknesses here inevitably impair the setting of expected results and standards of performance for CIDA and the other main players associated with development cooperation.

While all the elements of the model set out in the govenment's Management Accountability framework are interrelated, and while each has obviously had important roles, the elements "within the box" are more concerned with means than ends and are decisively shaped, for good or ill, by the strategic context. Many would argue that the same is true for many if not most areas of government activity; the case made here, though, is that the main parameters have been especially blurred in the case of development cooperation. Notably, too, these weaknesses have proved more persistent in Canada than in many other donor countries.[3]

As will also become clear below, the context set in Ottawa at the "constitutional" and policy-making levels has dictated extremely powerful incentives and interactions among the actors on the Canadian side of development cooperation relationships. As a result, the room for developing country "ownership" of these activities, or even for consequential interaction about them with developing country partners, has often been severely constrained. An extensive survey of many analyses over the decades of Canadian performance in this field reveals that the best explanations for this anomalous situation are those which focus on "governmental and bureaucratic politics" (Morrison 1998,[4] with reference to White 1974; Berry 1981; English 1984; Lavergne and English 1987). In one of the most blunt and enduring formulations, Canadian political scientist Kim Nossal concluded in 1988 that

> one can better account for Canada's ODA policies and programmes if a different set of interests are put into the mix of "politico-strategic" concerns of foreign policy-makers. Specifically, I will argue that if one substitutes the interests of state officials in prestige, organizational maintenance and limiting real expenditures for the orthodox trinity of motives [philanthropic, economic, political], one will have a more proximate explanation for the existence, nature and size of Canada's development assistance policies. (1988, 38)

From the very outset of development cooperation in the 1950s, a vacuum of strategic direction has helped perpetuate this situation. The confusion has resulted from ill-defined and unrealistic hopes and expectations among the public, combined with the political and official mindset in donor countries. Swirling around together were the following factors: a wider awareness of the realities of mass poverty and some spreading tendrils of solidarity; a global battle for "hearts and minds" in the context of the Cold War; and a broad range of traditional foreign economic, political, and prestige interests. Each set of motivations held greater or lesser appeal for different constituencies at home, and the mix of these ingredients, and the outcomes, varied among the different industrialized countries. While always echoing loudly the public understanding of humanitarian solidarity with very poor people as the basic motivation for development cooperation, successive Canadian government statements of foreign and development policy over the decades have been forced to accompany this with enough other purposes to allow wide leeway for other interests.

Initially, for Canada—which had only fragmentary "hard" interests at the time with developing regions other than the Caribbean and parts of Latin America—the mix was able to incorporate a slighter higher than average quotient of idealism. This blended smoothly with postwar Canadian aspirations for prestige and multilateral influence, which bloomed during the first major waves of decolonization and in the remarkable new arena of the Commonwealth. Building on the key Canadian role in establishing NATO as well as on a pivotal UN presence, a substantial aid program was a logical part of a budding "voluntarist"[5] tradition in Canadian foreign policy. This disposition—which also found expression in UN peacekeeping and in a continuing search for other "bridging" and system-building roles—was no accident: it was for many years a considered expression of the interests and identity of a middle power in the shadow (and sometimes the smotheringly close embrace) of a superpower neighbour.[6] The voluntarist impulse in Canadian international policy, with development cooperation as one of its pillars, has waxed and waned over the decades and right up to the present, with a number of key factors at play. Despite a great deal of fanfare and public enthusiasm, however, there is ample evidence that up until now both voluntarism and development have mainly been secondary, and often marginal, in the actual strategic management of Canada's national and international policies.

Probably the most solid indicator of the weakness and subordinate standing of development cooperation, and of its distinctive strategic direction, has been its position (or lack thereof) at the Cabinet table, with all the implications that flow from this under the Canadian system. From 1950 to 1960 the embryonic activities of foreign aid were handled as an economic and technical cooperation function under the Department of Trade and Commerce; then, for the next eight years, through the External Aid Office, which reported to the Secretary of State for External Affairs. Since 1968, CIDA has been the agency primarily responsible, under erratic and mainly short ministerial mandates. From the early stages, responsibility for multilateral assistance programs has often been a bone of interministerial contention, although the Department of Finance has always been able to reserve for itself direct responsibility for the largest programs, those of the World Bank. Throughout most of this period, the rest of Canadian development cooperation activity has been subject to junior status, split ministerial jurisdictions, and until quite recently the formal "droit de regard" (and often the "droit de seigneur") of several federal ministries and their clients, without development cooperation staff having any reciprocal right of influence over *their* policies and programs.[7]

While it may be easy to understand the early growing pains of such an unprecedented activity in foreign policy and government administration, it does not explain the persistence of this subordinate position for development cooperation over several decades and the failure of successive Canadian governments to take decisive action to reflect its real importance. This in spite of the substantial budgets, responsibilities, and risks being managed, strong public and parliamentary support, an unusual potential for Canadian leadership in the world, evidently growing interests at stake, and the relative substantive and managerial competence of different agencies in the tasks concerned.

A key to understanding Canada's foreign aid policy is the mismatch between intentions and executive capability and incentives. The rationale for this is highlighted by the findings of a survey conducted in the late 1970s of some three hundred ministers, MPs, and senior officials. Those surveyed saw the moral or humanitarian motive for development cooperation as the most important one. The cruel irony was that official Ottawa attached a "low priority to meeting the challenges posed by the Third World" precisely because it perceived Canada's participation in international development "to be essentially a matter of altruism ... and nothing in which Canada has a vital stake" (Lyon et al. 1979, 12, in Morrison 1998, 427). Interestingly, one of the authors of this survey had earlier concluded that talk about commercial and political objectives for aid was "essentially a tactical ploy to court public support" (Morrison 1998, 426, referring to Lyon 1976). In fact, there is evidence that such appeals, based on Ottawa's shallow and mechanistic perception of public opinion, proved counterproductive in that it further confused the mission and fed popular suspicions that vested interests were at work and thus weakened rather than strengthened the solid rationale for this work as a major pillar of Canadian foreign policy.

In sum, development cooperation has retained a sideshow status in Ottawa. It has been viewed as worthy, but it has been neither powerful enough nor adequately structured to resist all manner of interference and arbitrary changes in priorities and direction.

In terms of the record of management of Canadian development cooperation, the most important effect of the subordination of development policy to so many interests and masters for so long has been to impede the emergence of a clear and realistic mission for the whole program, and thus of results commensurate with the effort invested. Even today, a major bone of contention in this field in Canada relates to the pros and cons of putting in place a clear legislative mandate for the aid program's primary developmental mission. As the UK and others have demonstrated, legitimizing and protecting such a mission is the vital prerequisite for setting achievable goals, for mobilizing resources, for assembling the necessary organization and discipline, for pursuing serious strategies and programs to achieve established goals, and then for showing results that are sufficient to maintain engagement and support over the long periods involved in bringing about sustainable development impacts.

In short, the inability to develop or enforce a disciplined development cooperation mission has allowed the many powerful actors in the Canadian arena to erect—and redecorate with baffling frequency—a "Christmas tree" of a program that is overburdened with favoured recipient countries; economic, political, or other interests; pet sectoral or thematic cure-alls; and multilateral, non-governmental, and other "partners." For long periods, those concerned with pursuing long-term development were compelled to pursue defensive strategies of damage limitation—to avoid confrontation, resist or delay encroachments, and balance and appease non-developmental interests when the pressures became irresistible, all the while struggling (often under the radar) to protect and implement at least a core of long-term developmental bilateral programming where possible.

As evidence of the enduring character of these struggles, the first of several "grand bargains" was drafted as early as 1972 by the Ministry of Industry, Trade and Commerce. This initiative proposed to separate out a "commercial aid program" with a specified share of the total aid budget, to be directed to more commercially oriented projects on soft-loan terms; the goal in this was to open up markets or match others' export subsidies in somewhat better-off countries (common features of most aid programs at the time). The quid pro quo was to be a more "hands off" approach to the rest of the aid program by Canadian commercial interests, with less or no linkage to Canadian procurement, and with non-interference in programming by the trade department. As with another set of proposals from the Ministry of External Affairs twenty years later (which was less well thought out and more threatening to the developmental mandate of the aid program), discussion of these or other options was curtailed by leaks to the media and by subsequent public controversy. Other and new encroachments have been broached periodically and have been fought case by case, with mixed results.

Given the overwhelming superiority of the bureaucratic forces ranged against a developmental program, and most importantly the lack of powerful and consistent champions at the Cabinet level, the defensive and confrontation-avoidance strategies of development policy-makers were often managed quite skilfully. But the result was that when budgets were steadily cut during the 1990s, Canada was left with the most scattered bilateral program of any donor (OECD DAC 2004, Table 32).

While the breadth and complexities of the development objective have often similarly hampered other donor countries, it was striking that in the mid-1990s Canada was one of the slower donors to get on board with the new International Development Strategy, which had been worked out in the context of the OECD DAC as the way to pull aid out of what was seen by many as a "death spiral" in the early 1990s. Above all it aimed to apply honest reforms and to communicate the central mission of development cooperation more clearly to practitioners, to parliaments, and to populations, by replacing the jumble of motives and activities that had prevailed in the past. Even as recently as the Canadian government's international policy review of 2004–5, which led to the International Policy Statement, there has been repeated evidence of a lack of basic understanding in key Ottawa circles as to what development cooperation actually can and cannot do, an understanding that should now be clarified by decades of well-documented experience.

The mismatch in Ottawa between the distribution of relevant knowledge and experience on the one hand, and influence over development policy on the other, is another enduring contextual reality and constraint. Canada's aid system to date has provided too few concrete incentives for officials to seek out and apply lessons learned by other countries and donors, and indeed from their own experience, in order continually to improve the effectiveness of Canada's aid (Wood 2004, 1). While Canadian representatives do take part, and make major contributions, in international exchanges of experience in development cooperation (through standing bodies such the OECD and many other networks), there is less institutional or systemic interest in taking up, adapting, and applying the learning of others to Canada's own actions in the area of development assistance than in many other fields of interest.

## Uphill Battle:
## Incentives Skewed against Host Country Ownership

The remaining sections of this chapter will leave aside further discussion of the management of multilateral and emergency aid, non-aid relations with developing countries, and foreign aid that supports NGOs and their programs (each of which merits its own chapter) in order to focus on the component of development cooperation where CIDA has had the most direct responsibility and influence: bilateral, country-to-country programs. To begin, it is crucial to note that in terms of scale, in 2004 (for example) well under 35 percent of total Canadian ODA was available for "normal" bilateral programming, and not even the largest country-to country programs received more than 2.5 percent of Canadian ODA.

For reasons of space, I will not attempt to trace the evolution of aid management through several decades. Instead I will work from a basis of the accepted standards of good aid management, testing how Canadian aid management measures up, with appropriate references to how it developed. It should first be stressed that this is not just imposing a standard retroactively. Most of the component good practices of this "new" paradigm have become clear to thoughtful analysts and practitioners over many years. They point to the following:

• applying the basic principles of local ownership;
• building capacity to ensure sustainability;
• striving for more genuine partnerships in the face of imbalances in bargaining power;
• civil society and private-sector engagement alongside government;
• an integrated approach to take account of political, economic, social, and institutional dimensions of development; *and*
• a results-based approach (focused on partner countries' priorities among the MDGs), with built-in monitoring and evaluation of programs and some mechanisms of mutual accountability.

Since these standards were building cumulatively until they were pulled together in the mid-1990s in "Shaping the Twenty-First Century" (OECD DAC 1996) and in subsequent multilateral declarations and action programs, it is both fair and possible to use most of them in both actual and normative assessments.

Table 2 represents an attempt to summarize graphically the range of key actors affecting Canadian bilateral aid programs, the incentives and constraints they face, and some of the most important linkages and implications. The Swedish study, referred to early in this chapter, mapped an "octangle" model of eight major sets of actors in development cooperation[8] as well as the interactions and incentives at work among them. The broad-brush analysis here of the key actors in Canadian bilateral development cooperation demands a much more prominent place for a larger number of Canadian actors and the incentives and constraints they face. This in turn yields a brutally clear picture of the overall pressures for "donor-led" Canadian bilateral cooperation as well as the formidable obstacles that work against moving from the current enclaves of "best practice" toward a full system that is led by the needs, priorities, and capacities of developing countries themselves.

TABLE 2

Canadian Bilateral Programs:
Key Actors, Incentives, and Constraints

| Actor | Interests | Incentive/Constraints | Implications |
|---|---|---|---|
| Donor government: centre of government (PMO, PCO) | Avoid bad news (e.g., scandals). | Always high-risk, especially in difficult environments overseas (although in fact CIDA has had rare public problems since a few in the 1970s and earlier). | The risk of most bilateral aid relationships has often come to be seen to outweigh potential international or domestic benefits. |
| | Maintain international respectability, and an occasional platform. | Without a significant ODA program, Canada (i.e., its representatives) would now have "pariah status" (Nossal 1988, 51). | Satisfy minimum public expectations and maintain minimum "dues." |
| | "Show the Canadian flag." | Minimize criticism by allies (e.g., in Afghanistan, Iraq) and domestic constituencies (e.g. Francophonie, Tsunami-hit countries, Haiti). | Often works against focused allocations, longer-term programs, and results. Fails to recognize the primacy of host countries' own efforts and the need for modest and coordinated help from external partners. As above, and sometimes difficult to fit with realities on the ground and longer-term programming. |
| | Provide vehicle for international "leadership" aspirations (e.g., Canada Corps), periodic international initiatives, and occasional strong constituency interests. | Outlet for top leaders' and other Ministries' interests and views on development. | |
| | Show sustainable contributions, with partner countries and other donors, to development results on the ground. | Little confidence in the capacity to do this, or appreciation of the advances in good practice that can help make it possible. | Limited readiness to forego some of the old ways. |
| Department of Finance | Serve as main gatekeeper of fiscal discipline and allocation of funding of federal priorities, emphasizing fiscal, economic, social, and security objectives. As an international window and | Maintain the "fiscal advantage" for Canada—never again permit ballooning deficits and debt. Apply the sharpest challenges to claims of "government priority" while, in the international development | When all are claiming to be "Government priorities," the gatekeeper's own interpretations and projected implications of financial commitments become even more powerful, short of decisive contrary |

Table 2, *continued*

| Actor | Interests | Incentive/Constraints | Implications |
|---|---|---|---|
| Department of Finance, *continued* | occasional lever, represent Canada in the Bretton Woods institutions. | field, favouring and forming its views through the Bretton Woods programs where Finance has its vested interest. | direction from the top. While Finance no longer intervenes in most bilateral work, it has little capacity or apparent interest in following closely. The conflict of interest in the Finance/Bretton Woods ODA funding link has never been tackled. |
| Central agencies: Treasury Board, Auditor General | Ensure financial and management accountability and risk management. | In spite of doctrines on modern management and mature management approaches to risk management, the main incentives and constraints (e.g., "gotcha" press and Opposition) and cultural reflexes in these institutions usually work for "command and control" systems and risk avoidance. | Impedes good management and mature parliamentary and public understanding in any field—crippling in the unfamiliar and high-risk terrain of international development. |
| International Development Agency minister and officials | Manage demands of PCO/PMO and others (i.e., avoid scandals and dangerous risks, provide platforms, support initiatives, juggle conflicting priorities. Manage demands of other Government departments and vocal Canadian constituencies, and resist diversions/encroachments). | Without a sufficiently clear and valued central mission, the struggle to satisfy all these demands often becomes in effect the primary yardstick of successful performance, for ministers, senior management, and the agency collectively. Normally, these requirements should be secondary "costs of doing business," but the main business of development cooperation has been so little grasped and respected in official Ottawa that these demands have often had to come first. | Since these demands can never all be satisfied (especially from the limited "discretionary" budget), the reflexive response of multiple disgruntled fund seekers has been to charge CIDA with failing to be a "team player." At the same time, failures to engage in pro-development action by others have been little noted. |

*Continued on page 238.*

Table 2, *continued*

| Actor | Interests | Incentive/Constraints | Implications |
|---|---|---|---|
| **International Development Agency minister and officials,** *continued* | Fully commit and disburse budgets within normal government fiscal years while meeting the process and risk "management' requirements of central agencies geared to work in Canada. | This is the primary tangible yardstick of performance for CIDA managers. Constraints are worst in times of rapid contraction or growth, but always severe because of changing directions, accommodating unforeseen demands. | CIDA managers and staff must be highly skilled and flexible in financial, project, and contract management and juggle changing pressures at home with the long-term requirements of development work on the ground. |
| | Shape and maintain a program with some prospect of showing development results in reducing poverty (e.g., focus, "ownership," coordination and harmonization). | Decades of experience show that this is the only defensible rationale and approach for development cooperation, and give confidence that it can be done well. However, neither point has yet been absorbed sufficiently by others. | A daily uphill battle to turn around, with the prospect of only medium to long-term rewards. From the bottom up, CIDA can muster sound analysis and country programming skills and systems (in line with current good practice) where program size justifies. But the aggregate problem has been compounded by many scattered programs without critical mass and by limited ministerial tenures. |
| | Practice continuous learning and meet international good practice standards for development cooperation. | Professional integrity, satisfaction and peer respect versus the fact that no one else in official Ottawa, or elsewhere in Canada, in fact cares much about these, and much of CIDA not very consistently in practice, with all the other pressures. | Enclaves of good practice, struggling to make a long-term impact, with as much protection as can be managed from the swirling pressures on the overall program. |
| | Inform and engage the attentive public in Canada in a mature understanding and support of the long and rocky road of development cooperation. | Need to overcome the lack of direct exposure by most Canadians, and respond to their openness to get beyond "charity," while avoiding the path of self-serving propaganda. | The starting-point is for the government to set and respect a clear enough mission and direction to be able to communicate them to the attentive public. |

Table 2, *continued*

| Actor | Interests | Incentive/Constraints | Implications |
|---|---|---|---|
| Donor government: other departments | Call on ODA resources for international programs and activities of interest to their mandates. Some broad connection to "development" preferred. | Difficulties in obtaining adequate funding to meet increasing international demands in globalized world versus apparently large and "soft" pool of funds in CIDA. | Persistent raid attempts on ODA, resulting in running conflict, diversion of aid, and/or frustration and denigration of the program. |
| Third party implementing organizations (e.g., NGOS, private contractors) | Call on ODA resources for international programs and activities of interest to their mandates and expertise. Often quite a strong developmental approach and capacity. | Variable willingness to work within Canadian government strategic directions where these exist. NGOS' independent fundraising, international linkages, and knowledge base are assets, and sometimes a source of tension (healthy or otherwise). | De facto, these have often become the most important "partners" for the Canadian program, especially with reduced budgets and scattered programs (see DAC 2003, *Peer Review* on how Canada has "led" in this respect). |
| Organized interest groups and civil society organizations within the donor country | Largely the same groups as implementing organizations above. | Perceived narrowness of base, commitment to their own approaches and interests—as well as unremittingly critical/crusading styles toward government action—have often undermined effectiveness of many. | Earlier rabid anti-aid interest groups have largely faded, although disgruntled bidders are vocal critics. Recent unprecedented awareness raising (e.g., Make Poverty History) may have updated and reinforced basic sympathy for development. |
| Recipient government ministries and agencies | Maximize supplementation of their often-insufficient resources to carry out their pressing sectoral or other development mandates with limited capacities. | Maintain maximum support and freedom of action vis-à-vis other parts of their own governments and external donors, individually and collectively. Balance urgent needs for help in achieving tangible results with the need to build up long-term capacity and sustainability. | When the donor community and the host government are working at their best together, these agencies can be well-served in working with them. Otherwise they have natural interests in competing with other claimants and promoting diversification and competition among their sources of support. |

*Continued on page 240.*

Table 2, *continued*

| Actor | Interests | Incentive/Constraints | Implications |
|---|---|---|---|
| **Organized interest groups and civil society organizations within the recipient country** | Very often the de facto proxy for hard-to-hear, hard-to-reach beneficiaries. Some well established, some still nascent counter-weights to overweaning and overloaded post-colonial states. | Working with donors can provide resources, credibility, sometimes protection, and sometimes dangers. | Capacities to work with grassroots are often strained, and they can lose touch. Local governments can often be a similarly, or even more, important set of partners. |
| **Targeted beneficiaries** | To receive tangible, enduring help to surmount some of their most pressing problems, as defined by themselves. Cut out as many "middlemen" and transaction costs as possible. | Working for better governance in real political economies, ultimately to improve their quality of life. The poor need to find ways and allies to break through and be heard on their challenges and ideas on solutions, backed by resources. Real holders of power and possible drivers of change need to be enlisted. Committed outside donors and domestic institutions need modesty, skill, and perseverance to back them effectively. | For bilateral donors, finding ways to hear the voices of the poor and build them into wider-scale programs has improved. But the distances and obstacles are still huge. This takes intensive, sustained, and sensitive investment of time, effort, and knowledge in real governance in real places. |
| **Recipient government** | Survive politically by managing the complex political economy of their own countries within the limits of scarce resources and capacity constraints. To a greater or lesser degree this will include strategies for development and poverty reduction—embraced and defined in some synthesis of their own political priorities and those of the international community. | Supplementary resources from outside often provide substantial and relatively easy support, although Canada has become a tertiary actor in most countries. In most cases, still struggling to keep track of, let alone provide strategic direction to, multiple interventions with sectoral ministries, agencies, NGOs etc. | To the extent that the centre of government and main donors put real weight on a serious development and poverty reduction agenda, the new paradigm of managing cooperation can be a net improvement over dispersed and uncoordinated assistance. Once Canada becomes a substantial actor in a smaller number of countries, it can make a difference in this "partnership." |

Table 2, *continued*

| Actor | Interests | Incentive/Constraints | Implications |
|---|---|---|---|
| **Other donors** | Make a more serious development impact while coping with many of the same pressures faced by the Canadian government. | While it is the widely accepted "right thing to do" for effective development coopera- tion, most incentives still work against coordinating, harmo- nizing and aligning to host countries' priori- ties and capacities. Showing the flag, expending quickly, using their own national resources, and meeting individ- ual donor govern- ments' demands for control and accounta- bility all work in the wrong direction. | CIDA has been seen as instinctively willing to cooperate on these fronts, conceptually and on the ground. It has sometimes even been an innovator, but has long lacked the critical mass to make a major difference in most countries, and has been impaired by formal procurement tying, heavy reliance on the "Canadian part- ner base," and limited capacity in countries. Greater focus will make it more impor- tant and possible to resolve these issues. |
| **Parliament in donor and recipient country** | At both ends of the development cooper- ation chain, elected representatives can provide crucial links of legitimacy, over- sight, outreach and informed engagement between citizens and government-to- government coopera- tion programs. | In their different set- tings, Canadian and many developing- country MPs must constantly struggle to bridge the dangerous "democratic deficit" in this work. In devel- oping countries, integrating donor programs into the budgetary framework and decisions on revenue-raising and spending priorities, as well as oversight, is essential. In the Canadian Parliament, the record of respon- sible and non-partisan policy contributions in this field has been strong for decades— at times outstanding— but little heeded. | With all its undoubted complications, perhaps the manifest need to do better in engaging elected representatives more effectively offers some powerful keys to improving the gover- nance of international development coopera- tion at both ends. |

## The Centre of Government

The ordering in Table 2 of the key actors at work in the Canadian bilateral aid system is intended to suggest a ranking of their relative importance, as is the ordering of the different interests attributed to them. One significant distinction is that while the "centre of Government" (the Prime Minister's Office and the Privy Council Office) and Department of Finance are ranked highest in terms of influence, their influence is felt mainly when overall limits, context, and prevailing conditions for Canada's programs are being set (with occasional bursts of activism), and only secondarily when individual country programs are actually being managed. In any case, it is only through strong support at this top level that binding and constraining strategies for effective bilateral development cooperation can be maintained—for example, in containing the tendencies to proliferation both in country eligibility and in country allocations.

## The Central Agencies

The activities of central agencies (the Treasury Board and the Auditor General) are intended to serve government-wide accountability purposes. The argument here is that in fact, for many years they have had a powerful direct impact—and a negative one—on efforts to make Canadian bilateral aid more responsive to good practice. The special conditions of working as a supporting partner on long-term development in aid-receiving countries require radically different approaches to the requirements for "risk management, stewardship, and accountability" than most government programs operating inside Canada. At various times, these needs have been recognized and accommodated by the central agencies' systems—for example, in CIDA's exemption for many years from the requirement to "lapse" and return unspent funds at the end of each fiscal year, and in some serious efforts by the Auditor General over a decade or so to try to work out and respect some realistic rules for assessing cida's contributions and accountabilities in its distinctive programs.

CIDA operates in uniquely high-risk environments; even so, it has managed to avoid major scandals and related problems for many years. This is partly because the agency has come to spread its risks among many small programs; but another reason, certainly, is its ability (largely unrecognized) to assess and manage risks to its programs, an ability embedded in the experience of its managers.[9] But it must also be noted that this scandal-free performance comes with a price: a sort of "self-censoring" risk avoidance by the agency, which takes the form of time-consuming, burdensome, and expensive procedures that encumber its basic work and yield only scattered results.

Like all government activities in Canada, development cooperation will be facing increasing pressure in the coming years to demonstrate soaring standards of accountability and risk management, and CIDA is giving high priority to strengthening its systems in these areas. If the trend toward sensationalistic public vivisection in official auditing continues, Parliament and the government of the day will need to define plainly the real level of tolerance for the inescapably high risks in development policy and will have to be prepared to weather the storms when even the best risk management fails to catch every problem. Also in regard to risks, it is important to counter an emerging impression that the recipient country–led programs of development cooperation that are increasingly being favoured (e.g., in greater sectoral and budget support) will incur higher risks than the multiple projects micromanaged by donors in the past. In fact, these approaches will actually *reduce* the most important risks confronting development cooperation programs up to now, the most significant of which are inconstancy of direction and the failure to achieve widespread and sustainable development results (see Wood 2004).

## Implications for CIDA

This section of Table 2 suggests a number of quite important conclusions to be drawn about the management of Canadian bilateral aid. The first is that the minister responsible and the agency share the same basic interests, incentives, and constraints in trying to shape and maintain a program with a serious prospect of showing results in poverty reduction programs.

A second conclusion relates to the importance placed on solid *policies and programs* in the government's overall management accountability framework. CIDA has had quite a respectable record in working out policies and delivering programs on the ground in its complex fields and risky laboratories, albeit within the most scattered program of any donor. Its people include a good number of skilled and flexible project managers who have the special practical knowledge required to operate in, and with, developing countries without making critical mistakes. At the same time, the government's "projectized" assistance, widely scattered programs, standard rules and regulations, long-standing heavy reliance on centralized administration, and use of the "Canadian resource base"[10] have not allowed the agency to develop the capacity to operate as a focused, substantial player on the ground in more country-led development programs. This latter approach would require more analytical capacity at the macrolevel in countries; solid, state-of-the-art strategies and resources in fields of concentration; and the authority, capacity, and incentives to work closely and responsively with host governments, civil societies, and private sectors and to coordinate and harmonize CIDA's actions with those of other donors.

## Decentralization: Part of the Answer

On the basis of the analysis above, it is apparent that several major changes are needed if Canada is to muster a substantial program of bilateral development cooperation that reflects and implements the principles of good practice now recognized in the field. This does not mean that Canada can or should jettison its bilateral program and rely on multilateral or other aid channels. Even if these other channels were impeccable models of effectiveness and efficiency, it would be impossible to conceive of a government of a significant country delegating to others all means of conceiving, prioritizing, delivering, and learning from its official development cooperation. Moreover, while the direct use of aid programs by donors to pursue national economic or political interests has historically proved ineffective and counterproductive, and while excessive flag waving contradicts and can undermine country ownership, there is a legitimate need for citizens in donor countries to see some direct and official relationship with countries where cooperation is provided in their name.

### Resources

Contrary to widespread assumptions, the facts show that for some time the long-term bilateral component of Canadian aid has not been the first claimant on the aid budget, but has in effect often had to serve as the flexible residual element of the overall expenditure, constantly adjusting to unforeseen demands elsewhere. Over the past fifteen or so years the bilateral share of Canada's ODA has fluctuated between two-thirds and three-quarters, but on average more than one-third of that share has gone to uses other than long-term bilateral development programming (OECD DAC 2006, and author's calculations).[11] Moreover, the amounts made available for purposes of long-term country-to-country development programming, even if they were not spread over so many small-country allocations, would still support only a third-class aid effort from a country with first-class capabilities. Economies of scale, as well as the achievement of results in line with current good practice, dictate that serious bilateral programs should probably each be able to disburse between C$50M and C$200M annually, depending on the size and needs of the country. The Canadian government in 2005 aimed by 2010 to have some twenty-five such programs with what CIDA called "core development partners," plus necessary opportunities for bilateral cooperation with other countries and subregions. Based on rough averaging at this stage, it is clear that a substantial program of long-term bilateral cooperation on this scale would call for a budget in the region of at least C$3.0–3.5 billion, compared to C$1.75 billion actually disbursed in similar programs in 2004.

It should also be stressed that any realistic possibilities for shifting resources from other channels would come nowhere close to offering the critical mass of funds needed for Canada to mount an adequate bilateral program. As has been shown, each of these different channels has its own substantive and political rationale—it is not entirely by accident that they have often had a priority claim. While substantial shifts and some reductions could be achieved over time, the aggregate budgets freed up would make only a small contribution to the resources needed for a world-class bilateral program, the scale of which, by the rough estimates above, would still be expected to fall well below that of the "high performers" among donors as a share of national wealth or government expenditure.

## Focus

As the government's 2005 International Policy Statement recognized, it is decades overdue for Canada to focus the lion's share of its bilateral spending on development aid in long-term partnerships with a manageable number of poor countries or subregions (i.e., no more than thirty) from what has become the most dispersed bilateral aid program in the world.[12] This is essential if Canada is to concentrate its attention, knowledge, and resources and work effectively with partner countries themselves and with other external partners so as to make a sustained difference (see also Wood 2004). Countries are still the main settings for policies and programs as well as for the framework conditions that either promote or impede development by their entrepreneurs and citizens.

All of the good practices mentioned earlier in this chapter, combined with the current emphasis among donors on greater alignment and harmonization of their programs, point toward this kind of focused, intensive, and sustained engagement with partner countries. This approach would also allow for the application of a serious sectoral or thematic focus to Canadian contributions, rooted in Canadian capabilities and general strategies. These contributions could then be deployed in CIDA's "core development partner" countries in line with their needs and priorities, and in an appropriate division of labour with other external partners.

These long-term relationships should not just be with "good performers." The attempts of some donors in recent years to dispense or withhold aid as a performance incentive have proved predictably simplistic and exaggerated. Need is an obvious determinant; so is the reality that performances (and thus the levels and types of Canadian engagement that will be appropriate) are likely to fluctuate over the years, but that Canada is there for the long haul work of development. Such a country focus is also key to making the program more understandable and transparent to Parliament and to the Canadian public at a meaningful level. This is a better approach than continuing to try to account for either vast global objectives or to aggregate the impacts of a myriad of scattered projects. Both a "whole of Canada" strategy and a focusing of bilateral aid in a few countries can and should be used to deepen the knowledge and ownership of the program in different regions and sectors of Canadian society. In this respect, Canadian international development could consider adapting and applying some of the innovative public involvement techniques being pioneered by such groups as the Canadian Policy Research Network and the Public Policy Forum.

## Decentralized Management Systems and Capacities

In relation to prevailing international standards over the decades, CIDA has generally been able to apply solid, and sometimes leading, approaches to needs assessment, consultation and coordination, country programming, and performance management in countries where Canada has had substantial bilateral programs. In general, delivery has often been more problematic, although some of Canada's difficulties in that area have not been unique.

This generally positive assessment must not be taken as grounds for complacency: since the mid-1990s it has been conceded that the prevailing international standards for development cooperation over the decades have been inadequate and often highly inappropriate. (Critiques of those standards are well documented in the next chapter by de Renzio and Mulley.) It is not surprising that fragmented, donor-led investments which run through parallel implementation units, which thereby undermine government capacity and relationships of domestic accountability, and which are tied to questionable conditionalities as well as unpredictable and insufficient levels of aid funding, have often failed to deliver sustainable development impact. The bar has been raised to new standards that are now working their way through difficult processes of implementation between partner countries and external donors. Though implementation remains uneven and requires ongoing critical review to promote genuinely recipient-led processes (as suggested by de Renzio and Mulley), these new standards are widely acknowledged today not just as desirable but as obligatory.

The new insistence on recipient-country ownership of development cooperation programs that are integrated with those countries' own development strategies and based on deeper analysis of country contexts and their development challenges, on greater citizen participation in development processes, and on other accepted good practice standards, points toward a need for donors to exhibit much greater knowledge, engagement, and responsiveness in the societies with which they are working. All of this has been recognized by "best practice" donors and has accelerated some trends already underway toward extensive decentralization of bilateral aid policy-making and implementation capacities to the countries of operation. Thus the UK's DFID and the Dutch and Danish aid administrations, as well as the World Bank (on a pilot basis), have made radical shifts of capacity and authority to the field, each within its distinctive structure and system. The results of these changes have been positively received both by developing country partners and by the agencies' own personnel.

Ironically, while many donors (including USAID) have experimented with elements and instruments of decentralized management over many years, Canada was perhaps the first to have opted (in the second half of the 1980s) for a wholesale shift toward decentralized administration. The idea built upon the findings and recommendations of the North-South Institute's independent evaluations of four CIDA country programs and was eventually endorsed by the Auditor General as well as by the Public Accounts and External Affairs Committees of Parliament. All, remarkably, realized that moves to decentralize personnel and authority to the field would result in increased administrative costs, but should be done anyway in order to improve aid effectiveness. The External Affairs Committee concluded that of all the suggestions to improve delivery, "none is so compelling or commands such widespread support as decentralization to the field" (SCEAIT 1987, 79, in Morrison 1998, 285; see also Morrison 1998, 303–12).

CIDA's top management had early reservations, based on skepticism that such a radical shift would ever be accepted by the government. They also noted that the existing system was comparatively cost effective in disbursing budgets, especially with a program so closely tied to Canadian procurement and with such limited Canadian commercial representation on the ground (both these factors were frankly acknowledged; see ibid., 253). It is also true that for some time the agency had been proceeding less formally to beef up its capacity in the field through field support units (FSUs) made up of contracted personnel, who were to be resident in countries and who were to provide ongoing support to major programs and projects. By 1987, however, CIDA's senior management had noted the critical mass of support for this proposal. With its own top priority being to cut through some extremely slow and complicated decision-making processes,[13] CIDA's top management ultimately embraced the decentralization plan in spite of continuing misgivings and foot dragging by some of its own senior managers in headquarters.

Even with its auspicious beginnings and strong ministerial support, all the perennial spoilers in the Canadian aid system (see Table 2) re-emerged with a vengeance. The impacts were felt in the ensuing processes of bitter interdepart-mental negotiations over terms, costs, and authorities (particularly with Trea-sury Board and External Affairs); in unsatisfactory compromises; and in albeit still promising implementation on the ground (with some resistance from senior managers within the agency); followed by the gradual unravelling of the entire scheme within four years of its launch—"a major casualty of cutbacks and bureaucratic politics" (ibid., 311).

As Morrison concludes in his epitaph for CIDA's short-lived leadership in decentralization, it "probably had the greatest potential [in many years] for changing CIDA's organizational thinking and behaviour" (ibid., 311). Canada's development community, Parliament, and ministers had been ahead of their time, and had overreached when confronted with obstacles and the lack of conviction and staying power in its overall governance system for develop-ment cooperation.

This brief review of the failed early Canadian experiment in decentraliza-tion raises a question: Some two decades later, could Canada now try again? The analysis here suggests that before any such moves take place, Canada's bilateral program would need to focus much more strongly on a manageable number of countries and subregions. Clearly, without a number of substan-tial long-term country programs, Canada cannot justify (in programmatic or economic terms) moving strongly to locate more staff and authority on the ground, not will it have the capacity to do so. Aid officers and experts can be deployed abroad at less cost than diplomats; even so, the overall cost of doing this is probably still on the order of three times the cost of deploying them at home. Since a critical mass of staff is also needed, the country programs in question would have to be in the C$50 to 200 million range before a case could be made for the additional expenditure.

Even more important, a determined commitment to make the hard deci-sions to achieve greater country focus and to embrace the other key directions of the recent International Policy Statement will be necessary if decentraliza-tion is to be worthwhile. A move toward decentralized management in turn could reinforce those key directions. A review of some of the problems of the earlier experiment provides some encouragement—as well as some warning notes.

## Conclusion

This chapter has examined and assessed the record of management in Cana-dian development cooperation in light of the heightened expectations for the next decade at least, by Canada and others, in terms of the impact, quality, and volume of assistance. The option of greater decentralizing Canadian aid management was singled out for specific attention. Like other chapters in this book, this one has attempted to analyze the incentives at work in the Canadian system in order to identify problems and potential improvements.

A number of stubborn constraints have hindered the various efforts undertaken over the years to improve the effectiveness of Canadian development policy. While these constraints are not necessarily "structural" (i.e., they fall below the level of what I have called the "grand forces" of political economy), they cannot be dismissed as mere administrative obstacles. Rather, as I have argued, they drive to the heart of the Canadian government's approach to "strategic management" and, more specifically, its management accountability framework. These parameters have consigned development policy to sideshow status in Ottawa, where it has been susceptible to frequent interference and arbitrary changes in priorities and direction. In parallel, CIDA and its officials have constantly been stereotyped and sidelined as naive "do-gooders," even while envied and resented for the substantial budgets they manage and the influence they exert in many countries on Canada's behalf.

Furthermore (see Table 2), the context set in Ottawa by the predominance of "governmental and bureaucratic politics" has dictated such powerful incentives and interactions among the actors *on the Canadian side of development cooperation relationships alone* that room for recipient-country ownership of these activities—or even for serious interaction about them with developing country partners—has often been severely constrained. This in turn yields a clear picture of the overall pressures for donor-led Canadian bilateral cooperation, and the formidable obstacles that will be faced in quite literally "turning around" this system so that it moves from the current situation of "enclaves of good practice" into a full system driven by the needs, priorities, and capacities of developing countries themselves.

In terms of the record of management of Canadian development cooperation, the most important effect of the subordination of development policy to so many interests and masters for so long has been to impede the emergence of a clear and realistic mission for the program as a whole, and thus of results commensurate with the effort invested. Legitimizing and protecting such a mission is the vital prerequisite for setting achievable goals; for mobilizing the resources, organization, and discipline required; for pursuing serious strategies and programs to achieve the goals; and then for showing the results necessary to maintain engagement and support over the long periods involved in realizing sustainable development impacts.

On the positive side, the shift of the whole aid paradigm to place recipient-country ownership at the centre means that radical measures to ensure much greater donor responsiveness are now the norm for respectable aid performance rather than the exception. The problem of a highly tied and centralized Canadian aid program, while not entirely overcome, has been reduced. At the very least, the idea that much sourcing and resources should shift to the field is incontestable today, as is the necessity for much greater knowledge, analysis, and engagement with a spectrum of actors in the countries in which Canada is working.

More debatable is whether the "rapport des forces" and understanding of development cooperation in official Ottawa has shifted sufficiently to allow a decentralized bilateral aid program to be set up and function effectively instead of being undermined as it was in the late 1980s. The analysis in this chapter of the key actors, incentives, and constraints involved in development policies highlights much evidence of outdated or uninformed attitudes, equivocal political commitment, and potentially obstructive bureaucratic positions that could make this cornerstone (and others) of a modern aid program for Canada unachievable.

## Notes

1   Without dismissing the role and importance of declaratory statements of principle and policy, such an analysis must recognize that they are especially susceptible in this field to grand ambition and rhetoric; thus, this chapter must go well beyond them to examine performance in practice.

2   This framework is applied retroactively, since most of the record under study here predated this particular framework of strategic guidance. On the other hand, many if not most of its elements were in play earlier, explicitly and/or implicitly.

3   This judgment is based on the author's long experience of comparative monitoring and analysis, especially during six years as director of the OECD/DAC Secretariat.

4   Morrison's in-depth history of Canadian development assistance has served as a key reference for this chapter.

5   This term, originated by Thomas Hockin, is not always used clearly. It is used here to denote a type of constructively intended community activism at the international level, typified by Canada after the Second World War, and later more consistently by the "like-minded" states of Scandinavia and the Netherlands. It is more subtle, and (as noted above) more rooted in enlightened self-interest, than are the pejorative "Boy Scout" or "do-gooder" appellations that are sometimes applied, especially by those who find a tendency to moral condescension among the voluntarist states.

6   There is a considerable, and evolving, literature on the place and roles of "middle powers" in the international system, a good deal of it referring specifically to the Canadian case. The best starting point is in the writings of John W. Holmes. See Holmes 1976 on the early life of this concept in the post–Second World War period

and its changing value. See also Cooper 1997; Cooper et al. 1993; Holbraad 1984; and Wood 1988 for interesting further references over the decades.

7  Experience in this area shows that formal institutional change may do little to shift power or decision-making, while particular individuals, and relationships, can make a substantial difference to formal and traditional arrangements. Thus, for example, 1982 to 1984 was a period of strong performance in development assistance policy when a dynamic and persuasive Margaret Catley-Carlson as CIDA president reported directly to a Minister of External Affairs, Alan MacEachen, who gave serious attention and authority to this part of his broad portfolio. From 1984 to 1991 an active and committed engagement by the Right Honourable Joe Clark as External Affairs Minister lent political clout at strategic moments, clout that was beyond the reach of his junior colleagues with day-to-day responsibility. Between 2003 and 2005, an energetic and influential Minister for International Cooperation, with some support from the centre of government, was able to wrest long-overdue government agreement to greater focus in the program, and began to give a more accurate profile to the importance of the portfolio and to the capacity of CIDA. At the time of writing, the jury remains out with regard to arrangements under the government and new Minister for International Cooperation in place since early 2006.

8  1. The donor government; 2. Recipient government; 3. Other donors; 4. A donor's international development agency; 5. Recipient government ministries and agencies; 6. Third-party implementing organizations (e.g., NGOs, private contractors); 7. Organized interest groups and civil society organizations within the donor and recipient countries. 8. Targeted beneficiaries.

9  Comparative assessment carried out by this author and a senior auditor colleague in 2004 confirmed a good capacity in CIDA's performance management systems relative to a number of other federal departments, especially in results-based management and evaluation.

10 This is a euphemistic term for a wide range of protected Canadian suppliers of goods and services for the aid program. Canada has traditionally maintained relatively high levels of aid tying, and has been criticized by its peers for its level of reliance on "Canadian executing agencies" for bilateral program implementation. It is fair to note that many of these CEAs, composed of (mostly) Canadian NGOs, private-sector firms, and other government departments, have over the years contributed respectably to the agency's programming record.

11 Bilateral figures here excluding Emergency and Distress or Humanitarian Relief, Contributions to NGOs, and the bogus item of first-year resettlement costs for refugees.

12 There is also room for serious analysis and discussion as to whether and how some such focus should also apply to the government's "Canadian partnership" funding.

13 Interview by the author with Margaret Catley-Carlson, 4 July 2005.

▲

# 11

## DONOR COORDINATION AND
## GOOD GOVERNANCE:
## DONOR-LED AND RECIPIENT-LED APPROACHES

### Paolo de Renzio and Sarah Mulley

The past ten years have seen considerable changes in the way the aid system in general, and relationships between donors and recipients in particular, function; and in the mechanisms used to ensure that aid resources are effective in achieving development results. Among donors, the adoption of the Millennium Development Goals (MDGs), the focus on "partnership" models of development cooperation, and the increasing emphasis on donor coordination have influenced the ways in which agencies see themselves and the ways in which they work. Recipients are moving toward more active management of aid, with some countries developing increasingly effective mechanisms for managing their relationships with donors. More coordinated aid practices and good governance in recipient countries have come to be seen as mutually supportive agendas. As a consequence, donor coordination, and its more formal expression in the harmonization and alignment (H&A) agenda, has been the focus of increasing attention in aid debates.

This chapter takes a critical look at these recent trends and assesses two alternative but complementary approaches to donor coordination. The first has mostly been led by donor countries at the international level and is associated with the work of the Development Assistance Committee (DAC) of the OECD, recently enshrined in the Paris Declaration on Aid Effectiveness, which is the focus of this chapter's consideration of the international level. The second is based on country-level coordination initiatives in individual countries, where the role of recipient governments has been more significant. The discussion of this country level in this chapter is based on the experiences of three recipient countries: Tanzania, Mozambique, and Afghanistan, which in recent years have tried to shift the terms of the aid relationship by establishing mechanisms to better manage or regulate aid inflows.

There are several ways in which donor coordination can have positive impacts on governance. Coordination can reduce transaction costs and thus free up political and bureaucratic capacity in the recipient country. When coordination takes the form of alignment to recipient country systems of policy development and administration, it can provide a strong incentive to improve those systems. Coordination can also make donors more effective in promoting good governance directly. All this said, it is important to note that the impact of coordination on governance is not unambiguously positive. If coordination strengthens accountability to donors at the expense of domestic accountability, or significantly reduces the scope of recipient governments to make political decisions over policy, it may have long-term negative impacts on governance. Finally, if donors, acting together, promote policies that are inappropriate to the country context, the cause of good governance may be undermined by poor development results.

## Background

The origins of recent debates about donor coordination and aid effectiveness can be traced back to a series of studies carried out in the late 1980s and early 1990s, which questioned the overall effectiveness of aid in contributing to positive development outcomes.[1] The end of the Cold War opened a unique political opportunity at the international level to take a fresh look at the nature and functioning of the aid system, and to reorient it from a system based mostly on geostrategic interests to one with a stronger focus on reducing global poverty levels. The persistence of poverty and economic stagnation in some regions, notably Sub-Saharan Africa, also led to a rethinking of the instruments being used by international agencies to channel aid resources.

The 1980s had been the decade of structural adjustment programs. During those years, much of the aid system, led by the international financial institutions (IFIS), was geared toward lending money to low-income countries that committed themselves to implementing a package of structural reforms—a package that included liberalization of prices and exchange rates, privatization of publicly owned enterprises, and, more generally, measures aimed at fostering a market economy. These policies (based on the "Washington Consensus")[2] were based on the belief that if governments retreated from the economic sphere and allowed market forces to operate freely, they would spur growth and in turn reduce poverty. Conditions attached to loans provided by the World Bank and the IMF, and to related balance-of-payments supports by a number of bilateral agencies, were the main instrument used to "buy" the policy reforms that were believed to promote development. Structural adjustment programs existed alongside a large number of other projects in different sectors; these were supported by various donor agencies and NGOs, with few efforts made at coordination.

By the mid-1990s the effectiveness of structural adjustment programs was being questioned for a number of reasons (Mosley and Eeckhout 2000). First, many countries had not implemented the required structural reforms, or had reversed them after having adopted them. This was viewed as a consequence of the fact that such reforms did not have strong support in recipient countries and that aid was rarely withdrawn from countries that did not comply with the conditions (Killick 1998; Mosley, Harrigan, and Toye 1995). Second, the effectiveness of the reforms was being questioned: in some of the countries that had implemented them, the results in terms of economic performance were often less than satisfactory. Finally, the *social cost* of adjustment was perceived to be very high, with worsening human development indicators blamed on rising unemployment and public expenditure cuts, which were often a consequence of the adjustment programs. Alongside this discussion of the effectiveness of structural adjustment programs, donor agencies were becoming more aware of the problem of "project proliferation" (Cassen and Associates 1994), which had negative consequences on recipient governments' human and financial capacities in terms of counterpart personnel and budget resources, and which undermined efforts at comprehensive planning and budgeting because interventions were too often fragmented and uncoordinated.

Another important element shaping the political agenda of donor countries at the international level in the early 1990s was the decline in aid levels (see Figure 1). For five or six years beginning in 1992, official development assistance (ODA) declined steadily both in terms of overall levels and, more dramatically, in terms of percentage of donor countries' national income. This was partly the result of fiscal pressures and tightening budget constraints in OECD countries; but there was also a perception that "donor fatigue" was beginning to creep in and that there was not enough political support for the aid enterprise as a whole, given some of the other factors outlined above in terms of foreign policy agendas and research on aid effectiveness.

FIGURE 1

Trends in Official Development Assistance from 1990

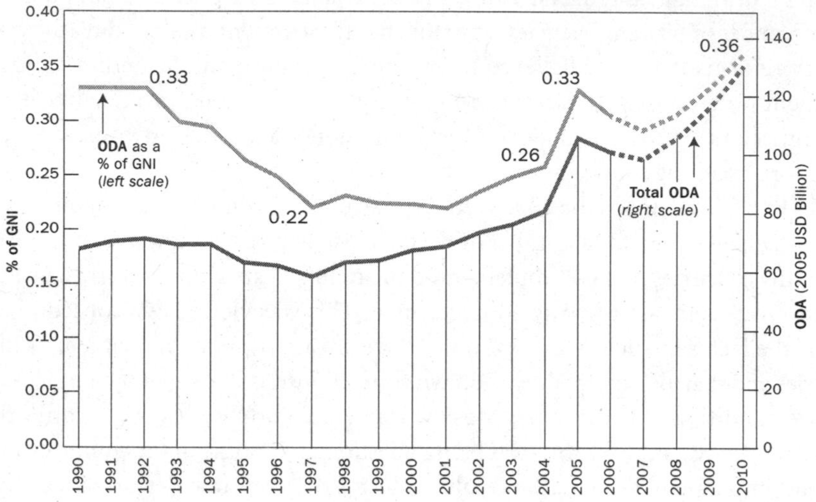

*Source*: www.oecd.org/dac/stats.

## Shaping the Twenty-First Century:
## Setting the Donor-Led Coordination Agenda

The Development Assistance Committee (DAC) of the OECD, established in 1960 as a forum to promote joint learning and coordination among the aid programs of all OECD countries, responded to this impasse by founding a *group de réflexion*, which drafted a strategy document, "Shaping the Twenty-First Century" (OECD DAC 1996), considered by many to be the basis for the developments that followed, which included a new approach to aid effectiveness based on the partnership model and the H&A agenda. The main purpose of the document was to restate the overall case for aid, which was to focus on fundamental, shared, and easy-to-understand objectives rather than on the obscure policy reforms attached to structural adjustment loans. A number of specific targets, borrowed from the ones identified by the UN conferences of the early 1990s,[3] were selected and put forward; these formed the basis for what would become the MDGs adopted by the UN Millennium Declaration in 2000. "Effective international support," argued the DAC, "can make a real difference in achieving these goals" (ibid., 2). The key to making a difference was identified as the establishment of development partnerships between donor and recipient governments, where a commitment to development and accountable governance by a poor country would be matched by donor commitments to:

- provide adequate resources;
- improve the coordination of assistance in support of locally owned development strategies; and
- achieve coherence between aid policies and other policies that impact on developing countries (such as trade).

The new approach was meant to address a number of problems. One of its most important objectives was to reverse the decline in aid flows by focusing on the fundamental contribution of development assistance to key objectives of human development and poverty reduction. Another was to recognize that "the linkages between industrialised and developing countries extend far beyond development assistance" and that the fiscal, environmental, defence, trade, and immigration policies of rich countries all have an impact on poor countries' development opportunities in complex ways. This is what would become MDG8, whose focus would be on "developing a global partnership for development" that would include issues related to trade, debt, and the roles played by the private sector and by technology.

But perhaps the most important aspect of the new approach, which gave rise to the so-called H&A agenda, was that it tackled some of the existing criticisms and contradictions of aid relationships and aid delivery mechanisms. These can be summarized as follows:[4]

- High transactions costs from the multiplicity of different reporting and accounting requirements, including tied aid.
- Inefficient spending dictated by donor priorities and procurement arrangements.
- Extremely unpredictable funding levels.
- Undermining of state systems through special staffing arrangements and parallel structures.
- Corrosion of democratic accountability as mechanisms were designed to satisfy donor rather than domestic constituencies.
- Hard-to-sustain positive impact beyond the short term, with high levels of reliance on donor funding undermining sustainability.
- Corruption, fraud, and rent seeking in the management of projects (not overcome by their independence from government).

"Shaping the Twenty-First Century" outlined a clear shift in the aid paradigm, based on a change in the conception and the language of aid (see Figure 2). In order to enhance the role and effectiveness of ODA, it was necessary to focus on building more effective partnerships between donors and recipients, with joint responsibilities and mutual commitments. In particular, donors would focus their efforts on low-income countries, rely on locally owned development

FIGURE 2

Paradigm Shifts through the Aid "Jargon"

| Recipient countries | Partner countries |
|---|---|
| Donor-led strategies | Partner-led strategies |
| Conditionality | Selectivity/Ownership |
| Project aid | Program assistance |
| Fragmentation | Coordination |
| "Upward" accountability | "Downward" accountability |

strategies, and support government programs as much as possible, avoiding project proliferation and shifting to program-based approaches.[5] Recipient governments, on their side, would create effective coordination mechanisms for managing development assistance and would improve their systems for managing public resources and monitoring development outcomes.

## A Brief History of the
## Donor-led Coordination Agenda

The publication of "Shaping the Twenty-First Century" marked the starting point for a series of subsequent initiatives and events, which stemmed from the increasingly widespread recognition of the new model of development assistance, with the DAC as one of the main players and forums where discussions were held and decisions were taken. In 1997 the first Development Partnership Forum was organized in The Hague in an attempt to systematically involve least developed countries (LDCs) in international events where issues relating to development assistance and its effectiveness could be discussed. In a paper prepared for a DAC high-level meeting in 1998, it was proposed that a Task Force on Donor Practices be created in order to promote consensus on the changes needed in the systems and procedures utilized by DAC donors and to look into ways to facilitate the necessary policy shifts for enhancing donor coordination and country ownership.

The Task Force was established as an ad hoc, time-bound body with an expected lifespan of two years. It included participation from a number of multilateral organizations and from a panel of sixteen developing countries, representing different geographical areas and different levels of development.[6] The Task Force had three working groups, which focused on issues relating to financial management and accountability, reporting and monitoring, and the pre-implementation phases of the project cycle, including country analytic work. Their main purpose was to compile good practice papers that would identify and document donor practices that could cost-effectively reduce the burden on recipient countries to manage aid, besides lowering the transaction costs involved. In this way they would help strengthen ownership and also crystallize the basic principles of a new way of working for donor agencies and recipient governments alike.

The years 1998 to 2002 saw a number of related initiatives, as other actors in the international aid system attempted to address the same problems as the DAC and to adapt to the new consensus on the partnership model of development assistance. In January 1999, after extensive consultations, the World Bank launched the Comprehensive Development Framework (World Bank 1999a), a new model of partnership-based collaboration with its client countries. This was aimed at recognizing the key role played by recipient governments in setting development strategies and policies; and at capturing the contributions of different actors, including donors, the private sector, and civil society. Recipient countries were asked to fill in a matrix that, for each main sector of the economy, would specify the key policies and actors. The UN tried to respond to the changing environment by introducing new instruments; the intent of which was to improve coordination of the activities of different UN agencies and other donors at the country level, while at the same time promoting their alignment to country policies and priorities. The Common Country Assessment (CCA) and the UN Development Assistance Framework (UNDAF) were also launched in 1999, in the hope that they would place the UN at the centre of efforts to make aid more effective.

It is another initiative, however, that has come to embody the international community's efforts to promote a different approach to development cooperation (Christiansen 2003). In late 1999 the boards of the World Bank and the IMF endorsed a proposal that would require highly indebted poor countries (HIPCs) willing to qualify for debt relief to draft poverty reduction strategy papers (PRSPs). These would link the additional resources made available through debt relief to specific poverty reduction efforts. PRSPs quickly became a useful avenue for operationalizing some of the basic principles underpinning the new model of development cooperation promoted by the DAC and embodied in the CDF and CCA/UNDAF initiatives. The fact that they were a requirement for accessing debt relief also provided a clear incentive for countries to engage in the process of drafting one. According to the five core principles that underlie PRSP development and implementation (IMF/World Bank 1999), PRSPs must be (a) *country driven*; (b) *results oriented*; (c) *comprehensive*;

(d) *partnership-oriented*, involving coordinated participation of development partners; and (e) based on a *long-term* perspective for poverty reduction.

While PRSPs emerged as the main operational instrument at the country level to enhance local ownership and donor coordination, the DAC working groups under the Task Force on Donor Practices continued collecting available evidence and best practices, in order to provide more concrete examples and general guidelines on what donors needed to do to transform the PRSP principles into practice and therefore move toward the new model of development cooperation. The good-practice papers were finally published in 2003 in a DAC document, "Harmonizing Donor Practices for Effective Delivery" (OECD 2003), after two significant international events that gave great impulse to the partnership model as well as to the H&A agenda. The Monterrey Conference on Financing for Development, held in Mexico in 2002, reinforced the emerging consensus by placing heavy emphasis on effective partnerships for aid effectiveness; it called for donors "to harmonize their operational procedures at the highest standard so as to reduce transaction costs and make ODA disbursement and delivery more flexible, taking into account national development needs and objectives under the ownership of the recipient country." The following year, the Rome Declaration on Harmonization built on that general statement and set out a number of ambitious commitments, including these:

- To ensure that harmonization efforts would be adapted to the country context, and that donor assistance would be aligned with the development recipient's priorities.
- To expand country-led efforts to streamline donor procedures and practices.
- To review and identify ways to adapt institutions' and countries' policies, procedures, and practices to facilitate harmonization.
- To implement the good practices principles and standards formulated by the development community as the foundation for harmonization.

In addition, in May 2003 the DAC created the Working Party on Aid Effectiveness to promote, support, and monitor progress on harmonization and alignment, with input from several partner countries. The Working Party, which is still in existence, has a broader multilateral participation than its predecessor (the Task Force on Donor Practices), as well as a wider mandate that covers public financial management, procurement, and managing for results. Since 2003 the Working Party has been highly active promoting a range of activities. These include surveys on progress achieved in implementing the commitments included in the Rome Declaration and the Paris declaration; the development of a Country Implementation Tracking Tool to provide information on country-level activities through a Web-based system;[7] and further

FIGURE 3

A Graphical Sketch of the H&A Agenda: The DAC "Pyramid"

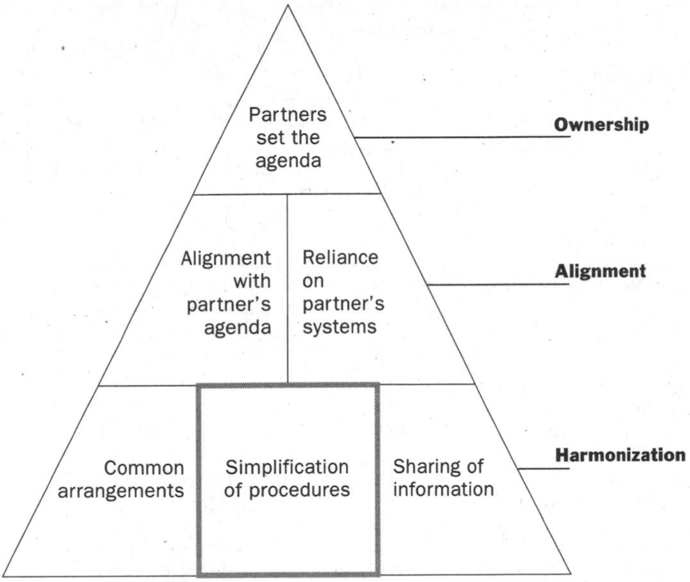

Source: OECD 2005c.

work on good-practice areas following the second High-Level Forum, which was held in Paris in March 2005.

Its work has allowed a clearer definition of the three principal dimensions of the Rome commitments (ownership, alignment, harmonization) (see Figure 3), added the two additional dimensions of mutual accountability and managing for results, and has facilitated agreement on the crucial set of indicators and benchmarks that form the core of the Paris Declaration on Aid Effectiveness and that will allow for a much more significant monitoring of progress both at global and country levels (see Table 1). These indicators, and the more specific targets associated with each, were endorsed by the UN during the Millennium Review Summit held in September 2005. A monitoring process has also been put in place to ensure the collection of relevant data at country level in order to track progress in meeting the targets. A follow-up High-Level Forum to review the status of implementation is scheduled to take place in Ghana in 2008.

TABLE 1

## Commitments and Indicators in the Paris Declaration

| Commitment | Indicator |
| --- | --- |
| *Ownership* | |
| Partners have operational development strategies | Number of countries with national development strategies (including PRSs) that have clear strategic priorities linked to a medium-term expenditure framework and reflected in annual budgets. |
| *Alignment* | |
| Reliable country systems | Number of countries that have procurement and public financial management systems that either (a) adhere to broadly accepted good practices or (b) have a reform program in place to achieve these. |
| Aid flows are aligned on country priorities | Percentage of aid flows to the government sector that is reported on partners' national budget. |
| Strengthen capacity by coordinated support | Percentage of donor capacity development support provided through coordinated programs consistent with partners' national development strategies. |
| Use of country systems | Percentages of donors and of aid flows that use partner-country procurement and/or public financial management systems in partner countries, which either (a) adhere to broadly accepted good practices or (b) have a reform program in place to achieve these. |
| Strengthen capacity by avoiding parallel implementation structures | Number of parallel project implementation units (PIUs) per country. |
| Aid is more predictable | Percentage of aid disbursements released according to agreed schedules in annual or multiyear framework. |
| Aid is untied | Percentage of bilateral aid that is untied. |
| *Harmonization* | |
| Use of common arrangements and procedures | Percentage of aid provided as program-based approaches. |
| Encourage shared analysis | Percentage of (a) field missions and/or (b) country analytic work, including diagnostic reviews that are joint. |
| *Managing for results* | |
| Results-oriented frameworks | Number of countries with transparent and monitorable performance assessment frameworks to assess progress against (a) the national development strategies and (b) sector programs. |
| *Mutual accountability* | |
| Mutual accountability | Number of partner countries that undertake mutual assessments of progress in implementing agreed commitments on aid effectiveness, including those in this Declaration. |

*Source*: OECD 2005b.

## Have Aspirations Been Met?
## A Critical Look at the Donor-Led Coordination Agenda

Any attempt at measuring the impact of the H&A agenda since its inception a decade ago is likely to run into a number of problems. While its final objective is clearly linked to development outcomes, much of its focus is on changing approaches and behaviours that may bring about results only over a much longer time horizon. It can be argued that the policy shifts advocated by the partnership model of development cooperation, while based on a clear perception of the problems they want to address, constitute an act of faith, in that there is scant evidence on their actual impact. PRSPs and their associated processes have been under increasing scrutiny in recent years. A series of studies and reports[8] have noted that in many cases the rhetoric behind the core principles of the PRSP has not been born out in practice: some donors are undermining local ownership, failing to streamline conditions, shifting substantial resources toward program modalities, and multiplying review processes and frameworks that continue to strain local policy-making and implementation capacities.

Recent evaluations of general budget support (IDD and Associates 2006; Lawson et al. 2005), the preferred aid modality for improving ownership, alignment, and harmonization, highlighted a number of positive outcomes in relation to macroeconomic management, quality of public financial management, and increases in key areas of public spending. They also pointed to a number of problems for which donors are still responsible, such as keeping high levels of fragmented project funding and structuring policy dialogue in ways that prevent genuine country policy ownership.

In 2004 the DAC carried out a survey on harmonization and alignment in fourteen countries (OECD 2004) in order to gauge both donors' and recipients' views on progress with the H&A agenda. The survey identified a number of shortcomings in donors' efforts to implement the commitments contained in the Rome Declaration. In particular, the survey found that "alignment will remain an unfulfilled promise if donors do not take steps to clarify how they should adapt their country programmes to reflect poverty-reduction strategies, and if they do not rely on country systems to deliver aid" (2004, 9). It also stated that "there is not enough evidence that harmonization initiatives have helped curb transaction costs. Indeed, over the short term at least, they may have actually increased these costs" (ibid.).

Despite some of this controversial evidence, dismissing the H&A agenda as impossible or unreasonable would be a mistake. Although slow to produce results on the ground, the drawn-out process through which DAC donors, multilateral agencies, and participating recipient countries have been negotiating the content of a different model for structuring aid relationships has been very important in bringing about a shift in the predominant consensus on aid effectiveness. The conceptualization work that underpins the definitions of the commitments and indicators in the Paris Declaration is in and of itself a very important achievement, especially in light of the consensual nature of the process. The DAC relies on the development of a shared language and of common understanding among its members, and it inevitably runs the risk of watering down its positions to reach a lowest common denominator that keeps everybody engaged.

It would be short-sighted not to recognize the different pressures faced by the various donor agencies and the incentives created by their existing structures in terms of promoting or hindering H&A-related efforts. A study of incentives for harmonization and alignment in six aid agencies carried out for the DAC (de Renzio et al. 2005) helped shed some light on why H&A rhetoric is often not matched by concrete changes in donor behaviour on the ground. Domestic political pressures for visibility, rigidity and resistance to changes in policies and procedures, and lack of individual incentives for staff to engage in harmonization activities are some of the factors that shape an agency's capacity to deliver on the H&A commitments it signs up to in international forums. While some agencies are able to tackle these different aspects all at once, others struggle. While some have taken the lead in pushing for a further deepening of the H&A agenda, others are clearly lagging behind, still unconvinced of its premises and usefulness.

The issue of monitoring and reporting on progress against the indicators and targets included in the Paris Declaration, especially at the country level, is going to be key in the near future to ensuring that the hard-won agreement does not remain unfulfilled. Work carried out since 2005 has highlighted the need to establish a clear baseline for many of the indicators that need to be monitored. The methodology that has been developed for collecting and analyzing information will determine the future significance of the H&A agenda.

Another fundamental issue is that of widening and deepening recipient-country involvement in the whole process. Only a very small subset of developing countries have taken part in the DAC process since the late 1990s, and the actual content of their contributions is questionable. Many more have signed the Paris Declaration and will be included in the monitoring process. To avoid the risk that a donor-led process will limit the scope and extent of recipient country leadership, clear mechanisms for mutual accountability need to be put in place, so that aid-receiving countries will be able to gain a higher degree of control over the ways in which aid flows are channelled, distributed, and managed.

## Reframing the Coordination Debate:
## Recipient-Led Coordination Approaches at the Country Level

The coordination of aid is often analyzed from donor perspective. The discussion above demonstrates the value of critically analyzing donor-led coordination efforts at the international level. However, if ownership is to be taken seriously, coordination on the ground must be led by recipients. In aid-dependent countries, aid is at the centre of political and economic systems. Aid flows, and associated conditions, dominate the work of many recipient country institutions. If recipient countries are to develop domestically owned policies and systems and promote good governance, their role in the aid relationship needs to change. If the coordination agenda is pushed forward solely by donors, an opportunity to develop recipient country ownership and governance will be missed and long-term progress in these areas may be undermined.

So reframing the coordination debate to focus on recipient country leadership is not about removing responsibilities from donors, but rather about (a) exploring the scope for building on recipients' interests in coordination in order to ensure that aid is appropriately coordinated, even where donors are unable or unwilling to do this; and (b) ensuring that coordination does not come at the expense of recipient-country ownership and governance capacity, but rather enhances it.

There are relatively few examples of recipients taking the lead in their aid relationship (e.g., by setting the terms under which they are prepared to accept aid)—an observation that is perhaps unsurprising, given the asymmetries of resources, power, and capabilities that characterize most relationships between donors and recipients. For most aid recipients, the perceived risk of losing aid is enough to prevent much assertiveness. That said, some interesting exceptions to this are emerging. It is worth studying these cases, for they demonstrate a range of approaches that can help recipients establish leadership in their aid relationships and thus improve donor coordination.

Some recipient countries have set hard conditions for the acceptance of aid, backed by the government's intention to reject aid that fails to meet these conditions, sometimes supported by legislation. Other recipients have sought to use information and transparency to change donor behaviour, through independent monitoring. This provides data that can be used by both donors and recipients, and can put pressure on both sides to improve their performance. Often based on independent monitoring, some countries have developed more formal mutual accountability systems in which donors and recipients are held accountable to targets or performance standards. Finally, almost all examples of recipient leadership are premised on the establishment of clear policies and systems by the recipient government that encourage alignment by donors.

Most notable current examples of recipient leadership employ a combination of these strategies. It is perhaps unsurprising that countries such as India, which are not aid dependent, have been able to set the terms under which they are prepared to accept aid (India now refuses any government-to-government aid less than $25M). More interestingly, some highly aid-dependent governments have been able to change donor behaviour in their countries and to improve coordination. The discussion below will focus on three cases: Tanzania, Mozambique, and Afghanistan. All three rely heavily on aid to fund their government expenditures yet have been able to exercise some degree of leadership in the aid relationship to improve coordination.

## Tanzania

Over the past ten years the Government of Tanzania (GoT) has taken steps to improve the quality of the aid it receives, based on a model that combines independent monitoring and elements of mutual accountability to promote Tanzanian leadership in the aid relationship. This process has been facilitated by the fact that the GoT has clearly stated preferences and strategies, as expressed in its Poverty Reduction Strategy (which is relatively long-standing—the first PRSP was agreed on in 2000). The government's priorities focus on three areas: reducing income poverty, developing human capabilities and well-being, and containing extreme vulnerability.

In 1994, in response to a breakdown of relationships with donors and declining aid volumes, the GoT (with financial support from the Danish government) commissioned an independent group of advisers to investigate the problems with the aid relationship and propose solutions. The subsequent report[9] led to the formulation by 1997 of "Agreed Notes" between the GoT and its donors; these set out the terms of the aid relationship and defined specific commitments on both sides to improve aid outcomes. Progress against these commitments was initially assessed in regular reports from the chair of the original Group of Independent Advisers; since 2000 it has been monitored through a formally constituted Independent Monitoring Group (IMG).

In 2002 the GoT's strategy for managing its aid was formalized as the Tanzania Assistance Strategy (TAS). The TAS "is a Government initiative aimed at restoring local ownership and leadership by promoting partnership in the design and execution of development programmes" (Tanzanian Ministry of Finance 2002). It outlines the undertakings of the GoT (e.g., improved financial management, anticorruption measures, domestic resource mobilization) and its donors (e.g., harmonization, aid untying, the use of central budgeting tools). The TAS Action Plan outlines specific actions to be taken on both sides, which focus on four priority areas: improving predictability, integrating aid into the budget, rationalizing and harmonizing processes, and capacity building for aid management. The TAS system is essentially a mutual accountability framework, with both sides being held to account through the work of the IMG.

Thus far the GoT has generally avoided rejecting aid that does not meet TAS standards. Tanzania's next move seems to be toward setting tougher conditions for accepting aid. The Government Loans, Guarantees and Grants Act (2003) has enshrined a minimum grant element of 50 percent for new borrowing, and the GoT has rejected loans that do not meet this standard. The latest report from the IMG also recommends that future project aid be subject to firmer conditions.

The TAS has now been used as the basis for developing a Joint Assistance Strategy (JAS), initiated by the GoT, DFID, and the World Bank. This aims to further improve donor coordination—including through the identification of donors' comparative advantages and the introduction of a single review cycle— and will replace the individual assistance strategies of the participating donors. The JAS may also confirm the move toward tougher conditions on the acceptance of aid, the aim being to create "a binding agreement between the Government of Tanzania and Development Partners for the duration of a JAS cycle" (Tanzanian Ministry of Finance 2005).

The JAS represents an ambitious coordination strategy. The GoT will commit to creating appropriately integrated structures to act as the basis of coordination (e.g., PRS and Budget, performance assessment frameworks), and donors will accordingly commit to alignment as well as to harmonization measures, including the identification of lead and delegating donors in each sector and increased use of budget support.

## Mozambique

The Government of Mozambique (GoM) has developed its role in the aid relationship, and improved donor coordination, through a model based on mutual accountability. As in Tanzania, the coordination of donors in Mozambique has centred on the GoM's PRS (the "Plano de Acção para a Redução da Pobreza Absoluta" [PARPA]). The PRS aims to reduce absolute poverty from 70 percent in 1999 to less than 60 percent by 2005 and less than 50 percent by 2010. However, it should be noted from the outset that leadership from the GoM has been less significant than in the Tanzanian case—donors have played a more significant role in defining the process.

Since the mid-1990s a group of "like-minded" donors has been relatively effective at coordinating their activities in Mozambique through multidonor budget support. Donors' concerns have done much to define their relationship with the GoM. For example, in 2000, concerns about banking crises and fraud (which led to a suspension of budget support) led donors to reassess their conditions and focus on "second generation" reforms to governance structures. This change in the substance of donor conditionality was one factor in the emergence of new structures for donor–GoM relations.

In 2000, budget support donors in Mozambique formalized their coordination efforts in the Joint Donor Program for Macro-Financial Support, superseded in 2004 by a Memorandum of Understanding (MoU) between the GoM and its program donors. This memo outlined commitments on both sides to improve the quality and effectiveness of program aid. Nineteen donor agencies providing budget support or other program aid (the so-called G-19[10]) have now signed up to the MoU. The MoU is based on donor commitments in six key areas: alignment to GoM policies and systems, increased predictability of aid flows, elimination of bilateral conditionality, reducing transaction costs, transparency of aid flows and conditions, and enhanced GoM capacity and leadership. The GoM has signed up to a Performance Assessment Framework (PAF), which provides the basis for an annual joint review process whereby donors assess GoM progress and make aid commitments for the following year in a coordinated way.

Since 2003, donors in Mozambique have themselves been assessed under the Program Aid Partners' Performance Assessment Framework (PAPS' PAF). A baseline for donor performance was defined in 2003. An annual reporting process monitors donors' progress toward meeting the MoU commitments. Although the PAPS' PAF has been criticized for failing to set firm targets in a number of important areas (e.g., alignment of medium-term aid commitments with GoM planning horizons), it does provide a degree of mutual accountability in Mozambique that is far ahead of that achieved in most aid-receiving countries.

The MoU and mutual accountability framework's main limitation is that it applies only to program aid and program aid donors (although other donors have "observer status" in the G-19). This leaves much of Mozambique's aid outside the system. There is some coordination of project aid through SWAPs, which are long established in Mozambique (the Agriculture SWAP was established as early as 1991), but problems are now arising regarding how to align sectoral initiatives with the MoU process amid concerns that line ministries with responsibility for delivery in key sectors are marginalized in the MoU process.

## Afghanistan

At the outset, the post-conflict aid effort in Afghanistan did not look promising from the perspective of recipient leadership. The aid architecture established in 2001 was designed when there *was* no government in Afghanistan, and the initial needs assessment and development framework was negotiated and agreed largely among donors. However, the Afghan Interim Administration was quickly able to gain some control in its relationship with donors through a combination of clear national policies and systems and some hard conditions for the acceptance of aid.

The National Development Framework (NDF) developed by the Afghan Interim Administration in early 2002 provided the basis for donor alignment around Afghan priorities and strategies. The NDF is based on three "pillars" (humanitarian assistance and human and social capital; physical reconstruction and natural resources; and private-sector development), with twelve associated national programs (including refugee return, education, transport, and public administration). In addition, the NDF identified three cross-cutting themes (governance, financial management, and administrative reform; human rights, security, and rule of law; and gender) that are priorities across sectors. The NDF formed the basis for the National Development Budget, around which donors were expected to align. The NDF also provided the basis for Afghan leadership in the aid relationship: after April 2002 the main donor implementation forum (the Afghanistan Reconstruction Implementation Group) was chaired by the Afghan Interim Administration. The new Afghanistan National Development Strategy is currently the subject of consultation: it will be finalized as Afghanistan's PRSP next year.

Besides creating strong policies and systems to which donors can align, the Afghan Interim Administration (and then the Government of Afghanistan [GoA]) sought from the outset to actively manage aid. The Assistance Coordination Authority (now the Development Budget and External Relations Unit) provided a focal point for this. The GoA set some hard conditions for the acceptance of aid, and this forced even normally recalcitrant donors to harmonize their activities to some extent. For example, the government limited the number of sectors any donor can work in, and it requires minimum contributions before donors can expand to new sectors. In 2004 the GoA submitted its own bid for resources to donors; in doing so, it was proactively seeking the resources it needed rather than managing preplanned donor projects and programs.

The Afghanistan Reconstruction Trust Fund, established in 2002 and managed by the ADB, IsDB (Islamic Development Bank), UNDP, and World Bank, is a pooled funding arrangement that provides coordinated funding for recurrent expenditures as well as for priority programs. This has become a key instrument of donor support, with some donors providing a significant proportion of their non-humanitarian assistance through the fund.

Although Afghanistan does not have a formally constituted mutual accountability or independent monitoring system as in Tanzania and Mozambique, transparency and the availability of data about donor behaviour have helped the GoA manage its donors. The Development Assistance Database now records over 90 percent of the aid coming into Afghanistan and makes data about donors' pledges and disbursements publicly available.

The case of Afghanistan demonstrates both the promise and the potential limitations of recipient leadership. Despite early success in establishing clear policies and systems for donors to align to, the GoA's control over aid inflows remains limited by the security situation as well as by the combination of humanitarian, military, and development assistance it receives. Although the establishment of hard conditions for the acceptance of aid did have an impact on donor behaviour, this approach may become less tenable if, as seems likely, Afghanistan faces significant shortfalls of resources in coming years.

## Preconditions and Limitations for Recipient-Led Donor Coordination

It is important to note that the models of leadership described above do not seem to be freely accessible to all aid recipients. Although the small number of successful cases limits our ability to draw conclusions about necessary prior conditions, the record to date suggests that certain types of aid relationships help recipient countries exercise leadership. Low levels of dependence on aid clearly provide recipient countries with more control over their aid—control backed ultimately by the ability to reject aid. Even countries that depend heavily on aid may gain "leverage" if they have access to large volumes of aid from a variety of sources. Finally, recipients who (possibly just for historical reasons) have aid relationships with like-minded donors who are able and willing to align with recipients' preferences may be able to take leadership with less fear that donors will reduce their aid.

It is interesting that the political systems and governance institutions of the cases discussed above are relatively varied. It does not seem to be the case that only recipients with well-established institutions and polities can take leadership. Indeed, the fact that Afghanistan's Interim Administration was able to establish leadership in its aid relationships and improve donor coordination, despite its fragile political position and post-conflict challenges, suggests that taking a leadership role in aid relationships can actually facilitate the development of stable political systems and governance institutions.

Having said that, there are clearly some political/governance preconditions. Ultimately, the ability of recipients to change donor behaviour rests on the willingness of donors to engage with the recipient government, which in turn clearly requires some level of donor-perceived credibility. This is not to say, however, that recipients need to have good relationships with donors in order to change the nature of those relationships. The Tanzanian case demonstrates that recipient leadership can actually improve relationships with donors, even from a low base.

## Can Recipient-Led Coordination Change Donor Behaviour?

The first measure by which recipient leadership in the aid relationship must be judged is whether it changes donor behaviour in ways which might not otherwise have been expected. Evidence from Tanzania, Mozambique, and Afghanistan suggests that recipient leadership can change donor behaviour at least to some extent; with the important caveats that we cannot know how donors would have behaved in different circumstances, and that many recipient-led processes are relatively recent developments, which makes long-term impacts impossible to judge.

Recipient leadership has in some cases been associated with the increased use of program assistance by donors and with budget support in particular. In Tanzania the level of general budget support rose from Tshs 274.6 billion in 2002–3 to 405 billion in 2003–4 and is over Tshs 430 billion in 2004–5 (Economic and Social Research Foundation 2005). Budget support (including debt relief) now accounts for around 50 percent of Tanzania's aid (Balogun 2005). Since the development of the PARPA in Mozambique, the number of donors providing budget support (and participating in associated mutual accountability frameworks) has risen from six to nineteen. In a 2007 review, seven donors met or exceeded the GoM's target for more than two-thirds of aid to come as program aid (Killick, Castel-Branco, and Gerster 2005). The picture in Afghanistan is less promising on this measure. At least one-third of the funds disbursed since 2001 have been for humanitarian projects rather than reconstruction (Rubin et al. 2003), and almost 80 percent of aid disbursed in 2002–3 was project funding.[11]

There is also some evidence that recipient leadership, and the closer relationships with donors that have been associated with it, have helped improve the predictability of disbursements. In Tanzania in 2003, around 70 percent of donors indicated to the GoT what their planned aid disbursements would be over the following three years; also, budget support disbursements in the first quarter of the financial year rose from 8 percent in 2002–3 to 80 percent in 2004–5 (Economic and Social Research Foundation 2005). In Mozambique, most of the donors participating in the MoU process now have multiyear arrangements in place. In 2004, twelve of them reported that disbursements took place on schedule (compared to six in 2003). Again, Afghanistan provides a less optimistic view. In 2002–3, donors disbursed less than $1.9 billion, despite committing more than US$4 billion[12] (ibid.), and future levels of aid are uncertain.

Donors have also been encouraged to make more use of national budgeting tools and systems. In Tanzania more than 40 percent of aid is now channelled through the national budget (compared to 30 percent in 2002), and estimates suggest that more than 75 percent of project aid is now recorded in the centralized budget system. Alignment of donors' calendars to the Tanzanian budget cycle has also been improved. In Mozambique the number of donors stating that they were fully aligned with Mozambican funding cycles rose from four in 2003 to eight in 2004 (Killick, Castel-Branco, and Gerster 2005). In Afghanistan the Development Assistance Database now records more than 90 percent of aid, although only a small proportion of aid actually flows through the government budget.

The evidence above suggests that there have been improvements in donor coordination and alignment around country systems in these cases, but even so, systems alignment remains far from perfect. One thousand projects accounted for only 17 percent of aid flows in Tanzania in 2003. Although Tanzania has reduced the number of reports it has to produce for donors from the much vaunted level of twelve hundred per year, it still received more than five hundred donor missions in 2002–3. There are also concerns that new coordinated arrangements (e.g., SWAPs, basket funds) simply add new structures and management requirements to existing ones (Ronsholt 2002). Tanzania's coordination mechanisms may now need coordinating! Similarly, in Mozambique, administration costs remain high (the GoM is estimated to have more than one thousand bank accounts due to donor requirements, and received 143 donor missions in 2004, excluding World Bank missions). Furthermore, more than half of aid to the country remains off budget and outside the mutual accountability arrangement. There are concerns in some quarters that the focus of attention on the budget support element of Mozambique's aid has reduced coordination in the rest of the portfolio. As noted above, Afghanistan continues to receive most of its aid as project funding, and although transparency and data have improved, most aid remains off budget.

The picture with respect to donors' alignment with recipients' policies is more complex. The harmonizing of donor positions on development policies (economic, social, or political) is not necessarily desirable from a recipient's perspective if alignment with country priorities and strategies is incomplete—it may increase donors' negotiating power at the expense of the recipient government and reduce the latter's scope to make policy independently. This makes "success" for recipient leadership strategies harder to define. Increased coordination of donor policies, which is relatively easy to observe, may be a good or bad thing; and real alignment of donor policies to country priorities and strategies is hard to discern, given the possibility that recipients will "pre-empt" donor preferences simply by presenting priorities and strategies that they expect donors to approve.

Afghanistan started with a clean slate with donors and has made impressive progress in establishing its own development plans and budgets as the central focus of policy. Although it is not clear that donors' priorities would have differed significantly from those set by the Interim Administration in the NDF, the fact that policies and strategies have been established in clearly government-led processes is significant. Having said all this, it remains to be seen whether the GoA will be able to build on this success and establish meaningful policy leadership in the long term, given the security concerns and other constraints it faces.

In Tanzania and Mozambique, donors had well established priorities and strategies that did not historically line up with government policies. There is some evidence that GoT priorities are now influencing conditionality in Tanzania. For example, the GoT's Letter of Intent to the IMF (July 2003) reflected priorities set out in the PRSP progress report of March 2003 (Peretz and Wangwe 2004). Having said this, some have argued that long-term dependence on donors has rendered real policy choice impossible in countries such as Tanzania (Harrison 2001). Similarly, there is some evidence that conditionality is being streamlined in Mozambique, giving the government more policy flexibility. The World Bank was persuaded not to add conditions to the established multidonor agreement, for example. However, more than half the G-19 donors maintain exceptions to the joint PAF and impose bilateral conditions. Also, some observers have questioned the nature of the apparent consensus between the GoM and donors in Mozambique. Killick, Castel-Branco, and Gerster (2005) have raised the possibility that the apparent lack of controversy on policy fundamentals in Mozambique could be a product of extreme dependence and "resignation" on the part of the government to the fact that it cannot affect major policy decisions. It is worth noting again that in the case of Mozambique, donor concerns have actually been a driving force in creating the system that now exists.

All of this raises the question of whether donor coordination and alignment with recipient government systems and policies is simply a slow process,
or whether recipient leadership faces fundamental limitations in changing
donor behaviour. Experience seems to suggest that progress over time is possible, but it is hard to see how recipients will ever be able to overcome the fundamental power imbalances of the aid relationship. In some respects, donors
continue to hold all the cards. Recipients, for the most part, lack the means to
enforce agreements made by donors. This means that mutual accountability,
for example, can only ever be partially "mutual" in the aid relationship. It also
underlines the continued importance of donors' willingness to take harmonization and alignment seriously.

Even where recipients can reject aid and set "hard" conditions on aid receipts,
sanctions on donors remain weak—limited, really, to reputational and peer
pressure impacts. Having said this, in the context of rising aid budgets and
donor agencies with incentives to disburse funds, certain recipients at least
may be gaining negotiating power. The latest report from the IMG in Tanzania argues that even if the introduction of hard conditions by recipients initially leads to donors withdrawing aid, donors won't be able to credibly with-
draw aid in the long term if recipients are merely implementing principles
signed up to by donors in Rome and Paris (Economic and Social Research
Foundation 2005).

Another fundamental asymmetry emerges when collective action by donors
is not met by collective action by recipients. Recipients typically have fewer
forums for formulating collective positions, in contrast to the multiplicity of
donor forums (OECD, G7, like-minded donor groups, etc.); and they face the
same kinds of incentive problems as donors when it comes to coordination
among themselves. The potential risks of this at the country level have been
touched on above (e.g., the risk that collective action by donors will simply reduce recipient countries' negotiating power), but there are also more systemic
problems. The lack of recipient input into international or headquarters-level
donor policy-making is a fundamental limitation on their impact on donor
behaviour. Some of the most significant remaining barriers to systemic alignment in the three cases set out above (e.g., tied aid) are often non-negotiable
at the country level. The limited role of recipients at the international level
also reduces the spillover effects of existing good practices in countries like
Tanzania, Mozambique, and Afghanistan.

## Donor Coordination and Good Governance

As noted in the introduction, a key benefit of donor coordination should be improving the quality of institutions and governance standards at country level, especially those related to policy-making and financial management. The long-term impact of donor-led and recipient-led donor coordination initiatives remains to be seen, but there are at least some suggestions that donor coordination and recipient leadership in the aid relationship can form part of a virtuous circle, with ownership, alignment, and harmonization acting as mutually reinforcing factors, as envisaged in the Paris Declaration. When government institutions and systems can be established as the central instruments of policy and decision making, domestic incentives to hold the recipient government to account are enhanced. This kind of effect is in addition to the direct impact of aid management experience on government capacity. The focus on specific country experiences, in this respect, is very useful, as ultimately the impact of donor coordination on good governance is a country-level issue.

The Tanzanian case, which is the longest-established of the three discussed here, provides some evidence of such virtuous circles. The most recent report from the IMG notes that GoT ownership has been strengthened as the role it plays in the aid relationship has changed. The national policy process has also become more participatory—the second-generation PRS has been more consultative and more national in character than the first. The quality of governance has also improved, with greater transparency and increased capacity at both national and local levels of government (ibid.).

Any judgment of whether changes such as these can be attributed to new models of aid management is beyond the scope of this paper. However, it does seem clear that at the very least, recipient-led harmonization and alignment initiatives should mitigate the risk that donor activities will have negative impacts on ownership and good governance, whether through a lack of coordination (e.g., where administrative burdens overwhelm recipient agencies) or through inappropriate coordination (e.g., where coordinated donor conditionality removes real policy-making power from the recipient government).

The real challenge for even the most proactive recipient government is to successfully move from *partnership* to *leadership* in the aid relationship, and from *ownership* of policies and systems to *sovereignty* over them. The three cases here are at different stages of this process. In Tanzania the government is increasingly leading the harmonization process, even though many initiatives were initiated by donors. The TAS and the emerging JAS are genuinely innovative structures. In Mozambique the government's role in harmonization can probably more fairly be described as ownership rather than leadership. For example, the government played only a limited role in the design of the PAPS' PAF. In Afghanistan the government has clearly played a leadership role in the aid relationship, but it remains to be seen whether this can be capitalized on, given other constraints.

## Conclusions

This chapter has provided an outline and an assessment of two approaches to donor coordination.

First, the history, aspirations, and progress of recent international discussions around donor coordination and the harmonization and alignment (H&A) agenda, from its inception to the recent Paris Declaration on Aid Effectiveness and its follow-up, were discussed. While progress has been made in creating a shared language and joint commitments on reaching clear targets, this process has been slow in making a difference on the ground and has suffered from limited participation and leadership from developing countries. The H&A agenda has so far failed to adequately address a number of issues and questions that are key for the wider objectives it aims to achieve.[13] These are related to, among other issues, engagement in so-called fragile states, building sustainable capacity to formulate, implement, and manage development policies, and the challenges of scaling up aid volumes.

Second, however, examples from Tanzania, Mozambique, and Afghanistan have shown how, when recipient governments take the lead, donor coordination can be delivered at country level and can bring about limited but significant improvements in institutions and governance.

The key question for donors is how to support recipient leadership in the aid relationship in a way that genuinely promotes recipient capacity and ownership and that also maximizes aid effectiveness. Although benefits can certainly be reaped from donor-led coordination exercises, experience suggests that progress on aid effectiveness made in this way will always be limited. There is a risk that donor-led coordination may undermine rather than support the emergence of good governance and ownership.

## Notes

1   Among others, see Cassen and Associates 1995, Mosley 1991, and World Bank 1998.
2   See Williamson 1994.
3   These include the ones on education (Jomtien 1990), children (New York 1990), the environment (Rio de Janeiro 1992), human rights (Vienna 1993), population (Cairo 1994), social development (Copenhagen 1995), and women (Beijing 1995).

4  Adapted from Lawson and Booth 2004.

5  These include Sector-Wide Approaches (SWAPs) and General Budget Support (GBS), and are characterized by four key elements: (1) leadership by recipient government, (2) a single program and budget framework, (3) donor coordination and harmonization of procedures, and (4) increased use of local procedures with regard to program design and implementation, financial management, and monitoring and evaluation (CIDA 2004).

6  The countries represented were Bangladesh, Bolivia, Cambodia, Egypt, Senegal, Guatemala, Kenya, Kyrgyz Republic, Mali, Morocco, Mozambique, Pacific Forum, Romania, Tanzania, Uganda, and Vietnam.

7  It can be accessed through the website www.aidharmonisation.org.

8  See, for example, Booth 2003, Driscoll et al. 2005, CIDSE 2004, Gould and Ojanen 2003, and Craig and Porter 2002.

9  "Report of the Group of Independent Advisers on Development Cooperation Issues between Tanzania and Its Aid Donors," more commonly referred to as the "Helleiner Report," after the group's chairman, Gerry Helleiner.

10  The G-19 comprise Austria, Belgium, Canada, Denmark, the EC, Finland, France, Germany, Ireland, Italy, Netherlands, Norway, Portugal, Spain Sweden, Switzerland, the UK, the World Bank, and the African Development Bank.

11  Data from Afghan Development Assistance Database.

12  Data from Afghan Development Assistance Database.

13  See Rogerson 2005 and Rogerson and de Renzio 2005.

▲

# 12

## CONCLUSION:
## CHALLENGES AND NEW DIRECTIONS FOR CANADA

### Jennifer Welsh[1]

As noted in the introduction to this book, good governance has been identified as an area where Canada's experience, combined with its perceived reputation as an impartial donor, provides the country with a comparative advantage with respect to other actors. Within the public debate in Canada, this view is stronger than an intuition; according to some, good governance is a fundamental feature of the Canadian identity and should be a key driver of Canada's foreign and development policy. In a speech to the Liberal Party Convention in March 2005, Michael Ignatieff proclaimed: "From Sri Lanka to Iraq, from South Africa to Ukraine, we can help promote democratic federalism for multiethnic, multilingual states. Exporting peace, order and good government should be the core of a disciplined foreign policy that concentrates on what we do best and shares the Canadian dream with the rest of the world" (Ignatieff 2005b). The idea that Canada's interest in and responsibility for promoting good governance somehow flows from the country's particular governance abilities also featured prominently in the federal government's 2005 International Policy Statement: "For those in countries where violence threatens to overtake political accommodation as the answer to competing interests, Canada's long history of accommodation of linguistic, ethnic and cultural differences ... offers a glimmer of hope. Our system of governance represents a laboratory full of intriguing experiments that can assist others engaged in the complex task of institution building" (Canada 2005a, 22).

Three aspects of this assumption about Canada's unique strength are worth highlighting and probing further. First, policy-makers should remember the

relatively recent nature of Canada's confidence about good-governance promotion. As Ian Smillie demonstrates in his chapter, neither of Canada's more
activist prime ministers on the global stage during the Cold War—Lester Pearson and Pierre Trudeau—considered good governance to be an essential part
of efforts at bringing about greater justice internationally. Even during the
1980s, the decade that sowed the seeds of so much political change in the former communist world, governance issues were framed through the narrow
economic lens of the so-called Washington Consensus. It was only in 1987,
with the publication of a comprehensive CIDA strategy on foreign aid, that
human rights and democracy received any sustained attention in development policy-making (CIDA 1987).[2] But with the exception of Canada's sanctions
against South Africa and suspension of aid to Zaire (now Republic of Congo),
this aspiration for linkage between governance and aid had to wait until the
start of Lloyd Axworthy's tenure as foreign affairs minister (in the mid-1990s)
for a strategic plan of action (CIDA 1996a). In short, Canada has had roughly
a decade of experience in integrating good-governance considerations into its
development assistance programming—hardly enough to support bold claims
about comparative advantage. As Smillie concludes, the question is not so
much whether Canada should be promoting good governance, but whether it
"knows enough yet to do it well, and whether it will commit adequate resources
in the future to do more."

Second, generating responsibilities from abilities does not necessarily provide a coherent blueprint for good-governance promotion. In its supporting
strategy for the International Policy Statement, CIDA highlighted the following attributes and skills that make Canada well suited to supporting developing countries' efforts to improve their governance: a broad base of experience
with democratic parties, elections, and legislatures; a demonstrated commitment to international human rights norms; gender equality expertise in policy-making; experience and capacity in child protection; a dual code of common law and civil law; a strong reputation in peacebuilding and conflict
prevention; and robust environmental assessment practices (CIDA 2005b, 12).
But how is Canada to choose where and how to make a contribution? The
preceding list can accommodate a huge array of policy initiatives and would
not necessarily encourage Canadian specialization. Moreover, how can Canadian policy-makers guard against the more negative aspects of technical assistance—namely, the tendency among donors to advance opportunities for
their own consultants, private-sector and civil-society actors, and academic
experts? The cases examined in this book suggest that while expertise can
sometimes act as a guide for constructive good-governance programming—
for example, Canada's legal reform and judicial training projects in Vietnam—
CIDA needs to prioritize the cultivation of recipient country expertise and

ensure, as Nilima Gulrajani warns, that it is "not unintentionally substituting for the capacity it is supposedly seeking to foster."

Third, a healthy dose of humility is in order: good governance is an extremely challenging objective to pursue through foreign and development policy. Indeed, as Easterly shows in his assessment of foreign aid, the pushing of Western countries' preferences through development assistance has often done more ill than good (Easterly 2006). Governance is arguably even more daunting a task than previous donor agendas (such as macroeconomic reform and human development) since it is harder to measure and is closely tied to countries' cultures and histories. In Smillie's words: "It [good governance] must be earned and learned, not just by those for whom it is intended, but by those who would help them." As the authors of our case studies have discovered, the process of allocating resources to good governance promotion remains fragmented and unsystematic, outcomes are difficult to define and determine, and the myriad of intervening factors and variables make it methodologically challenging to evaluate the impact of particular interventions. These obstacles to measurement are exacerbated, as Robert Muggah's study of Haiti demonstrates, "by Canada's restless conceptual approach to governance itself." How can results be assessed if the goalposts for what constitutes good governance are constantly moving? Moreover, the chapters show that there is no one "right" pathway to success. Aid can promote better governance either through specific good-governance programming (as in the case of environmental management in Vietnam) or through the wider impact of the aid relationship on the institutions of the recipient country (as in the case of Ghana). The story of Mauritius indicates that good governance may also emerge as a result of historically favourable circumstances and economic success, and have very little direct relationship to donor initiatives.

With these caveats in mind, the conclusion to this book has a more modest aim: to outline what objectives could guide Canada's good-governance policy as it goes forward; to analyze the constraints on Canadian policy-making; to suggest how the Canadian government might act on its commitment to make better governance a priority; and to recommend ways in which Canada's foreign aid could be managed to bring about greater effectiveness.

I

## The Goals of Aid for Good Governance

The first ambiguity faced by Canadian policy-makers in this realm concerns objectives: should good governance be a goal in and of itself or a means for achieving better development outcomes? The answer depends greatly on the degree to which political values serve as the key "export" of a donor's foreign policy.

Here, Canada would do well to learn from some of the mistakes and excessive ambition of its neighbour to the south. Since the end of the Cold War, successive US administrations have clearly viewed the establishment of democratic governments elsewhere as an intrinsically valuable foreign policy goal, for three interrelated reasons. The first is the Jeffersonian ideal that all parts of the world should enjoy the superior form of government enjoyed by the United States, which has a special responsibility for ensuring that spread. In other words, freedom and democracy are goods that must be shared. The second, which builds on Kantian ideas about a democratic peace, is the belief that the construction of "good" (liberal democratic) polities is the best guarantee of international security, since democracies tend not to go to war with one another (Williams 2001). Following the terrorist attacks on New York and Washington, this link between security and good governance morphed into a third variant and acquired a new sense of urgency: states that were collapsed or "failing" in their governance functions were now seen as potential breeding grounds for international terrorism. This perception helped forge the close connection in the minds of Bush administration officials between values and interests. The United States not only had a deeply held belief in freedom and democracy, but now also had a compelling interest in preventing their abuse elsewhere. As George W. Bush put it early in 2005 in his Second Inaugural Address: "Sixty years of Western nations excusing and accommodating the lack of freedom in the Middle East did nothing to make us safe."

Our conclusion is that Canada's allocation of resources toward promoting good governance will be most effective if linked directly to the achievement of better development outcomes rather than to the replication of a particular political model in various parts of the globe. There are four main reasons for this. First, promoting good governance for its own sake quickly becomes all about democratization—with all the associated problems and disappointments (see Carothers 1999; 2003). Scholars have shown that the attempt to export a specific set of political values risks garnering the tag of neocolonialism and creating top-down and unresponsive programs. Moreover, the drive to promote good governance becomes dangerously deterministic. A donor can easily drift into thinking that because it is a liberal democratic country, it must build institutions of a particular kind and in a particular way. This brand of identity-driven development policy may have benefits for the donor in terms of greater legitimacy and domestic support, but it is likely to downplay or even overlook the priorities of the recipient country—and decades of experience have shown that such priorities are vital to ensuring aid effectiveness.

Second, "foreign aid as democracy promotion" is tricky for Canada—a country whose history and foreign policy identity are associated with a commitment to pluralism. The original guiding principle of development assistance, even if unrealized in practice, was effectiveness. Those wedded to democracy promotion would argue that accountability—i.e., ensuring that citizens have direct input into the decisions that affect them—should now "trump" as the guiding principle. Yet, as our authors have shown, effectiveness and accountability must be carefully balanced through the development process. And this means that Western donors cannot always demand accountability mechanisms that are identical to those in Western-style democracies.

Third, in the current context, the export of political values has become too closely linked with a security imperative. Ngaire Woods shows in her chapter how the discourse and practices of Western countries since 9/11 have gradually securitized initiatives designed to assist weak and failed states, particularly those which are emerging from conflict. As a result, the establishment of stable, democratic polities has increasingly been defined as not simply desirable from the point of view of people in poor and war-torn societies, but as an important aspect of regional and global security. This trend is especially visible in Haiti, where in 2004 Canada adopted what Muggah calls a "security first" approach to its international assistance. But when reconstruction and development aid are justified with reference to the particular (geostrategic) interests of those providing it, there is a significant danger that standards against which impact is measured may be lowered. For example, the nature and level of stability required in Afghanistan to keep it from becoming a breeding ground for international terrorism need not (and probably is not) the same as that required for the basic well-being of local civilians. In addition, the security imperative can all too easily lead to a jettisoning of best-practice principles of development assistance, such as the value of recipient-country leadership. As Woods argues, security-driven aid packages can set in place a longer-term pattern of assistance that keeps local officials depending on donors instead of developing indigenous capacity.

Above all, a good-governance policy that is motivated by a concern with concrete development outcomes will force donors such as Canada to confront (instead of ducking) the complex relationship between governance, economic growth, and the just distribution of economic and social goods. The cases examined here suggest that the relationship between good governance and economic development runs both ways and that the "governance first" approach may not always be appropriate. To put it another way, a country such Canada can't skip straight to institutional transformation without first appreciating a particular country's prevailing incentive structures and how its existing (even

if informal) rules and institutions function. In so doing, it will be more likely
to avoid the temptation to reach for the latest fashion or fad in governance
promotion, and to develop instead a more nuanced understanding of the
processes of change occurring in the developing countries it seeks to partner
with. Such an approach also calls for greater coherence between bilateral aid
programs and non-aid policy, such as debt relief and market access, and a
breaking down of barriers between the various government departments
involved in development policy.

### "First, Do No Harm": The General Impacts of Aid on Governance

With these broad parameters for good governance policy established, the next
question that emerges is one of scope. When donors such as Canada talk of the
need to support good governance, what should they be aiming to achieve?
Our research suggests that the first operating principle guiding Canadian aid
for good governance should be a negative one: do no harm. Canada's international aid program, and its foreign policy more generally, need to be conceived
and implemented in a way that supports rather than undermines good governance. The point may seem obvious, but is all too often overlooked in discussions about development assistance.

All aid can have unintended consequences for a recipient country's economic and political institutions—not to mention its more informal mechanisms
of policy-making and implementation. This is particularly true in the area of
governance, where project-based aid and technical assistance programs can
unwittingly usurp the role and power of local actors, create new and burdensome bureaucratic hurdles for those actors to jump over, or draw those with
talent and experience away from government when they are most needed.
Here, the warnings of Ashraf Ghani, Minister of Finance in the first post-Taliban government in Afghanistan, are worth reiterating. When donors' activities compromise the sovereignty of countries that receive ODA, by interfering
with their control over the public budget and with their attempts to provide
economic and social rights to citizens, they risk undermining governance in
the target country in the longer term. The same pattern can be seen in Haiti,
another so-called failed state, where the presence of too many donors with
competing interests consumed the scarce energy and time of key recipient-
country actors and diverted them from the more important task of laying the
foundations for genuine self-government.

Such potential for collateral damage reinforces the earlier call for humility
in good-governance programming. But it also suggests that donors such as
Canada must make ongoing efforts to understand local challenges, priorities,
and incentives. This clearly has implications for how an agency such as CIDA

deploys and manages its human resources—a subject I return to at the end of this chapter. If one of the keys to effectiveness is an appreciation for how institutions and structures work *in practice* (as opposed to how they are conceived in theory or discussed in the manuals of multilateral institutions), then Canada should be striving to build a stronger presence in the field, where staff can accumulate the necessary local knowledge and are granted the authority to make timely adjustments based on local conditions.

## Political versus Administrative Goals

When we move beyond the "do no harm" principle to concrete choices about *how* to bring about better governance, the challenges facing Canada as it seeks to develop a coherent aid strategy seen to be formidable. Sue Unsworth's chapter points out that the good-governance agenda as currently construed by donors is so broad that it has become unwieldy. This is particularly true in the case of Canada, where five pillars were identified in the IPS as priorities for programming in this area: democratization (including electoral and legislative systems, citizen engagement, and civil society mobilization); human rights; rule of law (involving both legal and judicial reform); public-sector institution and capacity building; and conflict prevention, peacebuilding, and security sector reform.[3]

Our contributors suggest that a broad distinction can be made between political objectives on the one hand, and administrative or technical goals on the other. The former are aimed at deepening democratic processes, either by reforming core political institutions such as Parliament and the judiciary or by strengthening the relationship between the state and civil society; the latter are concerned mainly with the machinery of government and focus on the setting and implementing of policy priorities (e.g., through improved management of public expenditures). In the cases of Vietnam and Ghana, CIDA has been pursuing primarily administrative goals, driven by a belief that good *economic* governance is the key to success. In Haiti, Canada adopted a similar approach during the latter half of the 1990s—with heavy investments in training civil servants in the justice, finance, and social welfare ministries—but rapidly switched to a more overtly political strategy aimed at challenging the Haitian government and strengthening civil society.

However, to achieve greater aid effectiveness, two points should be recognized. First, neither set of objectives is uncontroversial. In certain contexts, administrative reform may be just as sensitive and contestable as the reform of political institutions. This is evident in situations such as Bosnia and Sri Lanka, where there are rival ethnic groups with a historical experience of either dominance or exclusion with respect to the public service. Similarly, as

Gulrajani shows in her analysis of Vietnam, CIDA initiatives aimed at strengthening the capacity of the central administration carry with them the potential to overlook non-state actors who are also important components of the country's governance architecture. This is a deeply *political* decision. As she writes, the "privileging of the state as CIDA's primary interlocutor and the desire to avoid sensitive discussions on political reform have meant that the attention paid to societal forces is usually a secondary concern in CIDA programs."

Second, political and administrative goals are often interdependent. While the historical record of capitalist transition seems to suggest that strong, undemocratic states are best able to manage the challenges of industrialization and globalization, donors need to question the assumption that effectiveness and accountability are mutually exclusive. In the longer term, the capable state is also the state that is embedded in the broader society that underpins it. In Arthur and Black's words: "Better governance in the 'machinery of government' sense is likely to depend on more robust democratic accountability, even if the results of this deepening of democracy are indirect and less neatly consonant with donor preferences." Their case study illustrates that one of the assumptions guiding CIDA's public-service and public-finance reforms in Ghana—that fiscal decentralization is the best way for local bodies to assume the management of development—needs more careful scrutiny. Is local ownership really being enhanced through this kind of devolution, or are deeply entrenched tendencies toward clientelism simply being reinforced? In most cases, technical reforms require a political impetus if they are to have any chance of success, and therefore they must be treated by donors as part of a wider political process.

There are also limitations to a "politics only" approach, particularly if it is focused on strengthening civil society. In the case of Bangladesh, a significant portion of Canadian aid has been directed at building the capacity of a particular set of NGOs, which are now widely viewed as constructive development actors in their own right. While this strategy has helped create an enabling environment for "pro-poor" growth in Bangladesh, it has been (necessarily) selective in its choices of NGO partners; as a result, it is less clear whether it has genuinely enhanced popular participation in development policy-making. Quadir's analysis also raises broader questions as to whether the focus on civil society has actually improved economic prospects or governance in the country. Half the population of Bangladesh still lives below the poverty line, and child and maternal mortality rates, while improving, are still among the worst outside of sub-Saharan Africa. There is a consensus among scholars and donors that Bangladesh's ability to meet the Millennium Development Goals requires a stronger public service, more robust efforts to combat corruption, and improvements to law and order throughout the country. If it is to be a constructive partner in building this foundation, Canada—alongside other donors such as DFID and USAID—should pursue initiatives that improve both administrative capacity and accountability vis-à-vis the Bangladeshi population.

If this lesson holds true in a context of relative stability, it is even more salient in the case of fragile states. In Haiti, as CIDA quickly discovered, there is nothing intrinsically benign about civil society. The agency's attempts to strengthen voluntary associations, cooperatives, trade unions, and NGOs yielded limited results, as these bodies not only proved unable to challenge public authority but also represented a heterogeneous set of interests that were difficult to reconcile. Muggah's chapter also shows how CIDA's move to empower non-governmental actors by making them the front-line delivery mechanism for social services did not necessarily improve efficiency. Instead, this decentralized approach simply created a parallel delivery system, raised the local costs of labour, and hindered the longer-term task of creating a state-wide capacity to provide social and political rights for the Haitian people.

### Aiming for "Good Enough Governance"?

These findings support Unsworth's broader conclusion that effective public institutions are created not by transposing models from the outside, through the export of technical governance expertise, but through a process of state–society bargaining. This requires both effectiveness *and* accountability, as well as an ability to institutionalize a set of *common* interests between the state and civil society. Governance cannot be installed in place or at the expense of a functioning indigenous government. The implication for donors like Canada is that more effort needs to be directed toward identifying and building on the incentives for different parties in a developing country to engage in collective action, rather than on trying to re-engineer the state and society parties themselves.

To put it another way, perhaps the goal for Canada's international assistance should be "good enough governance" (Grindle 2002). This principle of self-restraint would require the Canadian government (and CIDA in particular) to identify minimum standards of governance as a general guide to policy-making, but to show considerable flexibility in measuring progress. As Unsworth argues, this might mean accepting second-best solutions, or achievements in limited areas rather than across-the-board improvements. More specifically, progress would be assessed not just in formalistic terms (i.e., were certain institutions and processes created?), but also in terms of the quality of outcomes (i.e., were innovative and equitable policies generated?). A strategy aimed at "good enough governance" would also display sensitivity to the local political context as well as to the domestic and international constraints facing aid-receiving governments.

## II
## Assessing the Current Context
## for Canadian Development Policy

Of course, constraints operate at both ends of the aid relationship: donors and recipients. When discussing the challenges facing Canadian policy-makers in the realm of good governance promotion, resources tend to be top-of-mind for most analysts. It is undeniable that the decade of declining foreign aid disbursements (which saw Canada's ODA drop to the level of 0.22 percent of GNI) placed severe pressure on both CIDA and the broader capacity of the Canadian government to think in innovative ways about the links between international assistance and good governance.

These limitations on resources are now being partially removed. In the IPS, the Canadian government committed to doubling ODA from 2001 levels by 2010 (which would raise the international assistance budget to over C$5 billion per year), with Africa the largest recipient of that aid. But three caveats are in order. First, this increase looks substantial only when compared against the low baseline of 2001. The international assistance budget for 2005–6 was projected at C$2.46 billion, roughly equivalent to what was spent in 2004–5.[4] Compared to other industrialized democracies in the OECD, Canada's ODA as a percentage of GNI—0.34 percent in 2005 (OECD DAC 2006a)—is very much in the middle range. This comes at a time when Canada's federal government continues to enjoy record surpluses.

Second, more money alone will not guarantee impact. As Bernard Wood points out in his chapter, unless the Canadian government can reorient its development policy in a more strategic fashion—and focus its bilateral programs on a core set of countries—the resources allocated will still fall short of the critical mass required for measurable impact (a bilateral program in the range of $50 to 200 million, depending on the size of country and level of need). Moreover, as I suggest later, spending increases will need to be accompanied by a more expansive staff presence on the ground and by a greater level of authority for those staff, if relationships with strategically important "countries of concentration" are to have any hope of bearing fruit.

Third, while accountability has been an important operating principle for government agencies for some time, the new Conservative government in Ottawa elevated it to one its five guiding priorities in the 2006 federal budget. Accountability therefore forms a major part of the context for all policy-making. In the 2006 Speech from the Throne, Canada's government committed itself to a more effective use of Canadian aid dollars and to ensuring greater accountability in the distribution and results of Canada's international assistance. This commitment reflects a growing concern in some circles that recent trends in development policy, such as attention to recipient country needs and the channelling of assistance through multilateral institutions, have jeopardized the government's responsibilities to Canadian taxpayers. In the words of one commentator and former adviser to Prime Minister Stephen Harper, "when it comes to aid policy, the Canadian taxpayer has become a kind of cash cow funding overarching goals and objectives that are set outside of the government and the country" (Rempel 2006, 99). A similar sentiment is expressed by Gilmore and Mosazai in their chapter, where they argue (controversially) that the effectiveness of aid must ultimately be measured by how it supports a domestic (i.e., donor) agenda.

This view is a salient reminder of the tensions that exist in Ottawa between the objectives of CIDA on the one hand, and the preoccupations of other parts of the government with short-term fiscal management, national security, specific foreign policy goals, and commercial considerations on the other. Attempts to reconcile these, especially in the context of fragile states such as Haiti and Afghanistan (where both development and security imperatives are at work), frequently come up against entrenched bureaucratic "silos" and a lack of incentive for departments to collaborate constructively. In the case of Afghanistan, Canada's "3D" approach, encouraged from the centre by the Clerk of the Privy Council, went some way toward redressing the problem of coordination. For Gilmore and Mosazai, however, the best way to improve the effectiveness of Canada's engagement in Afghanistan would have been for key decision makers in Ottawa to identify specific *Canadian* interests in the region. Determining these, they argue, would have allowed officials to craft a more unified interdepartmental strategy that in turn would have facilitated better coordination of the defence, diplomatic, and development initiatives on the ground—including projects related to governance.

Beyond resources, two other contextual considerations work to shape what it is possible for Canada to achieve in the realm of good governance.

## The Politics of Democracy Promotion

This book has employed a definition of good governance that includes not only regime attributes (i.e., a democratic political system) but also broader capacities such as a functioning bureaucracy, the enforcement of the rule of law, control over the public budget, and the creation and regulation of a market. Nevertheless, any Canadian policy aimed at creating better governance in developing countries must contend with the highly politicized nature of democracy promotion in today's international climate. "Good governance" and "democratic governance" remain closely linked in the eyes of many countries on the receiving end of foreign aid generally and of post-conflict reconstruction assistance in particular.

The US-led war in Iraq, justified in part by a desire to create a beachhead for democracy in the Middle East, has been subject to intense criticism not only for the way in which the Occupation Authority managed postwar reconstruction but also for the particular view it took of what a democratic Iraq should look like. In the process, the international reputation of two powerful democracy promoters—the United States and the United Kingdom—has suffered a severe blow, and this has raised questions in the minds of many about both the "real" motives behind good-governance policy and the capacity of Western countries to craft and implement it. This skepticism will only increase as the Bush administration, chastened by its mid-term electoral defeat in 2006, scales down its definition of success in Iraq and focuses more on the creation of a *stable* government than on a democratic government.

In such an environment, Canadian policy-makers need to be wary of the latest fads in promoting democracy. Here, Smillie's cautions about Canada Corps are worth heeding.[5] In addition, those in CIDA and elsewhere in government should develop and articulate a clearer picture of the link between the different components of political reform they are seeking to advance: popular sovereignty, respect for human rights, and the rule of law. At the moment, as Smillie notes, a "shopping-list approach" to democracy dominates policy-making in Ottawa; a series of building blocks are listed, but there is no understanding of the dynamic relationships among the items in the basket. In fact, as I have argued elsewhere, democracy, the rule of law, and human rights do not all fit together neatly and may even conflict (Welsh 2004, 194–98). Third, policy-makers need to cultivate a much richer understanding of the forms of democracy assistance that have proven to be the most effective, and the differences in approach even among Western countries.[6] Finally, as suggested at the beginning of this chapter, Canada should keep the ultimate goal of better development outcomes firmly in its sight as the guide for policy-making, and avoid the more extreme forms of conditionality that engender so much suspicion among recipient countries.

In navigating the highly politicized waters of good governance, choosing one's language is critical to success. As Unsworth notes, donors have often missed opportunities for engaging powerful constituencies within developing countries simply on account of the way they have framed their agenda. While terms like "Millennium Development Goals" or "liberal democracy" may resonate with us, do they always inspire those in recipient countries? Other values and goals—such as national security, prosperity, fear of social unrest, or even reputation—may have much greater purchase. Richard Sandbrook's reflections on the success enjoyed by Mauritius underline a similar point about the need for a very broad approach to talking about governance. "People in poor countries," he writes, "overwhelmingly conceive of 'real' democracy as a system that tackles poverty, inequality, *and* powerlessness" (emphasis added).

## What Other Donors Are Doing

Although Canada is a G8 country, the absolute size of its economy—combined with the 1990s period of declining aid budgets—limits its overall weight in development policy internationally. Thus, even in the case of those countries which are on the list of the top recipients of Canadian aid, such as Bangladesh, Ghana, and Vietnam, Canada is at most a medium-sized donor and accounts for only a small share of those countries' overall aid income (just under 5 percent in the case of Bangladesh, and roughly 4 percent and 2.5 percent for Ghana and Vietnam respectively). In addition, while Canada was a key player in the Colombo Plan of 1951 (the first aid program for the developing world), it is no longer seen as being in the forefront of ODA strategy or programming internationally (Cohen 2003, chapter 4; Greenhill 2005, 15). Taken together, these facts suggest that the success of Canadian assistance for good governance is and should be partially dependent on the activities and priorities of other donors (whether other countries or multilateral institutions), and that the best strategy for aid effectiveness will often involve looking for opportunities to contribute to collective initiatives, rather than establishing and operating wholly Canadian-owned programs. For this reason, Canada has (rightly) given priority to the OECD DAC principles—set out in the Paris Declaration—which are designed to harmonize and align donors' bilateral aid programs. The Canadian government has also decided that multilateral institutions (which include regional development banks) offer a valuable way to deliver "audited aid" with reduced transactions costs.[7]

In an environment where accountability to taxpayers is paramount, and where Canada is battling the perception that its global role is declining, this reliance on other donors and institutions is perceived by some as a significant constraint. In short, the pressure for Canada to be "relevant" may complicate the strategy of multidonor collaboration. Renewed relevance calls for differentiation and clear visibility for Canada in its initiatives whereas successful multilateral efforts often require critical mass and a willingness to forgo the temptation to "fly the flag." Our research suggests that Canada needs to distinguish between "making a difference" (which aims at impact) and "striving for differentiation" (which aims at visibility), and concentrate its efforts toward the former. Given the number of active donors in the countries in question, and in some cases (such as Vietnam) the overabundance of ODA, it is often hard for a single external actor to make a unique contribution.

The majority of our contributors agree that, provided Canada remains engaged in efforts to reform these organizations—so that they address their deficiencies in efficiency and legitimacy—the multilateral avenue remains a crucial one for delivering good governance assistance. Rather than radically changing the balance between the bilateral and multilateral channels, the bet-ter strategy is to use both channels for their strong points in advancing over-all objectives, and to be demanding of their performance. Our authors also provide several examples of where, by working with other "like-minded donors," Canada has been able to extend its reach beyond what is possible through its own bilateral assistance program. CIDA's seat at the table of the LMDG in Viet-nam, for example, allowed it to acquire agenda-setting powers that its rela-tively small portfolio would not have warranted on its own. In the case of Afghanistan, a multilateral approach to reconstruction—driven by Afghans themselves through their National Development Framework[8]—was deemed highly successful, whereas uncoordinated donor activity threatened to dam-age the legitimacy of the nascent Afghan government. Thus, while in one sense Gilmore and Mosazai are right—had Canada been driven by a concern for relevance and visibility, it might have had an easier time accounting for its activities to the Canadian taxpayer—their perspective is arguably too narrow. The overall effectiveness of Canada's assistance program in Afghanistan would likely have been much lower had it not adopted a strategy of coordination.

### III
### Acting on Canada's Decision to
### Make Good Governance a Priority

In Section I, I argued that Canada's objectives with respect to governance should focus on creating the conditions for domestically controlled policy processes and political accountability in partner countries. This still leaves open the question of how Canada's priorities should be translated into action.

#### Identifying Specific Areas of Concentration

A consistent critique of Canada's foreign aid allocation over the past five years has highlighted its lack of focus. Whether the pattern of CIDA's disbursements is blamed on bureaucratic inertia (the more charitable reading) or on a polit-

ical imperative to appease ethnic communities at home, a number of scholars and journalists have called on the government to be more selective in its
list of recipient countries (Rempel 2005; Cohen 2003).

In 2003–4, Canada gave development assistance to 155 countries—a more
widely dispersed portfolio than that of any other donor. Approximately 54 of
those countries received less than $1 million per year, and only 18 received
more than $10 million. Whereas other members of the OECD give no less than
25 percent of ODA to their top 15 recipients, between 2000 and 2005 Canada gave
roughly 15 percent. This level of dispersion has undoubtedly made it harder for
CIDA to gain deep knowledge of the local factors that our case studies and
much of the OECD DAC literature show to be so critical to aid effectiveness,
especially in the context of governance. The proliferation of small-scale programs also places greater coordination and cost burdens on recipient countries.
Finally, and most obviously, the fragmentation of the aid programs increases
the management and costs for the Canadian government itself. This cost is
felt not just in financial terms, but also in terms of public ownership. A "story"
that involves a smaller set of countries receiving larger levels of ODA would be
more compelling for Parliament and Canadians in general than one based on
achieving a general set of global objectives, or one that tries to add up the
impact of a myriad of small projects.

In response, CIDA has rightly acknowledged the need for greater country
concentration. The recommendation in the IPS to focus on twenty-five "core
development partners" (fourteen of which are in Africa) is a welcome step. So
too is CIDA's introduction of a four-part "aid effectiveness agenda"—one aspect
of which commits the agency to making "careful choices in a complex world"
on countries where Canada can "make the most difference." However, there are
questions to be raised about how this declared strategic direction is actually
being implemented. The first thing to note is that only two-thirds of the bilateral portion of the aid budget (which is roughly 40 percent of the overall
budget for international assistance) is being directed to this set of countries.
This means that only 28 percent of the ODA budget will be governed by the
"new" concentration policy. The remaining dollars will go through multilateral channels and to a category of "other" bilateral partners—the latter of
which in recent years have been defined more by a security imperative. Indeed,
in 2003–4 the top two recipients of Canadian international assistance (by a
wide margin) were Afghanistan and Iraq.

Second, close inspection of the numbers reveals that the degree of change
from past practice is quite modest. In 2003–4 the top twenty-five recipients of
ODA were *already* receiving two-thirds of the budget for bilateral assistance. This
fact, combined with the five-year time horizon established for achieving concentration, suggests that a philosophy of incrementalism is driving the policy

(Stairs 2005). This is not to say that *no* change is occurring. The "old" list of twenty-five included China, India, Russia, Egypt, and Nigeria—countries that are powerful global and regional players and that do not fit easily with one of the key criteria for selection: absolute level of poverty.[9] The "new" list contains five more developing countries from Africa—which conforms to the government's stated goal of concentrating its international assistance more on that continent—and three from the Americas. But there are also some anomalies. For example, Afghanistan, Iraq, and Haiti have all apparently been dropped from the list of core partners, presumably because they fail to meet the criterion of a capacity to use aid effectively. But as noted above, these countries remain central to Canadian foreign and development policy and will likely receive large chunks of the CIDA budget over the next two fiscal years. They have simply been moved to another category of development assistance (Rempel 2006).

In sum, while the new policy of country concentration will help move the Canadian government up to an acceptable critical mass of resources for development partners (close to $60 million annually to each core partner, if 2004–5 dollars were divided evenly), there is still significant progress to be made toward real focus. In addition, it is clear that, as Denis Stairs has noted, "CIDA and the government have retained enormous freedom of manoeuvre in selecting their development assistance targets," meaning that domestic political considerations and bureaucratic inertia could continue to be obstacles to meaningful change (Stairs 2005, 18). Finally, CIDA will continue to face criticism over its method of choosing partners. Already, concern is being raised in some quarters about the Harper government's interest in concentrating more on Latin America and Caribbean (a function of economic and strategic concerns), allegedly at the expense of Canada's commitment to Africa. There is clearly a trade-off between operating in countries that are "good performers" with a number of "like-minded" donors working together to improve aid effectiveness, and working in countries that are neglected by other donors, where effectiveness may be less but where Canada might be able to have a more visible influence. Those who emphasize the need for differentiation and relevance will see the current approach to concentration as unsatisfactory. Clearly, CIDA is still grappling with how to operationalize the directive to concentrate. In her report to Parliament on Plans and Priorities for 2007–8, the new Minister of International Cooperation, Josée Verner, listed as one of her key objectives to "reach consensus on geographical concentration to allow long-term, predictable financial commitments" (CIDA 2007).

This raises the question as to whether another form of concentration—on function rather than country—might be a more productive path for Canadian policy. Some would argue that while a focus on fewer countries can help a donor achieve visibility, it is actually sectoral concentration that contributes most to aid effectiveness. This has been the experience of other donors, such as DFID in the United Kingdom.

Concretely, this would require Canada to focus the majority of its bilateral aid in three or four priority sectors—such as governance, health, private-sector development, and education—each with a further concentration in an area where Canadian capacity and excellence meet with real and acknowledged needs in developing countries. These subsectors or niche areas would be determined according to where Canada is equipped to make a maximum difference in response to partner countries' priorities and in coordination with others.[10] With each sector explicitly linked to one of the MDGs, the government could more systematically and accurately demonstrate Canada's contribution to meeting those goals, thereby assisting in the task of providing accountability to Canadians. Within the governance sector, some of our authors, most notably Gulrajani, see a real potential for Canada to focus on particular kinds of assistance, building on its domestic experience. For example, Canada has successfully built on two distinct legal traditions, thus putting itself in a strong position to help developing countries institute effective legal systems in multicultural societies.

However, four challenges confront Canada when it engages in sector concentration. First, governance is a slightly slippery category, and it is difficult to consider it as a "sector" like health or education. In practice, as our authors show, good governance is often an overarching objective that is crucial for advancements in other areas of public policy. Second, having identified specific areas of expertise, Canada will find it a challenge to walk away from other initiatives it has championed in the past. This will require discipline on the part of senior management within CIDA and a continued willingness to make significant changes to how financial and human resources are allocated. Third, any policy of concentration needs to be accompanied by a commitment to stable and predictable funding. One of the biggest drawbacks to good governance programming is its fungibility: it has given donors too much leeway to move from one fad to the next, and it has encouraged short-term rather than long-term time horizons. As an illustration, compare the volatile funding record of donors in Haiti with the more predictable approach to project funding in Ghana. Finally, in developing subsector expertise, CIDA must take care not to slip too heavily into "technical assistance mode." As Canada strengthens its capacity to deliver particular kinds of good governance assistance, it might be tempted to offer aid-receiving countries a specified bundle of predetermined technical and material assistance.

This latter risk is arguably the most significant, for it challenges policy-makers to problematize rather than accept the current way in which the discourse about development assistance is being framed in Canada. The emphasis on concentration and focus, while understandable given recent history, may overlook the more fundamental mind shift needed in good-governance programming. General Rick Hillier, a participant in our policy round table in October 2005, summed up the dilemma with reference to his experience in Afghanistan: "We spent far too much time saying to Afghans 'here's what we can do for you' and not nearly enough time asking 'what do you really need us to do?'" Those with extensive on-the-ground experience, such as Sue Unsworth, agree that the only effective approach to strengthening governance has to start with *listening* to what local populations say they need rather than advertising what donors have on offer. Numerous donors with different strengths to offer might easily drown out (or overwhelm the capacity of) a government expressing such needs. Moreover, the empirical record shows that much technical assistance is not effective, nor does it offer developing countries good value for money.

### Responding to Recipient Country Needs and Conditions

The chapters in this book make it clear that the goals of Canadian aid for good governance vary not only among countries but also within countries over time. While this may be an appropriate way to respond to local priorities and the locus of political/administrative change in each country, it does raise the question of how Canada can implement a coherent framework for its efforts to promote good governance. Those in the senior echelons of CIDA, who are concerned about better management, are right to raise this question. But they should also be open minded about where coherence might come from. If Canada is to get truly serious about partnering with developing countries, then striving for clarity and consistency in good governance programming may be self-defeating. Coherence will be found in the operating principles of local ownership and predictable funding, as well as in the outcomes achieved; the more specific modalities and goals of projects must be left to recipient countries themselves.

Such an approach may frequently set up a tension between policies that encourage recipient country leadership (e.g., budget support) and the desire to promote Canadian values in specific areas (e.g., gender equality). Given the discussion above about sectoral concentration, the most appropriate course for CIDA would be to develop a "menu of options" that focuses on areas of particular Canadian expertise, and then ensure that there is flexibility to focus on different goals at a country or local level. CIDA acknowledges that for such a strategy to work, it needs to become extremely adept at identifying recipient countries' priorities. Within the OECD DAC, a consensus has developed that a multilateral approach to understanding the needs of aid-receiving countries, and to distributing responsibilities among donors with different strengths, is the best way forward. But this does not mean that Canadian officials have no responsibilities or independent role in this process. While organizations like the World Bank and the IMF have developed some comparative advantage in defining the problems that donors should address, bilateral actors like Canada still have an important role to play in providing a counterweight to the policy diagnoses of these bodies and in serving as conduits for alternative views. Canada's experience in Afghanistan shows that representatives from DND, Foreign Affairs, and CIDA, working quietly to develop relationships of trust with officials in the aid-receiving country, can be useful and sympathetic "ears"— hearing what is needed and feeding that back into a coordinated multilateral process. Furthermore, the case of Haiti reveals that multilateral mechanisms are not always foolproof. The Interim Cooperative Framework established in 2004 to pool donor pledges and harmonize programming in Haiti was hastily cobbled together by the World Bank and the UN. As a result, Muggah argues, it was neither inclusive in its consultations nor truly "owned" by Haitians, and as a result its legitimacy and effectiveness were limited.

The trick for CIDA will be to determine whether it is actually succeeding in identifying and responding to recipient countries' needs. Scholars of development assistance have argued that four tests need to be met. First, have those within the recipient country articulated a demand for the aid and/or project? Second, are the recipients exercising some control over the resources that have been made available? Third, is the recipient-country government allocating some of its own resources to the project (so as to give it a stake)? Fourth, and finally, have recipients been assigned responsibility for the project, and do they participate in decisions about whether to continue or discontinue it? (See Ostrom et al. 2001; Woods 2006.)

Although recipient country leadership remains a crucial principle for aid effectiveness—in terms of both strategy setting and implementation—Canada must also ensure that it retains some levers to hold aid-receiving governments accountable. This delicate balancing act is particularly difficult when donor and recipient priorities seem to diverge. On the one hand, CIDA may have legitimate reasons to promote certain governance strategies; on the other hand, the recipient country's political processes need to be respected if governance is to be strengthened in the long term.

The chapter by Mulley and de Renzio suggests that mutual accountability mechanisms, where each side has clearly defined responsibilities and rights, constitute a promising way to resolve this tension. In Mozambique and Tanzania—two countries on the list of Canada's core development partners—recipient governments have taken the lead in setting the terms for aid and coordinating the activities of donors; in return, these governments have submitted themselves to an annual review process and promised improvements in areas such as financial management and anticorruption policy. In the case of Mozambique, Canada is one of eighteen donors to sign onto a Memorandum of Understanding with the recipient government, thereby promising, for example, to eliminate conditionality in its bilateral assistance, improve the predictability and transparency of its aid flows, and align its initiatives with national priorities. However, such mechanisms for mutual accountability require time to establish, as trust must be gradually built up between donors and local officials. As Mulley and De Renzio note, in the final analysis the accountability established can only be partially mutual: recipient countries will never be able to overcome the fundamental power imbalance of the aid relationship and will need to rely on donor agencies such as CIDA to take harmonization and local ownership seriously.

In the context of "failed states" such as Haiti, this power imbalance is even more obvious, as well as tempting for donors to exploit. In the lead-up to the disputed elections in 2000 in which Aristide was declared the winner, the Organization of American States (backed by key donors such as the United States and Canada) abandoned any pretext of recipient-country ownership and exerted considerable pressure on the president and his allies through threats, sanctions, and the withholding of development assistance. What is interesting to remember, however, is that these "sticks" did not enable donors to achieve their objectives: Aristide was re-elected, and much of the ODA dispersed during this period was effectively wasted. The Haiti example also illustrates that even when donors such as Canada are guided by the principle of recipient-country ownership, divided societies make it extremely hard to identify who, exactly, should "own" governance reforms.

## IV
### Managing Aid for Good Governance

The sections above implicitly argue that improvements in governance require donors to develop long-term relationships with recipients. This, in turn, requires continuity of policies and engagement in particular countries. Decentralized decision-making is also needed if governance strategies are to be tailored to a country's circumstances. But there are a number of characteristics of Canada as a donor, and CIDA as its key development agency, that make such maxims difficult to act on.

While Canada's aid portfolio is more widely dispersed than those of most of its peers, its management structure works in the opposite direction. Indeed, a peer review exercise carried out by the DAC in 2002 found Canada to be one of the most centralized bilateral donors operating in the realm of development assistance. Looking at the case of Vietnam, Gulrajani found that CIDA's country-based managers have much less authority to contract for project delivery and to disburse funds. Any project worth more than c$20 million requires approval by the federal government's Treasury Board Secretariat. Yet centralization is not accompanied by power at the centre of government. CIDA still lacks representation by a Cabinet-level minister—a situation that contrasts sharply with that in the UK, for example. Furthermore, it has had to withstand influence (and in some cases control) on the part of several federal ministries, without any reciprocal right of influence over policies and programs. Moreover, CIDA's activities are vulnerable to the vagaries of day-to-day politics; the agency has not been given a legislative mandate to pursue (and be held accountable for) a particular goal—such as poverty reduction.

The result of this inability to develop or enforce a coherent mission for development assistance is captured by Wood's image of a "Christmas tree": a foreign aid program weighted down by the interests, fads, and favoured partners of powerful actors within the Canadian political system. This outcome appears even odder when one considers the size of the budgets, responsibilities, and risks being managed, the strong levels of public support for development assistance, and the potential for Canadian leadership in this area. One of the keys to understanding Canada's foreign aid policy, Wood concludes, "is the mismatch between intentions and executive capability and incentives."

Centralized decision making has impeded CIDA's ability to respond to local priorities, to find the appropriate entry points in a country for its initiatives, and to coordinate its activities with those of other donors. It has also weakened the agency's capacity to take risks with new approaches to programming and aid delivery. This is why, as Wood argues, the time has come to revisit the question of a decentralized structure for managing aid. A shift of capacity and authority to the field—which was tried by CIDA in the late 1980s, but aborted after only four years—has recently been undertaken by the British, Dutch, and Danish governments as well as by the World Bank. Thus far the results are encouraging.

Nonetheless, a blanket move toward decentralization will not completely address the problems of responsiveness and innovation. The obstacles facing improvements to Canada's performance as a donor are not just administrative; they are part of a broader ethos of governance within Ottawa. A host of counteracting structures and incentives have prevented Canada from acting on the best practices identified by other donor countries and multilateral organizations. As an example, take Wood's discussion of how the current system for managing and delivering aid is skewed toward a Canadian-led rather than recipient-led strategy. This is due to the central role still played by the Prime Minister's Office in formulating foreign, defence, and development policy and to the power of the Treasury Board Secretariat to approve expenditures; it is hard to justify to these bodies—with their need to avoid scandal and their concern for stewardship—the risk levels that must necessarily be taken to develop a long-term development strategy with an overseas partner. Annual budget cycles, which create pressures to disburse funds within the financial year, have also been a barrier to the development of new approaches. Allowing for "end of year" flexibility of funds would encourage longer-term engagement at the country level and could promote the development of sustainable strategies in areas such as governance.

Once again, these changes must be understood against the backdrop of concerns about accountability. Long-term strategies and decentralized decision making may be needed to promote effectiveness but may also make it harder to account for the impacts of Canadian international assistance year to year. Furthermore, the Treasury Board has acquired the impression (one that is hard to counteract) that recipient-led development programs, which tend to involve more sectoral and budget support, are more risky than multiple projects micromanaged by donors. At the end of the day, foreign aid relies on political support within Canada, which means that successes need to be communicated. In general, public opinion surveys have been encouraging with regard to aggregate amounts of aid; there are high levels of support, for example, for Canada honouring the 0.7 percent of GNI standard (CRIC 2003; Dominion Institute 2005). However, Canadians have rarely been asked to trade aid against other public policy priorities (such as defence spending and health care improvements), nor have they been presented with alternative strategies for promoting development through international assistance.

These considerations do not necessarily rule out the kinds of reforms discussed above. Sustained political leadership by a high-profile minister, combined with a new International Development Act endorsed by Parliament, could provide both a clear structure of accountability and a degree of scope for long-term decision making—even in the face of changing political circumstances. More importantly, the bar of expectations has clearly been raised. Within Canada there has been much public discussion about the need for both higher volumes of foreign aid and greater impact through those aid dollars. Internationally, a consensus is consolidating around a set of standards for how donors, working in partnership with recipient countries, can contribute to better governance and bring about real progress in development outcomes. These forces could create a virtuous cycle—one that sees Canadian policy-makers absorbing the lessons from past experience, creatively managing the constraints that work against change, and overcoming the temptation to adopt quick fixes. By avoiding both undue pessimism (about the intractability of problems in the developing world) and unwarranted optimism (about the capacity of outside actors to transform poor countries through foreign aid), Canada, working in concert with others, can support the local actors and processes that ultimately hold the key to better governance in their societies.

## Notes

1   The author wishes to thank Ben Rowswell for his helpful comments on this chapter.

2   A year prior to the publication of CIDA's strategy document, a Special Joint Committee of Parliament (authored by Hockin and Simard) released a report, entitled "Independence and Internationalism," that recommended ways in which Canada could expand its aid program beyond economic development to address the broader political context in aid-receiving countries. The report also recommended the creation of the International Centre for Human Rights and Democratic Development.

3   CIDA appears to have dropped security from its current definition of governance, described on its website in 2007 as including four elements: freedom and democracy, human rights, the rule of law, and open and accountable public institutions.

4   CIDA's international assistance budget for 2004–5 was $2.5 billion. The actual allocation was $3.74 billion, accounting for the extraordinary relief contribution in response to the Indian Ocean tsunami. Projected expenditures at the time of writing were $2.46 billion for 2005–6 and $3.8 billion for 2006–7.

5   In October 2006, Canada Corps was folded into the new Office for Democratic Governance.

6   The recent report of the Standing Committee on Foreign Affairs and International Development, titled "Advancing Canada's Role in International Support for Democratic Development" argues that Canada should continually invest in learning from the experience of other donors. The committee conducted hearings in both Europe and the United States in order to better understand previous efforts at good governance promotion (Canada 2007).

7   This is why CIDA already relies on multilateral organizations to deliver more than 40 percent of its aid program.

8   Under the NDF, the Afghan Interim Administration limited the number of sectors any donor could work in, and required a minimum amount of aid before a donor could expand to new sectors.

9   The IPS sets three factors for selecting the core development partners: the level of poverty in the country, capacity of the country to use aid dollars effectively, and

a significant Canadian presence or knowledge of the country, relative to other donors (CIDA 2005c, 23).

10 Using the health sector as an example, where Canada's HIV/AIDS focus has enjoyed considerable success, CIDA could add other infectious and poverty-linked diseases (such as malaria or polio).

▲

# REFERENCES

▼

Abuza, Zachary. 2001. *Renovating Politics in Contemporary Vietnam*. Boulder: Lynne Rienner.

Adam, Heribert, and Kogila Moodley. 1992. *Democratizing Southern Africa: Challenges for Canada's Foreign Policy*. Ottawa: Canadian Institute for Peace and Security.

ADB (Asian Development Bank). 2005. "Rebounding Industry and Services Driving Bangladesh's Economy." April. Dhaka.

———. 2004. "Bangladesh's Economic Growth Outlook Upbeat in FY2004 and FY2005." April. Dhaka.

Alesina, Alberto, and David Dollar. 2000. "Who Gives Foreign Aid to Whom and Why?" *Journal of Economic Growth* 5 (March): 33–63.

Ali, S. 2004. *Bangladesh Civil Service: A Political–Administrative Perspective*, Dhaka: Dhaka University Press.

Allen, Richard. 1999. *Slaves, Freedmen, and Indentured Laborers in Colonial Mauritius*. New York: Cambridge University Press.

Allen, Richard, Salvatore Schiavo-Campo, and Thomas Columkill Garrity. 2004. *Assessing and Reforming Public Financial Management: A New Approach*. Washington, DC: World Bank.

Arthur, Peter. 2002. "Ghana: Industrial Development in the Post-Structural Adjustment Program Period." *Canadian Journal of Development Studies* 23, no. 4: 717–42.

Aryeetey, Ernest, Jane Harrigan, and Machiko Nissanke, eds. 2000. *Economic Reforms in Ghana: The Miracle and the Mirage*. Oxford: James Currey.

Asim, Attaulah, and Aidan Cox. 2004. "Aid Coordination in Afghanistan." Kabul: Ministry of Finance.

Austin, Dennis. 2001. "Good Governance?" *Round Table* 361: 497–505.

Axworthy, Lloyd. 2004. *Navigating a New World: Canada's Global Future.* Toronto: Vintage Canada.

Axworthy, Thomas, Leslie Campbell, and David Donovan. 2005. "The Democracy Canada Institute: A Blueprint." IRPP working paper, series no. 1005-02a (May).

Ayee, Joseph. 2000. "Ghana: The Continuing Search for Cures in the Fight Against Corruption," in Kempe Ronald Hope and Bornwell Chiluko, eds., *Corruption and Development: Lessons from Country Case Studies.* London: Macmillan, 183–97.

———. 1997a. "Local Government Reform and Bureaucratic Accountability." *Regional Development Dialogue* 18, no. 2 (Autumn): 86–104.

———. 1997b. "The Adjustment of Central Bodies to Decentralization: The Case of the Ghanaian Bureaucracy." *African Studies Review* 40, no. 2 (September): 37–57.

———. 1994. *An Anatomy of Public Policy Implementation.* Aldershot: Avebury.

Balogun, Paul. 2005. Working paper: "Evaluating Progress Towards Harmonisation." London: DFID.

———. 1998. "Brief on Canadian Assistance to Bangladesh." Dhaka.

Bangladesh Bureau of Statistics. 2004. *Local Estimation of Poverty and Malnutrition in Bangladesh.* Dhaka.

———. 1997. *Summary Report of the Household Expenditure Survey 1995–96.* Dhaka.

Bangladesh Development Forum. 2004. "Report on the Bangladesh Development Forum Meeting." May. Dhaka.

Bangladesh Planning Commission. 2005. *Unlocking the Potential: National Strategy for Accelerated Poverty Reduction.* Dhaka: General Economics Division.

Baranyi, Stephen. 2004. *What Next for Canadian Peacebuilding? Innovation and Effectiveness in a Time of Turbulence.* Ottawa: North-South Institute.

Bauer, Peter. 1984. *Reality and Rhetoric: Studies in the Economics of Development.* London: Weidenfeld and Nicolson.

Baviskar, S., and M. Malone. 2004. "What Democracy Means to Citizens and Why It Matters." *European Review of Latin America and Caribbean Studies* 76: 3–24.

Benn, Hilary. 2004. Speech by Secretary of State for International Development, Centre for Global Development, Washington DC, June 23.

Berry, Glyn R. 1981. "Bureaucratic Politics and Canadian Economic Policies Affecting Developing Countries: The Case of the Strategy for International Development Cooperation, 1975–1980." PhD diss., Dalhousie University, Halifax.

Bickerstaff, Karen, and Gordon Walker. 2001. "Participatory Local Governance and Transport Planning." *Environment and Planning* 33: 431–51.

BIDS (Bangladesh Institute of Development Studies). 2000. *Poverty: Bangladesh Human Development Report 2000.* Dhaka.

Birdsall, Nancy. 2004. "Seven Deadly Sins: Reflections on Donor Failings." Working paper no. 50, Center for Global Development, Washington, DC.

Black, David. 2004. "Canada and Africa: Activist Aspirations in Straitened Circumstances," in Ian Taylor and Paul Williams, eds., *Africa in International Politics*. London: Routledge.

Blair, Harry. 1986. "Ideology, Foreign Aid, and Rural Development in Bangladesh: Emergence of the Like-Minded Group." *Journal of Social Studies* 34: 1–27.

Boafo-Arthur, Kwame. 1999. "Ghana: Structural Adjustment, Democratization, and the Politics of Continuity." *African Studies Review* 42, no. 2: 41–72.

Bogdanovich, Walt, and Jenny Nordberg. 2006. "Mixed U.S. Signals Helped Tilt Haiti Toward Chaos." *New York Times*, January 29.

Booth, David, et al. 2005. "What are the Drivers of Change in Ghana?" Policy Brief no. 1. London: Ghana Centre for Democratic Development/Overseas Development Institute.

———. 2004. *Drivers of Change in Ghana: Overview Report*, London: Overseas Development Institute.

Booth, David, ed. 2003. *Fighting Poverty in Africa: Are PRSPs Making a Difference?* London: Overseas Development Institute.

Boulden, Jane. 2005. "Democracy and Peacebuilding." *Policy Matters* 6, no. 2 (April). Montreal: Institute for Research on Public Policy.

Bräutigam, Deborah. 2000. "Aid Dependence and Governance." Stockholm: Expert Gorup on Development Issues.

Brautigam, Deborah. 2004. "The People's Budget? Politics, Participation, and Pro-Poor Policies." *Development Policy Review* 22, no. 6: 653–68.

Brautigam, Dorothy, and Stephen Knack. 2004. "Foreign Aid, Institutions, and Governance in Sub-Saharan Africa." *Economic Development and Cultural Change* 52, no. 2: 255–85. http://www.sti.ch/fileadmin/user_upload/Pdfs/swap/swap 404.pdf.

Brown, Barbara. 1995. *Democracy and Human Rights: What Are We Learning?* Ottawa: Canadian International Development Agency.

Bulir, Ales, and A. Javier Hamann. 2003. Aid Volatility: An Empirical Assessment." *IMF Staff Papers* 50, no. 1: 64–89.

Bunwaree, Sheila. 2001. "The Marginal in the Miracle: Human Capital in Mauritius." *International Journal of Education and Development* 21: 257–71.

———. 1999. "Gender Inequality: The Mauritian Experience," in Christine Heward and S. Bunwaree, eds., *Gender, Education, and Development*, London: Zed Books.

Burnside, Craig, and David Dollar. 1997. "Aid, Policies, and Growth." Policy Research working papers no. 1777. Washington DC: World Bank.

Canada. 2007. "Advancing Canada's Role in International Support for Democratic Development." Report of the Standing Committee on Foreign Affairs and International Development. July. Ottawa.

———. 2005. February 23. Department of Finance. Budget. www.fin.gc.ca/ budtoce/2005/budliste.com.

Canada. 2004. Speech from the Throne, February 2. http://www.gvuas.ca/docu ments/resources/documents//speech%20from%20the%20throne%20feb 2004_e.pdf.

Canada. 2000. http://www.humansecurity.gc.ca/psh-en.asp.

Canada. 1995. *Canada in the World*. Ottawa, 1995.

Canada. 1994. Senate and House of Commons. Report of the Special Joint Committee of the Senate and the House of Commons to Examine Canada's Foreign Policy. November. Ottawa.

Canada. 1986. "Competitiveness and Security: Directions for Canada's International Relations." Ottawa.

Canada. 1975. *Strategy for International Cooperation 1975–80*. Ottawa.

Canada. 1970. *Foreign Policy for Canadians*. Ottawa.

Canada. Department of Finance. 2005. "The Budget Plan 2005." Ottawa.

Canada. Department of National Defence. 2003. Press Release: "John McCallum Speaks to the Royal Institute of International Affairs." December 3.

Capstick, Mike. 2005. "Strengthening the Weak: The Canadian Forces in Afghanistan." Canadian Institute of International Affairs, Occasional Papers 3, no. 5.

Carment, David. 2005. "Upheaval in Haiti: The Criminal Threat to Canada." Report commissioned by Criminal Intelligence Service Canada, Carleton University, Ottawa.

Carothers, Thomas. 2003. "Promoting the Rule of Law Abroad: The Problem of Knowledge." Working paper, Carnegie Endowment for International Peace, Washington, DC.

———. 2002. "The End of the Transition Paradigm." *Journal of Democracy* 13, no. 1.

———. 1999. "Aiding Democracy Abroad: The Learning Curve." Carnegie Endowment for International Peace, Washington, DC.

Carothers, Thomas, and Marina Ottaway, eds. 2000. "Funding Virtue: Civil Society Aid and Democracy Promotion." Carnegie Endowment for International Peace, Washington, DC.

Carroll, Barbara Wake, and Terrance Carroll. 2000. "Accommodating Ethnic Diversity in the Modernizing Democratic State: Theory and Practice in the Case of Mauritius." *Ethnic and Racial Studies* 23, no. 1: 120–42.

———. 1999a. "The Consolidation of Democracy in Mauritius." *Democratization* 6, no. 1: 179–97.

———. 1999b. "Civic Networks, Legitimacy, and the Policy Process." *Governance* 12, no. 1: 1–28.

Carroll, Barbara Wake, and S.K. Joypaul. 1993. "The Mauritian Senior Public Service Since Independence." *International Review of Administrative Sciences* 59, no. 3: 423–40.

Cassen, Robert and Associates. 1994. *Does Aid Work?* Oxford: Clarendon Press.

CCIC (Canadian Council for International Cooperation). 1994. "A Review and Analysis of the Report's Recommendations." Ottawa, November.

Centre for Applied Social Research. 2003. *Mauritian Social Attitudes Survey 2002: Report*. University of Mauritius.

Centre for the Future State. 2005. *Signposts to More Effective States: Responding to Governance Challenges in Developing Countries*. Brighton: IDS Sussex.

Chang, Ha-Joon. 2002. *Kicking Away the Ladder: Development Strategy in Historical Perspective*. London: Anthem Press.

Cheema, G. Shabbir. 2005. *Building Democratic Institutions: Governance Reform in Developing Countries*. West Hartford: Kumarion Press.

Christiansen, Karin. 2003. "The PRSP Initiative: Multilateral Policy Change and the Role of Research." Overseas Development Institute working paper no. 216. London.

Chua, Amy. 2003. *World on Fire: How Exporting Free Market Democracy Breeds Ethnic Hatred and Global Instability*. New York: Doubleday.

CIDA (Canadian International Development Agency). 2007. Reports on Plans and Priorities 2007–2008. www.acdi-CIDA.gc.ca/.

———. 2006. "Canadian International Development Agency." *Info Source*. June.

———. (Canadian International Development Agency). 2005a. "Statistical Report on Official Development Assistance, Fiscal Year 2003–2004." Gatineau.

———. 2005b. "Canada's International Policy Statement: Development." Gatineau.

———. 2005c. "CIDA Governance Sector Strategy." Information sheet. July. Gatineau.

———. 2004a. "Vietnam Country Development Programming Framework, 2004–2009." Gatineau.

———. 2004b. "Canadian Cooperation with Haiti: Reflecting on a Decade of 'Difficult Partnership.'" Gatineau.

———. 2004c. "New Corporate Strategic Approach." http://www.acdi-CIDA.gc.ca.

———. 2004d. "Consultations on the New Strategic Corporate Approach for Haiti." http://www.acdi-CIDA.gc.ca.

———. 2003a. "Bangladesh Country Development Programming Framework." Bangladesh Program, Asia Branch, Gatineau.

———. 2003b. "Departmental Performance Report." Gatineau.

———. 2003c. "Haiti: Country Development Programming Framework: A Strategic Paper." Gatineau.

———. 2003d (October). "Bangladesh Country Development Programming Framework: 2003–2008." Gatineau.

———. 2002. "Canada Making a Difference in the World: A Policy Statement on Strengthening Aid Effectiveness." Gatineau.

———. 1999a. "Bangladesh Programming Framework." Bangladesh Program, Asia Branch.

———. 1999b. "Projects/Program Activities in 1998/99 for Bangladesh." Gatineau.

———. 1999c. "Ghana Programming Framework: 1999/00 to 2004/05." Gatineau.

———. 1997. Internal working paper on governance strategy, Asia Branch.

———. 1996a. "Government of Canada Policy for CIDA on Human Rights, Democracy, and Good Governance." Gatineau, December.

———. 1996b. http://www.acdi-cida.gc.ca/cida_ind.nsf/0/120E9700965D51CE 85256919006BF1E5? OpenDocument.

———. 1990a. *Annual Report, 1989–90*. Gatineau.

———. 1990b. "Probing the 1990s: Topics for Discussions on CIDA's Environment in the 1990s." Gatineau.

———. 1988. *Annual Report, 1987–88*. Gatineau.

———. 1987. "Sharing Our Future: Canadian International Development Assistance." Gatineau.

————. 1986. *Annual Report, 1985–86.* Gatineau.

CIDSE (Coopération Internationale pour le Développement et la Solidarité). 2004. *PRSP: Are the World Bank and IMF Delivering on Promises?* Brussels.

Cohen, Andrew. 2003. *While Canada Slept: How We Lost Our Place in the World.* Toronto: McClelland and Stewart.

Collingwood, Vivien. 2003. "Assistance with Fewer Strings Attached." *Ethics and International Affairs* 17, no. 1: 55–68.

Communications Development, Inc. 2005. UN Millennium Development Project 2005: "Investing in Development: A Practical Plan to Achieve the Millennium Development Goals." Washington, DC.

Conway, Tim. 2004. "Politics and the PRSP Approach: Vietnam Case Study." Overseas Development Institute working paper no. 241. London.

Cooper, Andrew F. 1997. "Niche Diplomacy: A Conceptual Overview," in Andrew F. Cooper, ed., *Niche Diplomacy: Middle Powers after the Cold War.* New York: St. Martin's Press.

Cooper, Andrew F., Richard A. Higgott, and Kim Richard Nossal. 1993. *Relocating Middle Powers: Australia and Canada in a Changing World Order.* Vancouver: UBC Press.

Cornia, Giovanni, Richard Jolly, and Frances Stewart. 1987. *Adjustment with a Human Face: Protecting the Vulnerable and Promoting Growth.* Oxford: Oxford University Press.

Côté-Harper, Gisele, and John Courtney. 1987. Report: "International Cooperation for the Development of Human Rights and Democratic Institutions." Ottawa.

Cotler, Irwin. 2005. Quoted in Government of Canada, "Canada's International Policy Statement: Development." Ottawa, January 17.

Cousens, Elizabeth M. 2002. "From Missed Opportunities to Overcompensation: Implementing the Dayton Agreement on Bosnia," in Stephen John Stedman, Donald Rothchild, and Elizabeth M. Cousens, eds., *Ending Civil Wars: The Implementation of Peace Agreements.* Boulder: Lynne Rienner.

CPCC (Canadian Peacebuilding Coordinating Committee). 2004. "Multilateral Cooperation in Transition: Key Outcomes and Paths Ahead." Ottawa.

Craig, David, and Doug Porter. 2002. "Poverty Reduction Strategy Papers: A New Convergence." *World Development* 30, no. 12.

Crawford, Gordon. 2004. "Democratization in Ghana: Assessing the Impact of Political Aid (1997–2003)." POLIS working paper no. 8, School of Politics and International Studies, University of Leeds.

CRIC (Centre for Research and Information on Canada). 2003. "Canada and the United States: An Evolving Partnership." Montreal.

Culpeper, Roy, et al. 2003. "Architecture Without Blueprints: Opportunities and Challenges for the New Prime Minister in International Development Policy." *International Journal* 58, no. 4: 667–98.

Darga, Amedee. 1996. "Autonomous Economic and Social Development in Democracy: An Appreciation of the Mauritian 'Miracle.'" *African Development* 21, nos. 2–3: 79–88.

de Renzio, Paolo, et al. 2005. "Incentives for Harmonisation and Alignment in Aid Agencies." Working paper no. 248. London: Overseas Development Institute.

De Soto, Hernando. 1989. *The Other Path: The Invisible Revolution in the Third World*. New York: Harper and Row.

Department for International Development (DFID). 2006. "Eliminating World Poverty: Making Governance Work for the Poor." White Paper presented to UK Parliament.

―――. 2005. "Partnerships for Poverty Reduction: Rethinking Conditionality." http://www.dfid.gov.uk/pubs/files/conditionality.pdf.

―――. 2004a. "Departmental Report, 2004." London.

―――. 2004b. "Statistics on International Development 99/00–03/04." October. London.

―――. 2001. "Reforms in Budgeting and Expenditure Control: Evaluation. August. London.

DFAIT (Department for Foreign Affairs and International Trade). 2005. "Canada's International Policy Statement: A Role of Pride and Influence in the World." Ottawa.

Diamond, Larry. 2002. "Winning the New Cold War on Terrorism." http://www .stanford.edu/~ldiamond/papers/coldWarOnTerrorism.pdf.

Dollar, David, and Aart Kraay. 2000. "Growth Is Good for the Poor." Preliminary Paper. Development Research Group. The World Bank. Washington.

Dominion Institute and Canadian Defence and Foreign Affairs Institute. 2004. "Visions of Canadian Foreign Policy." Research conducted by Innovative Research Group, http://www.cdfai.org.

Donini, Antonio, Larry Minear, Ian Smillie, Ted van Baarda, and Anthony C. Welch. 2005. *Mapping the Security Environment: Understanding the Perceptions of Local Communities, Peace Support Operations, and Assistance Agencies*. Somerville: Feinstein International Famine Center, Tufts University.

Driscoll, Ruth, et al. 2005. "Progress Reviews and Performance Assessment in Poverty-Reduction Strategies and Budget Support: A Survey of Current Thinking and Practice." London: Overseas Development Institute.

Duffield, Mark. 2005. "Governing the Borderlands," in Rorden Wilkinson, ed., *The Global Governance Reader*. Abingdon: Routledge.

Dukhira, Chit. 2002. "History of Mauritius: Experiments in Democracy." Quatre-Bornes.

Duncan, Alex, et al. 2002. *Bangladesh: Supporting the Drivers of Pro-Poor Change*. London: DFID.

Easterly, William. 2006. *The White Man's Burden: Why the West's Efforts to Aid the Rest Have Done So Much Ill and So Little Good*. New York: Penguin.

―――. 2002. "The Cartel of Good Intentions: Bureaucracy Versus Markets in Foreign Aid." Center for Global Development working paper no. 4, Washington, DC.

Easterly, William, Ruth Levine, and David Roodman. 2003. "New Data, New Doubts: Revisiting 'Aid, Policies, and Growth." Working paper no. 26. Washington, DC: Center for Global Development.

Economic and Social Research Foundation. 2005. "Enhancing Aid Relationships in Tanzania: IMG Report 2005." Dar es Salaam.

———. 2002. "Enhancing Aid Relationships in Tanzania: Report of the Independent Monitoring Group." Dar es Salaam.

Elsenhans, Hartmut. 2001. "The Political Economy of Good Governance." *Journal of Developing Societies* 17, no. 2: 33–56.

English, E. Philip. 1984. *Canadian Development Assistance to Haiti.* Ottawa: North-South Institute.

ERD (Bangladesh Economic Relations Division), Ministry of Finance. 2006. "Flow of External Resources into Bangladesh." Dhaka.

European Commission. 2006. *Annual Report on the European Community's Development Policy and the Implementation of External Assistance in 2005.* SEC (2006)808. Brussels.

European Commission. 2004a. "Translating the Monterrey Consensus into Practice: The Contribution by the European Union." COM(2004)150. Brussels.

———. 2004b. "Building Our Common Future: Policy Challenges and Budgetary Means of the Enlarged Union, 2007–2013." Brussels.

Evans, Peter. 1995. *Embedded Autonomy: States and Industrial Transformation.* Princeton: Princeton University Press.

Fenton, Anthony. 2004. *Engineering the Overthrow of Democracy: Canada in Haiti.* Znet, http://www.zmag.org.

Ferguson, James. 1994. *The Anti-Politics Machine.* Minneapolis: University of Minnesota Press.

Ferguson, Niall. 2004. *Colossus: The Rise and Fall of the American Empire.* London: Penguin.

Fforde, Adam. 2005. "Vietnam: A Note on Instability, the Causes of Development Success, and the Need for Strategic Thinking." Melbourne: School of Devleopment Studies, University of Melbourne.

Fforde, Adam, and Doug Porter. 1995. "Public Goods, the State, Civil Society, and Development Assistance in Vietnam." Vietnam Update Conference. Hanoi.

Fowler, Robert. 2003. "Canadian Leadership and the Kananaskis G-8 Summit: Towards a Less Self-Centred Foreign Policy," in David Carment, Fen Hamson, and Norman Hillmer, eds., *Canada Among Nations 2003: Coping with the American Colossus.* Don Mills: Oxford University Press.

Freeman, Linda. 1997. *The Ambiguous Champion: Canada and South Africa in the Trudeau and Mulroney Years.* Toronto: University of Toronto Press.

Fukuyama, Francis. 2004. *State-Building: Governance and World Order in the Twenty-First Century.* Ithaca: Cornell University Press.

Gemmell, Norman, and Mark McGillivray. 1998. "Aid and Tax Instability and the Budget Constraint in Developing Countries." Research Paper 98/1. Nottingham: CREDIT, University of Nottingham.

Gerster, Richard, and Alan Harding. 2004. "Baseline Survey on Pap Performance in 2003." Report for the G-15 Programme Aid Partners and Government of Mozambique. N.p.

Ghani, Ashraf. 2005. Speech on Aghanistan given at IDRC, Ottawa, 9 March.

Ghani, Ashraf, Clare Lockhart, and Michael Carnahan. 2005. "Closing the Sovereignty Gap: An Approach to State-Building." London: Overseas Development Institute.

Gillies, David. 2005. "Democracy and Economic Development." *IRPP Policy Matters* 6, no. 2 (April) 8–26.

Gokhool, P.A. 1999. "The Trade Union Situation in Mauritius at the Eve of the Third Millennium." BSc paper, University of Mauritius.

Goldfarb, Danielle, and Stephen Tapp. 2006. "How Canada Can Improve Its Aid: Lessons from Other Agencies." Commentary no. 232. Toronto: C.D. Howe Institute.

Gottlieb, Allan. 2004. November. "Romanticism and Realism in Canada's Foreign Policy." C.D. Howe Benefactors Lecture, Toronto.

Gould, Jeremy, and Julia Ojanen. 2003. "'Merging in the Circle': The Politics of Tanzania's Poverty Reduction Strategy." *Policy Papers 2.* Helsinki: Institute of Development Studies.

Government of Afghanistan. 2002. "National Development Framework." Kabul.

Government of Mozambique. 2001. "Action Plan for the Reduction of Absolute Poverty." Maputo.

Government of Mozambique and Program Aid Partners. 2004. "Memorandum of Understanding Between Government of the Republic of Mozambique and the Program Aid Partners for the Provision of Direct Budget and Balance of Payments Support." Maputo.

Greenhill, Robert. 2005. "Making a Difference? External Views on Canada's International Impact." Toronto: Canadian Institute of International Affairs.

Grindle, Merilee. 2002. "Good Enough Governance: Poverty Reduction and Reform in Developing Countries." Cambridge, MA: Kennedy School of Government, Harvard University. http://www.grc-exchange.org/docs/HD32.pdf. Also discussion paper. Washington, DC: World Bank.

Grote, Juergen, and Bernard Gbikpi. 2002. *Participatory Governance: Political and Societal Implications.* Opladen: Leske and Budrich.

Gulhati, Ravi, and Raj Nallari. 1990. "Successful Stabilization and Recovery in Mauritius." Economic Development Institute, policy case series #5. Washington, DC: World Bank.

Haggard, Stephan, and Robert Kaufman. 1989. "Economic Adjustment in New Democracies." *Fragile Coalitions: The Politics of Economic Adjustment.* Washington: Overseas Development Council.

Haiti Democracy Project. 2003. "Mobilizing Resources for Development." http://www.haitipolicy.org.

Hammerstad, Anne. 2004. *African Commitments to Democracy in Theory and Practice: A Review of Eight NEPAD Countries.* Pretoria: African Human Security Initiative.

Hancock, Graham. 1989. *Lords of Poverty: The Power, Prestige and Corruption of the International Aid Business.* London: Macmillan London.

Hansen, Henrik, and Finn Tarp. 2000. "Aid Effectiveness Disputed." *Journal of International Development* 12: 375–98.

Harding, Alan, and Richard Gerster. 2004. "Learning Assessment of Joint Review 2004: Final Report." Report to the Program Aid Partners and Government of Mozambique. N.p.

Harmer, Adele, and Joanna Macrae. 2004. *Beyond the Continuum: The Changing Role of Aid Policy in Protracted Crises.* London: Overseas Development Institute.

Harper, Stephen. 2006a. "Address by the Prime Minister to the 61st Opening Session of the United Nations General Assembly," September 21. New York. http://www.pm.gc.ca/eng/media.asp?id=1329.

———. 2006b. Address to the Canadian Armed Forces in Afghanistan, March 13, 2006.

Harrison, Graham. 2001. "Post-Conditionality Politics and Administrative Reform: Reflections on the Cases of Uganda and Tanzania." *Development and Change* 32.

Hawrylak, Maciek, and David Malone. 2005. "Haiti, Again! A Tough Peacebuilding Task." *Policy Options* (September).

Hayter, Teresa. 1971. *Aid as Imperialism.* Harmondsworth: Penguin.

Head, Ivan, and Pierre Trudeau. 1995. *The Canadian Way: Shaping Canada's Foreign Policy, 1968–84.* Toronto: McClelland and Stewart.

Helleiner, Gerry. 2000. "Towards Balance in Aid Relationships: Donor Performance Monitoring in Low-Income Developing Countries." *Cooperation South* (2000).

———. 2001. "Local Ownership and Donor Performance Monitoring: New Aid Relationships in Tanzania." *Journal of Human Development* 3, no. 2.

Helleiner, Gerry, Ndula Lipumba, and Knud Erik Svendsen. 1995. "Report of the Group of Independent Advisers on Development Cooperation Issues between Tanzania and Its Aid Donors." Copenhagen: Royal Danish Ministry of Foreign Affairs.

Herrling, Sheila, and Sarah Rose. 2007. *Will the Millennium Challenge Account Be Caught in the Crosshairs? A Critical Year for Full Funding.* Washington, DC: Center for Global Development 2007.

Hirschman, Albert O. *Exit, Voice, and Loyalty: Responses to Decline in Firms, Organizations, and States.* Cambridge, MA: Harvard University Press, 1970.

Hobsbawm, Eric J. 2004. "Spreading Democracy." *Foreign Policy* (September–October).

Holbraad, Carsten. 1984. *Middle Powers in International Politics.* New York: St. Martin's Press.

Holmes, John W. 1976. *Canada: A Middle-Aged Power.* Ottawa: Carleton University Press.

Houbert, Jean. 1982–83. "Mauritius: Politics and Pluralism at the Periphery." *Annuaire des Pays de l'Océan Indien* 9: 225–65.

Hutchful, Eboe. 2002. *Ghana's Adjustment Experience: The Paradox of Reform.* Geneva: UN Research Institute for Social Development.

————. 1989. "From Revolution to Monetarism: The Economics and Politics of Adjustment Program in Ghana," in John Loxley and Bonnie Campbell, eds., *Structural Adjustment in Africa*. London: Macmillan. 92–131.

IDD (International Development Department) and Associates. 2006. *Evaluation of General Budget Support: Synthesis Report*. Birmingham: IDD, University of Birmingham.

IDEA (Institute for Democracy and Electoral Assistance). 2000. *Democracy Forum 2000: Regional Workshop Reports*. Stockholm: IDEA.

Institute of Development Studies (IDS). 2005. *Signposts to More Effective States: Responding to Governance Challenges in Developing Countries*. Sussex: Institute of Development Studies.

Ignatieff, Michael. 2005a. "Who Are Americans to Think That Freedom Is Theirs to Spread?" *New York Times Magazine*, June 26.

————. 2005b, Speech to Liberal Party Convention, March 3, Ottawa. http://www .liberal.ca/news_e.aspx?type=news&news=934.

————. 2004. "Peace, Order and Good Government: A Foreign Policy Agenda for Canada." Skelton Memorial Lecture. http://www.dfait-maeci.gc.ca.

International Commission on Intervention and State Sovereignty. 2001. *The Responsibility to Protect: Report of the International Commission on Intervention and State Sovereignty*. (December). http://www.iciss.ca/report2-en.asp.

International Monetary Fund and World Bank. 1999. *Poverty Reduction Strategy Papers: Operational Issues*. Washington, DC: IMF.

Islam, Roumeen, and Claudio E. Montenegro. 2002. "What Determines the Quality of Institutions?" World Bank Policy Research Working Paper No. 2764. Development Research Group. The World Bank. Washington.

Islam, Nasir, and David Morrison. 1996. "Introduction: Governance, Democracy, and Human Rights." *Canadian Journal of Development Studies* 30 (special issue): 5–18.

ISSER (Institute of Statistical, Social, and Economic Research). 2004. *The State of the Ghanaian Economy in 2003*. Legon.

Japan. Ministry of Foreign Affairs. 2001. White Paper: *Japan's Official Development Assistance*. Tokyo: Economic Cooperation Bureau, MFA.

Jiménez, Marina. 2006. "Author of Lancet Article on Haiti Investigated: Writer Critical of Canadian Peacekeepers Worked at Orphanage Founded by Aristide." *Globe and Mail*, September 7.

Johnson, Alison, Matthew Martin, and Hannah Bargawi. 2004. "The Effectiveness of Aid to Africa since the HIPC Initiative: Issues, Evidence, and Possible Areas for Action." Background Paper for the Commission for Africa. London: Development Finance International.

Kates, Jennifer (Kaiser Family Foundation), José-Antonio Izazola (UNAIDS), Eric Lief (CSIS). 2006. *Financing the response to AIDS in low- and middle-income countries: International assistance from the G8, European Commission and other donor governments*. www.data.unaids.org/pub/Presentation/2007/2007 0605_unaids_kff_ppoint_en.pdf.

Kaufmann, D., Aart Kraay, and Massimo Mastruzzi. 2005. "Governance Matters IV: Governance Indicators for 1996–2004." Washington, DC: World Bank.

Kaufmann, Daniel, Aart Kraay, and Pablo Zoido-Lobaton. 1999. "Governance Matters." Policy research working paper series no. 2196. Washington, DC: World Bank.

Knack, Stephen, and Philip Keefer. 1995. "Institutions and Economic Performance." Economics and Politics 7: 207–27.

Khan, Mushtaq. 2002. "Corruption and Governance in Early Capitalism: World Bank Strategies and Their Limitations," in Jonathan Pincus and Jeffrey Winters, eds., Reinventing the World Bank. Ithaca: Cornell University Press.

Killick, Tony. 1998. Aid and the Political Economy of Policy Change. London: Routledge.

———. 1989. A Reaction Too Far: Economic Theory and the Role of the State in Developing Countries. London: Overseas Development Institute.

Killick, Tony, Carlos Castel-Branco, and Richard Gerster. 2005. "Perfect Partners? The Performance of Program Aid Partners in Mozambique." Report to the Programme Aid Partners and Government of Mozambique.

Kithinji, Kiragu, Rwekaza Mukandala, and Denyse Morin. 2004. "Reforming Pay Policy: Techniques, Sequencing and Politics," in Brian Levy and Sahr Kpundeh, eds., Building State Capacity in Africa: New Approaches, Emerging Lessons. Washington, DC: World Bank Institute.

Kolbe, A., and R. Hudson. 2006. "Human Rights Abuse and Other Criminal Violations in Port-au-Prince, Haiti: A Random Survey of Households." The Lancet 6736 (2006).

Lambertson, Ross. 2005. Repression and Resistance: Canadian Human Rights Activists, 1930–1960. Toronto: University of Toronto Press.

Lambi Fund of Haiti. 2004. Enquete sur l'intégrité: l'état des lieu de la corruption en Haiti. Port-au-Prince: Centre pour l'éthique et l'intégrité publique et privée.

Lange, Matthew. 2003. "Embedding the Colonial State: A Comparative-Historical Analysis of State-Building and Broad-Based Development in Mauritius." Social Science History 27, no. 3: 397–423.

Large, Tim. "Cash-Strapped Japan Rethinks Foreign Aid." Reuters AlertNet, October 20, 2003. http://alertnet.org/thefacts/reliefsources/106665138683.htm.

Lavergne, Réal, and E. Philip English. 1987. Canadian Development Assistance to Senegal. Ottawa: North-South Institute.

Laville, Rosabelle. 2000. "In the Politics of the Rainbow: Creoles and Civil Society in Mauritius." Journal of Comtemporary African Studies 18, no. 2: 277–94.

Lawson, Andrew, and David Booth. 2004. Evaluation Framework for General Budget Support. London: ODI.

Lawson, Andrew, David Booth, Meleki Msuya, Samual Wangwe, and Tim Williamson. 2005. Does General Budget Support Work? Evidence from Tanzania. London: ODI; and Dar es Salaam: Daima Associates.

Leftwich, Adrian. 1993. "Governance, Democracy, and Development in the Third World." Third World Quarterly 14, no. 3: 605–24.

Levy, Brian. 2004. "Governance and Economic Development in Africa: Meeting the Challenge of Capacity Building," in Brian Levy and Sahr Kpundeh, eds., *Building State Capacity in Africa: New Approaches, Emerging Lessons*. Washington, DC: World Bank Institute.

LFHH. 2004. *Enquete sur l'intégrité: l'état des lieu de la corruption en Haiti*. Port-au-Prince: Centre pour l'Ethique et L'Intégrité Publique et Privée.

Liang, Lung Chong, J. 1998. "Globalisation and Female Workers in the Textiles and Clothing Industry." BSc paper, University of Mauritius.

Lipset, Seymour Martin. 1981. *Political Man*, rev. ed. Baltimore: Johns Hopkins University Press.

Lledo, Victor, Aaron Schneider, and Mick Moore. 2004. "Governance, Taxes and Tax Reform in Latin America." Institute of Development Studies working paper no. 221. Brighton.

Lockhart, Claire. 2004. "From Aid Effectiveness to Development Effectiveness: Strategy and Policy Coherence in Fragile States." Background paper for the Senior Level Forum on Development Effectiveness in Fragile States. London: Overseas Development Institute.

Lumsdaine, David. *Moral Vision in International Politics*. 1993. Princeton: Princeton University Press.

Lyon, P.V. 1976. "Introduction," in P.V. Lyon and T.Y. Ismael, eds., *Canada and the Third World*. Toronto: Macmillan of Canada.

Lyon, P.V., R.B. Byers. and D. Leyton-Brown. 1979. "How 'Official' Ottawa Views the Third World." *International Perspectives*, January–February.

Mackie, James, and Celine Rossini, European Centre for Development Policy Management. 2004. "A Changing EU: What Are the Development Implications?" *In Brief* 8 (April).

Mahbub ul Haq Human Development Centre. 1999. *Human Development in South Asia*. Dhaka: Dhaka University Press.

Martin, Matthew, and Alison Johnson. 2005. "Empowering Developing Countries to Lead the Aid Partnership." London: Development Finance International.

Martin, Paul. 2004a. Transcript of speech at the Sun Valley 2004 Conference. July 7. http://www.pco-bcp.gc.ca/default.asp?Language=E&Page=archivemartin&Sub=speechesdiscours&Year=2004.

———. 2004b. April 29. Speech by the Prime Minister, April, Washington, DC. http://pm.gc.ca/eng/news.asp?id=192.

Mathur, Raj. 1997. "Parliamentary Representation of Minority Communities." *Africa Today* 44, no. 1: 61–82.

Mauritius, Central Statistical Office (cso). 2002. *Economic and Social Indicators: Household Budget Survey*. No. 394, November 5. Port-Louis: Government Printer.

———. 2003. *Economic and Social Indicators: Labour Force, Employment and Unemployment*. No. 402, March 10. Port-Louis: Government Printer.

Mauritius, Ministry of Commerce and Cooperatives. 2003. *Cooperatives: Road to Prosperity*. Port-Louis: Government Printer.

Mauritius, Ministry of the Environment. 2002. *Meeting the Challenges of Sustainable Development*. Port-Louis: Government Printer.

Mauritius, Ministry of Health and Quality of Life. 2001. *Health Statistics 2001*. Port-Louis: Government Printer.

McGregor, Sarah. 2006. "Sticking With Haiti." *Embassy: Canada's Foreign Policy Newspaper.* http://www.embassymag.ca.

McKechnie, Alastair. 2003. Working paper: "Humanitarian Assistance, Reconstruction, and Development in Afghanistan: A Practitioner's View." Syracuse: Center for Policy Research.

McRae, Rob, and Don Hubert, eds. 2001. *Human Security and the New Diplomacy*. Montreal and Kingston: McGill-Queen's University Press.

Meisenhelder, Thomas. 1999. "The Developmental State in Mauritius." *Journal of Modern African Studies* 35, no. 2: 279–97.

Migliorisi, Stefano. 2003. *The Consequences of Enlargement for Development Policy: Development Strategies*. Brussels: EC.

Miles, William F.S. 1999. "The Mauritius Enigma." *Journal of Democracy* 10, no. 2: 91–104.

Ministry of Defence. 2006. *Ministry of Defence Annual Report and Accounts 2005–6*. www.mod.uk/DefenceInternet/AboutDefence/Corporate Publications/AnnualReports/MODAnnualReport0506/.

Minna, Maria. 2000. Speech to Session of the Organization of American States on Human Security, Windsor, Ontario, June 5. http://www.acdi-CIDA.gc.ca.

Mistry, Percy. 1999. "Mauritius: Quo Vadis?" *African Affairs* 98, no. 393: 551–69.

Mitzberg, Henry. 1994. *The Rise and Fall of Strategic Planning*. New York: The Free Press.

Montas, R. 2003. "Haiti: Les Causes de augmentation de la pauvreté entre 1981 et 2003." Mimeo.

Moore, Mick. 2004. "Taxation and the Political Agenda, North and South." Forum for Development Studies, 31, no. 4: 7–31. Centre for the Future State, Univrsity of Sussex. Brighton.

———. 1998. "Death Without Taxes: Democracy, State Capacity, and Aid Dependence in the Fourth World," in Mark Robinson and Gordon White, eds., *The Democratic Developmental State: Politics and Institutional Design*, Oxford: Oxford University Press. xiii, 353.

———. 1993. "Declining to Learn from the East? The World Bank on 'Governance and development.'" *IDS Bulletin* 24, no. 1: 39–50.

Moore, Mick, and Anuradha Joshi. 2004. "Institutionalised Co-production: Unorthodox Public Service Delivery in Challenging Environments." *Journal of Development Studies* 40, no. 4.

Moore, M., and Sue Unsworth. 2006. "Britain's New White Paper: Making Governance Work for the Poor." *Development Policy Review* 24, no. 6 (November): 707–15.

Morrison, David R. 1998. *Aid and Ebb Tide: A History of CIDA and Canadian Development Assistance*. Waterloo: Wilfrid Laurier University Press.

Mosley, Paul, and Marion Eeckhout. 2000. "From Project Aid to Programme Assistance," in Finn Tarp, ed., *Foreign Aid and Development.* Microsoft Reader ebook. http://www.ebookmall.com/ebooks/foreign-aid-and-development-tarp-ebooks.htm.

Mosley, Paul, Jane Harrigan, and John Toye. 1995. *Aid and Power: The World Bank and Policy-Based Lending,* 2nd ed. London: Routledge.

Mosley, Paul, John Hudson, and Arjan Verschoor. 2004. "Aid, Poverty Reduction, and the 'New Conditionality.'" *Economic Journal* 114 (June).

Muggah, Robert. 2005a. "More Arms No Solution for Haiti." *Globe and Mail,* April 7.

———. 2005b. "Securing Haiti's Transition: Assessing the Prospects for Disarmament, Demobilization, and Reintegration." Occasional paper no. 15. Geneva: Small Arms Survey/Swiss Department of Foreign Affairs.

Muggah, Robert, and Keith Krause. 2006. "A True Measure of Success: The Discourse and Practice of Human Security in Haiti." *White Journal of International Diplomacy and International Relations* (Winter–Spring).

Mulroney, Brian. 1991. "Notes for a Speech by Prime Minister Brian Mulroney." October 16. Harare: Commonwealth Heads of Government Meeting.

New Partnership for Africa's Development (NEPAD). n.d. "What Is NEPAD?" http://www.nepad.org.

Noriega, Richard. 2004. Remarks before the Subcommittee on Western Hemispheric Affairs: "The End of a Chapter in Haiti and a New Beginning," March 3. Washington, DC: US Department of State.

North-South Institute. 2005. *Canadian Development Report 2005.* Ottawa.

———. 2004. *Canadian Development Report 2004: Investing in Poor Countries.* Ottawa.

———. 1985. "Rural Poverty in Bangladesh: A Report to the Like-Minded Group." Ottawa.

———. 1980. "In the Canadian Interest? Third World Development in the 1980s." Ottawa.

Nossal, Kim Richard. 1988. "Mixed Motives Revisited: Canada's Interest in Development Assistance." *Canadian Journal of Political Science* 21, no. 1.

ODI (Overseas Development Institute). 2004. "Senior Level Forum on Development Effectiveness in Fragile States: Harmonisation and Alignment in Fragile States." London.

OECD (Organization for Economic Co-operation and Development). 2005a. "Statement to the Follow-up of the UN Millennium Declaration and Monterrey Consensus." Paris.

———. 2005b. Paris Declaration on Aid Effectiveness. Paris.

———. 2005c. *Aid Harmonization and Alignment: Summary of Initiatives.* Paris.

———. 2005d. *Development Cooperation Report 2004.* Paris.

———. 2005e. "Harmonisation, Alignment, Results: Report on Progress, Challenges, and Opportunities." Background Paper for the High-Level Forum on Aid Effectiveness. February 28–March 2. Paris.

———. 2004. *Survey on Harmonisation and Alignment: Preliminary Edition.* Paris.

————. 2004. *Harmonizing Donor Practices for Effective Delivery.* Paris: OECD.

————. 2002. "Development Cooperation Review: Canada." Paris.

OECD DAC (Organization for Economic Co-operation and Development, Development Assistance Committee). 2006a. *2006 Development Co-operation Report* 8, no. 1. Paris.

————. 2006b. "Policy Paper on Anti-Corruption: Setting an Agenda for Collective Action." DCD/DAC/GOVNET(2006)3/REV.

————. 2006c. *Development Co-operation Report 2005.* Paris.

OECD DAC (Organization for Economic Co-operation and Development, Development Assistance Committee). 2005. *Security System Reform and Governance.* Paris. http://www.oecd.org/dataoecd/8/39/31785288.pdf.

————. 2004a. Statement adopted by members of OECD, DAC, at high-level meeting, April 16.

————. 2004b. *Development Co-operation Report 2003.* Paris.

————. 2003a. *Development Cooperation Report 2003.* Paris.

————. 2003b. *Development Co-operation Review: Canada.* Paris.

————. 2002a. "Report of the Donor Public Sector Working Group." April 22–23, DCD/DAC/GOVNET. Paris.

————. 2002b. "Canada DAC Peer Review: Main Findings and Recommendations." Paris.

————. 2002c. "Working for Development in Difficult Partnerships." Paris.

————. 1998. "The Limits and Scope for the Use of Development Assistance Incentives and Disincentives for Influencing Conflict Situations. Case Study: Rwanda." Paris.

————. 1996. "Shaping the Twenty-First Century: The Contribution of Development Cooperation." Paris.

————. 1993. "DAC Orientations on Participatory Development and Good Governance." Paris.

————. 1989. "Development Cooperation in the 1990s." Paris.

OED. 2005. *Country Assistance Evaluation Retrospective: An OED Self-Evaluation.* Washington, DC: World Bank.

————. 2004. "Mainstreaming Anti-Corruption Activities in World Bank Assistance: A Review of Progress Since 1997." Report No. 29620. Washington, DC: World Bank.

Oodiah, Malenn. 1991. *Mouvement Militant Mauricien: 20 Ans d'Histoire.* Port-Louis: Electronic Graphic Systems.

Orlandini, Barbara. 2003. "Consuming 'Good Governance' in Thailand." *European Journal of Development Research* 15, no. 2: 16–43.

Ostrom, Elinor, Clark Gibson, Sujai Shivakumar, and Krister Andersson. 2002. "Aid Incentives and Sustainability: An Institutional Analysis of Development Cooperation." *Sida Studies in Evaluation* 2, no. 1: 1.

Ottaway, Marina, and Thomas Carothers, eds. 2000. *Funding Virtue: Civil Society Aid and Democracy Promotion.* Washington, DC: Carnegie Endowment for International Peace.

Pearson, Lester B. (chairman). 1969. *Partners in Development: Report of the Commission on International Development.* New York: Praeger.

Peretz, David, and Samuel Wangwe. 2004. "Monitoring Donor and IFI Support Behind Country-Owned Poverty Reduction Strategies in the United Republic of Tanzania." Report for the Commonwealth Secretariat, London.

Picciotto, Robert. 2004. Background paper: "Policy Coherence and Development Evaluation." Paris: OECD.

PNUD. 2005. *DSRP—Gouvernance.* Port-au-Prince: UNDP.

Pratt, Cranford, ed. 1990. *Middle Power Internationalism: The North South Dimension.* Montreal and Kingston: McGill-Queen's University Press.

Priest, Dana. 2003. The *Mission: Waging War and Keeping the Peace with America's Military.* New York: W.W. Norton.

Pritchett, Lant, and Michael Woolcock. 2002. "Solutions When the Solution Is the Problem: Arraying the Disarray in Development." Center for Global Development working paper, Washington, DC.

Przeworski, Adam. 2004. "Institutions Matter?" *Government and Opposition* (October): 527–40.

Putnam, Robert D. 1993. *Making Democracy Work: Civic Traditions in Modern Italy.* Princeton: Princeton University Press.

Quadir, Fahimul. 2004. "Going Beyond the Mainstream Discourse: Democratic Consolidation and Market Reform in Bangladesh," in Fahimul Quadir and Jayant Lele, eds., *Democracy and Civil Society in Asia: Democratic Transitions and Social Movements,* vol. 2. London: Palgrave, 86  106.

Radelet, Steven. 2005. "From Pushing Reforms to Pulling Reforms: The Role of Challenge Programs in Foreign Aid Policy." Centre for Global Development working paper no. 53, Washington, DC.

Radelet, Steven, and S. Herrling. 2003. "The Millennium Challenge Account: Soft Power or Collateral Damage?" *Center for Global Development Brief* 2, no. 2: 1–7.

Reddi, Sadasivan J. 1997. "The Making of a British Colonial State in Nineteenth-Century Mauritius." Paper presented to the "British Legacy" Conference, Mahatma Gandhi Institute, Réduit, May 6–9.

———. 1989. "The Development of Political Consciousness Among Indians, 1870–1930." *Journal of Mauritian Studies* 3, no. 1: 1–15.

Reis, Elisa, and Mick Moore, eds. 2005. *Elite Perceptions of Poverty and Inequality.* London: Zed Books.

Rempel, Roy. 2006. *Dreamland: How Canada's Pretend Foreign Policy Has Undermined Sovereignty.* Montreal and Kingston: McGill-Queen's University Press.

Robert Cassen and Associates. 1994. *Does Aid Work?* 2nd ed. Oxford: Clarendon Press.

Rodrik, Dani, ed. 2003. *In Search of Prosperity: Analytic Narratives on Economic Growth.* Princeton: Princeton University Press.

Rogerson, Andrew. 2005a. "What If Aid Harmonization and Alignment Occurred Exactly as Intended? A Reality Check on the Paris Forum on Aid Effectiveness." Overseas Development Institute draft paper, January 28.

———. 2005b. "Aid Harmonisation and Alignment: Bridging the Gaps Between Reality and the Paris Reform Agenda." *Development Policy Review* 23, no. 5.

Rogerson, Andrew, and Paolo de Renzio. 2005. "The Seven Habits of Effective Aid: Best Practices, Challenges, and Open Questions." ODI *Opinions*. London.

Ronsholt, Frans. 2002. "Tanzania: a Country Case Study." Prepared for the OEDC DAC Task Force on Donor Practices. Paris.

Rubin, Barnett, Abby Stoddard, Humayun Hamidzada, and Adib Farhadi. 2003. "Building a New Afghanistan: The Value of Success, the Cost of Failure." Center on International Cooperation, New York University, in cooperation with CARE.

Sallot, Jeff. 1995, "Choosing Quiet Diplomacy over Megaphone Diplomacy," *Globe and Mail*, July 1.

Sandbrook, Richard. 2005. "Origins of the Democratic Developmental State." *Canadian Journal of African Studies* 39, no. 3.

———. 2000. *Closing the Circle: Democratization and Development in Africa*. London: Zed Books.

Saumier, A. 2003. "The Impact of Research on Public Policy: IDRC's Programs in Vietnam." IDRC Working Paper. Ottawa.

SCEAIT (House of Commons Standing Committee on External Affairs and International Trade). 1987. *For Whose Benefit? Report of the Standing Committee on External Affairs and International Trade on Canada's Official Development Assistance Policies and Programs*. Ottawa: Queen's Printer.

Scharfe, Sharon. 1996. *Complicity: Human Rights and Canadian Foreign Policy*. Montreal: Black Rose Books.

Schmitz, G. 1995. "Democratization and Demystification: Deconstructing 'Governance as Development Paradigm.'" In David Moore and Gerald Schmitz, eds., *Debating Development Discourse: Institutional and Popular Perspectives*. London: Macmillan. 54–90.

Schmitz, Gerald, Marcus Pistor, and Megan Furi. 2003. "Aid to Developing Countries." http://dsp-psd.pwgsc.gc.ca/index-e.html.

Seegobin, Ram, and Lindsey Collen. 1977. "Mauritius: Class Forces and Political Power." *Review of African Political Economy* 8: 109–18.

Sen, Amartya. 2000. *Development as Freedom*. New York: Anchor Books.

Stairs, Denis. 2005. "Confusing the Innocent with Numbers and Categories: The International Policy Statement and the Concentration of Development Assistance." Calgary: Canadian Defence and Foreign Affairs Institute.

Stevens, Michael, and Stephanie Teggemann. 2004. "Comparative Experience with Public Sector Reform in Ghana, Tanzania, and Zambia," in Brian Levy and Sahr Kpundeh, eds., *Building State Capacity in Africa: New Approaches, Emerging Lessons*. Washington, DC: World Bank Institute.

Stiglitz, Joseph E. 2002. *Globalization and Its Discontents*. New York: W.W. Norton.

Stokke, Olav, ed. 1989. *Western Middle Powers and Global Poverty: The Determinants of Aid Policies of Canada, Denmark, the Netherlands, Norway and Sweden*. Uppsala: Scandinavian Institute of African Studies.

Subramanian, Arvind, and Devesh Roy. 2003. "Who Can Explain the Mauritian Miracle? Meade, Romer, Sachs, or Rodrik?" In Dani Rodrik, ed., *In Search of Prosperity.* Princeton: Princeton University Press. 205–43.

Grimm, Sven, with Bettina Woll. 2004. "Political Partnership with the South." *European Development Cooperation to 2010: ODI/EDC Briefing,* May.

Tanzanian Ministry of Finance. 2005. "Draft JAS Concept Paper." Dar es Salaam.

———. 2002. "Tanzania Assistance Strategy (a Medium Term Framework for Promoting Local Ownership and Development Partnerships)," final draft, January.

Tarp, Finn, ed. 2000. *Foreign Aid and Development: Lessons Learnt and Directions for the Future.* London: Routledge.

Teelock, Vijayalakshmi. 2001. *Mauritian History: From Its Beginnings to Modern Times.* Port-Louis: Mahatma Gandhi Institute.

Tendler, Judith. 1997. *Good Government in the Tropics.* Baltimore: Johns Hopkins University Press.

Tettey, Wisdom, et al. (2003). "Ghana and the Experience of 'Development,'" in Wisdom Tettey, Korbla Pupamplu, and Bruce Berman, eds., *Critical Perspectives on Politics and Socioeconomic Development in Ghana.* Leiden: Brill. 1–18.

Thacoor-Sidaya, Indira. 1998. "Women and Development in Mauritius." *Indian Quarterly* 54, nos. 1 and 2.

Thede, Nancy. 2005. "Human Rights and Democracy: Issues for Canadian Policy in Democracy Promotion." *Policy Matters* 6, no. 3 (May).

Therien, Jean-Philippe, and Carolyn Lloyd. 2000. "Development Assistance on the Brink." *Third World Quarterly* 21, no. 1: 21–38.

Tomlinson, Brian. 2006. "Aid Flows, MDGs, and Poverty Eradication: More and Better Canadian Aid," in *Canadian Development Report 2005: Towards 2015: Meeting Our Millennium Commitments.* Ottawa: North-South Institute.

Tomlinson, Brian, and Pam Foster. 2004. "At the Table or in the Kitchen? CIDA's New Aid Strategies, Developing Country Ownership, and Donor Conditionality." CCIC/Halifax Initiative briefing paper, September. http://www.nsi-ins.ca/english/pdf/cdr2005_e_2.pdf.

UDNP (United Nations Development Programme). 2005a. *UNDP Development Cooperation Report 2005.* Hanoi.

———. 2005b. *Human Development Report 2005.* New York: Oxford University Press. 118–25.

———. 2004a. "Overview of Official Development Assistance in Vietnam." Hanoi.

———. 2004b. *Human Development Report.* Oxford: Oxford University Press.

———. 2002. *Human Development Report 2002.* New York: Oxford University Press.

———. 1997a. "Governance for Sustainable Human Development." New York.

———. 1997b. *Human Development Report 1996.* New York: Oxford University Press.

———. 1997c. "Reconceptualizing Governance." New York.

United Kingdom, Ministry of Defence. 2003. *Operations in Iraq: Lessons for the Future*, chaps. 11 and 12. July. London.

UNSC (United Nations Security Council). 2005. Report of the Secretary-General on the United Nations Stabilization Mission in Haiti. s/2005/313. May 13.

Unsworth, Sue. 2005. "Focusing Aid on Good Governance: Can Foreign Aid Instruments Be Used to Enhance 'Good Governance' in Recipient Countries?" Working paper, Global Economic Governance Programme, Oxford.

———. 2003. "Better Government for Poverty Reduction: More Effective Partnerships for Change." DFID Consultation Paper. London.

Uppiah, S.L.D. 2000. "Impact of Retrenchment of Women Working in the EPZ Sector: Case Study of KFI Ltd." BSc paper, University of Mauritius.

USAID. 2007. Fiscal Year 2008 Budget Request. www.usaid.gov/policy/budget /cbj2008/.

USAID. 2006. Budget Summary: Bangladesh. http://www.usaid.gov/policy/budget/ cbj2006/ane/bd.html.

US Department of State. 2003. *Country Commercial Guide for Bangladesh*. Washington, DC.

Uvin, Peter. 2004. *Human Rights and Development*. Bloomfield: Kumarian Press.

Van Rooy, Alison. 1998. *Civil Society and the Aid Industry*. London: Earthscan.

Van de Walle, Nicolas. 2001. *African Economies and the Politics of Permanent Crisis*. Cambridge: Cambridge University Press.

Wangwe, Samuel. 1997. "The Management of Foreign Aid in Tanzania." Economic and Social Research Foundation, discussion paper no. 15, Dar es Salaam.

Ward, Christopher, and William Byrd. 2004. "Afghanistan's Opium Drug Economy." South Asia Poverty Reduction and Economic Management (SASPR) Working Paper Series.

Watts, Michael. 1998. "Recombinant Capitalism: State, Decollectivization, and the Agrarian Question in Vietnam," in John Pickles and Adrian Smith, eds., *Theorizing Transition: The Political Economy of Post-Communist Transformation*: London: Routledge. 450–505.

Weart, Spencer R. 1998. *Never at War: Why Democracies Will Not Fight One Another*. New Haven: Yale University Press.

Welsh, Jennifer. 2004. *At Home in the World: Canada's Global Vision for the Twenty-First Century*. Toronto: HarperCollins.

White, G. 1994. "Civil Society, Democratization and Development (1): Clearing the Analytical Ground." *Democratization* 1, no. 3 (Autumn).

White, Gordon. 1998. "Constructing a Democratic Developmental State," in Mark Robinson and Gordon White, eds., *The Democratic Developmental State: Politics and Institutional Design*. Oxford: Oxford University Press. 17–51.

White, John. 1974. *The Politics of Foreign Aid*. New York: St. Martin's Press.

Whitfield, Lindsay. 2003. "Civil Society as Idea and Civil Society as Process: The Case of Ghana." *Oxford Development Studies* 31, no. 3: 379–400.

Williams, David. 2000. "Aid and Sovereignty: Quasi-States and the International Financial Institutions." *Review of International Studies* 26.

Williamson, John. 2004. *The Political Economy of Reform*. Washington, DC: Institute for International Economics.

Williams, Michael C. 2001. "The Discipline of the Democratic Peace: Kant, Liberalism and the Social Construction of Security Communities." *European Journal of International Relations* 7, no. 4.

Windsor, Jennifer L. 2003. "Promoting Democracy Can Combat Terrorism." *Washington Quarterly* (Summer).

Wood, B. 2004. "Goodbye Columbus: Getting Serious about Development Cooperation." Discussion paper prepared for the Canadian Department of Foreign Affairs, April 2004.

———. 2001. "Best Practices in the Strategic Management of National Development Cooperation Programs." Report prepared for CIDA, Policy Branch. Ottawa.

———. 1988. *The Middle Powers and the General Interest*. Ottawa: North-South Institute.

Woods, Ngaire. 2006. *The Globalizers: The IMF, the World Bank, and Their Borrowers*. Ithaca, NY: Cornell University Press.

———. 2005. "The Shifting Politics of Foreign Aid." *International Affairs* 81, no. 2 (March).

———. 2000. "The Challenge of Good Governance for the IMF and the World Bank Themselves." *World Development* 28, no. 5: 823–41.

World Bank. 2007a. *Global Development Finance 2007*. Washington, DC: World Bank.

World Bank. 2007b. "Data and Statistics." http://worldbank.org/data.

———. 2006a. "Global Monitoring Report 2006." Washington, DC.

———. 2006b. "Strengthening Bank Group Engagement on Governance and Anti-corruption." Paper prepared for the Development Committee, September 8, 2006.

———. 2005a. "World Bank Governance Indicators 2005." Washington, DC.

———. 2005b. "Bangladesh PRSP Forum Economic Update: Recent Developments and Future Perspectives." November. Dhaka: World Bank.

———. 2005c. "Governance Indicators: 1996–2004." Washington, DC.

———. 2005d. *The World Bank in Bangladesh: Country Brief*. Dhaka.

———. 2004a. "Global Monitoring Report 2004." Washington DC.

———. 2004b. "African Development Indicators 2004." Washington, DC. http://devdata.worldbank.org/dataonline.

———. 2004c. Transitional Support Strategy for the Republic of Haiti. Washington, DC.

———. 2002a. "Poverty in Bangladesh: Building on Progress." Washington, DC.

———. 2002b. Report no. 23637: "Haiti Country Assistance Evaluation." Washington, DC.

———. 2000. "Reforming Public Institutions and Strengthening Governance." Washington, DC.

————. 1999a. "A Proposal for a Comprehensive Development Framework." Washington, DC.

————. 1999b. "Bangladesh: Key Challenges for the Next Millennium." Washington, DC.

————. 1998a. *Bangladesh:* "From Counting the Poor to Making the Poor Count." Washington, DC.

————. 1998b. "Assessing Aid: What Works, What Doesn't, and Why." Washington, DC.

————. 1997. *World Development Report 1997: The State in a Changing World*, Oxford: Oxford University Press.

————. 1989. "Sub-Saharan Africa: From Crisis to Sustainable Growth." Washington, DC.

————. 1981. "Accelerated Development in Sub-Saharan Africa: An Agenda for Action" (Berg Report). Washington, DC.

World Bank, Operations Policy and Country Services Department. 2003. "Harmonization Follow-Up: Global Architecture and World Bank Activities."

▲

## NOTES ON CONTRIBUTORS

PETER ARTHUR is Assistant Professor of Political Science at Dalhousie University. His research focuses on African political economy and development, and he has written a number of articles and papers on the multilateral trading system, private sector development, and the role of the small-scale sector in economic development.

DAVID BLACK is Professor of Political Science and International Development Studies at Dalhousie University, and Chair of the Department of International Development Studies. His current research focuses on Canada and Sub-Saharan Africa.

PAOLO DE RENZIO is a doctoral candidate in the Department of Politics and International Relations at Oxford University, and a Research Associate at the Overseas Development Institute, where he previously was a Research Fellow. He holds degrees from Bocconi University (Italy) and the London School of Economics, and has worked as an economist, lecturer, and consultant in Papua New Guinea and Mozambique.

SCOTT GILMORE is the Executive Director of Peace Dividend Trust, a non-profit foundation dedicated to making peace and humanitarian operations more effective, efficient, and equitable. He was formerly a Canadian Foreign Service Officer. As Deputy Director for South Asia, from 2002 to 2004, he focused on the development of Canada's diplomatic, defence, and development operations in Afghanistan.

NILIMA GURAJANI is a lecturer in the Department of Government and Development Studies Institute (DESTIN) at the London School of Economics. Her doctoral research (completed at Trinity College, Cambridge) examined management reforms in large aid agencies with operations in Bolivia and Vietnam.

JANAN MOSAZAI was born and raised in Kabul, Afghanistan. He worked for the BBC and the UN Assistance Mission in Afghanistan (UNAMA) between 2001 and 2005. He immigrated to Canada in early 2005, where he is currently pursuing a master's degree in journalism at Carleton University in Ottawa.

ROBERT MUGGAH is at the University of Oxford and is research director of the Geneva-based Small Arms Survey. He works in several countries on post-conflict, security, and development issues, including Haiti, Sri Lanka, the Philippines, Nepal, Uganda, Sudan, and Congo. He is the author of two forthcoming books, *Relocation Failures: A Short History of Displacement and Resettlement in Sri Lanka* (Zed Books) and *Securing Protection* (Routledge), as well as *No Refuge: The Crisis of Refugee Militarization in Africa* (Zed Books, 2006).

SARAH MULLEY is Coordinator of the UK Aid Network, working with UK NGOS to improve their research, policy, and advocacy work on aid. She was previously a Research Associate at the Global Economic Governance Programme in Oxford, and a Senior Policy Analyst at the UK Treasury. She holds an M.Phil. in International Relations from Oxford University.

FAHIMUL QUADIR is Associate Professor in the Division of Social Science at York University in Toronto. He is the director of York's Graduate Program in Development Studies. He has recently published on governance, civil society, democratization, economic liberalization, and microfinance.

RICHARD SANDBROOK, a professor of political science at the University of Toronto, has focused his recent research on the political economy of market reform, democratization, and neoliberal globalization. He has published numerous scholarly articles and ten books, including most recently *Social Democracy in the Global Periphery: Origins, Challenges, Prospects* (coauthor–2007); *Civilizing Globalization: A Survival Guide* (2003); and *Closing the Circle: Democratization and Development in Africa* (2000).

IAN SMILLIE was a founder of the Canadian NGO Inter Pares, and is a former Executive Director of CUSO. His most recent books are *Managing for Change: Leadership, Strategy and Management in Asian NGOs* (with John Hailey) and *The Charity of Nations: Humanitarian Action in a Calculating World* (with Larry Minear). He is currently Research Coordinator for Partnership Africa Canada's "Diamonds and Human Security Project" and a participant in the forty-five-government Kimberley Process. He was appointed to the Order of Canada in 2003.

SUE UNSWORTH spent many years working as a development practitioner with DFID, latterly as Chief Governance Adviser. She is now a freelance consultant and a Research Associate with the Institute of Development Studies, University of Sussex.

JENNIFER WELSH is Professor of International Relations at Oxford University and a Fellow of Somerville College. She is the author and editor of several works on International Relations theory and Canadian foreign policy, including most recently *Humanitarian Intervention and International Relations* and *At Home in the World: Canada's Global Vision for the 21st Century*. In 2006 she was named a Trudeau Fellow, and is currently researching changing conceptions of sovereignty in international relations.

BERNARD WOOD heads his own international consulting firm, drawing on his long experience in development, political, and security affairs. He was the founding CEO of the North-South Institute, headed the Canadian Institute for International Peace and Security, and then the secretariat of the OECD/DAC in Paris. He was educated at Loyola College in Montreal and the School of International Affairs at Carleton University. He did doctoral work at the University of London and was a Fellow at Harvard University in 1992–93.

NGAIRE WOODS is Director of the Global Economic Governance Programme and Dean of Graduates at University College, Oxford University. She has written numerous articles on international institutions, globalization, and governance. Her most recent book is *The Globalizers: the IMF, the World Bank and their borrowers*. In 2005–6, Ngaire Woods served on a three-person panel to report to the IMF Board on the effectiveness of the IMF's Independent Evaluation Office. Since 2002 she has been an Adviser to the UNDP's Human Development Report.

▲

# INDEX

*Page numbers in italics refer to diagrams and graphs.*

donors, 112; and poverty reduction, 105–106, 108; and social development, 105, 106, 107, 108, 113; and work with NGOS, 106, 110, 111, 112–13, 286

Bangladesh, CIDA governance aid to, 106–107, 108–16; amount of, 113–14, 115; assessment of, 111–14; for banking research capacity, 110; for environment/water management, 109–10; for gender equality, 111; for legal/electoral reform, 110, 117n17; and need for anticorruption measures, 115; and need to encourage participatory governance, 115–16; and need for judicial autonomy, 114–15; and need to strengthen public institutions/civil service, 113, 114; for political reform/accountability, 110, 111–12; recommended improvements in, 114–16; as selective, 113–14

Bangladesh Development Forum (BDF), 112, 115, 118n21

Berg Report (World Bank), 47

Bosnia-Herzegovina, 5, 285

Brahimi, Lakhdar, 149

Broadbent, Ed, 52

Bush, George W., 7, 9, 282, 290

## C

Cambodia, 11, 45; UN intervention in, 56, 148, 179

Canada, foreign aid by. *See* foreign aid, Canadian, *and subsequent entries.*

Canada, foreign policy of: and human rights, 45–47, 50, 52, 53–55, 68, 80; and human security, 54–56, 70; and International Policy Statement, xiv–xv, 43, 44–45, 59, 68, 108–109, 234, 245, 248, 279, 280, 288; joint Senate–Commons committee on, 52–53; in post-9/11 era, 61–64; and postwar foreign aid, 45–47; and realism vs. romanticism, 41–42, 70; and spending on good governance, 43–44, 67; and spread of democracy, 42–43; and state sovereignty vs. intervention-

ism, 61–62; "three Ds" of, 62–64, 144, 154, 155–56, 159–60, 164, 165–66, 297; and "voluntarist" tradition, 231, 250n5. *See also* CIDA.

Canada, and pursuit of good governance: acting on, 292–98; and assessment of current development policy, 288–92; challenges/issues for, 280–81; as focus of sector concentration, 294–96; and goals of aid, 281–88; and human rights, 45–47, 50–52, 52–53, 58, 68, 80; and International Policy Statement, xiv–xv, 43, 44–45, 59, 68, 108–109, 279, 280, 285; and lessons from US experience, 282, 290; managing aid for, 298–301; and need to accept "good enough governance," 287–88; and need to "do no harm," 284–85; and political vs. administrative goals, 285–87; in postwar era, 45–47, 280; as relatively recent, 280; since 1990, 52–56, 68–71; spending on, 43–44, 67

Canada Corps, 69–70, 236, 290

Canada Fund for Africa (Chrétien government initiative), 124

*Canada in the World* (Chrétien government document), 53, 58

Canadian Forces: in Afghanistan, 151, 152, 157–58, 166n7; in Gulf War, 61; in Haiti, 180, 186. *See also* Afghanistan; DND.

Canadian International Development Agency. *See* CIDA.

Carroll, Aileen, xiv, 150

Carter, Jimmy, government of, 46

Catley-Carlson, Margaret, 251n7

Cédras, Lt.-Gen. Raoul, 170

Central America, 46. *See also* Latin America.

China, 10, 47, 79, 294; CIDA work in, 64; economic growth of, 32, 57; and growing influence in Africa, 31; human rights abuses in, as opposed by Canada, 50–51, 52, 58

Chrétien, Jean, and government of, 52–